Garden and Labyrinth of Time

Germanic Studies in America

(Supersedes German Studies in America)
Founded by Heinrich Meyer

Edited by Katharina Mommsen, Stanford, California

Advisory Editorial Board
Sigrid Bauschinger (Amherst) - Eckehard Catholy (Toronto) - Peter R. Frank (Stanford) - Ingeborg Glier (Yale) — Michael Metzger (SUNY Buffalo) - Herbert Penzl (Berkeley) - David Pike (North Carolina) - Maria Tatar (Harvard) - Ulrich Weisstein (Indiana) - Theodore Ziolkowski (Princeton)

No. 56

PETER LANG
New York · Berne · Frankfurt am Main · Paris

Gerald Gillespie

Garden and Labyrinth of Time

Studies in Renaissance and Baroque Literature

PETER LANG
New York · Berne · Frankfurt am Main · Paris

CIP-Kurztitelaufnahme der Deutschen Bibliothek

Gillespie, Gerald:
Garden and labyrinth of time: studies in
Renaissance and baroque literature / Gerald Gillespie.-
New York; Berne; Frankfurt am Main; Paris: Lang, 1988.
  (Germanic studies in America; No. 56)
  ISBN 0-8204-0727-5

NE: GT

© Peter Lang Publishing, Inc., New York 1988
All rights reserved.
Reprint or reproduction, even partially, in all forms such as
microfilm, xerography, microfiche, microcard, offset strictly prohibited.

Printed by Weihert-Druck GmbH, Darmstadt (West Germany)

"To search with wandering quest a place foretold..."
> ——Lucifer, in Canto II of John Milton, *Paradise Lost*

" 'Come'è bello il mondo e come sono brutti i labirinti!' dissi sollevato.
" 'Come sarebbe bello il mondo se ci fosse una regola per girare nei labirinti,' rispose il mio maestro."
> Adso da Melk (and Guglielmo da Baskerville), in ch. 2 of Umberto Eco, *Il nome della rosa*

"The best way, as I have heard, to get out of a labyrinth, is to retrace one's steps."
> The Cosmopolitan in ch. 36 of Herman Melville, *The Confidence Man*

TABLE OF CONTENTS

Foreword 9
1. Education in Utopia 15
2. Alcofribas on the Nile, Britomart at the Temple of Isis, Zeno in the Garden of the White Goddess: Illustrations of Poetic Anthropologies in the Renaissance and Baroque .. 33
3. Cosmic Vision in Lohenstein's Poetry 63
4. Primal Utterance: Observations on Kuhlmann's Letters to Kircher, in View of Leibniz' Theories 89
5. Scientific Discourse and Postmodernity: Francis Bacon and the Empirical Birth of "Revision" 117
6. The Rebel in Seventeenth-Century Tragedy 153
7. Time and Eternity in Andreas Gryphius' *Catharina von Georgien* 169
8. Lohenstein's *Epicharis*: The Play of the Beautiful Loser 193
9. Dream and Calculus in European Baroque Drama 225
10. Transformations of the Female Delinquent in Fiction 253
11. Estebanillo und Simplex: Two Baroque Views of the Role-Playing Rogue in War, Crime, and Art (with an Excursus on Krull's Forebears) 279
12. Erring and Wayfaring in Baroque Fiction: The World as Labyrinth and Garden 297

Acknowledgments 325
Index of Names 327

FOREWORD

The comparatist cannot escape from a daunting awareness of how imperfect and provisional are all summary labels imposed on such a large and variegated cultural domain as Europe — not to speak of the diversity of the German territories in their own right. Of course, the terms "Renaissance and Baroque" in my subtitle, announcing the general timeframe of the essays collected here, sound sweepingly vast if one reads into them the many critical debates concerning, and the entire historical pageant of, the several centuries usually understood under those banners. But my purpose here is not to erect a theory of literary history based on the evidence of the Renaissance and Baroque era or even to propose a detailed refinement of our extant period definitions.

I find myself, nonetheless, in agreement with the spirit of Claudio Guillén's chapter "Second Thoughts on Literary Periods" in his still invaluable book *Literature as System* (1971). It is in some measure because I share his view of the Renaissance era as multiple in its energies, as "a plural number or cluster of temporal processes, 'currents,' 'durations,' rhythms or sequences" (Guillén, p. 464) that I have undertaken to examine habits, conventions, and tendencies sometimes as they appear concretized in single texts, and sometimes as strands transversing actual or supposed geocultural, temporal, and generic boundaries. I have commented at more length on the characteristic theses and findings of German scholarship after World War II, when tackling the problem of periodization, in an article entitled "Renaissance, Mannerism, Baroque." Since that assessment served as the opening chapter of the widely disseminated book, *German Baroque Literature: The European Perspective*, edited by Gerhart Hoffmeister (1983), the reader can readily find there my discussion of the German picture within the European context, as well as a select bibliography of relevant Anglo-American, French, German, Iberian, and Italian writings on literary history and theory.

The pairing of terms in the main title of the present volume, *Garden and Labyrinth of Time*, implicitly acknowledges the persistent association of these poetic spaces with the themes and structures of error, development, and education in the literary works into which most of my ensemble of studies look. Another purpose of first reinvoking the master-images of the "garden" and "labyrinth" and next joining them with the concept of "time" is to indicate that the volume focuses not on the earlier, but on the later Renaissance and what is now widely called the Baroque, when the ongoing Humanist revision of history had already borne much fruit and when a frequent preoccupation of imaginative literature was to scrutinize the dynamism and perplexities of temporality. The center of gravity of the literature revisited in my essays does not lie in the great building of Renaissance aspirations and themes beyond Dante (of which, e.g., Thomas M. Greene speaks in *The Light in Troy: Imitation and Discovery in Renaissance Poetry* [1982]); it is located somewhere closer to the moment of an intesifying, often perplexing awareness of the accrued Renaissance experiences and accomplishments and the rise of an art that is proudly autonomous and self-referential (to which, e.g., James V. Mirollo addresses our attention in *Mannerism and Renaissance Poetry: Concept, Mode, Inner Design* [1984]).

In certain senses, the "garden" and the "labyrinth" capture two versions or ways of regarding human experience. The garden was inherently a more positive orientation, the labyrinth more negative, but as both orientations proved capable of being subtly deceptive or destabilized, both were challenging to the imagination of writers who wanted to resituate mankind in a history and cosmos altered by Humanism and advances in science. Poets of the Renaissance discovered that neither as garden nor as labyrinth was their world exempt from the power of time. Insofar as movement within the framework of either the "garden" or "labyrinth," or from one to the other perception of the world, might intimate important aspects of mankind's groundedness in the creation, the conventions associated with the master-images garden and labyrinth could be pressed into service in literature about education and history.

All this being said, my chapters nonetheless do not revolve around questions of imagery. Neither do they concentrate on one mode of writing. Rather, they cut across several genres and touch on a number of important areas relevant for literature, such as linguistics, anthropolgy, and cosmology. At times, my approach to the thought and writing of the sixteenth and seventeenth centuries is deliberately from an oblique angle, because it was that peculiar angle that caught my attention and renewed my pleasure in the special qualities of the poetic imagination of the age.

Several of my essays deal exclusively or principally with one or a few German authors, rather than a cross-section of Europe, but the overarching aim is to locate the German works in the larger European context without diminishing their particular attributes. I trust it is self-evident that certain essays pursue key themes, while others examine the features of specific genres, and yet others combine these two tasks.

The first five essays move back and forth between what today, in retrospect, sometimes rejecting the original generic understanding involved, we tend to regard as canonical literature, on the one hand, and para-literature or non-literary discourse, on the other. But, as is rather obvious in certain cases (e.g., More's *Utopia*, Rabelais' books of Gargantua and Pantagruel), the new uses to which Renaissance writers put "non-literary" materials caused fascinating shifts in the sense of genre. In the creative rupture and élan of the Renaissance, there was far more than a zeal to restore lost or decayed literary values; new forms, too, sometimes sprang from inventive parasitism and a new openness to the vast trove of materials in the total heritage — one thinks, e.g., of the principle of "polyglossia" proposed by M.M. Bakhtin, the principle of "quotation" proposed by Herman Meyer, and related descriptions of such auto-critical and creative reorderings.

In chapters one and two, the boundaries between fiction and philosophy and the educational or political treatise and scientific imagination are seen as frequently blurred. Chapter three brings a more extended discussion of particular cosmological and metaphysical concerns in the Protestant North, and chapter four goes into a debate about the nature of language, with wider long-range significance, between a late Renaissance polyhistor and a chiliast mystical poet. Chapter five deliberately assumes a polemical stance vis-à-vis the "postmodernist" critique of the European and Anglo-American tradition, but it does so in order to highlight ways in which the obsession to harness language and to invent a program to stabilize the key instrument of progress, the human mind, are interconnected in that tradition (both before and after Walter Shandy's pondering of the efficacy of the modal verbs).

The four essays that follow and are devoted to the drama stand out as a "generic" block. Two of them are discursive, general treatments of European playwrighting which bracket concentrated analyses of plays by Gryphius and Lohenstein, the two major German dramatists before Lessing, plays wherein we can observe the breakthrough of the Humanist discovery of history as one of the driving forces in the introduction of tragedy, a key Humanist genre. Since Robert J. Nelson's *Play within a Play: The Dramatist's Conception of His Art, Shakespeare to Anouilh* (1958), down to the present, the epochal European dimensions in the rise of the German drama have regrettably been ignored outside the ranks of German comparatists. Therefore it seems justifiable to draw the attention of non-Germanists to the value of comparative treatments taking German dramaturgy into account.

The last three essays more loosely constitute a second "generic" block dealing principally with kinds of narrative fiction. The range is from the picaresque tale to the grandiose Baroque romance and early forms of the novel. And the final essay returns to aspects of narration broached in the very first two essays, so that the volume closes a larger bracket around the interposed chapters on historical and cosmological imagination and the drama.

In several cases in essays included in *Garden and Labyrinth of Time*, where I have sought to suggest formal and thematic linkages, as well as discontinuities, between older and newer literature, or to indicate the relevance of older literature in contemporary debates about the nature of art, culture, and history, I have decided not to truncate the original presentation. Thus "Scientific Discourse and Postmodernity," "Transformations of the Female Delinquent," and the excursus in "Estebanillo and Simplex" carry into the twentieth century.

While one essay is effectively new and others are substantially revised or recast in English, most chapters retain the basic form in which they originally appeared. However, the variant styles of citation have been unified, older orthography has been slightly modernized when that would not violate primary textual qualities, minor errors have been silently corrected, annotations have been modestly augmented in some instances, and some small cuts have been made to avoid inevitable redundancies. But I have ordinarily chosen to leave thematic overlappings intact as nodular junctures unifying the volume.

I am grateful to many friends, colleagues, and former students who by their incidental suggestions and conversations over the years have helped create the nurturing climate in which this book started to take shape.

My interest in the Baroque and *Siglo de Oro* was first awakened by the good fortune of having Wolfgang Kayser as a teacher during my undergraduate years at Harvard. But it was Walter Naumann who gave me my first thorough introduction to the German Baroque during graduate studies and who encouraged me to continue a more programmatic pursuit of British, French, Italian, and Spanish literature at Ohio State University, shortly before he returned to Germany to found the Institute of Comparative Literature at the University of Darmstadt. He brought intact from his days as a student of Ernst Robert Curtius a remarkable love for literature and the arts that overleapt the centuries, national frontiers, and narrow specialization. Whether discoursing on Virgil, Walter von der Vogelweide, Dante, Shakespeare, Stifter, Mallarmé, or Gottfried Benn, he imbued his students with confidence in the humane enterprise of which he offered such a high example.

I add to this list of stimulating voices Bruce Wardropper, Rodolfo Cardona, Alexander A. Parker, Anthony N. Zahareas, Franke J. Warnke, Harry Levin, René Wellek, Claudio Gullén, Harold Jantz, Albrecht Schöne, Giorgio Tonelli, Harold B. Segel, Leonard Forster, George Steiner, Peter Skrine, Brian Vickers, Marc Fumaroli, Thomas R. Hart, Kurt and Florence Weinberg, Ailene Goodman, Tibor Klaniczay, Lewis W. Spitz, Alberto Martino, Lowry Nelson, George C. Schoolfield, Hans-Jürgen Schings, Klaus Garber, Joachim Dyck, William Kennedy, Giles R. Hoyt, Hans P. Braendlin, Gerhard Strasser, Aldo Scaglione, Gerhard Hoffmeister, and Yang Zhouhan; and no doubt further names should be acknowledged.

For their help at various stages of my research, I want to express my gratitude especially to the Widener and Houghton Libraries at Harvard University, the Bayerische Staatsbibliothek in Munich, the Sterling and Beinecke Libraries at Yale University, the Bibliothèque Nationale and Bibliothèque de l'Arsenal in Paris, the British National Library, the Lilly Library at Indiana University, the Central Library of Cambridge University, the Zentralbibliothek of the Canton and University of Zurich, the Bancroft Library at the University of California in Berkeley, and the Green Library at Stanford University. The School of Humanities and Sciences and the Graduate Division of Stanford University have awarded a grant toward the publishing costs of this volume. A special word of thanks is due Professor Katharina Mommsen, editor of the series *Germanic Studies in America*, for her collegial encouragement of this project. She has once again graciously opened the series Germanic Studies in America to a comparative study.

1. EDUCATION IN UTOPIA

An intense interest in proper education must certainly count among the most characteristic concerns of the Renaissance. Three broad streams of writing exhibit the passion for defining and reforming the aims, substance, and practice of education on all levels of society. First, there are the famous treatises ranging from Baldassare Castiglione's *Il Cortegiano* (1528), which sets forth the aristocratic ethos of self-cultivation, to Roger Ascham's *The Schoolmaster* (1570), which reflects the ideals of Protestant Humanism. Erasmus' urbane, ironic *Colloquia* (1518ff.), addressed to the general learned public, deliberately hover between compact storytelling and didacticism. Second, there are the explicit novels of education, such as Jörg Wickram's *Der jungen Knaben Spiegel* (1554), contrasting the moral and social achievements of contemporary youths who follow the right educative pathway with the failure of those who succumb to dissolute behavior; or John Lyly's *Euphues: The Anatomy of Wit* (1579), transposing this basic story-line to foreign parts and criticizing key institutions thinly veiled (e.g., the University of Oxford). The educational journey of a young nobleman, often interacting with a guide or mentor, is a branch of the genre increasingly favored from the late Renaissance through the Enlightenment. Such allegorical tours of educational problems and principles, or encyclopedic reviews of religious, metaphysical, scientific, political, social, and psychological ideas – for example, in Baltasar Gracián's *El Criticón* (1619), François Fénelon's *Les aventures de Télémaque* (1695), and Andrew Michael Ramsay's *Les voyages de Cyrus* (1727) – ordinarily are set in the symbolic spaces of the quester romance or Antiquity.[1]

Beginning with Thomas More's *Utopia* (1516), which provided the generic name, the Renaissance brought forth a third kind of writing which combined elements of the didactic treatise and the fabulous voyage of discovery. In a letter of June 9, 1508, Erasmus claims jestingly that his friend's name, by association with the Greek *moria*, has inspired the *Praise of Folly (Encomium Moriae)*; and in this same spirit, More's Latin term "Utopia" establishes an ironic ambivalence (punning on Greek *eutopia* "good place" and *outopia* "nowhere"). More updates Lucian's traveler, the Cynic philosopher Menippus, as the modern searcher Raphael Hythlodaeus ("purveyor-of-Nonsense") and lets him start out on the imaginary trip from a far point reached during the historical voyages of Amerigo Vespucci in 1504. The still scarcely known New World provides unlimited opportunity to erect a satirical foil to the Old World under the license of fiction. More frames his fantastic tale and concocted samples of Utopian poetry in the transparent hoax that these materials were narrated to himself and a Humanist friend, Peter Gilles, an official of Antwerp, during an actual diplomatic mission in Flanders. Their source, the learned "foreigner" Raphael, is amazingly well-informed about English society and politics too. In Book I, in the presence of the late Primate John Morton, Archbishop of Canterbury and Lord Chancellor, he ventures protests on the cruelty of hanging thieves instead of creating needed jobs, the burden of supporting parasitical noblemen, the ruinous English penchant for war, the relentless enclosure of lands destroying rural communities, and other pernicious dislocations and abuses, and proposes reforms of the system of justice with a view toward rehabilitation of most offenders and expansion of prosperity. In further dialogue with More, Raphael posits hypothetical approaches to English problems of statecraft and national welfare with illustrations from the realm of Utopia and then expatiates on the Utopians' more advanced political and economic system in Book II.

The island Republic, founded some eighteen centuries earlier by a benevolent conqueror Utopos, practices a communism which in many respects suggests the orderliness of a Benedictine establishment, secularized and extended as a national way of life. Housing and land are equitably distributed; work is mandatory; by social preference, meals in town are taken in communal dining halls; there are no dens of iniquity or luxury industries; surveillance by the elected authorities thwarts anti-social deviance; and repeating shirkers or criminals must labor as slaves, earning their reacceptance as citizens. The carefully monitored economy and surplus alow all the people to have the use of equipment or means as well as time for healthful recreation, vacations, and education. Although the use of free time is "voluntary," Utopian men and women tend to flock to various lectures. A restricted, carefully selected number of both sexes are legally exempted from ordinary work so that they can concentrate on their studies, but if they produce disappointing results they must go back to the working class, whereas workers, by hard study, can get promoted into the intelligentsia, the class from which diplomats, priests, scholars, and magistrates are recruited. The cultural atmosphere is determined by communal discussion, public reading of literature, and music-listening. Education fits needs and aptitudes, is continuous, and occurs in their native language.

In a standard Humanist thrust, Raphael's account notes that, while the Utopians have independently discovered much the same principles in the arts and sciences as the Ancients and advances in astronomy, meteorology, etc., they have failed to come up with the tortured scholasticism of the Moderns. Their ethics stress the pleasure principle at the base of reality and reject gloomy asceticism in favor of natural, true happiness on both rational and religious grounds. They approve of bodily pleasures, especially positive health, as well as aesthetic and higher mental pleasures. It comes as little surprise to learn that, under Raphael's tutelage, they have rapidly taken to studying Greek literature and philosophy in the original texts, since there is some linguistic evidence of a remote Utopian tie to the Greeks and Persians, nor that they have instantly grasped and independently replicated the new bookprinting technology of Europe. Utopian national unity is guaranteed by religious tolerance, and their deep irenic sentiments are reflected in skillful avoidance of war, and in just as clever measured conduct of hostilities forced upon them. The priesthood — among them some women — divides into two major sects vaguely along Catholic and Protestant lines, one celibate, vegetarian, and fervently laboring, the other approving of marriage and accepting normal pleasures. This highly moral ecclesiastical minority represents no political danger and renders invaluable service in curbing warfare or mitigating its pains in times of crisis. Utopian churches contain no visual representations of God so as to allow every citizen to participate without prejudice to his own particular creed or imagination, but — with some exotic touches lifted from contemporary voyage reports — the worship service reinforces communal cohesion and oversight of the congregation's deportment is of equal importance to ritual.

More's *Utopia* introduced a stimulating element of speculation into Renaissance didactic literature, as readers had to argue what the final meaning or teaching was since More's other writings often stood in contradiction, and this aspect of his work became all the more intriguing with the rapid development of the Protestant movement under the leadership of Martin Luther just a few years later.[2] If scholarship has perennially debated whether More's view in *Utopia* was essentially Catholic or Protestant, controversy over the position of François Rabelais has remained, down to the present, as perplexingly variegated as his great five-part novel *Gargantua and Pantagruel* which conflated many specific motifs from More and Erasmus and pushed their Humanist biases further with radical energy. Enjoying such diverse patronage as that of Gallican Cardinal du Bellay and the protectress of Protestants, Marguerite of Navarre, and condemned alike by the reactionary theologians of the Sorbonne and by John Calvin in Geneva, Rabelais' satire now captivated and now offended many elements of the French public. Even to outline the question of Rabelais' beliefs exceeds the scope of this essay, and here it must suffice to concentrate on his humoristic treatment of education within a modified utopian framework. Important is the fact that in Books I, II, and III the territories of the Gargantuan race are vaguely congruent with those of France. There is never any withdrawal from rough-and-tumble reality into the prophylactic safety of an island, and although exuberantly fantastic, and replete with allegories, the island-by-island search for the temple of the Divine Bottle in Books IV and V, an entertaining voyage of discovery in remote waters, ultimately symbolizes the Renaissance quest for experience and knowledge on one's home grounds.

Toward the end of Book II, actually the first published (1532), the clever and benevolent statecraft of the young prince Pantagruel not only limits the destructiveness of war unleashed by Anarchus, but completes the fusion of the Utopian (More) and Dipsodic (Erasmus) realms in civilizing conquest. Rabelais uses the "lie" convention of fabulous tales to full advantage for amusing while teaching. The pristine vigor of the Gargantuan race, whose gigantism and lusty appetites represent Renaissance vitality, is traced from the Flood in a jocoserious addition to myth and Scripture in the opening chapters. But the account of Pantagruel's prodigious childhood rather soon leads, by way of his tour of French provincial universities, to the capital in the company of his Humanist tutor Epistemon. In the celebrated catalogue of books in the Library of St. Victor in Paris (ch. 7) and the elegant letter in Ciceronian style sent by Gargantua to guide his son (ch. 8), Rabelais contrasts the barbaric muddle of medieval learning and his new Renaissance ideals and program. With Pantagruel, we sense, as his father says, standing on the border between two ages of mankind:

> [...] Le temps estoit encores tenebreux et sentant l'infelicité et calamité des Gothz, qui avoient mis à destruction toute bonne litterature. Mais, par la bonté divine, la lumiere et dignité a esté de mon eage rendue es lettres, et y voy tel amendement que, de present, à difficulté seroys je receu en la premiere classe des petitz grimaulx, qui, en mon eage virile, estoys (non à tort) reputé le plus sçavant dudict siecle.
> [...]
> Maintenant toutes disciplines sont restituées, les langues instaurées: Grecque, sans laquelle c'est honte que une personne se die sçavant, Hébraïcque, Chaldaïque, Latine. Les impressions tant elegantes et correct en usances, qui ont ésté inventées de mon eage par inspiration divine, comme à contrefil, l'artillerie par suggestion diabolicque. [...] (Book II, ch. 8)

> [(...) However, you can readily understand that the times were not as suited and favorable to learning as today, nor did I have the likes of the teachers you have had. We were still in the dark ages and suffering the misfortune and calamity caused by the Goths when they brought about the destruction of all good literature. But, through divine grace, light and dignity have been restored to letters in my lifetime, and now I witness such improvements that, although I was rightly reputed in my manhood the century's leading scholar, I would at present find it difficult to enter the bottom class in grammar school.
> (...)
> Nowadays all the branches of learning have been revived, and the classical languages restored: Greek, without which one is ashamed to count himself a scholar, Hebrew, Chaldean, and Latin. We now use the elegant and accurate

products of the art of printing, whose invention was prompted by divine inspiration in my lifetime, as contrarily, artillery sprang from demonic suggestion. (...)]

A not unimportant aspect of Pantagruel's practical education is his encounter with Panurge, the incarnation of the big-city schemer and trickster, who becomes his foil, stimulus, and boon companion. It is Panurge who helps Pantagruel consult the whole range of European experts on the question whether Panurge should marry in Book III and thus becomes an *alter ego* and co-searcher of the Renaissance hero in Books IV and V.

Taking up the experiences of the older generation in Book I, Rabelais expands on two central Utopian themes: proper education, and the benefits of peaceful cultivation. Gargantua's childhood is painted in more lavish and earthy terms, but every detail of his behavior and upbringing has symbolic value. For example, his love of wine exhibits his "complexion divine" and his attunement to "les joyes de paradis" (I, ch. 7), just as his blue and white clothes signify "joye, plaisir, delices et resjouissance" and "choses celestes" (ch. 9); in his hat he wears the emblem of the androgyne, his family's "mystic" badge from Plato's *Symposium* (ch. 8); his naive generosity and furious riding of his hobbyhorses (ch. 12) demonstrate spontaneous, imaginative involvement in life, as do his romping in the dirt and adolescent sexual explorations with his nurses (ch. 11); and father Grandgousier, far from being upset, interprets Gargantua's scatological experiments (ch. 13) as a sign of genius. But when Grandgousier tries to have his son educated under the care of the typical pre-Renaissance savant, a "theologian and sophist," the ponderous medieval ways — without benefit of printing — turn Gargantua into a dunce (ch. 14), and finally newer-style tutors, Eudemon ("happiness through reason") and Ponocrates ("vigorous"), must be hired to accompany the prince to the polyglot world center, Paris. The reactionary preceptors of the Sorbonne, epitomized by Janotus, decry reason and again threaten to turn Gargantua into a dolt and slouch (chs. 20, 21). But Ponocrates intervenes to implement, step by step, Rabelais' humanist philosophy and encyclopedic plan for education (chs. 23, 24). Gargantua's penchant for playing games (ch. 22) is exploited both mentally and physically. No hour is wasted, but the routine is pleasurable and varied by athletics and perfecting of artistic skills, excursions to learn the nature of trades and occupations or witness public events and performances, making scientific observations and visits to learned experts and travelers, and well-timed vacation outings.

Because the foolish Picrochole refuses to negotiate an end to hostilities (chs. 25 ff.), Grandgousier is finally compelled to interrupt Gargantua's formal studies, and the prince assumes direct responsibility for pursuing the war and then his duties as ruler. The Utopian-Dipsodic house acquires a valuable ally in the new-style, tough-minded monk, Friar John of the Funnels, who for heartiness, large appetites, and valor is immediately appreciated by the prince and his Humanist mentors (chs. 39 ff.). Book I concludes with the collaboration of Gargantua and Friar John in founding the Abbey of Thélème ("free will"), a utopian educational institution of revolutionary character built in the heartland of Utopia not only to replace the corrupt, outmoded monastic system, but to serve as a model for the formation of a secular elite (ch. 52 ff.). In contrast to other utopian establishments of the Renaissance era, Rabelais forcefully advocates an open society governed by positive freedom and the imperative of self-perfection. There are no monastic walls nor regulation by the clock; instead, taste, tact, spontaneity, and good sense determine the daily round of activities, and the men usually defer to the women in choices. Like the monastic vows of chastity, poverty, and obedience, the separation of the sexes is abolished. The students have the right to marry, get rich, and be free. Thélème is no dumping ground for the deformed, misfit, and disadvantaged; rather, it selects the shapely, natural, and gifted, and graduation ordinarily occurs when a compatible couple decides it is time to embark, in marriage, into the adventure of the real world of France and Europe. Rabelais' innovative "abbey" copies the grand Renaissance *châteaux*, with splendid grounds, excellent lighting, munificent decor and appointments. While acquiring the whole range of courtly graces, the Thelemites can repair to the core of the institution, its libraries in Greek, Latin, Hebrew, French, Italian, and Spanish. The enigmatic poem uncovered in digging in the foundations of the old abbey — the import of which Gargantua tersely characterizes as "le discours et maintien de vérité divine" — hints guardedly at the collapse of the old order, a fusion of the codes of Nature and Scripture, and the rebirth of human glory (ch. 58).

In the late Renaissance, however, Utopia again was detached from the immediacy of the European homeland and projected onto the New World or the symbolic island of quester romance. One of the most striking cases is the abstract, idealized sanctuary depicted in Tommaso Campanella's *La Città del Sole* (1602), which he wrote in the same year as his condemnation to perpetual imprisonment by the Inquisition for his active leadership in a conspiracy to overthrow Spanish and clerical rule in Italy. Narrated as a dialogue between a much-traveled Hospitaler and the pilot of Christopher Columbus, the *City of the Sun* reverts to the dream of a highly structured communist republic to express Campanella's revolutionary program. The City, supposedly set on the island of Taprobana in the Indian Ocean, mentioned by Diodorus Siculus, is symmetrical, with four gates at the cardinal compass points, and consists of seven fortified rings named after symbolic planets. The rotond temple of Metaphysics, set on the spacious plain crowning the summit in the city's midst, is the seat of the leader called Sole ("sun") who combines spiritual and temporal authority and governs with the help of the three Principi, officers and "principles," Pon (*potenza* "power"), Sin (*sapienza* "wisdom"), and Mor (*amore* "love"). "Power" is in charge of military matters, while "Love" oversees procreation, education, medical care, food, housing, and clothing. "Wisdom" has the broad responsibility for the liberal arts and sciences, with subordinate officers for astrology, cosmography, logic, rhetoric, grammar, medicine, physics, politics, and morals. Rather than bearing emblems of divinity, the altar of the temple is surmounted by two charts depicting the heavens and earth, and the greater stars are shown in the cupola.

The communal existence of the City is regulated in detail, and thus proper generation and education are fundamental to is success. Not only are all class distinctions abolished, but starting at the age of three, each citizen is taught all the arts possible, from work in the fields to mechanical and martial skills, and the sciences — all labor having dignity and access to political service on the supreme Council. Since dwellings, meals, clothing, and recreation are in common, children undergo socialization by the people at large. Public concern for hygiene, vigorous exercise by both sexes, and the disinterested pursuit of virtue guarantee a high level of physical and mental health, the virtual absence of crime. The main work of magistrates is to raise consciousness through public lectures dealing with confessed shortcomings which are reported anonymously up the ladder of authority. The chief task of the priests is to read stellar movements and set auspicious dates for procreation, sowing crops, harvesting, etc. Public worship and ceremonies betray an exotic formalism whose traits Campanella combines eclectically so as to suggest their descent from an ancient tradition. Although the inhabitants of the City have heard about Christ and are familiar with newer theoreticians such as Copernicus, Campanella drops names from antiquity and deliberately cloaks the citizens' reverence for the natural cosmos and their focus on the key symbol of God, the sun, in an indefinite Neoplatonic mystique. While basic propositions such as the immortality of the soul and the rule of divine Providence are upheld unequivocally, the solar race regards many other elements of Christian belief, such as the Trinity and the Adamic Fall, to be poetic stories reflecting metaphysical principles.

In the last few pages of *La Città del Sole*, the European discussants turn their minds to the turbulent, but dynamic world scene. The Hospitaler draws the lesson that the natural law being followed by the solar race amounts to the essence of Christianity and that divine providence has been using both noble searchers like Columbus, modern prophets of truth, and the base avarice of the Spaniards to expand the scope of that core relevation. Columbus' pilot asserts that their age

> hà piú storia in cento anni che non ebbe il mondo in quatro mila; e piú libri si fecero in questi cento che in cinque mila; e dell'invenzioni stupende della calamita e stampe ed archibugi, gran segni dell'union del mondo; [...].

> [has seen more history in 100 years than the world had known in 4000; and more books were created in these 100 than in 5000 before; and there have been astonishing inventions of calamity, both printing presses and blunderbusses — great signs of the coming unification of the world; (...)]

The cosmic conjunction seems to portend "grande monarchia nova, e di leggi riforma e d'arti, e profeti e rinovazione" ["great new rulership, reform both of laws and arts, both prophets and renovation"]. The heresies, errors, and outrages of the age are the death throes of a world advancing toward rebirth. Campanella's Protestant admirer, Johann Valentin Andreae, reformulated the imperative of a radical reeducation of humanity in *Reipublicae Christianopolitanae descriptio* (1619), which was even more widely read following its delayed translation into German by David Samuel Georgi as *Reise nach der Insel Caphar Salama und Beschreibung der darauf gelegenen Republik Christiansburg* (1741).

Andreae grew up in an atmosphere of religious tolerance, inbued with Neoplatonic mysticism, alchemical experimentation, and Paracelsan nature philosophy, in the circle of his prominent Humanist family in Württemberg. A polymath with a sense of mission, he was attracted to the Rosicrucian movement by the learned quester Christoph Besold, who later converted to Catholicism. The young Andreae became a member of the religious society "Civitas solis", traveled extensively in Europe, and gathered further broadening knowledge, before he turned from Rosicrucian aspirations to a distinguished career in education and government. Eventually his accomplishments included the codification of church laws in Württemberg, reconstitution of theological studies, and foundation of the Tübinger Stift. Andreae's best known work of his youthful period in German is the *Chymische Hochzeit Christiani Rosenkreuz anno 1549* (1616), probably written to defend the Rosicrucians against the suspicion of pursuing political goals such as Campanella's. This allegorical fable of an initiatory journey to heaven during Eastertime conflates motifs and imagery from ancient, Biblical, Oriental, medieval, and Humanist lore. The most variegated symbolic systems are brought together to exhibit the stages in the spiritual process, to praise positive forces, or to render criticisms of actual persons and ideas in the contemporary world. The learned first-person narrator of Andreae's utopian novel of state, *Reipublicae Christianopolitanae descriptio* or *Christianopolis*, relates the discovery of an ideal society already structured around the form-giving core of education. This remote Southsea state has evolved out of the aspirations of refugees who have fled various religious persecutions in the Old World.

Like Campanella's island-city, Christianopolis demonstrates its order and harmony through its hierarchical symmetry. The core is, conspicuously, the massive College containing in its center the Temple, on the very top of which is the City Hall. Whereas some two dozen sections of the book deal with the organization of agriculture, distribution of foodstuffs, exploitation of mineral resources, crafts, manufacturing, housing, wages, public streets and gardens, policing, water and sewage system, care for the sick and aged, worship, elections of magistrates, and communal activities, some seventy sections are concerned with education and furtherance of science. Christianopolis is communistic and egalitarian, but power is exercised from the center by a theocratic triumvirate. Andreae terms the division into three authorities, each with his own consultative senate, and the selection of officers and advisers from an elite of talent, "aristocratic" in distinction to the "monarchical" form of government. A Chancellor communicates the separate or joint pronouncements. Subordinated to the spiritual leader, who is both Chief Theologian and Priest, is a Deacon in charge of education of the young and general pastoral duties. Second in prestige is the Judge, or political leader and police authority; under him works an administrative chief responsible for the economy and public welfare. Third in the triumvirate is the Erudite, unpedantic overseer of learning and science. However, his scope is enormous, for the College is vast, physically and spiritually a state within the state. In accord with irenic hopes, the Library is the real heart of the College (section 39), while the Armory has been converted into a museum to remind citizens of the ghastly side of human behavior in the as yet unreformed outside world (s. 40). A center for the maintenance of the chronicles and documents serves as a bulwark against the falsification of history (s. 41), and the printing establishment is supervised to weed out noxious and frivolous literature (s. 41) — in contrast to the disorder of the European market.

Apparently, the wide seas are not a sufficient sanitary cordon, despite the boast that the island has no need of the old law and cultivates historical studies only as an important record of human error and development (s. 80). Intensive surveillance and counseling of men and women students in their respective dormitories are employed to counter bad attitudes brought from unenlightened homes and to prevent the contamination of the innocent (s. 80). The church is also a theater where edifying drama is enacted, religious art is displayed, and "Davidic poetry" uplifts the community (s. 82, 85). The City Hall contains depictions of great moments in world history, the Protestant heroes, and the contrasting godly and hellish realms, and allegories of reward and punishment to replace outmoded heathen myths and other unworthy subjects (s. 92). If all this well-calculated machinery — if finally public discussion of shortcomings, reproof, and even corporal punishment (s. 54) — fail to socialize an errant citizen, ostracism and excommunication is the most terrible penalty (s. 87). There may be pleasant public gardens inside and outside the city (s. 94); the eight subject-area lecture halls may be cheerful, comfortable, and shielded from noise (s. 51); universal coeducation, sound hygiene and medical care, adequate good food (s. 53), the promotion of manual skills and household arts, regular opportunity for sports and recreation (s. 54), support for widows and orphans (s. 91), and a guaranteed decent funeral (s. 100) may promise considerable well-being. But we are a long way from Rabelais. There are also strict laws against loose and boisterous living (s. 88), and although all jobs are honorable, citizens wear certain colors of clothing to designate their social functions (s. 84)!

Far from being inimical to the natural sciences, Protestant puritanical utopianism, as typified in Andreae, regarded research and technology as means to buttress and expand a genuine Reformation.[3] Notable among the scientific installations of Christianopolis are its chemical and pharmaceutical laboratories, anatomical theater, museum of natural history, and observatory with mathematical instruments, the newly invented telescope, geological models, and planetarium (s. 44-50). The importance of visualization for the furtherance of science is underscored by the presence of a studio for the art of painting in the same complex (s. 48). Andreae counts command of mathematics among the indispensible attributes of genuine humanistic learning and extols the practice of scientific skills and the use of models and aids to stimulate the scientific imagination of the young. The elaborate division of formal education into eight subject areas or "lecture halls" (s. 55-78) reflects the encyclopedic penchant seen in other Northern savants such as the German Calvinist millenarian Johann Heinrich Alsted. Thus, on the one hand, the entire fifth auditorium (s. 67-69) is devoted to the science of astronomy, which the Christianopolitans pursue boldly, even leaving open the possibility that other stars are inhabited.[4] On the other hand, they accept a higher kind of symbolic astrology as a legitimate branch of research, emphasizing the study of divine order and man's ultimate "rule" over the stars. The configurations of this occult heaven reveal wondrous correspondences, patterns in world and church history accessible only to true Christians. The same sort of relationship pertains with the sixth auditorium of natural philosophy (s. 70-72). On the one hand, the constitution of every thing and event in the animal, vegetable, mineral, and sidereal realms is eagerly investigated; the double goal is to overcome man's shameful ignorance, and to perceive divine goodness in the real world. Hence the study of world or human history and church history belong here as branches of natural philosophy, since it is also their task to overcome the legacy of man's ignorance and confusion, the millenia of bondage to devilish concepts, tyranny, and strife, and thereby to realize the ordained redemptive principle of "freedom."

Other traits in common with the scientifically oriented segment of British Protestantism appear in the traditional fields. The first auditorium, devoted to grammar, encompasses the immense field of rhetoric as well as the acquisition of classical and modern foreign languages and linguistics proper (s. 55-57). But Andreae insists on the utility and value of the native language as the primary instrument, the first that should be cultivated, and places quality and content of discourse in any tongue, including the native German, above superficial multilingualism. The province of the second auditorium, for dialectic, similarly ranges over metaphysics to theosophy (s. 58-60), that is, from the general utilitarian instruments of "method" over the definition of essential categories — the true, the good, the beautiful, unity, order, etc. — to the higher esoteric insights, and occult knowledge, beyond the reach of the Aristotelian mind. The habit is confirmed when the third auditorium, for arithmetic, houses not only noble geometry which scans micro- and macrocosmic dimensions, but also mystical-cabalistic numerology, which reveals secret relationships, ineffable harmony.⁵ No profane entertainment or dancing, only sacred, prophetic music is tolerated in the fouth auditorium (s. 64-66); Andreae notes that the musical instruments also have an honored place in the mathematical theater, and he stresses the importance of choral performance as a communal act of reverence. The seventh auditorium, for ethics, incorporates as a special branch a new kind of politics such as genuine Christians require — the anti-Machiavellian, anti-prudentialist-absolutistic, and puritanical, utopian mode — based on "Christian poverty," that is, theocratic communism (s. 73-75). In the eighth auditorium, for theology, philological acuity is prized, but wrangling over interpretation of Scripture is shunned, since the danger of speaking out of a personal temptation or confusion rather than out of God is well recognized (s. 76-78). Pauline "folly" (so appreciated by Erasmus) generally saves the day; and even though the islanders admit occasional genuine instances of modern prophecy, they hold that sufficient revelation by the Holy Ghost already has been vouchsafed for guiding humanity, if men will only work with it.

Far more controversial down to the present, and for good reason, has been Francis Bacon's *New Atlantis* (1627) which pushed the utopian vision decisively toward science. Because of Bacon's importance as an exponent of the inductive method in such seminal works as *The Great Instauration and New Organon* (1620), he has been forgiven his own inadequacies as a scientist and so wrong a conclusion as that the heliocentric theory was rationally untenable. Bacon proposed that, in order to guarantee the continuing progress of the scientific revolution of his own times, the inherited repertory of human knowledge had to be sorted out and regrounded in such a way that exclusively the verifiable components would be deemed to constitute a reliable body of information. Such a radical new start could not be subverted again by the inherited tendency of the mind to deceive and muddle itself. The *New Atlantis* posits the situation that the human race has managed "to recover that right over nature which belongs to it by divine bequest" (*New Organon*, Book I, cxxix), but envelopes it in the mystique of the survival of an ancient tradition. In the early pages, the shipwrecked Europeans learn that "the great Atlantis (that you call America)" suffered from a calamitous flood which eradicated its civilization, but from the thriving commerce and navigation some three millenia ago derived the happy outpost in the South Seas that has learned to shield itself from the decay of the aging world. The device of having the narrator mention a small remnant population of Jews, who believe that the island nation was founded by another son of Abraham called Nachoran and that "Moses by a secret cabala ordained the laws of Bensalem which they now use," lends a patent of authority to this ideal mirror for the Judaeo-Christian West.

By noting that the Bensalemites' literature celebrates Adam, Noah, Abraham, and Christ, Bacon effectively bypasses the intervening dismal record of Christianity and transfers the emphasis to the symbolism of elitist guidance of the society descending from their ancient Hebrew king Solamona to whom lost scientific works were attributed. The most important public observance is the Feast of the Father, in which the patriarchal heads of families are confirmed in their authority. But the key institution, with its supreme Father, is "an Order or Society which we call 'Salomon's House'," also "the College of the Six Days Works [...] for the finding out of the true nature of things [...]." Certain of the Fellows or Brethren of the College are selected to undertake the regular twelve-year voyages, passing disguised through other nations, by mean of which Bensalem remains in complete intellectual touch, while prophylactically protected against unwelcome persons or ideas. When the regal Father of Solomon's House relates its true state to the narrator, our imagination enters the realm of science fiction: cavernous depths, dizzying towers, vast installations and laboratories. There are miracles of science: efficacious cures; speedier and more bounteous crops; inventive breeding of beasts, fish, fowl, and plants; superior foods, beverages, medicines; means to replace the heat energy of the sun; devices to multiply, combine, manipulate, and apply the factors of light, sound, aromas, and tastes; higher-powered engines; improved instruments; apparatus for creation of illusions. Besides combing world literature for ideas, trying new experiments, compiling and analyzing results, and formulating laws that interpret nature, the officers of Solomon's House maintain two collections: one of the memorable inventions, another of statues of great inventors and discoverers, including Columbus, Gutenberg, Galileo, et al. Clearly, science not only helps mankind; it is a new cause and purpose in itself, and thus the protagonists of science are heroicized, having the rank in this society that saints and statesmen occupy elsewhere.

Breaking off with the theme of recognition of scientific greatness, the utopian "fragment" by Bacon (1561-1626) has a decidedly secular tone. It is as unmistakable as the secular praise of the arts and sciences and the great inventors — Prometheus, Cadmus, Minos, Gutenberg, Galileo, et al. — in Canto X of *L'Adone*, by his contemporary Giambattista Marino (1569-1625). For all their differences, the English philosopher, sober puritan rationalist, and the Italian Baroque poet, flamboyant celebrator of the marvels of the real cosmos, share — as do so many men of the late Renaissance — a conviction in the epochal mission of the sciences. Marino is quite frank in his avowal of the benefits of schooling by the senses, in a hierarchy from sensation to sentiment. Bacon never espouses specific forms of education in New Atlantis, but he is confident that "we cannot command nature except by obeying her" (*New Organon*, I, xccix).

The tradition of reconcilement with nature lived on in radical and puritanical Protestant utopias such as *A Description of the Famous Kingdom of Macaria: showing its excellent Government, wherein the Inhabitants live in great Prosperity, Health and Happiness* [...] (1641), by the British-German savant Samuel Hartlib, who was close to the Baconians, to reformers such as Amos Comenius, and the circle of the Royal Society. In Johann Gottfried Schnabel's popular four-volume novel, *Wunderliche Fata einiger See-Fahrer* [...], later known as *Insel Felsenburg* (1731-43), the idea of a new world, where the superior types of Northern European Protestants would combine into a vigorous race in harmony with nature and establish a thriving commonwealth under utopian circumstances, expressly reminiscent of Old Testament glory, was set forth in an expansive romance. Here the emphasis was on the Protestant work ethic, on practical arts and sciences, and on the prosperity these fostered, as well as on means of defense. But *Insel Felsenburg* overlapped with the appearance of a second edition of Daniel Casper von Lohenstein's two-volume polyhistoric novel *Arminius* (originally 1689-90), in which the rationalist vision of a utopian idyll under natural laws and of the high mission of theoretical science is restated (Book V) as part of the encyclopedic tour of the philosopher-prince Zeno, who discovers the impressive scientific research center of Prometheus.[6] Lohenstein fitted the utopian projections of a "pure" state of Nature and "pure" Science as separate subgeneric moments into the larger framework of educational journeying.[7] While the eighteenth and nineteenth centuries brought forth a variety of rationalist, socialist, and/or scientific utopias out of whole cloth — and religious utopias by no means disappeared as a distinct kind of literature — utopian materials were readily subsumed or conflated in newer kinds of fiction with a more general claim to verisimilitude. The fundamental pattern of the modern *Bildungsroman*, the explorations and encounters of a developmental protagonist or group, made it very inviting for the novelist to insert a sojourn in some special utopian environment — for example, the "Pädagogische Provinz" in Goethe's late work *Wilhelm Meisters Wanderjahre* (written 1825-29).

Notes

1   I have treated the relationship of the Renaissance *Bildungsroman* in relation to the quester romance in an essay on "The Incorporation of History as Content and Form: Anticipations of the Romantic and Modern Novel," in *Proceedings of the Ninth Congress of ICLA*, IV (Innsbruck, 1983), pp. 29-34. This excursus on the utopian strain, which intersects, is now appended as a tribute to Walter Naumann whom so many grateful students thank for his encouragement and guidance in the spirit of Erasmus and Rabelais.
2   The lasting German interest in More throughout the sixteenth and seventeenth centuries has been examined by Gilbert Waterhouse in ch. IV, "The Latin Novel," of: *The Literary Relations of England and Germany in the Seventeenth Century* (Cambridge, 1914).
3   In *The Rosicrucian Enlightenment* (London and Boston, 1972), Frances Yates asserts in a more daring form the thesis that seventeenth-century British-German cultural relations and affinities — echoed in some French and Italian sentiment — help explain the particularly favorable climate for Protestant acceptance of a scientific élite and furtherance of the Royal Society. The importance of millenarian expectations for a break-through of empirical science in Britain is convincingly and thoroughly documented by Charles Webster in *The Great Instauration: Science, Medicine and Reform 1626-1660* (London, 1975).

31

4   On the importance of the idea of a plurality of worlds in the Renaissance, Baroque, and Enlightenment, see Karl S. Guthke, *Der Mythos der Neuzeit: Das Thema der Mehrheit der Welten in der Literatur- und Geistesgeschichte von der kopernikanischen Wende bis zur Science Fiction* (Berne and Munich, 1983); Guthke does not cite Andreae, but treats Campanella at length.
5   Andreae's treatment of music, mathematics, astronomy, and city planning clearly reinstates the "comprehensive order" of a Renaissance correspondence between microcosm and macrocosm. On the elements of this tradition, see S.K. Heninger, Jr., *Touches of Sweet Harmony: Pythagorean Cosmology and Renaissance Poetics* (San Marino, Cal., 1974).
6   The importance of Lohenstein's work as a bridge to German Enlightenment fiction is discussed in my essay, "The Function of Myth in Lohenstein's *Arminius*: The Case of Egypt and Prometheus," *Argenis*, 2 (1978), 187-228.
7   The Renaissance and Baroque roots of the major German eighteenth-century novel of education before Goethe's *Wilhelm Meister* are treated in my essay on "Wielands *Agathon* als Bildungsroman zwischen Barock und Romantik," in *Akten des 6. IVG-Kongresses* (Bern, 1980), Bd. 3, 344-352.

Bibliography

Encyclopédie de l'utopie, des voyages imaginaires, et de la science fiction, ed. by Pierre Versins (Lausanne, 1972).

Les Utopies à la Renaissance: Colloque international (avril 1961), ed. by Jean Lameere (Bruxelles/Paris, 1963).

Bauer, Hermann, *Kunst und Utopie: Studien über das Kunst- und Staatsdenken in der Renaissance* (Berlin, 1965).

Braunthal, Alfred, *Salvation and the Perfect Society: The Eternal Quest* (Amherst, 1979).

Freyer, Hans, *Die politische Insel; eine Geschichte der Utopien von Platon bis zur Gegenwart* (Leipzig, 1936).

Manuel, Frank E., and Fritzie, P., *Utopian Literature: A Bibliography, with a Supplementary Listing of Works Influential in Utopian Thought* (Lawrence, 1977).

Manuel, Frank E., and Fritzie, P., *Utopian Thought in the Western World*. (Cambridge, 1980).

Münster, Georg, *Idealstädte: Ihre Geschichte vom 15.-17. Jahrhundert* (Berlin, 1957). Studien zru Architektur- und Kunstwissenschaft, 1.

Penrose, B., *Travel and Discovery in the Renaissance 1420-1620* (Cambridge, Mass., 1952).

Trousson, Raymond, *Voyages aux pays de nulle part: Histoire littéraire de la pensée utopique* (Bruxelles, 1975).

2. ALCOFRIBAS ON THE NILE, BRITOMART AT THE TEMPLE OF ISIS, ZENO IN THE GARDEN OF THE WHITE GODDESS: ILLUSTRATIONS OF POETIC ANTHROPOLOGIES IN THE RENAISSANCE AND BAROQUE*

> You will take special note of the marvellous independence and true imaginative absence of all particular space or time in the Faery Queene. It is in the domains neither of history or geography; it is ignorant of all artificial boundary, all material obstacle; it is truly in land of Faery, that is, of mental space. – S.T. Coleridge[1]

The penchant of Renaissance and Baroque writers to fuse pictorial and conceptual patterns of great complexity is widely appreciated. The intricacies of allegorical quests, of emblematic expression, of extended conceits, of the meditative process come readily to mind in illustration. Ernest B. Gilman has demonstrated how, as twinned phenomena, literary and pictorial wit gained the perspectival dimensions which came to obsess not only the visual arts and optical science of the age, but its very thought processes.[2] Gradually, the newly posited perspectivism of history and of the mind were invested with a perspectival theatricality as intense as that in the British, Spanish, French, Dutch, and German world theater flourishing from about 1580 to 1680. I shall look here at several moments of perspectivism which exhibit the remarkable intellectual suppleness of major writers in their approach to the plethora of disparate pieces of evidence from the history of religions. I hope to suggest why specific habits of imagining such pictorial and symbolic references taken from the tangle of older myths and cults could serve as the cultural training ground for later elaboration of "scientific" anthropological models in the European Enlightenment.

I take as my starting point the network of mythological and hermetic associations in François Rabelais' books of Gargantua and Pantagruel which have been examined so ably by G. Mallary Masters and again by Florence Weinberg.[3] For the purposes of my argument, I assume that *Le Cinquiesme Livre* was substantially drafted by Rabelais even if an editor, seeking to complete the work in the author's spirit, put it together. Although Rabelais drops his pseudonym Alcofribas after Books I and II, this playful authorial persona, with whom Rabelais, Doctor of Medicine, allows himself to be identified, is implicitly copresent as one of the explorers and "abstractors"-elect in the remote and recondite spaces being opened by the Renaissance. That is clear from the narrator's repeated return to the first-person plural as an internal observor of those happenings which are otherwise related as third-person events. As befitting an approach to the higher contemplation of cosmological order in Book V, our jocoserious mystagogue conducts us more decisively, not only through a longer, open exposition of the myth of Bacchus in civilizatory triumph as depicted in the mosaics of the temple of the Dive Bouteille, but also through the mathematical and astronomical imagery of the temple's construction.

Before we are privileged to hear the epileny and witness the voyagers' seizure by the breviary wine or Logos, Rabelais has gradually introduced us to many variations upon his Dionysian Christ. These range from the symposiast Silenus-Socrates in the Prologue of Book I to gross Priapus, "raising his red, flaming, cocksure head" in the Prologue of Book IV.[4] Unmistakable in the latter sexual image is a conflation of the common diurnal and the alchemical reference to the solar principle. We already know that the ultimate decision for marriage by the philautic trickster Panurge reaffirms universal harmony; that outcome is predicated by the meaning of the Androgyne in Book I, ch. viii, where the Gargantuan-Pantagrueline emblem of "l'umaine nature a son commencement mystic" bears as motto in "Ionic" script Saint Paul's words, "'ΑΓ ΆΠΗ Ο'Υ Ζ'ΗΤΕ˜Ι Τ 'Α 'ΕΑΥΤ˜ΗΣ." ("[Charity] seeketh not her own," I Corinthians 13:5). Feminine tutelary spirits dominate the mysterious realm of Lanternland and the Bottle which the male questers finally enter.

Characteristically, Rabelais as "abstracteur de quinte essence" prepares us for an abstract level of perception of the androgynic relationship, once the seekers have passed "beyond" ("la routte d'Outre" [V. 17]) and reached the port of "Matheotechnie, peu distant du palais de la Quinte Essence" (V. 19). Ambiguously, they land at "vain science," but perhaps also at "maththeo-technics," in a prelude to the Pythagorean numerological mystique of the shrine of the Bottle (e.g., V. 36, 41).

The newly appointed Abstractors experience such "technic-(que)s" in their most silly and exalted form through witnessing the lavish "bal joyeux en forme de tournoy" staged by their hostess, Quinte Essence (V. 24-25). One one level, through this queen and her followers, Rabelais pokes fun at the empty forms of Aristotelianism. Her courtiers are inefficacious except in the realm of medicine. But simultaneously Rabelais pursues a higher symbolic understanding. This ballet entertainment is a musical chess game between a golden and a silver troupe of dancers, the ruler of each side standing on and defending squares of symbolically opposite color: the gold king on white and his queen on yellow, the silver king on yellow and his queen on white. The elegant motions and accompanying music of the battle reveal the interaction of a masculine and feminine principle. The key players with the subtlest moves are the respective queens, and their roles continue since they are recreated as a series of individuals in the flux of defeats and victories. The silver forces win two games, but in the third and closing round, during which Queen Quintessence mysteriously disappears, the golden king at last emerges triumphant. I agree with Weinberg that this marks a deeper transformation, passage beyond even the perfection of nature or the material world. Rabelais pushes the "Aristotelian" allegory of his source, Francesco Colonna's *Hypnerotomachia Poliphili*, in which love triumphs as the highest of the three virtues, in the direction of a Platonic, Orphic, and Bacchic mystery.[5] The combat is a celebratory ritual, and the mystagogic elegance borders on open comedy, such as we encounter in the later lighthearted chess game in canto XV of Marino's *Adone*.[6]

Not surprisingly, Rabelais cites Nicholas de Cusa to explain the strange perception that the spinning dancers both appear to rest in their motion as dots of color, yet also trace a line of being in time: "[...]son mouvement est repos, elle semble quiete, non soy mouvoir, ains dormir [...]. Et y figurant un point de quelque couleur, semble à nostre veuë non point estre, mais ligne continue, comme sagement l'a noté Cusane, en matiere bien divine"(V. 25). The new abstractors have just glimpsed several difficult truths. One is the Cusanan doctrine of the coincidence of opposites. Another is the pardox of the multiplex motions of existences versus the divine rest of God as

35

perfect center.⁷ Yet a further sense is the ancient, and again also Cusanan, theory, mentioned in the following "Isles of Odes" chapter (V. 25), that "earth turns about the poles, and not heaven about a stationery earth, despite all the appearances to the contrary" ("[...] la terre veritablement autour des poles se mouvoir, non le Ciel, encores qu'il nous semble le contraire estre verité [...]"). Like his contemporary Copernicus, Rabelais cites the Pythagorean philosopher Philolaus in support of terrestial rotation.⁸ The penetration to these insights has been prepared ritually in the chess ballet with the restoration of the proper relationship of the masculine solar to the feminine lunar aspect. There the sun symbolizes both the creative core of mind-energy and intellectual clarity, while the moon symbolizes not only the reciprocal cosmic manifoldness and energy-recipient nature, but also a reflected, hence sometimes misleading light. The voyagers learn ever more about the complexity of cosmic and terrestial pathways, "Car les chemins cheminent comme animaux et sont les uns chemins errans, à la semblance des planettes: autres chemins passans chemins croissans, chemins traversans" (V. 26). This shift to an organistic metaphor for the seeming erring of heavenly bodies, motion which is actually a cosmic weaving, associates the confusing drama of earthly ways with the greater tapestry of divine providence in all its manifestations.

With irony as consumately swift as the stream along whose bank heretic pathbreakers are seen being burned at the stake, the narrating voice draws the comparison that "when we sailed down the river Loire, it seemed to us that the near trees and shore moved; but it was really we and our boat moving" ("[...] comme estans sur la riviere de Loire, nous semblent les arbres prochains se movoir, toutesfois ils ne se mouvent, mais nous per le decours du batteau"). Moreover, "The way, we heard, was that which followed the banks of the Nile in Egypt" ([...] c'estoit le chemin des aggeres et levées du Nil en Egypte"). All at once, we are no longer in the remote waters near Laternland. This sudden allusion, like the ripple of a current that as suddenly disappears, ties the still fresh theme of the erring heavenly body (that body is Man as well as his earth) with the belief in a secret channel, an ancient tradition to be rediscovered. When transfixed by passing Renaissance eyes, though its banks proffer the horrid spectacle of intellectual martyrdom, the pathway of their native Loire is also invisibly that of the Nile. Roads and people "err." But the Renaissance explorers sail on a perduring Nile that ever flows through archaic superstition and modern fallenness, carrying us onward toward "rebirth," restoration of the inner core of wisdom. Not only are we encouraged to dare to think anew as explorers of the natural cosmos, but in our mapping we are advised to use as helpful coordinates the secret hieroglyphic wisdom of Egypt, of which Pantagruelism, or Bacchic Christianity, is a "modern" expression.

Rabelais does more than slip in mention of Cusanus' radical view of the nature of the universe, then quickly let it drop as a dangerous topic. He imbeds the provocative Cusanan references in the larger context of Humanist syncretism and seems confident his more learned readers can instantly change from one register to another and follow the specific allusions to Egyptian lore. A. Kent Hieatt has analyzed a related process of impressively fluid mythopoeic imagination in Spenser's treatment of the principal Egyptian myth of Isis and Osiris in *The Faerie Queene.*[9] Spenser's daring use of Egyptian motifs to transcribe psychological as well as cosmological principles would have been virtually unthinkable, or the poet might have held back, if the effort to digest and assimilate such materials had not been so vigorously pursued throughout the sixteenth century as to prepare an audience for his work. The main line of development of the materials after Boccaccio is evident in commentated iconologies such as Georg Pictorius' *Theologia Mythologica* (1532), Natale Conti's *Mythologiae* (1567), Vincenzo Cartari's *Le Imagini dei Dei degli antichi* (1571), and Charles Estienne's *Dictionarium Historicum, Geographicum, Poeticum* (1595). The last was used by Spenser as a standard reference source.

I shall concentrate for the moment only on the anthropological tendency in the poet's application of the idealized system of references whereby Osiris was the Egyptian Bacchus, bringer of wine and law, a civilizing power, and associated with the sun and divine energy, while Isis, his sister and bride, associated with the moon, was nature. Within the cycle of the seasons, their marriage symbolizes the harmonious and dynamic synthesis of contraries, a union which the Renaissance also represented in such concepts as the alchemical hermaphrodite.[10] The simplified elements of the Egypt myth are these: When Osiris is dismembered by his fiery destroyer Typhon, the grieving Isis must search for her consort's male member in order to complete his reassemblage; that is, the creation yearns for the return of the Creator who both enables and is manifested by the life of nature, cosmic order, and the creative process. Osiris' surrogate and son, Horus, does battle with Typhon, who assumes the shape of a crocodile; in removing the crocodile's male member or Typhon's power, Horus restores the creative purpose. In some accounts, Horus and Typhon are good and evil brothers, and their tragic contest is resolved by the rebirth of Osiris as third stage. Cartari typifies the matured Renaissance manner of identifying protagonists from a variety of traditions as figurations of Christ and coordinating other elements of the respective myths to fit this interpretation. The result is that, by comparison with other myths of the southern and eastern Mediterranean, the Christ role acquires stronger cosmological dimensions which vie with the standard theological interest. Cartari relates the rending of Bacchus by the Titans to that of Osiris by Typhon, but he as unhesitatingly associates the son Horus in the aspect of Priapus with all stories of fertility and germination, and on the same principle he claims that the cult of Osiris is connected with the cult of Proserpina and Ceres.[11]

John Erskine Hankins has examined in detail the physical allegories in Spenser's use of the Isis-Osiris and Venus-Adonis myths.[12] Without rehearsing the analogies between various micro- and macrocosmic manifestations and symbolic functions of the All-Mother and All-Father, I note the fundamental agreement of Hankins, Hieatt, and others on the sense of the moral allegory when Britomart kills Radigund, the rabid man-hater, and releases Artegall and her other prisoners. Spenser draws the distinction, as Hankins says, that "True chastity in the soul deliberately destroys the impulse toward female domination and unites with justice in determining on wifely submission. The wedding of justice (Artegall) and chastity (Britomart) is not the external marriage. It is the union of impulses within a woman's soul that determines her to be a true and loyal wife."[13] In the celebrated episode in the Temple of Isis (V. vii), Britomart falls asleep by the silver statue which represents Isis as standing on Osiris who is in the form of a crocodile, the corcodile's tail reaching up and embracing Isis' waist. By implication, in an image of power as this dragon-like appearance connotes, Osiris is mysteriously merged with his "rival" Typhon. "Britomart dreams that the crocodile begs to have coition with her, that she consents, and that she afterwards gives birth to a lion." A priest of Isis explains that "the crocodile represents Artegall, who will restore her to the crown of her country. She will marry him and bear a lion-like heroic son."[14] The corollary allusion to the supreme champion, Christ, lends the aura of sacred dignity to the standard romance prophecy that a great national hero will someday appear.

But as Hieatt points out, Spenser introduces daring new elements in his imaginative conflation of various contemporary representations of Isis and Osiris. Whereas, when Cartari syncretically composes attributes from various authorities, Isis wears the traditional shining disk or sphere of the moon on her head, Spenser has her wear an unmistakable sun emblem:

> Vppon her head she wore a Crowne of gold,
> To shew that she had powre in things diuine;
> And at her feete a Crocodile was rold,
> That with her wreathed taile her middle did enfold.
> One foote was set vppon the Crododile,
> And on the ground the other fast did stand,
> So meaning to suppresse both forged guile,
> And open force: and in her other hand
> She stretched forth a long white sclender wand.
> Such was the Goddesse; [...] (V. vii. 6 ff.)

Numerous critics have suggested classical models for such a triumphant containment, such as the virgin Minerva standing on a dragon. I would add the obvious Christian analogue laden with Isis-associations: the Virgin Mary as the new Eve, standing on the Serpent, and on the lunar crescent. The adjectival participle "rold" recurs as an important motif in Milton's depiction of the Serpent in relation to Eve.[15] In the traditional iconography, with the Christ child in her arms, Mary in fact also exhibits the solar principle and upholds the restoring and restored Father in the divine Son.

A parallel, momentary division into the negative and positive femine also occurs when Radigund assumes the extreme witchlike, vengeful role and "Like as the Moone in foggie winters night,/ Doth seeme to be her selfe, though darkened be her light" (V. xii). Conversely, then, the figure of the crocodile can subsume the ambivalence of Bacchus or Osiris — of the God associated with both violence and fertility. And while the crocodile incorporates both the primordial raging of Typhon and the redeeming control by Horus, it is Isis, as mother of Horus or the redeemer son, who is shown as the channel for his divine role by manifesting his emblem and performing the symbolic act of control. This interlaced figure of Isis and Osiris thus suggests and is the poet's independent attempt to create a legitimate universal symbol, since each polarity reveals the presence of the other in achieved harmony. Furthermore the complete figure is a magisterial restatement of the mystery of the Incarnation. Spenser could rely on reader appreciation of the thematic connections interwoven with such fundamental iconic paradigms. For example, through consulting Estienne's *Dictionarium* they would find the implications of justice and right rulership associated with Osiris, "Cujus nomine non solum Sol intelligebatur apud Aegyptos, verum etiam Dionysius sive Bacchus, Jupiter quoque pater, justus, & dux, quique unà cum Anubi. Gigantes ex Italiâ expulisse legitur."[16] On grounds of the Elizabethan mystique, Kermode sees the imagery of the Isis episode as underscoring the association between the themes of "justice" and "empire."[17]

After Spenser, who confidently treats such mythological allusions as elements of a poetic vocabulary appreciated by an elite audience, we cross the threshold into Baroque poetry. I have discussed elsewhere the cases of the secular poet Marino and the religious poet Milton who span the first three quarters of the seventeenth century and through whom mythological imagination found one of its most important major channels to the future.[18] It is on the same basis as in the Anglican Spenser's poetry that we grasp in the Catholic Marino's *L'Adone* the meaning of the wound which, reciprocally, Venus as primal matter, sustains when smitten by the beauty of Adonis, as divine form. The inverted love relationship can stand poetically on its own as a metaphysical truth in secular humanism, or we can read it still as a Christian allegory in which, of course, Adonis is a Christ-figure. In Marino's poem, nature yearns for the Logos which informs her, even though that means divine form must undergo a martyrdom through nature — a travail presaged long before the death of Adonis by Venus' dream of him as covered in blood or in the symbolic transformation of the rose. Calvinist Protestantism was predisposed by its patriarchal bias against expanding poetically on the idea of a divine matrix, but it could not hold out against the attractive suggestions of Renaissance art in which Venus and the Virgin Mary had long coexisted as archetypes of cosmic wholeness, decorum, elegance, and vitality. Thus the survival of the All-Mother in her late Baroque guise as Eve in Milton's *Paradise Lost* (1667) was an event of enormous, immediate significance for the literature of Northern Europe and eventually for modern literature more widely, because through Eve the roles of Venus and Mary were bridged poetically.[19] Milton's own appreciation of Marino is a factor too little regarded in contemporary scholarship because of the slippage in the reputation of the Italian poet over the past two centuries in the North, once displaced by such Protestant giants as Shakespeare and Milton.[20]

I have discussed elsewhere the cosmological vision of another Protestant admirer of Marino in the late Baroque, the Silesian poet and playwright Daniel Casper von Lohenstein.[21] Here I shall consider the manner in which, in the same writer, the cosmological function of myth is subordinated to encylcopedic knowledge by a newer spirit of rationalism that was to crest in the Enlightenment. Lohenstein composed his polyhistoric romance *Arminius* (publ. 1689-90) at a time when vastly expanded information on wholly alien civilizations, such as those of India and China, — not to mention the exotic observations resulting from contacts with peoples of the newly colonized Western Hemisphere — was being added to the Egyptian and Near Eastern lore already retrieved by Renaissance savants.[22] The work of the influential Jesuit scholar Athanasius Kircher illustrates why it was becoming ever more difficult to integrate such materials into a reassuring pattern for Christian belief and why the drive to find abstract coordinates in universal history would yield the modern fields of comparative religion and anthropology.

Like so many intellectuals of the seventeenth century, Kircher was fascinated by the possibility of elaborating a combinatory art and universal character. In *Turris Babel* (1679), he applied equally to Biblical stories and ancient myths his general combinatory method of arranging data in tables in such a manner as to suggest the permutations of basic expressions or perceptions of divinity. Since any one axis of analogies can be coordinated with other axes, entire sets of relationships are generated in a kind of cultural calculus. On p. 136 of Book III, for example, Kircher sets forth a simple diagram of coordinated sets of brother-sister divine spouses and their principal offspring, triplicate brothers who enact the drama of the life-process and who can also be interpreted either euhemeristically or understood symbolically as generalized abstractions of forces of nature, stages of existence, etc. On p. 143, Aegyptian, Babylonian, Chaldean, Hebrew, Greek, and Latin gods and goddesses are exhibted in tabular profusion suggesting the combinatory production of variants upon basic themes.

As a final example, I adduce Kircher's "Speculum Geneatheologicum Sive Theotechnia Hermetica" on p. 144.[23] It by no means exhausts the treasure of materials one could cite to show how, in Kircher's mind, the superabundance of mythological data has begun to fall into place as scientific evidence, as surface phenomena which indicate a natural variation that has resulted from humanity's striving to represent basic insights. Striking is the resemblance of Kircher's model to the contemporary planisphere — whereby the diagram acquires a scientific aura. However, his allusion to the solar system is still geocentric. Framed by the square of the seasons, as well as by the zodiac, such circularity remains here comfortably imbedded in Pythagorean symbolism and the familiar tropes of the stations of the year and the marriage of heaven and earth. The fundamental reality, which generates all others, is the posited "solar" or masculine principle; it brings forth and interacts with aspects of a corresponding "lunar" and "terrestial" or feminine principle. At its symbolically supreme station, the sun as Apollo or heat-energy works through Venus as seminal matrix. This is the familiar relationship of Adonis and Venus on the level of the physical allegory in Spenser's *The Fairie Queene*. Each such relationship has its reciprocal inversion or transformation in Kircher's diagram; for instance, the solar fullness of Apollo as divine energy and mind, as against Venus as informable matter, has its positive complement in Minerva, the full moon illuminated by the sun, and in the healing power of a sun working through nature under the aspect of Aesculapis. The solar and lunar cycles are counterpoised in a manner which renders the phases less exact as simplistic correlates to actual physical stages during the year of nature, but hence more satisfactorily in coordination for symbolic purposes.

The inner scheme, we must remember, is "theotechnical" and "hermetic"; that is, anthropological. Kircher is constructing a complex model in order to understand the deeper rules underlying the apparent arbitrariness of myth. The appeal of the rationalist inferences one can draw from this kind of approach lasts right into modern times. For example, in his essay *Les Dieux antiques: Origine et développement de la mythologie* (1880), the poet Stéphane Mallarmé reendorses the eighteenth-century theory that the attempts of primitive peoples to comprehend natural events gave rise to the earliest myths and that one can analyze the structural clues for the logic underlying their diversity. Benjamin Hederich's *Gründliches Lexikon Mythologicum* (1724) represents the ancestral moment when the vast Baroque network of citation or allusion, such as Lohenstein practiced – a palimpsest of reiterated classical references, "modern" poetic views, densely woven iconological details, and predigested sixteenth- and seventeenth-century scholarship – is collapsed together into an "easier" encylcopedic handbook for enlightened readers. Easier, because of the ruling assumption of rationalism, as when Hederich confidently states in his introduction, that mytholgy is just "another kind of history." No less a poet than Goethe, epitome of a very different era, consulted this register while engaged in writing his *Faust*.

Lohenstein's fusion of historical romance and encyclopedic knowledge in the *Arminius* was the major German achievement in serious philosophical fiction before Christoph Martin Wieland, in *Die Geschichte Agathons* (1766 ff.), transposed the searchings of the eighteenth century to the Greek classical world.[24] Lohenstein interpreted the foundations and destiny of European civilization as revealed in the confrontation of peoples and creeds in the axial first century A.D. Today we must reconstruct many relationships obvious to the original readership, and they depended to some extent already on the editor's appended tables and charts which elucidated the multilayered historical references in this *roman-à-clef*. But even at some distance the cultural threats posed in the novel by oppressive or imperial peoples, such as the Egyptians or Chinese, bear recognizable analogy to that of the Turks in the seventeenth century. And in parallel, the contest between Rome and the ancient Germans prefigures Europe's internal cultural choices, and often specifically the rivalry between a centralized France and a divided German realm. The Celts and other races hostile to Rome and Rome's analogues are revealed to possess spiritual affinity to or indeed to be the allies or lost branches of the Germanic family. Moreover, we discover seventeenth-century Germany's main orthodox forces, Catholicism, Lutheranism, Calvinism, and "Stoic" and "Cartesian" Rationalism, under the guise of the Druiden, Barden, Eubagen, and Greek wisemen (Weltweisen) of yore. Through a variety of internal observers, such as the eloquent itinerant philosopher and exile Zeno, Lohenstein constantly shifts authorial perspective in a skeptical quest for truth. With copious invention – using the chauvinistic strategy of a number of French and British exponents of Ancient Theology – he exploits the advantage that the German-Celtic religious heritage was almost exclusively unwritten, so far as savants of the seventeenth century were aware. In the *Arminius*, worthy Germanic nobles discourse with their foreign guests about religious matters or listen spellbound to eyewitness accounts of worship in exotic and also scriptural settings close to the year zero in the calendar of Europe.

In effect, Lohenstein gives his own twist to the general theory of religious antiquity elaborated by Athanasius Kircher in *Oedipus Aegyptiacus* (1652 ff.). Kircher thought a comparison of doctrines, myths, and cults showed the spread of Egyptian beliefs to all nations, including the cultures of the New World.[25] We recognize the similarity to Kircher in Lohenstein's scope, taking in all of the Celto-Germanic north, the ancient Mediterranean basin, and the farthest reaches of the Orient, likewise in Lohenstein's derogation of Egyptian superstition. But Lohenstein denies to Egypt her special role as the first cradle of religion. This honor actually belongs to the Hindus and the Germans. The criticism of Egypt is, in the novel, voiced mainly through the Brahmin priest Zarmar, with whom Zeno has earlier journeyed to important points of the Mediterranean world. Zeno recounts in profuse detail in Part One, Book Five, Zarmar's explanation of the outward resemblances in religious custom and symbolism which connect such diverse peoples as the Persians, Chaldeans, Egyptians, Greeks and Romans; the surface always conceals profounder meaning. Zeno, of course, already accepts the principle that the Egyptians, Chinese, and Indians, among others, employ "dark symbols" to protect wisdom from the profane; his listener, the Cherusker prince Herrmann readily agrees, adding the Druids to the general list. But, as Zeno narrates, Zarmar is quite severe in distinguishing as perverse the Egyptians who

> alle ihre Weissheit von unsern Vor-Eltern erlernet; aber mit grossem Undancke ihre Lehrer nicht nur verschwiegen / sondern die Lehre selbst verfälschet / und unter einem ertichteten Alterthume ihnen selbst den Ursprung zugeeignet [haben]. (I.v. 666a)

> [learned all their wisdom from our forefathers; but with the greatest ingratitude not only kept silent as to their teachers but falsified the teaching itself, and even appropriated its origin for themselves under a fictitious antiquity.]

In addition, he criticises Pythagoras for having spoilt the doctrine of immortality through his concept of numbers, plurality of gods, and transmigration of the soul; much of this false understanding derives from Egypt, that is, ultimately out of the law book of the Jews, but it has been corrupted in transmission and then hopelessly falsified "in den Sümpfen der Griechischen Weltweisen" [" in the swamps of the worldly Greek philosophers"] (I.v. 666b). Major ancient disciples of what the novel emphasizes to be "Indian" teaching, such as Hermes and Zoroaster, are deemed similarly to be misunderstood. In sharp contrast, Zarmar exhibits special reverence before the memorials to Plato and Socrates and the inscription to the unknown God in Athens. When Zarmar links "der grosse Brahma / das Wort / oder wie Plato nachdencklich redet / der Sohn Gottes" ["the great Brahma, the Word, or as Plato says thoughtfully, the Son of God"] (I.v. 666a), his view of the highest aspect of godhead as Logos disturbs both the sophisticated Greek worldlings and the primitive mind of Cheremon, priest of Isis. There follows a remarkable confrontation.

Zarmar publically expresses indignation over the attempt to introduce the cult of Isis as a supreme deity in the Roman empire. Though Zeno attempts to soothe him with the ready irenic, rationalist argument that this will merely symbolize the divine maintenance of the world (I.v. 704b), for Zarmar it represents something more, the triumph of corruption at a late moment and necessary turning point in the evolution of religious awareness. Specifically, Augustus, modelling himself on a vicious Jupiter, wants to justify his own evil passions by making "aus einer geilen Venus eine heilige Isis" ["a holy Isis out of a lewd Venus"] (I.v. 704b). In answer to Cheremon's claims regarding the universal powers and aspects of Isis, Zarmar not only argues that God is indivisible and that any mere representation of Nature only mirrors this completeness, but he issues a stunning challenge. He offers to prove his conviction irrefutably before the altar of the unknown God. There in a farewell which fulfills his mission, Zarmar immolates himself on a pyre, proclaiming he sees

> die siebende Erscheinung Gottes unter dem grossen Ramma und Kristna für Augen / und allen Völckern ein Licht auffgehen; für welchem unser Verstand Finsterniß / unsere Weißheit Thorheit seyn / der aber allhier als unbekannt verehrte Gott offenbahr werden wird.   (I.v. 714b)

> [the seventh apparition of God after the great Ramma and Kristna rising before his eyes, and a light for all peoples; before whom our understanding is darkness, our wisdom folly, but who will be made manifest in this very place as the revered unknown God.]

Even Augustus must bow in tribute and has the saint's ashes preserved in an urn with an inscription acknowledging his sacrificial confirmation of the truth according to the custom of his land. Ironically, Zarmar is reconciled to "Isis" by being honored with a place in "Ceres'" temple.

Zarmar concedes that popular Hinduism exhibits an admixture of delusion similar to that which confuses Egyptian and Greek religion, but his most generous view is that the Greek philosophers may have been seeking to hold the "Poefel" ("rabble") in control by veiling sublime mysteries as superstitious fables (I.v. 668b). For example, initiation into the Eleusinian mysteries is directly equated with the favorite Osirian pattern in the Renaissance tradition of the Ancient Theology:

> Diese Einweihung wäre einerley mit der Egyptischen der Isis. Diese hätte Orpheus sowohl / als die Weihe des Bacchus / welche mit der des Osiris überein käme / aus Egypten in Griechenland gebracht. Bey der Eleusinischen Weihe würden alle diesem Gottes-Dienste beywohnende/insbesonderheit aber die Neulinge gebadet / ja auch die Bilder der Götter gewaschen / und die Strassen / wodurch sie ihren Umbgang hielten / mit Weih-Wasser besprenget. (I.v. 689b)

> [This initiation was one and the same as the Egyptian mystery of Isis. Orpheus had brought both this and the hallowing of Bacchus, which corresponded to that of Osiris, to Greece out of Egypt. In the Eleusinian mystery all attending this rite, most especially the novices, were bathed, indeed even the images of the gods were washed, and the streets through which they held their procession were sprinkled with holy water.]

In rapid succession, the suggestion of ritual analogies to the eucharistic sacrifice is followed by that of analogies to baptism, even though Zeno has no knowledge of Christ's story. A reference to Christ is hidden even in the idolatrous inscription to Isis claiming "Meine erste Frucht / die ich gezeuget / ist die Sonne" ["My first fruit I have engendered is the Sun"] (I.v. 704a). Zeno experiences Zarmar's rejection of the corrupt, outward aspects of extant religious teachings and is deeply moved by the example of inward, intense faith in a higher form of understanding which can and must finally be achieved. But his own way of facing the challenge which the complexity of religious history presents is through positive, constructive doubt (I.v. 715-ab). The way Zeno experiences the adventure of religious exploration often masks authorial attitudes, and we can read fairly accurately from the dramatic intensity of certain moments witnessed by him how involved Lohenstein becomes in their resolution. Clearly, one of the most crucial series of episodes, finally shaping an aesthetic correlative of monumental proportions, is Zeno's expedition to refind the domain of Prometheus. For the prince actually takes us into and through remote territories of mankind's lost start and unfulfilled future. The religious and philosophical systems of the more accessible parts of the ancient world reflect aspects of a present status, that is, distortions of sounder belief which Zeno tells of finding in the isolated fastness of the Caucasus. There the past and future, and two necessary levels of awareness, symbolized in a feminine and masculine cult, coexist poetically in pure form as a potential in humanity.

The tensions inherent in that polarity are quite diversely represented in the real world of antiquity and in the company of ladies and gentlemen at Herrmann's court. Their commentary interrupts Zeno's narration and establishes a larger philosophic framework for it in Part One, Book Five. Thus even though Lohenstein orchestrates certain climaxes through his captivating Armenian, the interior narrator Zeno, the Baroque readers must constantly return to and interpret from the fictional plane of the narrative present (which can be related to the historical present of their own age). The thematic bridge to Zeno's adventure of making contact with a "pure" feminine versus "pure" masculine religious heritage first appears in the guise of a lively discussion, as his preceding account of experiences among the Amazons is gradually closed off. All the talk about masculine traits in women and feminine in men helps carefully qualify principles which, in the ideal balance of the sexes, can achieve a harmony. That is one level of meaning of the terms "brain" (masculine) and "heart" (feminine) in Zeno's own argument upholding the dignity of the human "eye" as one organ not quite earthly like the other senses. His words, – in this regard anticipating his strong personal attachment to the memory of Prometheus as later narrated, – very clearly set forth a paradigm of hierarchical relationships by which man's lower nature properly subserves his higher nature and in turn the latter finds a channel to the supernatural (I.v. 546a).

The exact time in which Prometheus existed is deliberately never made explicit; however, Zeno recounts thinking of the legend that Hercules freed him, which makes Prometheus seem *humanly* close, though dead and revered. Since Hercules appears in the Amazon matter as an actual man, being deified by credulous admirers, Lohenstein's euhemerism is quite overt. The *spiritual* remoteness of Prometheus is conjured instead by the ritual of many days' journey over high mountains, often in clouds, and by Zeno's having to pass through the intervening stage of discovery. This takes the symbolic form of a protected valley of plenty, a virtual paradise deserving the name "der Garten der Welt / und ein Meister-Stuecke der Natur" (I.v. 551b). Zeno decides the party should recuperate under the favorable circumstances of this literal Arcadia, but soon is fascinated by the fact that

> der Überfluß aller Dinge macht hier alles gemein/ diese Gemeinschafft aber stellte die Wahrheit der ertichteten güldenen Zeit / das von Milch und Honig flüssende Land der glückseligen Inseln [...] für. (I.v. 551b)
>
> [the superfluity of all things made everything here common, and this communality demonstrated the truth of the fabled golden age, the land of the blessed islands flowing with milk and honey.]

This isolated folk has heard that, outside their valley, the whole world worships Fortune and has invented a multitude of idols based on its phenomena, even on the vices. In contrast, they themselves worship a white goddess in a sacred grove, "das alabasterne Bild ihrer einigen Göttin / nemlich der Natur" ["the alabaster image of their sole goddess, namely Nature"] (I.v. 552a). Her foot rests on a glass sphere representing the feminine basic elements of earth and water; she is adorned with sun, moon, stars, and the zodiac; her breasts spurt wine and milk, her vagina, water; she bears a horn of plenty and is replete with symbols of the metals, minerals, and elements — in short she possesses Great Mother, Isis, and Venus attributes. Zeno's sole negative observation is that her back is covered with Pythagorean cyphers, a point which will gain in significance once he reaches the temple of Prometheus.[26]

Meanwhile the priest of Nature asserts

> Diser Gottes-Dienst wäre so alt als die Natur selbst / und darumb auch der reineste ja nicht allein den Menschen / sondern allen Geschöpfen gemein.
> (I.v. 552 b)
>
> [This worship is as old as Nature itself, and thus is also the purest worship common not only to human beings but indeed to all creatures.]

And he launches into a catalogue of creatures and events large and small, any one of which could suffice as evidence there exists a creative godhead. Though even the baffling immensity of stellar space cannot contain the majesty of godhead, the variety and complexity of Nature do exhibit divine wisdom. In his exposition of theodicy, this predecessor to Barthold Heinrich Brockes teaches that God attracts us to love and recognition of his purpose by an inner impulse and that the great chain of being, ranging from the light of stars to the light of human understanding, forms a single design unit. The priest's long poem contrasting the deception, malice, and unrest of court and city with natural morality sounds like a preview of Englihtenment teaching. There is the pre-Anacreontic endorsement of a genuine pleasure principle, when "Vergnügung und Vernunfft sich in ein Bette leget" ["satisfaction and reason lie down in one bed"], but also pre-Rousseauian suspicion of society's corrupting power, because "Wo man das Gold nicht kennt / da ist die güldne Zeit" ["where gold is unknown, there is the golden age'] and "Die Liebe selber wird bey Hof' ein Ungeheuer" ["at court even love becomes a monster"] (I.v. 556a-557a). The lines on the absence of artificial rank in a state of nature might almost be from Albrecht von Haller's *Die Alpen* (I.v. 558a).[27] Actually, under Meherdates' exotic priestly garb, we have an educated, sensitive personality who has withdrawn from the big bad world of antiquity into a privileged philosophic refuge and learned a purer attitude from his adopted people. Our appetite is whetted when, in passing, he himself contrasts Prometheus with others who foolishly criticize Nature for imperfections and mistakes. He reassures Zeno that the exotic image of the goddess is only a mirror of Nature, while Nature in turn is but a mirror of God (I.v. 552b). Meherdates' firm rejection of polytheism does not, however, lead into pantheism, but rather into a veiled, virtually deistic admiration for natural order. Meherdates is a living example of one stage of Zeno's spiritual maturation, just as the cult of Nature exhibits an ideal understanding of man's primal context.

In this sense, the memory of Prometheus is lodged indeed as a moral thorn in the flesh of Asia; it is both a lost beginning and a high challenge. Prometheus is the mythic forebear whose fatherly wisdom is said to have saved his son, the Scythian Deucalion, and Deucalion's wife Asia, and their children from a universal deluge (I.v. 565a). Thus his temple nests on top of the world, higher even than Deucalion's Arc on Ararat; and as we continue with Zeno toward that very special goal, the earlier mountains shrink into molehills by comparison, pack animals must be left behind, and our party passes through ice and snow and clouds into the cool clear peaks of the Caucasus which reflect the wiseman's divine mind. The final stretch to the "age-old temple" is traversed in a manner remarkably reminiscent of the exhilaration of Nietzsche's Zarathustra (I.v. 566a). Hollowed by either nature or a workmaster in the rock cliff, this dome could have been a model for the Pantheon had Agrippa ever glimpsed it, and is in fact an observatory and planetarium in a space rather suggestive of the human skull. A globe showing all of earth's lands, oceans, and rivers known to Zeno's age and some unknown, yet beyond doubt more ancient as well as more beautiful and accurate than any so far documented charting, rests on the central altar. The support is inscribed with a One; that is, earth is a symbol of unity and perfection, and also a literal base number for astronomical measurements (I.v. 566b).

For the temple of Prometheus is an active scientific center. The poured gold image of the sun there bears an indication it is 140 times the size of the earth, though other opinions of largeness are also given. Contrary to the belief of the "Weltweisen" — i.e., sophistical Greeks — the sun does not go around the earth, but turns on its own axis in 27 days at a speed far greater than earth's rotation, and deeply influences the earth which goes around it (ibid.). Excited by the theories of "Prometheus," the editor of the 1731 edition of the *Aminius* cannot resist placing this footnote:

Die des Copernicus Lehr Sätzen folgen, welches heut zu Tage von den meisten geschiehet. Die Gründe derselben folgen unten im 82sten §. da der Herr von Lohenstein unter der Person des Meherdates denselben ebenfalls Beyfall zu geben scheinet. (AA, I.v. 527a)

[Copernicus' theses follow, which nowadays are admitted by most people. The reasons in favor follow below in section 82, where Lord von Lohenstein appears likewise to give his approval in the person of Meherdates.]

Indeed, we even learn a rather Newtonian version of gravitation, though with a slighly exaggerating "Promethean" twist:

> [...] der Mittelpunct jedes Sternes eine magnetische Krafft in sich hat / welche / wie es die Erde unter alle Eingeweide in den Thieren thun / alles seinem Wesen gleichgeartete an sich zeucht; also daß da ein Stück von dem Monden mit Gewalt auf die Erde käme / selbiges so wohl zu dem Monden klimmen / als ein Stein aus dem Monden zur Erde fallen würde.
>
> (A, I.v. 574b)

> [(...) the center of every star has in itself a magnetic force which, just as earth does beneath the insides of the animals, pulls everything of like constitution toward itself; so that if perforce a chunk of the moon came on earth, the same would as soon climb to the moon as a stone would fall out of the moon to earth.]

There are complete models of each body in the solar system. The priest of the temple has a clear concept of the fluid structure of the sun, its fire storms, production of solar energy, the related composition of comets, and much more of the like, as well as of the planetary system with its various orbiting bodies (I.v. 567 et seq.).

Zeno is profoundly impressed by the "Promethean" cosmology (I.v. 575b et seq.). Under the guidance of the priest-scientist, he perceives — contrary to the Ptolemaic theory — the amazing number and variety of size and type of stars. He discovers them in the mere interstices of large constellations, beyond reckoning in the Milky Way, and in the southern skies. He learns that earth is a *spaceship* moving in the immensity of the universe, whose vast distances create the illusion that most of the heavens are fixed, whereas in reality they too exhibit a tendency and direction. The ancient imagery of sailing — used by Rabelais-Alcofribas to make his Cusanan point — recurs once again and is unmistakably Copernican:

> Meinen falschen Augenschein die Bewegung der Dinge zu unterscheiden / solte ich aus einem Schiffe wahrnehmen / da mich bedüncken würde: Das Ufer fliehe für mich / und nicht für ihn. So geschehe auch die Bewegung der Erde in viel mehrer Gleichheit / als eines Schiffes bey dem besten Winde / darinnen alles so unverrückt bliebe / wenn es auf der See fort segelte / als wenn es im Hafen angebunden stünde / ob schon die Erde wohl mehrmals sich erschütterte / offmals nicht nur Berge einbrächen / sondern auch an einen fernen Ort gar fortgesetzet würden.   (I.v. 567a)

[In order to discriminate the motion of things as against the false appearance to my eyes, I should be perceiving as from a ship, since I would bethink me: the shore were receding before me and not my eyes from it. Even so does the motion of the earth occur with a far greater resemblance to that of a ship under the fairest wind. Everything on board remains undisturbed as it sails ahead on the sea, as if it were standing docked in harbor. No matter whether the earth were to quake repeatedly, and mountains were not only to collapse but even to be shoved a far distance.]

Movement of bodies in celestial space, gravitational fields, relativity of viewpoint, constant processes on large (geological) and small (biological) scale — these are "mysteries" which Lohenstein contemplates with an intensity that suggest even today the vertigo produced by the initial grasp of and belief in the majestic propositions of new science in Europe.

It is a veritable orgy of vision, the human eye linking the mind with an awesome panoply. And the capacity to face, accept, and grasp the total picture constitutes the glory of Prometheus. Hence, though mortal, this sublime scientist has survived in the superstitious mind through myth (I.v. 577b et seq.). Ironically, the volcanic action, about which Zeno has learned in such thorough detail in the thereby now destroyed temple, corroborates the validity of Prometheus' genius: Before Zeno's very eyes, the decaying powers of mutability have attacked man's Promethean heritage (I.v. 586a). As Zeno leaves the high valley, we realize that the vestiges of evidence of the Promethean mission will crumble and disappear. Access to them as in the case of the Ark on Ararat, is blocked by natural forces; they are swallowed by time. With unmistakable pathos, Lohenstein symbolizes the decay of ancient wisdom which moderns are only beginning to reconstruct again; that is, he projects in strata of ruins and debris the encumbrance thwarting realization of the potential of the human mind. Because the Scythian astronomer-geologist's work antedates the status quo of classical antiquity, Prometheus does not need to be presented as a rebel. Rather, the various "ancient" orthodoxies have only partially caught up with him in spirit and share in a muddled way, at least as an inner doctrine, his monotheistic concept. If we translate the equation, however, that means the scientific drive is radically in advance of divided and divisive Christianity. Or in other words, so far as the future of mankind is concerned, the closest thing to true religion is the truth of science, nobly striven after by lofty intellect.

We have come a long way from the expansiveness of Spenser's poem as a literary microcosm to the encyclopedism of Lohenstein's historical romance. In retrospect, the former seems dense in its symbolic patterns and their final symmetry, while the latter is consciously burdened by the discerned debris of the historical process into which it probes for a ground-pattern capable of surviving the unmistakable polycentrism and fragmentation of belief in real Europe. Outside of the reminders of cosmological harmony at intervals in the novel, Lohenstein's universalism depends in large part on his confidence in a principle of direction, rather than completed order; hence the importance of the image of the compass throughout his works. The popularity of a story of spiritual questing and touring, transposed in romance form to antiquity, — one of the major strands in the Zeno component of the *Arminius*, — helped European Neoplatonic sentiment survive into the eighteenth century (the example of the *Agathon* has already been cited).[28]

The title hero of Ramsay's *Les Voyages de Cyrus* (1727), translated as the *Travels of Cyrus* (1730), a book bridging the English and French traditions, exhibits a marked degree of affinity with aspects of Lohenstein's Zeno, because both authors drew upon common sources and background. Prior to accepting his role as ruler, Ramsay's highminded young prince from the mountains of Persia travels many years throughout the nations and encounters every form of religious thought and the cultural analogues thereof. He has the singular advantage of meeting, among others, Zoroaster, Pythagoras, Anaximander, and even Daniel. In his Preface to the 1795 edition of the *Travels of Cyrus, To Which is Annexed a Discourse on the Theology and Mythology of the Pagans*, Ramsay tells us outright what Ficino and others surmised, that

> all the Pagan Divinities may be reduced to one supreme God, the principle of all beings, a Goddess his wife, sister, or daughter, and a middle God, who is his son, his representative or viceregent. (p. x) [Furthermore:] The errors which prevail at this day resemble those of former times. [Therefore,] in order to set him [Cyrus] right, the different philosophers with whom he

converses successively unfold to him new truths mixt with errors. Zoroaster confutes the mistakes of the Magi [i.e., Spinozistic "atheism"]; Pythagoras those of Zoroaster; Eleazar those of Pythagoras [i.e., stages of "deism"]; Daniel rejects those of all others, and his doctrine [i.e., the inner essence of Christianity] is the only one which the Author adopts. The order of these conversations shows the progress of the mind [...]" (p. xix).

But, interestingly, Ramsay — like Lohenstein — invokes the paradigm of a fall from the purity of the originial heritage:

Tradition strikes in with philosophy: the Author has endeavoured to shew that the earliest opinions of the most knowing and civilized nations come nearer the truth than those of latter ages; that the theology of the Orientals is more pure than that of the Egyptians, that of the Egyptians less corrupted than that of the Greeks, and that of the Greeks more exalted than that of the Romans; that the primitive system of the world was that of one supreme Deity; that in order to adapt this idea to the capacity of the vulgar, the divine attributes were represented by allegories and hieroglyphics; that mankind sinking into matter quickly forgot the meaning of those sacred symbols, and fell into idolatry; that idolatry brought forth irreligion; that rash and inconsiderate minds not being able to distinguish between principles and the abuse of them ran from one excess to the other. (p. xvii)

Lohenstein, too, accepted that there was some originial basis in nature and the universality of the human mind for the existence everywhere of analogous mythologies and doctrines, what Ramsay terms "the foundations of Noah's religion [...] tranmitted to his children" and "[...] spread throughout all nations" (p. xviii).

The "progress of the human mind" certainly continues to be a central concern of eighteenth-century literature. But the larger story tends to find more forceful embodiment in philosophic treatises and didactic poems, rather than in works of fiction. Narrative poems and novels after 1700 concentrate more effectively on the shorter matter of one protagonist's education and sentimental development. The awesome learned apparatus of Baroque encyclopedic fiction is largely abandoned, and its materials survive in specialized reference works. For example, on a smaller scale, there are the mythological handbooks of the Renaissance which reappear as rationalized dictionaries in the early eighteenth century. On a larger scale, we see the great Renaissance encyclopedia, — as represented by Johann Alsted's seven-volume work (1630), with its supposition of a highest pneumatic level and its schematization of all knowledge by combinatory art, — eventually being replaced by a yet more secularized form. However, the underlying structure of a grandiose *arbor scientiae* remains. This is still strikingly evident in Jean-le-Rond d'Alembert's "Système figuré des connoissances humaines," in the *Discours préliminaire de l'encyclopédie* (1751).[29] The Romantic theory of the novel as a potential *Gesamtkunstwerk* will reinstantiate encyclopedism as a potent principle of fiction. Meanwhile, a sign of the new literary aesthetic of the dawning Englihtenment is the reduction of the quest story to a single plotline in Fenélon's *Télémaque*. By the time of Rousseau, the dichotomization is far advanced between the learned treatise, which grapples with the big outline of human development, and sentimental fiction, which by preference examines the immediate spiritual situation of contemporary men and women, the experiencing sensoria on whose education the fate of the race hinges. As we reach the flatlands of edifying prose, far below the Promethean peak in Lohenstein's *Arminius*, we have also crossed the boundary that separates the dark conceits of Renaissance romance from the sweet reasonings in the early days of modern myth studies.[30]

Notes

*   This essay is based on several earlier conference papers which dealt with the Egyptian fascination in European letters; by their genesis, which is roughly the inverse of the present order of the expanded and revised materials, these were: "The Myth of Egypt in German Baroque Literature: The Case of Lohenstein," heard by the Division for Comparative Studies in Renaissance and Baroque Literature of the Modern Language Association at New York in 1974; "Illustrations of Poetic Anthropologies in the Renaissance and Baroque," given at the congress of the British Comparative Literature Association at Canterbury in 1980; and " 'Theotechnical Hermetics' in Poetic Anthropologizing of the Renaissance and Baroque," read at the meeting of Philological Association of the Pacific Coast at Eugene in 1982.

1   *Coleridge's Miscellaneous Criticism*, ed. by Thomas M. Raysor (London, 1936), p. 36., cited by S. K. Heninger, Jr., *Touches of Sweet Harmony:*

Pythagorean Cosmology and Renaissance Poetics (San Marino, Cal., 1974), p. 376. Heninger's final ch., on the "Poem as Literary Microcosm," brilliantly argues Spenser's creative freedom in achieving the "orderly arrangement of a diversified whole," "archetypal form," an act of making that "reproduces the divine act of creation" and thus is an "esthetic in the framework of cosmology"; as a "comprehensive order," *The Faerie Queene* aspires to be reread by readers who participate in a search for "cosmic truth."

2 Ernest B. Gilman, *The Curious Perspective: Literary and Pictorial Wit in the Seventeenth Century* (New Haven and London, 1978).

3 G. Mallary Masters, *Rabelaisian Dialectic and the Platonic-Hermetic Tradition* (Albany, 1969), or his earlier essay focussing on Book V, "The Hermetic and Platonic Traditions in Rabelais' Dive Bouteille," *Studi Francesi*, 28-30, (1966), 15-29; and Florence M. Weinberg, *The Wine and the Will: Rabelais' Bacchic Christianity* (Detroit, 1972).

4 Unless otherwise noted, all translations used in this essay are my own. References to Rabelais, henceforth indicated in parentheses by roman numeral for book and arabic for chapter, follow the two-volume Garnier edition by Louis Moland and Henri Clouzot, *Oeuvres de Rabelais* (Paris, 1956).

5 For a more detailed examination, consult Florence Weinberg, "Chess as a Literary Idea in Colonna's *Hypnerotomachia* and in Rabelais' *Cinquiesme Livre*," *Romanic Review*, 70 (1979), 321-335.

6 In Marino's urbane depiction (based on Marco Girolamo Vida's poem *Scacchia Ludus*), Adonis is drawn in to complete the game when Mercury is caught cheating by a determined, resourceful Venus. A mock-epic on the warring of love, the chess match directly concentrates on the union of the true "king" and "queen."

7 The pivotal position of Cusanus between Plato and the Renaissance is examined by Vincent Martin, O.P., "The Dialectical Process in the Philosophy of Nicholas of Cusa," *Laval Théologique et Philosophique*, 5 (1949), 213-268; Martin concludes that "Cusa has conceived of God as both the universal predicate of all things, and as a subjective possibility which has been actualized from all eternity. [...] By reifying a distinctively human mode of cognition, Cusa has, in reality, made man the measure of all things." For a view of Cusanus as a bridge between medieval and modern thought, but without widespread influence in his own times, see Eugene F. Rice, Jr., "Nicholas of Cusa's Idea of Wisdom," *Traditio*, 13 (1957), 345-368.

8 On this so perceived anticipation of Copernicus by Philolaus of Croton, see Heninger, *Harmony*, pp. 127-132; Cusanus and Rabelais are not mentioned.

9 A. Kent Hieatt, *Chaucer, Spenser, Milton: Mythopoeic Continuities and Transformations* (Montreal, 1975), ch. 9, "Isis and Osiris."

10 Cf. Heninger's treatment of the hermaphrodite as nucleus of the tetradic cosmic pattern (e.g., diagram reproduced on p. 157) and the importance of

such emblematic guides in the work of Sidney and Spenser (e.g., pp. 287-288, 305-316).

11 Cartari marshalls all these associations cogently on pp. 402-407 of *Le Imagini* [...] (Padoa 1608). The trope of the marriage of heaven and earth, with the attendant operation of the great chain of being in the seasons, is the governing ground-figure. Hence, in one depiction by Cartari, a mercurially winged Horus, holding a phallic staff and betraying a covered erection, with the solar disk behind him, receives this capsule description: "Imagine d'Horo dio delli Egittij, che e Priapo, & Bacco ancora, il quale viene inteso per la virtu seminale, & per il Sole, con il disegno del Disco signicante la rotundita del mondo, che viene dal Sole illuminato, & à cui il Sole influiße la virtu sua" (p. 406).

12 Hankins, *Source and Meaning in Spenser's Allegory: A Study of "The Faerie Queene"* (Oxford, 1971), pp. 241-285.

13 Hankins, p. 154.

14 Hankins, p. 154. Also see Elizabeth Bieman, "Britomart in Book V of *The Faerie Queene*," *University of Toronto Quarterly*, 37 (1966-67), 156-172. Bieman believes that "history" is left on the threshold of Isis' church and, through Britomart's dream, we penetrate into ancient mysteries. In this numinous vision, her reaction to the destructive force of the world (Typhon) enables the higher aspect (Osiris) to prevail, and the female emerges "as a being of a higher order and a potential channel of grace when she is united with the male principle" (pp. 166-167).

15 See my essay, "Erring & Wayfaring in Baroque Fiction: The World as Labyrinth and Garden," *Revue de Littérature Comparée*, 58 (1984), 277-299; on Milton, pp. 293-295.

16 Charles Estienne, *Dictionarium* (Oxford, 1671), p. 590.

17 Frank Kermode, *Shakespeare, Spenser, Donne: Renaissance Essays* (London, 1971), ch. 2, especially pp. 54-56, stresses the association of the thematics of justice and equity with the imperial mythology cultivated at the court of Elizabeth I; in her glory as the imperial virgin Astraea, Elizabeth united "imperium" and "sacerdotium."

18 See my essay "Erring and Wayfaring in Baroque Fiction" mentioned above.

19 In ch. 11, "Adam Unparadised," of *Shakespeare, Spenser, Donne*, Kermode appreciates the poetically potent, "illogical" complexity of the "Venus-Eve-Mary triad" presiding over the Garden of Love (pp. 264-266).

20 A happy exception is the firm reminder of Marino's importance as regards Milton in Claus Uhlig, *Theorie der Literarhistorie: Prinzipien und Paradigmen* (Heidelberg, 1982), pp. 185-188. On the wide, varied, and poetically powerful influence of the English religious epic in the German territories, see J. Hermann Tisch, "Milton and the German Mind in the Eighteenth Century," in *Studies in the Eighteenth Century*, ed. by R.F. Brissenden (Canberra, 1968), pp. 205-229.

21 I have commented on the structure and thematics of the *Arminius* in

reviews/review-articles on the recent critical renascence enjoyed by the German Baroque novel in general, and Lohenstein's work in particular, e.g.: Dieter Kafitz, *Lohensteins "Arminius": Disputatorisches Verfahren und Lehrgehalt in einem Roman zwischen Barock und Aufklärung* (Stuttgart, 1970), in *Germanistik*, 12 (1971), 96-97; Elida Maria Szarota, *Lohensteins "Arminius" als Zeitroman: Sichtweisen des Spätbarocks* (Berne and Munich, 1970), in *Journal of English and Germanic Philology*, 70 (1971), 502-507; Gerhard Spellerberg, *Verhängnis und Geschichte: Untersuchungen zu den Trauerspielen und dem "Arminius"-Roman Daniel Casper von Lohensteins* (Berlin and Zurich, 1970), in *JEGP*, 71 (1972), 413-418; Bernhard Asmuth, *Lohenstein und Tacitus: Eine Quellenkritische Interpretation der Nero-Tragödien und des "Arminius"-Romans* (Stuttgart, 1971), in *Daphnis*, 1 (1972), 223-228. The following paragraphs are a condensed version of my more extensive treatment in an article entitled "The Function of Myth in Lohenstein's *Arminius*: The Case of Egypt and Prometheus," *Argenis*, 2 (1978), 187-228.

22 This aspect of his thought is treated in my article entitled "Primal Utterance: Observations on Kuhlmann's Letters to Kircher, in View of Leibniz' Theories," in *Wege der Worte: Festschrift für Wolfgang Fleischhauer* (Cologne, 1978), pp. 187-228.

23 See figure on p. 61.

24 On the persistance of the genre, see my article "Wielands *Agathon* als Bildungsroman zwischen Barock und Romantik," in *Akten des VI. Internationalen Germanisten-Kongresses, Basel 1980* (Berne, 1980), III, pp. 344-352.

25 On the stimulating effect of Egyptian studies on European thought, and Kircher's role, consult Don Cameron Allen, *Mysteriously Meant: The Rediscovery of Pagan Symbolism and Allegorical Interpretation in the Renaissance* (Baltimore and London, 1970), ch. 5.

26 I treat the rise of the Promethean myth in European Renaissance and Baroque literature and art in the opening section of my article "Prometheus in the Romantic Age," in *European Romanticism: Cross-Currents and Leading Protagonists*, ed. by Gerhart Hoffmeister (ca. 1988).

27 On the new direction taken by Protestant cosmological imagination and the specific Lohensteinian inheritance, see my article "Anticipations of Rousseau in the Philosophic Poetry of his Countryman Albrecht von Haller," in *Festschrift for A. Owen Aldridge: Esthetics and the Literature of Ideas*, ed. by François Jost (Urbana, Ill., [ca. 1987]).

28 The best treatment of the syncretist fusion of pagan and Christian "theologians" is D.P. Walker, *The Ancient Theology: Studies in Christian Platonism from the Fifteenth to the Eighteenth Century* (London, 1972).

29 On the importance of the heritage of "encyclopedism" for the Romantics, and its pathways in the seventeenth and eighteenth centuries, see especially chs. 2 and 5 of John Neubauer, *Symbolismus und symbolische Logik: Die Idee der Ars combinatoria in der modernen Dichtung* (Munich, 1978).

The new approaches to the organization of knowledge in the eighteenth century, leading to and influenced by the French *Encyclopédie*, are treated by Giorgio Tonelli, "The Problem of the Classification of the Sciences in Kant's Time," *Rivista Critica di Storia della Filosofia*, 3 (1975), 243-294.

30 Excellent as a guide on views of mythology from the Baroque to the triumph of the Higher Criticism is the commentated collection ed. by Burton Feldman and Robert D. Richardson, *The Rise of Modern Mythology 1680-1860* (Bloomington and London, 1972). The contest and interplay between the appeal of ancient classical literature and that of the Bible is the subject of Joachim Dyck, *Athen und Jerusalem: Die Tradition der argumentativen Verknüpfung von der Bibel und Poesie im 17. und 18. Jahrhundert* (Munich, 1977). The further development of Biblical criticism, the Romantic reversal of pejorative views of myth, and the bases of modern myth studies are treated in E.S. Shaffer, *"Kubla Khan" and "The Fall of Jerusalem": The Mythological School in Biblical Criticism and Secular Literature 1770-1880* (Cambridge, 1975).

SPECULUM GENEATHEOLOGICUM
Sive
THEOTECHNIA HERMETICA
Quam
Hebræi à Chaldæis, Græci ab Ægyptiis primò,
Latini à Græcis acceperunt.
Et qua Deorum Dearumque gentilium omnium nomina ad vnitatem, quâ Solis, quâ Lunæ, revocata exhibentur.

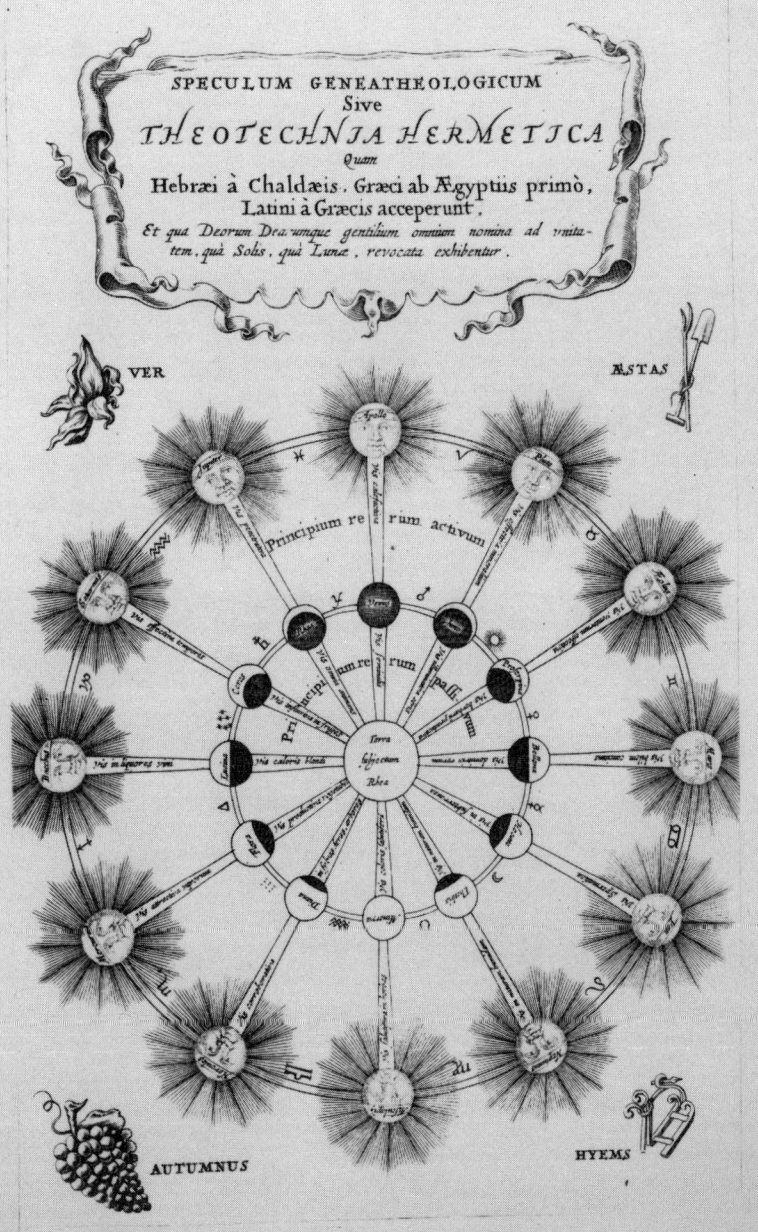

VER   ÆSTAS

AUTUMNUS   HYEMS

3. COSMIC VISION IN LOHENSTEIN'S POETRY

During the 1960s and 1970s, the remarkable and bonteous renascence of critical interest in Daniel Casper von Lohenstein (1635-1683) concentrated on him as a playwright and novelist, not as a poet. Treatments of his poetry were less frequent, but the appearance of several such studies in anticipation and on the occasion of the three hundreth anniversary of his death has stimulated a fresh awareness.[1] My purpose here is not to render an account of research on all the topics concerning the poetry which more recently have attracted attention, but to return to the matter of the poet's cosmic vision in particular.[2] The major contributions in this domain have been Charlotte Brancaforte's commentated critical edition of Lohenstein's *Venus* (1966, 1974), D.M. Moore's wider edition of the *Blumen, Geistliche Gedanken,* and *Venus* (1969), and Pierre Béhar's extensive article on Lohenstein's world view as a Renaissance theosophy (1978).[3] Other initiatives indirectly bearing also on the worldly and spiritual lyrics have included such studies as Albrecht Schöne's chapter on symbolism in Lohenstein's *Sophonisbe* (1964), a monograph by Wilhelm Vosskamp on Lohenstein's and Gryphius' conception of time and history (1967), and another by Elida Maria Szarota on late Baroque perspectives in the *Arminius* (1970).[4] As I hope to indicate below, the findings of these and other scholars have considerably enhanced our ability to correct the distorted picture of Lohenstein as an "artificial" poet which has come down to us almost directly from the tastemakers of the German Enlightenment.

In the only major work exclusively dedicated to the "lyrics" during the first half of the twentieth century, Helmut Müller (1921) treated older formal questions without opening new areas of investigation and failed to probe the poet's themes as indicative of a world view with distinct nuances.[5] It is revealing that, for example, Wentzlaff-Eggebert's subsequent attempt (1931) to rehabilitate Lohenstein's religious lyrics as "explanatory" and "objective" founders precisely through an overzealous reaction to the commonplace charge of empty rationalism. Whereas the younger Lohenstein admittedly excels in mastery of psychology, scholarly imagination, and linguistic virtuousity rather than deep religious feeling, his stoic ethos is supposedly shaken at the height of his artistic achievement, while writing the *Arminius*, so that he grasps for a surer hold besides reason.[6] But the sole forceful evidence which Wentzlaff-Eggebert adduces is a histrionic sonnet expressing desperation and disgust over corporeal vileness. Its sentiments are not at all foreign to Hofmannswaldau, especially in old age, nor to Günther when plagued by doubts; yet both of these Silesian worldlings depict themselves much more frequently and convincingly as downcast self-martyrs. The point is simply that we must be cautious about concluding that Lohenstein changes his temperamental and intellectual allegiance because he touches – as indeed he does a number of times – a religious theme shared by a genuinely pious contemporary such as Gryphius. For, down to the end, he also shares far more with Hofmannswaldau, as we see in the eroticism and urbane wit of his heroic epistles.[7]

The increased attention to Lohenstein as poet has as yet by no means yielded a settled understanding of his personal convictions and how they were shaped over time. The lack of a complete historical-critical edition continues to present a serious obstacle. The debate tends to revolve around two main questions: the extent or kind of "secularization" represented in Lohenstein's *oeuvre* and the precise degree and kind of beliefs held by him. Thus Urs Herzog can pick the poem "Weynacht-Lied" as the capstone of the *Himmel-Schlüssel* and argue that, quite the opposite of a mere exercize, it is in fact inventive and intimate, written with a genuine intention to serve real congregations and in the true spirit of Protestant hymnody. In turn, Gary Harris analyzes the long *Geistliche Gedanken über Das LIII. Capitel des Propheten Esaias* as a treatise in verse with a complex narrative perspectivism. The persona whose voice we hear may indeed mediate understanding of central mysteries – notably, Christ's crucifixion – by a highly emotional, dramatic approach, as prescribed in meditative poetry; but by raising man's intellect, as in effect equatable with the Holy Ghost, to the level of Godhead, the poem constitutes a "rejection of the ineffability of the divine" and "points the way to the mancentered cosmology of the Enlightenment." Somewhat analogously, Franz Eybl detects in Lohenstein a typical Baroque will toward synthesis through the fusion of sensual and spiritual registers; however, the poet's remarkable mastery in treating one of the age's favorite figures, Mary Magdalene, brings about a "problematic harmony" imposed on a "simultaneity of diverging contexts" – hence his poetic ingenuity masks the latent thought of the Enlightenment.[8]

One of the dangers in our attempting to evaluate Lohenstein's poetry from one or the other side of an imaginary divide between maintenance of Christian belief and abandonment of Christian belief is that we are predisposed to dismiss important alternatives, before they, too, can be tested in any adequate detail. For example, the Silesian author may belong to one of several Janus-headed species who – in Germany as elsewhere in Europe, according to the varying rhythms of specific geocultural terrains – were indispensible for the transformation of historically "advanced" Christianity into what we call, in our critical shorthand, the Enlightenment.[9] He may not have perceived, or only seldom have been disturbed by, any profound contradiction for himself in clinging, on the one hand, to essential Christian and Neoplatonic tropology and embracing, on the other hand, the hubristic promise of reason as a supreme redemptive instrument. A parallel peril for criticism is to assume that somewhere between 1650 and 1700 there existed, and poets recognized, some absolute watershed, a division of allegiances to specific topological and stylistic choices as reflections of belief. That assumption ignores the reality that many of the finest writers of the age, such as the "metaphysical" poet John Donne (d. 1631), like Shakespeare before him, used the most complicated systems of ideas as vocabularies at their disposal and prided themselves on their ability to move swiftly from one one set of references to another. It goes against the implications of the newer European poetics of *ingenium* and daring conceits (*conceptos, concetti*), formulated in such treatises as Baltasar Gracián's *Agudeza y arte de ingenio* (1642) and Emmanuele Tesauro's

Il cannochiale Aristotelico (1654). It does not take into account Lohenstein's own prominent theme of prudential disguise and practice of poetic occultation. I shall return to this point eventually in connection with the theses propounded by Béhar.

Critical preoccupation over Lohenstein's often impugned sincerity is misleading if we are mainly interested in vindicating his "heart" at the expense of his "head." For although he may seldom achieve a religious emotion which approaches those of Gryphius, he consistently attains insights of a convincingly complex order in another sphere. Lohenstein's best verse, whether ostensibly sacred or secular, expounds a *cosmic vision*. When he speaks of the structure and dynamics of the creation, he thinks of a highest creative principle – of Godhead rather than a Creator. When he speaks of eternity, we detect not primarily a linear concept which strictly continues Christian eschatology or buttresses Enlightenment theodicy. Instead, Lohenstein is fascinated by his own aesthetics of restoration of dignity and sees a cyclical pattern of time in line with stoic thought. His universe must return – at least symbolically – into primeval fire; ultimate catastrophe hovers over all; and there is a deep sympathetic parallel between the death-doomed individual, historically limited civilizations, and the cosmos. Leaving aside for now the matter of other levels in Lohenstein's stratified concept of fate (*Verhängnis*), it is clear that on the highest level the creation manifests for him an implicit purposefulness. Yet because he spins an elaborate network of relativizing comparisons in his works, some critics are tempted to overlook the system underlying it.[10]

A dominant mentality shapes Lohenstein's presentation of the most diverse subjects, and everything, including the Christian world view, is subordinate within his larger polyhistoric framework. This shift in the order of values is evident in two long poems among his *Himmel-Schlüssel*.[11] The first, "Wunder-Geburt unsers Erlösers," is neither warmly Christological, as would be characteristic of Pietistic writing, nor expresses drastic estrangement from this world in Gryphian mood; rather, it examines the concept of how God has "made this universe out of nothing" (1n.2). Fascinated by the enitre scheme of human knowledge, Lohenstein cites ancient lore, the scriptures, history, the sciences, everything "in the book of nature"

(1n.128), which he is studiously footnoting. When he finds fault with heathen and Jewish concepts, it is really to show his command of the entire subject matter today known as the history of religion. Despite a more emotional evocation of the divine birth (1n. 315 ff.), the sole important point is that something has happened to mankind, "daß Gottes Geist in Menschen sey gestiegen" (1n. 339) and that "Die Menschheit ist vermischt mit seiner Gottheit Glantze" (1n. 367). Following Italian models, the poet extols the Virgin as a "not small part of the miracle" (1n. 564), cloyingly portrays her purity and motherhood, and ends with touches of sensualism (e.g., 1n. 592 ff.) which infuses many Baroque treatments of saints by Catholic authors or those influenced by Catholic literature. Of course, sentimental bourgeois critics complained vociferously a generation later about his mixing of such "cold" historism and "hot" sensuality.[12] But what they either failed to grasp or no longer were willing to accept was the symbolic role of Woman — and most especially that of the Virgin — as the human analogue to a vital macrocosm which could bring forth being.

This seventeenth-century context, implicit for Lohenstein but fading as his century waned, is indispensible for understanding the new symbolic role of Christ in the second, superior poem, "Leitung der Vernunfft zu der ewigen Zeugung und Menschwerdung des Sohns Gottes." It widens rapidly into an explanation of the infinite creative principle which resides in Godhead and the purpose of a finite universe. It describes the totality of creation as a process in which the stage of the Son is a transitional means of fulfillment of the original, generative impulse of the Father. The Christ-theme has become a metaphor for the mysterious happening in which mankind participates, because Lohenstein is really broaching the idea of a system of spiritual energy, cosmic flow toward a higher state. The arcane moving principle called Love has a specific analogy in the processes of human thought during the generation of a positive resolve:

> Wie der Verstand gebiehrt in der Vernunft den Willen/
> So rührt ein Drittes noch von Sohn und Vater her;
> Umb die Vollkommenheit des Zeugens zu erfüllen/
> Dis ist der Liebe Geist und unerschöpflich Meer.

Béhar agrees in identifying the basic correspondences between pronouncements of Zarmar in the *Arminius* and the hermetic-theosophical trinitarianism so prominent in Lohenstein's poetry. Lohenstein's imagery draws nourishment both from Renaissance savants, such as Agrippa von Nettesheim, Justus Lipsius, and Athanasius Kircher, and from earlier sources from Cusanus to Porphyry and Macrobius.[13] It also draws on the nature philosophers and mystics of his own era, most notably Paracelsus and the Böhmean tradition.[14] The hypostatized stages of the cosmic drama are the Father as source of all being, the Son or Word as creative, regulating Logos, and the operative Holy Spirit or World Soul of which, as in Neoplatonic doctrine and Paracelsan thought, individual souls too are fragments. Béhar demonstrates the compatibility of Lohenstein's seemingly static, favorite imagery of cosmic perfection and divine rest, the circle and sphere, with his more vital, equally favorite imagery of cosmic activation and directedness, "fire." The latter is the metaphysical essence and impelling cosmological principle which we encounter at various levels in the universe and nature, for example, in the stars and in the sun as embodiments of the World Soul, in the generative interaction between the masculine and the feminine elements in the great chain of being. In my earlier essay on Lohenstein's use of mythology, I pointed out that the astronomer Prometheus, in his adoration of the sun, must be read as a multilevel, polyhistoric equation. Not only are his expressly masculine "eye" and "head" as parts of his mortal body in conformity with the orb of the sun and receptive to its rays (just as, in his system, feminine earth conforms to the sphericity of the cosmos and is fructified by sunlight); his immortal "mind" and "spirit," too, are in tune with the Logos and *anima mundi*.[15]

Béhar's analysis of the levels of the physical allegory and of the symbolic values in Lohenstein's universe is correct and helpful to this extent. But then, for reasons which, as I remark above, are familiar in Lohensteinian scholarship, this excellent interpretation is carried astray to conclusions not warranted by the full evidence. Béhar is so impressed by the poetic appeal of the Platonic-Ptolemic system of the spheres that he forgets this system came to be perceived as an aesthetic-symbolic construct, but as not true in fact, even while it continued to be used, by numerous poets of the seventeenth century. Among them were Marino, Milton, and Lohenstein. Béhar tries, however, to define Lohenstein as a writer who was looking backwards toward the Middle Ages from one side of the divide in cosmological thought, rather than as straddling that divide in the manner his works indicate. The critic perceptively finds that the symmetries within Lohenstein's dedicatory poem to the *Sophonisbe* replicate numerologicaly the threefold division of this older cosmos into the astral realm, the sublunary realm, and the world of man, as if it came down almost straight from Macrobius. Doubtless, this soul-satisfying, symbolic framework is relevant to our appreciation of the actual drama as "en effet le paroxysme du jeu universel," but it is only one of several frameworks even within the dedicatory poem.[16] It does not justify the assertion that "Le cosmos de Lohenstein n'est donc [...] celui de Copérnic [...] son cosmos, d'inspiration ptoléméenne, est celui de l'Antiquité classique" or that Lohenstein's reference to Galileo in the poem on Gryphius "ne fait aucunement gloire au grand astronome d'avoir défendu contre l'astronomie classique celle de Copérnic," when the praise is explicit.[17]

It is curious, moeover, that Béhar can ignore the fact Gryphius celebrated Copernicus in a poem entitled "über Nicolai Copernici Bild" that referred with unmistakable approbation to his heliocentric theory:

>   Du dreimal weiser Geist! Du mehr denn großer Mann!
>   Dem nicht die Nacht der Zeit, die alles pochen kann,
>   Dem nicht der herbe Neid die Sinnen hat gebunden,
>   Die Sinnen, die den Lauf der Erden neu gefunden;
>   Der du der Alten Träum und Dunkel widerlegt
>
>   Und recht uns dargetan, was lebt und was sich regt:
>   Schau! Itzund blüht dein Ruhm, den als auf einem Wagen
>   Der Kreis, auf dem wir sind, muß um die Sonne tragen!
>   Wann dies, was irdisch ist, wird mit der Zeit vergehn,
>   Soll dein Lob unbewegt mit seiner Sonnen stehn.[18]

John Milton dares to mention Galileo in a positive context as a human analogy for the seraphic gaze of Raphael in canto V of *Paradise Lost* ("as when by night the glass/ Of Galileo," line 261f.).

When Raphael answers Adam's question in canto VIII, he (through him, Milton) hedges on "whether Heaven move or Earth" (line 70), but he carefully leaves open the possibility that the newer picture of the cosmos is valid:

> Whether the sun predominant in Heaven
> Rise on the Earth, or Earth rise on the sun,
> He from the east his flaming road begin,
> Or she from the west her silent course advance
> With inoffensive pace that spinning sleeps
> On her soft axle, while she paces even,
> And bears thee soft with the smooth air along —
> (lines 160-166)

It is evident Milton cannot be equated with earlier conservative Calvinists who still cling to the older model of a stationary earth around which move the spheres, as one finds, e.g., in Johann Alsted's *Compendium philosophicum*.[19] Lohenstein, too, belongs to this newer Protestant generation among Lutherans. Moreover, Béhar's claim that the spirit of Lohenstein's age would have prevented him from appreciating the implications of the scientific revolution in astronomy is contradicted by Lohenstein's own lavish treatment of Prometheus as an intellectual hero identified with that astronomy in the *Arminius*. This was already abundantly clear to the editor of the 1731 edition who noted:

> Die des Copernicus Lehr Sätzen folgen, welches heut zu Tage von den meisten geschiehet. Die Gründe derselben folgen unten im 82sten §. da der Herr von Lohenstein unter der Person des Meherdates denselben ebenfalls Beyfall zu geben scheinet. (AA, I.v. 527a)

The principal educational protagonist in the novel, convinced by the teachings of Prometheus, corrects his own earlier misconceptions and reaches the unambiguous conclusion:

> [...] der Mittel-Punct war die Sonne/ umb diese lieff im ersten Kreise Mercur/im andern Venus/im dritten rennte die von mir für den unbeweglichen Mittel-Punct gehaltene Erde/ und umb diese in einem absondern kleinen Circkel der Monde herumb. Den vierdten Kreiß hatte Mars/ den fünften Ju-

piter/umb welchen in vier Circkeln vier Sternen umblieffen/ den sechsten Saturn/ umb den in zwey Circkeln zwei Sterne umbeileten/ inne. (I.v. 575 et seq.)

Far from being immobile, earth is discovered to be a spaceship! [20]

The poet's predilection for the symbolism of the older cosmic model obviously did not block his reception of the newer universe. But, by the same token, we should not apply in reverse the kind of critical "censorship" of values which I have just illustrated. It would be an egregious error not to take seriously the traditional cosmological references through which Lohenstein imbues his world with value, and those references include a large set of erotically colored observations on the relationships and events in the great chain of being. He is fascinated not just by celestial Love in the macrocosm, but by natural love in the microcosm. The favorite Baroque mystery of "incarnation" ("Menschwerdung") is central to Lohenstein, too, as a confirmation of the purposefulness of human existence and striving. The immediate parallel in the poem "Leitung" (p. 30) is between the creative involution of mind (Godhead) in matter and the housing of man's spirit in his body. The higher parallel is between the creation of the entire universe and the birth of Christ, for the mating of God and the Virgin is a representative marriage of Heaven and Earth (p. 40). Since "der Liebende" is also "die Liebe selber" and "sein Lieben nun auch ein selbständig Wesen" (p. 33), we have the trinity as an evolutionary metaphor on every level. A network of symbolic relationships links all phenomena: Christ as God-man represents man as soul-nature, and man "the little world" lives in correspondence to the universe infused with divine creative energy.

Lohenstein's interpretation of the Virgin is not daring; he merely uses a theme familiar in Silesian thought — as may be illustrated by Friedrich von Logau's couplet, "Der Mai":

> Dieser Monat ist ein Kuß, den der Himmel gibt der Erde,
> Daß sie jetzund seine Braut, künftig eine Mutter werde.[21]

Behind this trope of the marriage of Heaven and Earth is the serious view of Woman as epitome of beauteous, fertile nature. The greatest talents such as Paul Fleming, drawing on both the Paracelsan and

Petrarchan traditions, celebrated the female of the species as the true embodiment of the "perfection" and "charm" and "divinity" in God's creation[22]. Precisely because they were so self-explanatory, a poet could manipulate many formulas of glorification as effectively compact terms in briefer lyrics. Many epithalamia of the day did, however, give fuller attention to them, expatiating on the correspondences between human sexuality and the operations of nature and the universe.

The ecstatic bridal song closing part one of *Arminius* reveals how deep and positive is Lohenstein's fascination with such a vitalism. No disappointed rationalist turning back to religion exults over the splendor of life in these lines:

> Was ist nun herrlicher als dieser Erden-Kreiß?
> Was ist der grossen Himmels-Kugel gleiche/
> Der Sternen Burg/der Götter Königreiche?
> Sie zwey sind aber stets von Liebe glüend-heiß
> Kein Blick vergeht: dass sie von süssen Flammen
> Nicht flüssen gleichsam schmeltzende zusammen.
> Der Himmel is der Mann/die Erd ist Braut und Weib
> Sein Saamen ist die Glut/
> Ihr Saame Saltz und Flut/
> Und ihre schwang're Schoß ein stets gebehrend Leib.
> (ln. 42-51)

Composed in a form anticipating eighteenth-century hymnic free verse, this paean to love stands midway between Fleming and Brockes in its rhythms and subject matter, omitting no sector of the animal, vegetable, and mineral kingdoms in its survey of amorous pulsations. Lohenstein's works contain many notable images of circles, wheels, clocks, and chains, expressing the interlocked, finite natural order.[23] But one of the most pithy usages is a statement in this poem which fuses the Baroque vitalistic (Lucretius, Paracelsus) and mechanistic (Descartes) explanations:

> Kurtz alle Regung der Natur
> Ist eine wahre Liebes-Uhr
> (1n. 38-39)

The poet carefully hedges his statement about the correspondence between the macrocosmic and microcosmic expression of the power of love, so that his mythological references will be broadly acceptable to rationalists, Neoplatonists, and most Christians. The Baroque metaphor of "dream" takes on overtones of Englihtenment pleasure in the rational deciphering of the secrets in the mythological heritage, even while it reassures the more orthodox readership that the entrancing pagan stories are less valid because prior to the awakening of the gospel:

> Dis ist's Geheimnüs und der Kern/
> Das in den Schalen steckt geträumter Götter-Liebe.
> Denn in dem Himmel steht kein Stern
> Den nicht die Unter-Welt zeucht zu so süssem Triebe.
> (1n. 70-73)

As expression of deeper sympathetic attunement that reaches from the astral level to the lower regions, Lohenstein reinvokes the traditional music of the spheres:

> Ja alle Regungen des Himmels-Harffe sind
> Der Liebe Seitenspiel/ ihr Werck und ihre Gaben. (1n. 90-91)

The human arts and communal rites of the proto- or pre-Christian Germans in the *Arminius*, the "Braut-Lied" and the "Täntze" (I.v. 1425b) at the wedding celebration of the hero and heroine, Arminius and Thusnelda, exhibit this all-pervading impulse. Love impregnates not just earth with vitality, it also makes the stars pregnant ("Das auch die Sternen schwanger macht" [1n. 94]), imbues them with "soul" ("Weil die Gestirne doch sonst keine Seele haben" [1n. 102]). Love is the principle which gave rise both to the primordial cosmic egg and to the continuous hatching therefrom:

> Sie haben gelegt des Himmels grosses Ey/
> Aus welchem die Natur itzt alle Sachen hecket. (1n. 98-99)

Venus is associated with the divine concord that knits together the great chain of being:

> Der Sterne Würkungen sind die unsichtbaren Ketten/
> Der Venus Gürtel/ der die Welt
> Zusammen knipfft/ und in der Eintracht hält. (1n. 110-12)

Isis is the image of fruitful nature in the microcosm, responsive to her bridegroom the sun ("Und durch ihr Licht der Isis Bild/ die Erde Befruchtet" [1n. 176 f.). By commemorating the cultural identity of the German people before the advent of Christianity, Lohenstein situates his cosmology in a framework that tacitly subsumes the important archetypes of later European religion alongside those of past religions.

There were two main streams of Protestant cosmological poetry before 1700, and on occasion these currents intermingled. One was the Calvinist creation epic, as practiced by Guillaume de Salluste du Bartas (1544-1590) in *La Semaine* or *Création du Monde*, which no longer found fertile ground in the inhospital culture of France during the long reign of Louis XIV but throve in England. Via John Milton's masterwork *Paradise Lost* (1667), successfully translated into German by 1696, this tradition (re)entered the German lands and took firm root there. However, one of the consequences was the displacement of the native Baroque writers such as Lohenstein, even though his influence persisted as one element in the work of Albrecht von Haller (*Die Alpen* [1729]) and Barthold Heinrich Brockes (*Irdisches Vergnügen in Gott* [1721 ff.]).[24] The other stream, which flowed through such Lutheran writers as Harsdörffer, Hofmannswaldau, and Lohenstein, was the urbane exploration of nature, the human estate, and psychology inspired by the Catholic writer Giambattista Marino's *Adone*.[25] It was in this sophisticated Italian context that Lohenstein composed his epic encomium *Venus*, published without open attribution by Benjamin Neukirch in his famous anthology.

In some 1900 lines, Lohenstein celebrates a nature suffused with erotic vitality. There can be no mistaking it: he sings the entire range of earthly sentience, everything from the sexual drive to the refined sentiments. Yet, typically, this unabashed acceptance of life in the flesh which constitutes one level of the poem is undergirded by an argument through allusion to higher religious and cosmological principles that rehabilitates and justifies earthly joy. The tone anticipates the reasoning of the Rococo apologists of pleasure as educative and socializing under natural law and natural morality. His argument invokes not only the Neoplatonic and the Paracelsan paradigms, but also the transcribable drama of mythology as a poetic vocabulary for an elite readership. A key passage reads:

> Und daß das minste ja nicht unverliebet bliebe/
> So liebt die Königin der liebe selbst die liebe/
> Die grosse göttin dient dem selber / dessen frau
> Und mutter sie doch ist. Dann solte wohl ein bau
> Noch sonst was / dessen sich der meister wolte schämen/
> Jemanden wolgefall'n? Wer wolte früchte sämen/
> Dafür man eckel hat? Zwar als der götter schaar
> Einmal in Amatheus bey ihr zu gaste war/
> Und ihr der nectar-safft stieg etwas in die stirne/
> Gab sie sich zwar / aus schertz (wie offt noch manche dirne)
> Für eine jungfrau aus: doch als der vater sie
> Darüber schnell sah'an / sprach Juno die noch nie
> Viel seide mit ihr span / sie hätte sich wohl müssen
> Mit wasser aus dem qvell des Canathus begiessen /
> Durch dessen krafft sie selbst die jungferschafft vielmahl
> Schon hätte wiederkriegt: [...]

Behind this elegant, amusing play with the situation when Venus and her rival Juno banter, Lohenstein also weaves important themes together — and the rationalist mind, through the power of wit, reads the passage simultaneously as a conceptual play with religious archetypes. That is, Venus and Juno are two mythological aspects of the feminine, or the created material world through which God, the masculine principle, is manifested. In Silesian poetry of the seventeenth century the Virgin Mary is interpreted as the cosmic analogy to pure primal materia. Here Venus, masking the poetic function of the Virgin, has to love and serve love herself, since God is Love and she His instrument. Also, she is — as in the Christian religious myth — both the "wife" of God (Father aspect) and "mother" of God (Son aspect). The "master" alludes to one of Lohenstein's favorite concepts, the "Werkmeister" or God as cosmic artificer and designer. The term "sämen" is a key element in that part of his vocabulary deriving from the Paracelsan tradition and shared by many German theosophists and philosophers who drew on Renaissance nature philosophy.

The "feminine" here is both the pure creation and the matrix of which Paracelsus spoke: it brings forth life out of itself, once impregnated by God; is "corrupt" insofar as it represents the organic, limited time-process; but it is ever-renewed in the cycle of nature and life, a paradigm of real and figurative rebirth. Hence the jocund restoration of "virginity" by a bath of water drawn from a wellspring has its analogy in baptism, the sacramental rebirth flowing out of God. In a later passage, lines 1604 ff., similarly, we learn of a "virgin" (Cynthie) who is in love with Adonis, that perennial Christ-analogue in Western poetry. This virgin goddess, like Earth in other contexts, dreams of "him," a beautiful hero who "heals" her "wound" and receives a counter-wound in the process. The reciprocal love of Christ and his World peeks through the situation, and we can scarcely miss the double-entendre when the favorite theosophical imagery of the rose (Adam/Christ) is associated with Adonis.

Is it going too far, if we accept that Lohenstein entertained the serious possibility of doing what he (like others) surmized certain ancients had done? —

> [die] vor-welt / welche schon / o brunn der freundigkeit
> O wohlthats-stifterin! zu des Saturnus zeit
> Aus deinen würkungen und deiner hold hat müssen
> Durch schlüsse der natur die gottheits-würde schliessen.
> (V. 1026 ff.)

That assumption is not so farfetched if love informs every page in the great book of the world (V. 916 f.): "Der dinge brunn / die zeit / Wird von sich selbst hinfort schon meine flamme sämen." Such a creation can and does directly transpose for Lohenstein metaphysical propositions in his "Leitung der Vernunft zu der ewigen Zeugung der Menschwerdung des Sohns Gottes" (*Himmel-Schlüssel*). Far from having to import all elements of the Renaissance "love religion" and "love cosmology," German poets could relate these to native analysis of the Virgin as pure creation and Sophia. E.g.:

> Gott der Vater hat ein Weib gehabt vor allen Dingen. Wenn er kein Weib gehabt hätt, so hätt er den Sohn nit gehabt. Also wäre der Heilig Geist auch

nit. Das beweist, daß sie die Frau Gottes gewesen ist. [...] Diese Jungfrau hat Gott geborn wider alle Natur. Und das Mirakel wider die Natur ist auf die Geburt Mariae geredt. Denn dasselbige Mirakel ist größer denn das Mirakel Christi, die Geburt Christi, in dem der Gott Mensch ist worden. — Gedenk, daß ein Frucht muß ein Boden haben, ein Erden, ein Acker. Nun ist Christus die Frucht, Maria der Acker, der ihn getragen hat. Gott ist der Samen.[26]

The opening words of Lohenstein's prose-poem "Vereinbarung der Sterne und der Gemüther" (*Rosen*, p. 116) gives a distinctly Paracelsan slant to the favorite Renaissance trope of the marriage of heaven and earth and the idea of micro- and macrocosmic correspondences. The poet emphasizes hidden processes, mysterious affinities, an innate charm in life:

Der weise Baumeister dieses Allen hat theils eine ergätzende Widerwärtigkeit gewissen Sachen eingepflantzet/ meist aber die grossen Geschöpffe der Welt mit einer wunderbaren Kette der Eintracht vereinigt/ und ihre an sich selbst wiederwärtige Eigenschafften durch eine annehmliche Zusammenstimmung mit einander vermählet.

This coincidence of opposites occurs not only in the cosmos, but in the attraction of two hearts. His image for the "something" that guides us is a needle in the psyche (p. 126). Man's purpose is guaanteed through internal correspondence with universal laws as well as external analogy to the macrocosm: "Die allergröste Gleichförmigkeit aber hat der Mensch / als ein ewiges Geschöpffe mit der Eigenschafft des Himmels" (p. 124).

Ordinarily, the poet identifies this "property of heaven" with man's spirit or reason. Excited by his own thoughts in the poem "Leitung," Lohenstein describes reason as the Zoroastrian winged soul, a motif familiar to seventeenth-century readers in the emblem of the eagle which can soar into the sun:

Kanstu's begreifen nicht / Vernunft? So schwing die Flügel
Zur Sonne / die ihm Gott zum Schatten hat erkiest.
Sie zeugt das Licht in sich / und wird ihr eigen Spiegel;
Nun lerne: dass auch Gott ein Licht und fruchtbar ist.
(p. 34)

This imagery of apotheosis rings not with religious joy, but with the pride of the mind on the crossroads of scientific discovery. The collection of memorials called *Hyacinthen* makes it abundantly clear that Lohenstein no longer speaks of the "soul" just in the Christian sense, but of man's all-conquering intellect. These poems too are replete with allusions to the sidereal origins of "fiery" reason and recall pre-Socratic doctrines of an aether which motivates the world and Lucretius' theory of an activating impulse.

Lohenstein's finest eulogy, "Die Höhe des Menschlichen Geistes: über das Absterben Hn. Andreae Gryphii," begins unmistakably as a hymn to man's divine intelligence:

> Wohin hat sich der Geist der Menschen nicht geschwungen?
> Die kleine Welt reicht hin / wie weit die grosse gräntzt.
> Denn ist der spriede Leib gleich nur von Thon' entsprungen/
> So sieht man doch: das Gott aus diesen Schlacken gläntzt.
> Dass ichtwas Himmlisches beseele das Gehirne/
> Der Uhrsprung sey von Gott/das Wesen vom Gestirne.
>
> Die Sonne der Vernunft / das Auge des Gemüttes/
> Macht uns zu Herrn der Welt / zu Meistern der Natur.
>
> (p. 23)

Illustrations of man's sciences since ancient times, tributes to all forms of exploration, to colonization and civilizing acts follow. The poet comments with satisfaction:

> Ja eines Menschen Geist kan tausend Wunder stifften/
> Wenn Fleis die Sinnen schärft / und Weisheit den Verstand.
> Die Welt / das Grosse Buch / steckt in gelehrten Schrifften/
> Daraus uns der Natur Geheimnis wird bekant;
> Ja ein scharfsichtig Geist is fähig diß zu lernen/
> Was über die Natur / was auser Welt und Sternen.
>
>   In dem Gehirne steckt's Register der Geschichte/
> Und sein Gedächtnis ist die Mappe gantzter Welt/
> Er zeucht Wald/Stein und Wild durch Harffen und Getichte
> Schafft durch Beredsamkeit: Daß Grimm und Pöfel fällt.
> Zwingt durchs Gesetzes Zaum der rauhen Völcker Sitten;
> Dass tausend Ländern kan ein einig Haupt gebitten.
>
> (p. 24 f.)

The preface to the panegyric concludes asserting that man can even interpret the nature of God:

> Jedoch sind alles dis ihm noch zu enge Schrancken
> Weil er von Gott herkommt / so schwingt er sich zu Gott/
> Vergeistert Andachts-voll die Himmlischen Gedancken/
> Umbarmt die Ewigkeit umbschränckt mit Angst und Tod/
> Durchforscht die hohe Schrifft/in der uns Gott heist lesen/
> Ja Glaub' und Liebe fast der Gottheit tieffes Wesen.
> Herr Gryphens Seele war ein Muster solcher Geister [...].
> (p. 26 f.)

Of course, the pansophic idea of interpreting the "books" of the world — Nature and Scripture — on a universal plane in an ongoing triumph of the exuberant European mind was already thoroughly developed by great Christian educationalists like Comenius; and even Lohenstein's description of the brain as "the register of history" and "portfolio of the entire world" has nothing revolutionary about it, so far as contemporary thought was concerned. Earlier polyhistors such as Johann Heinrich Alsted had already laid the foundation for the encyclopaedism of the eighteenth century, whose first monument is roughly Pierre Bayle's rationalist dictionary of 1699. It is not the hubristic aspiration for immense scope which sounds novel in Lohenstein. Rather, it is the intense, fervent ring in his praise of the heroic quality of the intellect winning freedom from transitoriness that seems to fluctuate between the Baroque and Enlightenment registers.

Gryphius will live on "in tausend Seel'n/ als reinen Tempeln," that is, in the minds of humankind's elite. Gryphius' soul has climbed so high that, even after time is over, it will be building itself in eternity "ein neues Siegs-Altar" (p. 31). As this hyperbole asserts, there is no rest for ambition, no limit to the scope of heroism, but only striving. Man's divine spark makes him virtually godlike in an endless expansion of innate powers as he participates in a titanic drama of discovery, which is also the realization of his own mission — and earns him apotheosis! Lohenstein's special gift is his ability to link wisdom and activity, creating a dynamic area of freedom within the acknowledged limitations of nature, so that he does not fall back on a passive or purely contemplative view of virtue.[27] If we now relate this poem on Gryphius to "Leitung," the Platonistic tone of the imagery of a return to origins, an imagery that recurs throughout Lohenstein's works, assumes a more dynamic sense. In his view, the creation, a rationalistic *natura naturans*, is actually transfigured through the meaningful actions of humanity.

If we may even use Wentzlaff-Eggebert's term "crisis," the evidence shows not so much religious, as intellectual reservations, on Lohenstein's part, regarding reason. His conception of fate (*Verhängnis*) is not at all times entirely synonymous with providence (*Vorsehung*) and often incorporates elements from antiquity. Positively, reason is a potential for response to the world in whatever particular constellation the reasoner discovers it, but reason can only "play" with the shifting situation given by destiny. Negatively, reason is merely one factor — albeit an exalted one — among a variety of factors; and Lohenstein's trust in its powers weakened to the extent that he probed the significance of the affects and the mind as wellspring of irrational impulses, too. This development is more discernible in his plays and, unfortunately, lies outside the province of this chapter. It must suffice here to point to the connection between his poetic fascination for erotic themes and overall tendency to relativize values. The "epical" celebration of love in Lohenstein's long poem *Venus* exhibits his interest in passion and suggests an ideal of ultimate harmony with reason. This is a thought which also occurs in the *Arminius*. Though the motifs of light, fire, flame, sun, and similar terms have a distinct set of functions in seventeenth-century love poetry, Lohenstein is not infrequently tempted to associate the religious-philosophical ("soul," "mind," "reason") with the amorous-vitalistic ("love," "passion," "life") meanings. This imagery finally provides a formalistic bridge over the chasm separating the spirit and the flesh, as we notice so strinkingly in the play *Sophonisbe*.[28] Here Lohenstein interprets the Venus principle, too, as deriving from the primal fire that moves all things, thus truly divine.

But, in spite of its attractiveness, life is still held under the polyhistor's ironic glass for examination in poems which, like the often anthologized "Aufschrift eines Labyrinths," offer pure definitions. This conceptual tour de force with the motifs of a path and deviations ends in a neutral epigram, because it utters established truth and natural law. The poet's severe gaze at transitoriness is in itself an example of an act of heroic intellect, needing no further personal endorsement. The Pauline race of which Gryphius speaks is matched by Lohenstein's picture of the dark labyrinth — the labyrinth that we discover both externally in the maze of the world, and internally in the maze and amazement of the human brain.

The poem typically presents "vice" as the anti-principle manifest in the various weaknesses of the ages of man, a creature in confused motion between birth and death. Yet the implication of the "structure" of the "temple" (body/world) is positive: though the finite microcosm and macrocosm are subject to decay, they reveal infinity and essence. For the temple, as the title already states, bears an "inscription" or signature, whose meaning can be deciphered. Through reason — as Lohenstein once again reiterates with his standard metaphor of the winged soul — man can ascend to the Godhead, return to the wellspring of being.

The motif of the labyrinth in later German poetry is so familiar that today's reader will, in recalling Wieland's "Labyrinth des Lebens," Goethe's "Labyrinth der Brust," and other variations, not fail to detect in Lohenstein's formulation a hint of things to come:

> Wer aber durch den Bau vernünftig irregeht,
> Wird seines Heiles Weg, der Wahrheit Richtschnur finden.
> (In. 17-18)

The phrase "vernünftig irregehen" suggest the dark urge of Faustian striving not because Lohenstein generated the idea, but because he was affected here by the language and thought of his times, out of which eventually emerged the organic view. Its roots are in late Renaissance nature philosophy and mysticism (Andreae, Böhme, Comenius, et al.). Intrigued by Mediterranean lore, humanists introduced into educated speech in the sixteenth century terms such as "labyrinth" and "hieroglyph" which were destined to expand poetically and serve in the expression of that peculiarly German sort of metaphysical quest for a key to unity and inner illumination. What is notable in Lohenstein's cosmological vision in the *Himmel-*

Schlüssel is the lack of an obsessive central issue. One clearly emerges in the early decades of the eighteenth century when Albrecht von Haller (1708-1777) writes his famous poem "Über den Ursprung des Übels" with a related, but intenser, grandiloquence. Though Lohenstein touches on the fundamental and troublesome paradox that "Aus dieser Liebe [i.e., the Creator's] wächst die Wurtzel alles Bösen" ("Leitung," p. 37), he never penetrates deeply into the Böhmean idea of man's story as a drama of love contending against hate. We perceive the pattern of dialectical processes in Lohenstein, but his emphasis is constantly on man's triumphant return self-transfigured to his origins.

Despite careful approbations, and even some ecstatic glorification, of earthly love, Lohenstein still elsewhere portrays the "soul" in an older pose of martyrdom as the imprisoned divine likeness. His ambivalent attitude rests on a clear hierarchy of humane attributes, among which heroic fortitude (*virtus*) is supreme. It is thus Hofmannswaldau, rather than Lohenstein, who lays the more immediate groundwork for urbane worldly lyricism, a poetry of certainty about the goodness of the body as man's instrument. The Baroque yearning for apothesosis begins to look ridiculous to those confident in terrestial progress, the faith of the Enlightenment. A new generation of celebrators of the pleasure principle and civilizing instincts relapses less and less into despising friendly nature, because in and through it, they believe, the whole human race can achieve an implicit spiritual evolution. Lohenstein, as polyhistor, contributes to the formulation of natural in place of theological law, but he is not an advanced exponent of all the poetic corallaries. Gradually, his kind of glorification of individual "superhumanity" seems to transgress the beneficent order of the creation; and, inevitably, the true forerunners of Enlightement attitude broach the matter. Hofmannswaldau, for example, specifically disabuses himself of his own era's exhausted conception of grandeur and reinterprets it with gentle irony in the poem "Seine Geliebte wolte ins Kloster gehen," wittily pillorying motif by motif the whole metaphor complex of ascension — Lohenstein's favorite means to express the dignity of Heroic Reason.

If Lohenstein ever read this poem in manuscript, he doubtless enjoyed his friend's elegant argument, which depends for its effect on contemporary familarity with the values and form being mocked. And as a participant in the gallant mode, Lohenstein himself sometimes chides unreasonable, i.e., inappropriate, behavior by fleshly mortals. There is, however, no evidence of decisive personal wavering in his belief that the mind could transcend the human situation and the human past. — But the new age favors acceptance; it rebukes man for struggling against his own nature; pleasure even becomes duty; and reason grows tender. The tense days of the generalisimo and cavalier and other sorts of *viri clari* cede to the calmer times of burgher satisfaction. The validity of heroic transcedence is refocused upon an elitist idyll of human happiness in the short-lived Arcadia of Rococo lyrics. Gallant wit is tempered in sociable playfulness. As the connections to Lohenstein's poetic temperament fade, he becomes a kind of representative anachronism.

These remarks have attempted to sketch how Lohenstein's lyrics resemble his dramas and novel in their treatment of traditional philosophic and religious materials as relative, at times almost decorative, elements to be manipulated by intellect. His cosmic vision of the creation and of Love's operations conveys primarily his own excitement over a new capacity in man for dialectical perceptions of vast complexity. We can detect in his exultant command of disparate and exotic "facts" a new principle — the autonomy of the creative mind, loosened from the ideological contexts with which it plays.

Notes

1 Included in *Studien zum Werk Daniel Caspers von Lohenstein: Anläßlich der 300. Wiederkehr des Todesjahres*, ed. by Gerald Gillespie and Gerhard Spellerberg (Amsterdam, 1983; same as *Daphnis*, 12, nos. 2-3) are: Urs Herzog, "*Himmelschlüssel*: Lohensteins geistliche Lyrik," pp. 3-22; Franz M. Eybl, "Problematische Harmonie: Lohensteins *Thränen der Maria Magdalena zu den Füssen unsers Erlösers*," pp. 23-46; Gary Harris, "Technical and Ontological Reason in Lohenstein's *Geistliche Gedancken*," pp. 47-65; Barton W. Browning, "*Heldenbrief* and *Helden-Rede*: Lohenstein's Lyric in the Heroic Mode," pp. 67-77); Lathrop P. Johnson, "Dramatic Structure and Epic Breadth in a Lyric Poem? — Generic Synthesis in Lohenstein's *Venus*," pp. 79-304.

2   The earlier version of the present essay appeared under the same title in *Neophilologus*, 53 (1969), 413-422. I have also treated comparative religion and mythology as elements of polyhistoric fiction in "The Function of Myth in Lohenstein's *Arminius*: The Case of Egypt and Prometheus," *Argenis*, 2 (1978), 187-228; and I draw on this later essay, as well, in augmenting my argument here.

3   Charlotte Brancaforte, *Lohensteins Preisgedicht "Venus": Kritischer Text und Untersuchung* (Diss. University of Illinois, 1966; publ. Munich, 1974), which I have discussed in *Argenis*, 2 (1978), 363-368; D.M. Moore, "*Blumen, Geistliche Gedanken, Venus*" (Diss. University of Hull, 1969) and "Lohenstein's *Venus*," *New German Studies*, 1 (1973), 51-66; Pierre Béhar, "La *Weltanschauung* de Lohenstein: Une Théosophie de la Renaissance?," *Daphnis*, 7 (1978), 569-615. Having overlooked my explicit thesis of Lohenstein's hermetic-theosophical proclivity (1969), Béhar arrived at a similar sense of the general philosophic color of the lyrics and of the quester story within the *Arminius*, but at a quite different assessment of Lohenstein's cultural position and intellectual allegiances.

4   Albrecht Schöne, "Das Spiel der Sinnbilder in Lohensteins *Sophonisbe*," in *Emblematik und Drama im Zeitalter des Barock* (Munich, 1964), pp. 98-114; Wilhelm Vosskamp, *Zeit- und Geschichtsauffassung im 17. Jahrhundert bei Gryphius und Lohenstein* (Bonn, 1967); Elida Maria Szarota, *Lohensteins "Arminius" als Zeitroman: Sichtweisen des Spätbarock* (Berne and Munich, 1970).

5   Helmut Müller, *Studien über die Lyrik D.C. von Lohensteins* (Diss. Greifswald, 1921).

6   Friedrich-Wilhelm Wentzlaff-Eggebert, *Das Problem des Todes in der deutschen Lyrik des 17. Jahrhunderts* (Leipzig, 1931), pp. 183-192. Starting with such efforts as Szarota's above mentioned book and Gerhard Spellerberg's *Verhängnis und Geschichte: Untersuchungen zu den Trauerspielen und dem "Arminius"-Roman Daniel Caspers von Lohenstein* (Bad Homburg v.d.H., 1970), a far more promising trend in recent criticism has been to bring to bear on the longer-range question of the poetry numerous lessons gained from attempts to establish relationships between Lohenstein's altered understanding of history in his late years and his artistic treatment of generic possibilities of the romance, i.e., synthesis on a grandiose scale.

7   In his above-mentioned article, "*Heldenbrief* and *Helden-Rede*," Barton Browning sees the hand of the dramatist much in evidence in the love poetry, less supple or light than that of the fellow Ovidian, Hofmannswaldau. Useful not just because it forms an exception among areas of interest pursued by Lohenstein investigators, but for its detailed commentary on features of language and style related to the heroic epistles and other love poems, is Browning's dissertation at the University of California, "Artifice Visible: Literary Mannerism in the Dramas of Daniel Casper von Lohenstein" (Berkeley, 1970).

8   See note 1 for citation of the authors mentioned in this paragraph.
9   The sketch by Siegfried Wollgast, "Philosophische Strömungen in Deutschland im 17. Jahrhundert: Einige Grundlinien," *Daphnis*, 12 (1983), 1-65, serves to illustrate (in this particular instance, from a Marxian perspective) the task of replacing the grossly oversimplified schematizations of cultural periods (inherited from *Geistesgeschichte*) with a more adequate awareness of the actual variety of interacting and contending currents.
10 An examination of the cross-currents in Lohenstein that reaches an implicitly negative, though distinctly modern and in many respects quite helpful, assessment is Edward Verhofstadt, *Daniel Casper von Lohenstein: Untergehende Wertwelt und ästhetischer Illusionismus* (Bruges, 1964). Verhofstadt argues that no really stable reference points exist in the imposing edifice of Lohenstein's polyhistorism, which he ably investigates in detail, and that it therefore is empty of genuine values. The poetry is dismissed completely.
11 Henceforth, unless otherwise indicated, Lohenstein's poems will be cited, according to pagination or lines as given in each respective grouping, from the collection brought out by Fellgibel (Breslau, 1680). However, his poem *Venus* will be cited following the 1974 edition by Brancaforte (see note 3).
12 The complex story of the shift in tastes is best told by Manfred Windfuhr, *Die barocke Bildlichkeit und ihre Kritiker: Stilhaltungen in der deutschen Literatur des 17. und 18. Jahrhunderts* (Metzler, 1966).
13 Vide, e.g., in Béhar, "La *Weltanschauung*," pp. 573, 576 (note 8), 571, 570 (note 3), 574, 606.
14 Cf. Béhar, pp. 579 ff.
15 I have discussed the light-sun and eye-head motif complex in my essay "The Function of Myth," e.g., pp. 207 ff.; also, Sophonisbe's attempt at final re-identification with "fire" and "light" in relation to the Promethean drive, pp. 198 and 204. On the latter figure (without mention of Prometheus) cf. Béhar, p. 586: Dido seeks out the sun's rays, "parce que le soleil est l'incarnation de l'Âme du Monde, cette troisieme personne de la divinité qui porte inscrit en elle l'ordre du monde qu'elle a pour charge de conserver."
16 Béhar, p. 613.
17 Béhar, pp. 600, 598, 603.
18 (Cited from *Deutsche Barocklyrik*, ed. Max Wehrli [Basel, 1956], p. 12.) Béhar's weak argument from a supposed inhibiting spirit of the age — "en un temps ou l'héliocentrisme n'était qu'une hypothèse dédaignée et l'infinité du monde une théorie pour initiés" (p. 601 — might well apply to an ordinary citizen, but such timid behavior certainly cannot be presupposed for members of the intelligentsia, to which assuredly Lohenstein belonged. Wollgast, "Philosophische Strömungen," p. 25 f., indicates that the cautious reception of Copernicus was underway in Protestant territories by the second half of the sixteenth century; the case of Kepler (pp. 30 ff.) demonstrates that for strong-minded Protestants there was no inherent barrier between pursuing scientific speculations and feeling oneself to be a believer,

even if in the confessional of one's own mind none of the existing churches seemed acceptable. The early chapters of Karl S. Guthke, *Der Mythos der Neuzeit: Das Thema der Mehrheit der Welten in der Literatur- und Geistesgeschichte von der kopernikanischen Wende bis zur Science Fiction* (Berne and Munich, 1983), show that — contrary to Béhar's assumption — the theory of a plurality of worlds, too, was a topic widespread among the German intelligentsia.

19 Johannes Henricus Alstedius, *Compendium philosophicum, exhibens Methodum, Definitiones, Canones, & Quaestiones, per universam philosophiam* (1626), pp. 645 ff., in the "Compendii Uranoscopiae Sectio Prima, Exhibens Compendium Sphaerae coelestis."

20 For more detail, see my article "The Function of Myth in Lohenstein's *Arminius*," pp. 207 ff., 211-217; and in this volume, the ch. "Alcofribas on the Nile," pp. 49-54.

21 *Deutsche Gedichte des 16. und 17. Jahrhunderts*, ed. Werner Milch (Heidelberg, 1954), p. 106. Modern readers will scarcely have any difficulty in recognizing that this trope is still alive in Eichendorff's famous poem "Mondnacht," beginning:
>Es war, als hätt' der Himmel
>Die Erde still geküßt,
>Daß sie im Blütenschimmer
>Von ihm nun träumen müßt.

22 Lucretius' influence on Renaissance nature philosophy, the poetic treatment of love's cosmic significance, and woman's special microcosmic divinity are well treated in Hans Pyritz, *Paul Flemings Liebeslyrik: Zur Geschichte des Petrarkismus* (Göttingen, 1963), pp. 233-261.

23 Cf. Wilhelm Vosskamp, *Zeit- und Geschichtsauffassung*, pp. 167 ff. As Vosskamp points out, Lohenstein draws much from ancient thought, e.g., Pythagoras and the Stoics, for his cosmology. No adequate study yet exists of the penetration of Cartesian thought *per se*, but it appears to have affected Germany rather late in the seventeenth century; Lohenstein's sense of the dynamics of a system embracing the totality of the universe probably evinces only certain minor affinities, but no filiation with Descartes.

24 I have discussed the transition to Enlightenment cosmological poetry in Germany in an essay entitled "Anticipations of Rousseau in the Philosophic Poetry of His Countryman Albrecht von Haller," in *Esthetics and the Literature of Ideas* (see p. 59, n. 27 of present vol.).

25 I argued the significance of Marino as a model for modern "erotic" cosmological thought in the paper "Lohenstein als Marinist," delivered at the second congress of the Internationaler Arbeitskreis für Barockliteratur held in Wolfenbüttel in 1976.

26 Cited from the Reclam selection of Paracelsus' writings, *Vom Licht der Natur und des Geistes*, ed. by Kurt Goldhammer (Stuttgart, 1970), pp. 163 ff.

27 Vosskamp, *Zeit- und Geschichtsauffassung*, clearly explicates Lohenstein's view of man as *both* subject *and* object of history (p. 173), the polarity of "fortune" and "virtue" (manliness) (p. 201 f.), and the primacy of intellect in fulfilling the mandate of the "occasion" (p. 209).

28 Lohenstein's idea of "vernünftiges Spielen" from the foreword-poem to *Sophonisbe* is discussed by Vosskamp (p. 210 f.) and in my study *Daniel Casper von Lohenstein's Historical Tragedies* (Columbus, 1965), p. 115 f. The emphasis on striving and on a reciprocal engagement with the world-process characterizes Lohenstein's view, despite its disillusionism, as a kind of Neoplatonic "eros," as this is defined by Irving Singer in *The Nature of Love*, II: *Courtly and Romantic* (Chicago, 1984), ch. 6, "Neoplatonism and the Renaissance" (pp. 165-208).

4. PRIMAL UTTERANCE: OBSERVATIONS ON KUHLMANN'S CORRESPONDENCE WITH KIRCHER, IN VIEW OF LEIBNIZ' THEORIES

Quirinus Kuhlmann's learned interest in numerological and linguistic principles was inseparable from his religious quest to comprehend the dialectic in the unfolding of the Word. Even though he turned from the intellectual world in the 1670's, he did not really cease to share the general poetic concerns of his age. Thus ideas about language advanced in the precocious lyrical experimentation of his *Himmlische Libes-Küsse* (1671) continued to manifest themselves in his pseudo-scriptural *Kühlpsalter* (1684ff.). Testifying to the poet's synthesis of rational and inspirational understanding of language is the closeness of his *Neubegeisterter Böhme* (publ. 1674) and correspondence with the renowned polyhistor Athanasius Kircher.[1] Proudly issued as *Quirini Kuhlmanni Epistolae duae, Prior de Arte magnâ Sciendi sive Combinatoriâ, Posterior de Admirabilibus quibusdam Inventis; è Lugduno-Batavâ Romam transmissae cum Responsoria Viri in Orbe terrarum quadripartito celeberrimi, Athanasi Kircheri. Lvgd. Batavorum. Imprimuntur pro Auctore & venduntur à Lotho de Haes 1674*. [*Two Letters of Quirinus Kuhlmann, the First on the Great or Combinatory Art of Knowledge, the Second on Certain Wonderful Discoveries; Sent from Leyden to Rome with the Response of the Man most Celebrated in the Four Quarters of the Globe, Athanasius Kircher. Leyden. Printed for the Author and sold by Lotho de Haes 1674.*], this remarkable exchange illustrates not only the artistic logic in Kuhlmann's approach to language, but also the contrasting scientific approach championed by Kircher, representative of forces which enabled modern philology to emerge from the tangle of seventeenth-century speculation.[2]

Kircher's influence on Kuhlmann appears to have started shortly after publication of the former's *Ars magna sciendi sive combinatoria* in Amsterdam in 1669. In a commentary on his own experimental sonnet "Der Wechsel menschlicher Sachen" in the *Himmlische Libes-*

Küsse, and again in the "Vorgespräch" to his *Geschicht-Herold* (1672), the poet emphasized the importance of the polyhistor's fusion of logical and rhetorical principles in a kind of calculus. He even attempted to apply Kircher's conceptural series, transferring the order of various tabulated categories directly into poetry in many sonnets of the *Himmlische Libes-Küsse* and quite notably in the Pindaric ode in chapter one of the *Geschicht-Herold*.[3]

Kuhlmann's first letter to Kircher, dated January 4, 1674, reveals the extent of his craving for an art of arts and a method of methods. Citing a wide list of late-Renaissance interpreters of a universal system, he views them all as striving with more or less success toward a comprehension of things adumbrated by the peerless Raymond Lull. However, unlike their great predecessor, their insufficiencies result from various failures to derive knowledge from the "universal center" (*ED* 5). This expression characteristically relates the Lullian method of generating terms from a few irreducible tenets to the Böhmean belief in an original creative core in man and nature. Just as the Böhmean seeks the meaning under the signature of things, so the true Lullian — in Kuhlmann's view — harkens to the spirit, not the letter: "sic Lullum scire non est Artis alphabeta verbalia cognoscere, Syllogisticè illa proferre, sed realem vim sub illis ex universo Naturae libro latentem intelligere, & omnibus posse applicare" (*ED* 5). [Thus, to know Lull is not a matter of acquiring knowledge of the verbal alphabets of his Art and working them out in Syllogisms, but of perceiving, from the whole book of nature, the force hidden under them and being able to apply it to all things.] It is not long before Kuhlmann proposes to Kircher his own "Universalem libros *scribendi Artem*, vera à falsis discernentem, ultimo mundi aevo reservatam" (*ED* 6) [*Universal Art of writing books*, for distinguishing the true from the false, and reserved for the final age of the world], an art which will not only utilize the Lullian alphabets according to Kircher's method, but also demonstrate *all* books, written or to be written, by many thousands of methods reduced from unity into multiplicity and vice versa. As in the *Himmlische Libes-Küsse*, the creative potential of such a matrix-method makes the poet's head swim ("heu, quantus numerus!" [*ED* 7]). Hopeful of sympathetic response and eventual patronage, he promises to send scheduled volumes of his proposed encyclopedic undertaking and dedicates its start to Kircher. This announced *Ars sciendi combinatoria* in philology, oratory, poetics, history, ancient and modern philosophy of the Hebrews, Gentiles, and Christians, supernatural, Biblical, and natural theology, divine and secular law, and hermetical medicine was, of course, never pursued. Kuhlmann subsequently channeled his energies into his mission as a prophet, and the *Kühlpsalter* was to embody his insights *"de Philologiâ variâ & verâ,* in qua omnis *Oratoria, Poësis, Historia, & c.* consideratur" (*ED* 7) [on true and diverse Philology, in which we deal with *Oratory, Poetry, History*, etc., in their entirety]. The primacy of language as direct sacred utterance thus replaced, but also reaffirmed, the primacy of "philologia" or love of the Word as the generative proposition in Kuhlmann's system.

Kircher's kind, diplomatic reply on February 8 was not sufficiently reticent to dampen Kuhlmann's ardor. The poet did not read as friendly hints the polyhistor's references to the few sheets in German received as a sample, expression of confidence in Kuhlmann's eventual success in penetrating the labyrinth to the treasures of Lullian art, request for a more modest wording of any dedication, and assurance of continued good will even if Kuhlmann felt it necessary to disagree with certain of his views, an abstract of which he forwarded for purposes of clarification. What Kircher envisions is the rational establishment and integration of a repertory of structural definitions, the sets of which can be correlated and manipulated, as a means to solve existing questions and to generate further capacity to solve questions yet to be posited. Kircher's concept actually foreshadows the modern idea of "structure" and of a process of symbolization underlying both verbal and non-verbal codes or languages, while his ultimate device suggests today's computer:

Methodus autem *in hoc consistit.* Cistam conficimus in varia receptacula distinctam, in qua omnium scientiarum rationes ita exhibentur in tabulis conscriptae, ut de eo quispiam argumento disserere fuerit interrogatus, per variam tabellarum translocationem, applicationesque multiplici combinationum serie factas, innumera mox

Now, *the method consists herein:* We made a box divided into various compartments, in which the theoretical bases of all the sciences are set forth in tables in such a way that, no matter what subject anyone may be asked to speak about, he will, by various shiftings of tables and applications of a complex series of combina-

argumenta, ad quaestionem propositam quàm fusissime per syllogismos universales & demonstrativos deducendam, sit reperturus; Haud secus ac in *Musurgia* nostra praestitimus, qua unusquique etiam Musicae imperitus ad quamlibet melodiam artificiosè concinnandam, vel unius horae spatio, aptus fit. Iterum eodem prorsus modo & ratione qua quispiam vel *unico* solummodo *idiomate* instructus, cum omnibus tamen totius mundi nationibus & populis per literas communicare & correspondere posse docetur; quod novum repertum A. 1663. per Librum cui titulus *Polygraphia nova & universalis*, publici juris feci.... Veluti 1.2. *Duplex modus novi artificii linguarum omnium;* quorum prior docet, omni linguarum genere epistolas conscribere; alter est, omnium linguarum ad unitatem reductio, Artificium mirificum non nisi palmari arculâ conclusum, quo quispiam cum totius orbis nationibus reciprocâ negotiatione communicare poterit. 3. Hoc excipit *Steganographia universalis*, quâ quispiam cum altero correspondente occultos animi conceptûs communicare poterit, tantâ secreti profunditate, ut nullus adeò sit sagax humani ingenii conatus, qui arcanum mentis negotium penetrare possit; idque innumeris modis et rationibus. (*ED* 13-14).

tions soon find countless arguments with which to elaborate any proposed question in all possible fullness through universal and demonstrative syllogisms. Likewise, we have shown in our *Musurgia* ["method of composing music"] how anyone, even if he has no knowledge of music, can in the space of a single hour become capable of skillfully producing any melody you like. Again, in just the same way, by our method even a man who knows just a *single language* can be taught to be able to communicate and corre*spond in w*riting with all the nations and peoples of the whole world. I made this new discovery public in the year 1663 in a book entitled *New and Universal Polygraphy*. For instance, 1.2. *A two-part method for a new system of mastering all languages:* The first part teaches how to compose letters in any kind of language; the second is a reduction of all languages to their unity, an extraordinary contrivance, especially when contained in a box the size of your hand. By this device anyone will be able to carry on mutual business in writing with the nations of the whole world. 3. Next follows the *Universal Steganography* ["secret writing"], which makes it possible for anyone to share the hidden ideas of the mind with a correspondent in such a degree of secrecy that no attempt of human ingenuity is acute enough to be able to penetrate the secret business of the mind — and this [may be carried on] in countless ways.

The "method" can yield inexhaustible material for writing or speaking; and the astounding paradox is that it will ultimately enable even children and idiots to apply accrued knowledge beneficially. (Perhaps we are about to test this last assumption in the twentieth century.) Through the "method," Kircher promises control of other branches of knowledge such as mathematics, medicine, and chemistry, too. Once the generative terms of the system are put in order creative invention will flow: "Innumera alia ex hisce inveniri poterunt" (*ED* 15). [It will be possible to derive countless other things from these.][4]

Kuhlmann's response on April 19, however, returns obsessively to the theme of providential guidance. Exhilarated, he explains to Kircher that he will not be writing the proposed dissertations by his own choice, but rather through divine inspiration; in fact, he only writes according to a continuous revelation directly from God; and this occurs in his works as in his life in *quinaries*, with which other significant numbers are correlated – the pattern dominant a decade later in the *Kühlpsalter*! As the consummation of the world approaches, what was hidden under the Apocalyptic seals is being brought forth "centraliter" (*ED* 18) in his books. Kuhlmann's millenary madness is almost touching when he attempts to sway Kircher, as a God-sent collaborator, to abandon what he now more openly criticizes as the contradictory, imperfect, tedious Lullian doctrine and to embrace the higher "*Sapientiam simplicem Universalem*" (*ED* 18); all other arts depend on and are resolved in his own "Arte methodicâ centrali" (*ED* 20), Kuhlmann asserts. While tentatively accepting the possibility of a Kircherian "box" (*cista*) which would allow even children and idiots to select correct answers, the poet points out that such a device – like the various calculatory "wheels" (*rotae*) already invented – remains a machine. It could never deal with inner substance, but only manipulate reality outwardly and remain just a game:

Sed. lusus est ingeniosus,*Ingeniose Kirchere*, non methodus, primâ fronte aliquid promittens, in recessu nihil solvens. Sine cistâ enim puer nihil potest respondere, & in cistâ nihil praeter verba intelligit; tot profert, quot audit, sine intellectu.... (*ED* 21)	But it is just an ingenious game, *Ingenious Kircher*, not a method, promising something on the surface, but solving nothing deep down. For without the box the boy can answer nothing, and with the box he understands nothing but words. He produces whatever he hears, without understanding, like a parrot.

To this artificial production of mere "*Scientes*" instead of "*Sapientes*," Kuhlmann contrasts recognition of the true deriving from the "centrum rerum" (*ED* 22). If his program, too, incorporates instruction in the principles of grammar and eloquence, this involves not sterile rote learning, but training in the actual generation of a surprising abundance of words and forms from the hidden potential of language, that is, the creative act of adding to language by deriving variety from essentials. The law of analogy determines that the same principle of variation operates in history, logic, etc. Long before Hamann, Herder, and the Romantic theorists distinguish the poetic from the prosaic vision, Kuhlmann separates creative "poetry" from "versification," i.e., from mere perception, appreciation, or mechanical imitation. Most important and for him Biblically grounded, is the fact that poetry, the "science of wisdom," springs from man's inward or Adamic core:

Poësis nec discitur, nec docetur: *Versificatoria* quidem *metrica* facillimè discitur & docetur, sed haec serva *Poësios*, non *Poësis est*, quae nec metro indiget, *Grammatici, Historici, Logici, Rhetoris*, sive sermoninantis, narrantis, disputantis, exornantis munere ficto fungens. Nulla autem Scientia Sapientiae proprior divinâ Poësi: nulla magis hactenus ignota, cum tamen nulla magis nota. Haec versus metricos fundens, versu sola cunctas artes scientiasque exprimit, poëticans autem, quâ poësis propriè est, omne scibile humanum excedit. *Genius versificatorius* multis contigit, *Poëticus* paucissimis, qui in *Davide ac Salomone* maximè eminuit. Si puer ingenium versificatorium possideret, versificatoriam in paucis tabellis inclusam interpretarer, methodumque docerem extemporales versûs fundendi, sed versûs, non poëma: si verò simul haberet poeticum ingenium, indicarem ex omnibus rebus praesentibus *artis magnae Poetices fontes*,

Poetry is neither learned nor taught. *Metrical versification* is, of course, easily learned and taught, but this *is the servant of Poetry, not* Poetry, which does not require meter, but fulfills what are falsely claimed as the functions of *Grammar, History, Logic, and Rhetoric*; that is, carrying on conversation, telling a story, making an argument, embellishing a discourse. No Science is closer to Wisdom than divine Poetry; none has been more unknown up until now, at the same time as none has been more widely known. As the producer of verses in meter, it alone can express all the arts and sciences in verse, but as the maker of poems, which is the proper function of poetry, it surpasses all human knowledge. Many have had *genius* in writing verse, but few *in in writing poetry*, of whom *David and Solomon* stood out most prominently. If a boy possessed natural talent for writing verse, I would ex-

quos Versificatores possunt gustare, Poëtae solùm exprimere. (*ED* 23f.)	plain versification in a few tables, and teach the method of producing verses *ex tempore* — but it would be verses he then produced, not a poem. If along with this he really had natural poetic talent, I would show him the *sources of the great art of Poetry* in the immediacy of all things. Versifiers can appreciate these sources, but Poets alone can express them.

Kuhlmann's thesis of "analogy" implies that the creative flow of language is the deepest, most authentic expression of the mind. Poetic inspiration indeed occupies the seat of theology in its precedence over science and philosophy. As a reading of the book of Nature, Kuhlmann asserts, "Naturaescientia" teaches about outward, visible things past, present, or future. As a reading of the book of Scripture, "Naturaeprudentia" teaches the ethical application of the microcosmic and macrocosmic combinatory "wheel." But, from reading the book of Conscience, "In Naturaesapientia verò causam originemque mundi, ut extiterit, existit ac extiturus sit, *ex ipso creationis centro* in unitate trinitateque dicerem, ac hic simul, quae *Salamon* scivit." [In accordance with the wisdom of nature I would tell of the cause and origin of the world, how it was, is and will be, from the *very center of creation* in unity and trinity, and also this, that *Solomon* knew.] That is, in poetic knowing as in the creation itself inheres a universal potential: "*Omnium enim artifex docuit me Sapientia*" (*ED* 25). [For *Wisdom, the maker of all things, has taught me.*] Yet despite Kuhlmann's vaunting of the superiority of his own "method" and the unmatched creative endowment of his own "combinatory wheels" (*ED* 27), we detect his concern over the improper priority of linguistic interests which he infers from Kircher's work. He reasons that if one first teaches how to write in every kind of language, and then derives from all extant languages their unifying or underlying structure, one will be dealing with an unwieldy repertory of invented, artificial modes as well as with an overwhelming plethora of the past, present, or potential natural forms. This notion is elsewhere very tempting for the poet, as evidenced by his fascination for projecting astronomical calculations according to various theoreticians. But here, either unable to grasp or unwilling to accept the possibility of a rational, abstract language-code, he fears that the scientific mind — in the quest for an artificial language — is ignoring the source and goal of natural harmony and thereby further intensifying the confusion of tongues:

> Liberè dicam: *Omnes suo voto exciderunt, linguarum harmoniam naturalem minimè attendentes, maximamque confusionem in linguas introducentes.* (*ED* 28)

> I shall speak frankly: *They all lost sight of their own wish, paying not the slightest attention to the natural harmony of languages, and introducing the greatest confusion into languages.*

Nonetheless, despite reservations, Kuhlmann eagerly probes with questions as to how soon and in which order Kircher proposes to enable writing in all languages or to reduce them to unity. The gift of tongues at Pentacost is cited as a rare instance of the revival of universal speech, and obviously such capacity excites his imagination. A genuine universal language would, in Kuhlmann's view, have to partake of the qualities of the real, lost original tongue of the human race or a later, relatively less corrupt instance of it.

> Minime est imposibile linguâ Universali artificiali cum omnibus mundi Populis agere; sed qualis qualis haec est, Spuria est *linguae sensualis desperditae*, quâ Primiparens Adamus, ejusque liberi ante confusionem Babylonicam locuti, quâ Apostoli in festo Pentacostes loquebantur, quam omnes Gentes intelligunt. Haec justâ Dei paenâ in tot linguas se transfudit, ut Mater linguarum hodiè nesciatur, quamquam in verbo *Jeova* sive quinque vocalibus occulta jaceat. Hanc artificialem Linguam naturalem Universalem in Lexico Universali Harmonico, & Corpore Adagiorum Harmonico tradere me voluisse in Quinquennalium Admirandorum Commemoratione senties. (*ED* 28f.)

> It is not in the slightest impossible to treat with all the Peoples of the world by means of an artificial Universal language. But whatever sort of thing that may be, it is a bastard offspring of that *lost sensual language* in which our first parent Adam and his children spoke before the confusion of Babel and in which the Apostles spoke on the feast of Pentecost and which was understood by all Races. By God's just punishment this was changed into so many languages that the Mother of languages is today unknown, although it lies hidden in the word *Jeova*, or the five vowels. You will sense that in my calling to mind of the Wondrous Quinaries I wanted to render this artificial Language natural and Universal in a Harmonious Universal Lexicon

and a Harmonious Body of Proverbs. [Note: Babel actually appears under its association with Babylon in this passage.]

Kuhlmann's linkage of his sense of the simplest, primal, but also real utterance, and of his predestined "fiveness," will be discussed below. In his second letter to Kircher he already contemplates the creation of a numerologically satisfying polytrope Song — the future quinary, pseudoscriptural *Kühlpsalter* — in which expression of the combinatory potential of language will take shape:

Unum Carmen Polytropon, centum millibus versus constans, meditabar aliquando, quot versus, tot erant & similitudines & inter se Combinationes metro materiâque per tot millia milium Combinationum semper ilaesâ. Argumentu tam mirificissimi Poematis *Deo, divinoque Amori* consecrabam; *qui Scopus unus unicusque* verae *Poesios.* (*ED* 30f.)	I once considered a Much-wandering Song ["epic"] consisting of a hundred thousand verses. The number of verses was matched by number of comparisons and interrelated Combinations, and yet the meter and the subject matter remained unimpaired through so many thousands of thousands of Combinations. I consecrated the subject of this most wonderful poem to *God and His divine Love*, which is the one unique Goal of true poetry. [Note: Kuhlmann may intend a wordplay associating *scopus* also with *scop*, i.e., God as supreme bard.]

In turn, Kircher replies tactfully that he feels himself to be incapable and inept in Kuhlmann's described sublime science and that all his own writings have been accomplished by ordinary human means:

Quae scripsi ego, divinâ adspirante gratiâ, *humano more*, id est, studio & labore adquisitâ Scientiâ scripsi; non divinitùs inspiratâ aut infusâ, cujusmodi puram inter Mortales dari non existimo. (*ED* 42).	I have written these things with the favour of divine grace, but in the *human way*: that is, I have written from Knowledge obtained by study and hard work, not from knowledge divinely inspired or infused, and do not believe that knowledge purely of that sort exists among men.

He sends a descriptive bibliography of completed or committed works with the objective of clarifying his purpose and inducing due caution:

Ecce, *Vir praestantiβime*, haec Tibi pro meâ sinceritate & amore verè germano indicanda duxi, ut in arcanis, antequam lucem videant, debitâ cautelâ utaris. (*ED* 43)	You see, *most excellent Sir*, that out of my sincere and truly brotherly love I thought that these matters should be made known to you so that you would employ the appropriate degree of caution in your private writings, before they saw the light of day.

Kuhlmann takes the bait and proudly prints this impressive list.[4] Besides studies on magnetism, light, volcanic action, stellar space, geography, the critical history of numerological concepts, subterranean nature, physiology, medicine, analogical symbolism, musical theory, mathematics, sound, combinatory methodology, etc., there are numerous works on the Egyptian language, hieroglyphic writing, religion, and civilization. Kuhlmann gives no indication of being aware of the latter works' scientific context and their direct relation to the polyhistor's books on China and the Etruscans. Kircher's researches as the founder of German Egyptology, for example, his magnificent three-part *Oedipus Aegyptiacus* (1652-54), bridge the realms of the Renaissance tradition of the Ancient Theology and modern linguistics, anthropology, and comparative religion.[5] But the scriptural associations suggested by Kircher's *Arca Noë* (1673) and extensive *Turris Babel* (1673) overwhelm all other consideration of Egypt for Kuhlmann, and he concludes his printing of the transmitted bibliography with his own outburst of prophetic railing against the "Horrendum Babylonis" (*ED* 50), that is, rulers, academicians, orthodox theologians, established schools of medicine and science, and misguided mankind in general. He again casts huge numbers about to indicate the power of his own theosophical speculations, which can only be resolved *"in vero Centro"* (*ED* 51).

When four years later Kuhlmann celebrates and dedicates his own birthday as a sacred event, he describes his own first utterance as the primal sound out of the unfathomable center of being:

> Gelobet seistu, Gott, von mir in diser Stund,
> Darinn mit Aa zuerst verherrlicht dich mein Mund!
> Der du gantz wunderlich das Leben mir gegeben,
> Und wunderlicher noch dich lässest itz erheben.
> (*Kps.* 16; 4-8)

God elevates himself marvellously in the vowel A, the surviving Adamic cry of the innocent child, because it is the irreducible, yet generative core of all language. Harsdörffer had dealt with "Die I. Frage. Warumb das A der erste Buchstab in dem Abc seye?" and duly noted that it begins all known alphabets.[6] As his copious citations of linguistic speculation elsewhere show, this passing mention implicitly reminded the reader of the concept that the A, as primal start, remained intact despite all the irregularities and changes which set in after the confusion of tongues. As a sign of the origins, the A hinted at and anchored the order underlying the seeming confusion. Harsdörffer also cited Kircher's explanation that the A provides a total diagram of existence, because its five points contain latent the primary numbers and sounds.[7] Kuhlmann believes with deadly earnest in the symbolic sum of these (1,2,3,4,5) as fifteen or the quinary and quintessence interacting with the trinity. As he writes to Kircher, the five vowels are the constitutive elements of the potent holy name of IEOVA: "... in verbo *Jeova* sive quinque vocalibus [Mater linguarum] occulta jaceat" (*ED* 28). [... in the word *Jeova* or five vowels [the Mother of languages] lies hidden]. In Disquisitio IV of the *Specimen philologiae germanicae* (1646) [*Source Book of Germanic Philology*], Harsdörffer had also cited, among others, Scaliger's hypothesis that mankind could have invented or discovered the primal idea of the Creator in its first use of sound by combining the first vowel and consonant, A + B yielding Aba or "father". Kuhlmann now embraces as meaningful the widely held concept of the combinatory potential of sounds represented in the alphabet, which Harsdörffer had done much to popularize in his teaching "Vom Buchstabenwechsel."[8]

Both in his *Lehrreiche Weißheit-Lehr-Hof-Tugend-Sonnenblumen* (1671) and *Geschicht-Herold* (1672), Kuhlmann shows himself predisposed to fuse two contemporary ideas: that of a generative "calculus" of letter-number, and that of the "Japhethic" exclusion of German from the full repercussions of the confusion of tongues, with a resultant survival of its potential as a *sacred* language. Harsdörffer had discussed noncommittally the chauvinistic theory of the sixteenth-century scholar Goropius Becanus that, contrary to calumny, the barbarians, i.e., *babeles*, were actually the Greeks and Romans;

and that, moreover, the Romans were only "half," and in this sense decadent, Greeks, whereas the older heroic Greek language, and ethos, bears a closer resemblance to German (*Specimen*, Disquisitio VIII).[9] But in Kuhlmann's pseudo-scriptural writings, the primacy of German in any final revelation is definitely programmatic. We hear it in such wordplays as the refrain of *Kühlpsalm* 40, "Als er betrachtete des Babylonischen Antichristenthums Athenienser, Apollossöhne und Delosfreunde" while anchored in Greek waters in 1678:

> *Babel schlug Abel um den Bel:*
> *Babel schlägt Abel durch das El.*

Kuhlmann tends to associate sound patterns with concepts, feelings, and motions of spirit throughout his work. But at times his mind is so focused on naming, exhorting, rebuking, or narrating that referential musicality recedes or virtually disappears, and at other times he varies and combines levels. Here a magical incantation or litany seems to predominate over numerological, anagrammatic, and other features, and he approaches the intensely song-like lyrical writing of the Nuremberg school.[10] Thus we are justified in trying to interpret the "musical" associations in such powerful rhyming terms as the diminishing series Babel, Abel, Bel, and El, since Kuhlmann regards himself to be the leader of the "Abelzunft."

The following remarks make no claim to completeness or finality and serve only to suggest further work in this direction. We can hypothesize that, in the refrain, the false god Bel (Baal) is struck down by El, or the uncorrupted God who appears under one of His ancient designations in Hebrew scripture. In other places in the *Kühlpsalter*, a capital L. stands for London or Paris as new centers of the living Spirit where Kuhlmann operates; e.g., "A.L.L.E.S." refers to Amsterdam, London, Lutetia (Paris), Edinburgh, and Smyrna (e.g., *Kps.* 62-66). When Abel strikes through El, the B drops from the corrupt or confused form, and Abel is thus redeemed or reemerges from Babel. The name Abel probably reflects for Kuhlmann, among other things, a dialectic process in which the condition [b] attaches to primal being [A] and is the intervening problematic stage separating Adamic man from God [El]: A-b-El. In the relationship Babel/

Abel/Bel/El, Babel becomes Abel and Bel becomes El when the secondary reflective element b (a consonant or *Mitstimmer*) is overcome and transcended by the primary element A (vowel or *Stimmer*). This dialectic occurs, for example, in the realization of the primal utterance when, as in Scaliger's example cited by Harsdörffer, God is named as Father: Abba. "El" is also the significant letter of the alphabet which, in Kuhlmann's ABC poems, appears as "Lib-," "Leid," "Licht," "Leuchte," etc., that is, in a positive manifestation of processes or forces through which the Böhmean dialectic of Man goes forward. The associational complex of the L joined with the bright, high vowels and diphthongs often conveys masculine energy or the Holy Spirit; the association of the diphhong *ei* is already, in effect, given in the name of this person or aspect of God as "der He*i*lige Ge*i*st." In one sense, when Bel is overcome, Abel actually returns to the irreducible state of A, the primal unity of the Word in and as the simplest childlike sound. In poetic terms, however, all these "changes" (*Wechsel*) occur in the musical permutations of the refrain; they are enabled by virtue of the surviving deep correspondences in the German language.

In the ABC poems, the letter Q always introduces the Böhmean wellspring and welling terminology (*Qual, quellen, Qualität*, etc.), which through its sheer musical — and false etymological — associations expresses the mysterious story of man's fall and suffering, both an agony and an emergence, both a transfiguration and a return to origins. Serious wordplay achieves uncanny felicity in certain moments as in strophe 16 of *Kühlpsalm* 53, when Kuhlmann unquestionably *feels* God's breath inspiring Adam:

> Qual Gott in Adam nicht unendlich?
> *Sein Geist ist uns nur allzukändlich,*
> *Darinnen Gott qualificirt,*
> *Und den er himmlisch hat durchrührt*
> *Der geist, den Gott durch Adams nasen*
> *Nach sich aus sich ihm eingeblasen*
> *Im Paradischem lustgefild*
> *Nach seinem eignem Ebenbild,*
> *Das er von Gott mit Gott durchgottet,*
> *Solt ewig leben unzerrottet.*

After the terrible setback ending his mission to Turkey, Kuhlmann craves confirmation of the flowering of the Word; for, "Sprach sich nicht aus das Wort durch Worte?" (*Kp.* 53, str. 18). The alphabet, an irreducible code of generative primal elements of speech, gives comfort; its order, a seemingly arbitrary chain or series, embodies and conceals all the potent mysteries of the unfolding Word. Thus everything — the real historical juncture, the cycle of nature, the phases of revelation, the dialectic of divine and human aspects and transformations — can converge in the title of this complex ABC poem of some 50 pages:

> *Sibeiniges allgemeines Abend- Nacht- Morgen- Mittagslid aus dem sibeinigem allgemeinem güldenem ABC; sibeinig zum lobpreis Jehova-Jesus und Aufmunterung des sibentzigsibeinigen JaphetSemHam, nach recht der ewigen unendlichen gebährung im höchsten thone der 168 wechselungen angestimmet zu London im Sept. und das 5. 6. 7. den 16. 17. 18. Octob. 1679.*

From our vantage in the twentieth century, Kuhlmann's poetic skein exemplifies the unresolved tangle of ontological and mechanistic views of the potential of the human mind in the Baroque. The diverging of these strands will bring dramatic shifts and oppositions in German eighteenth-century literature — for example, between exponents of ratiocination as the supreme instrument for a moral education of the human race, and believers in organic developmental patterning. To cite a preeminent case, the German predilection for ontological explanations and resistance to exclusively mechanistic ratiocination already appears in Leibniz. Though insisting on the need for a more comprehensive ontological awareness of language and gaining a progressively deeper grasp of the organic, sensual aspects, Leibniz like Kircher nonetheless also continues the epochal trend toward a scientific view of language. Because Leibniz so rapidly grew beyond his own start as a proponent of a combinatory art in the train of Lull and Kircher, scholarship earlier doubted the extent of the connection between his brilliant linguistic insights and his creation of the calculus and method of inventing further science. Students of Leibniz still disagree not only on the question whether his "general science" was an unfulfillable utopian hope, but also on whether he indeed was dealing, in his own terminology, with matters such as deep structure and generative and transformational grammar. These issues can be cited here only by reference to other investigators.[11] More recent awareness of the interconnection of Leibniz' early interest in an artificial international language and logical calculus, and of his later concept of an Indo-European family tree, an original common language and start of the human race, and the natural superiority of German as a preserver of the good qualities of that *lingua adamica*, is broadly synthesized in D.P. Walker's excellent article, "Leibniz and Language."[12] Walker demonstrates that Leibniz' reductionism, in simplifying language to its minimal logical elements, and his psychological-epistemological and etymological studies in the *Nouveaux Essais* and *Collectanea Etymologica*, reflect one and the same concern to discover the *natural* patterns inherent in language.[13]

The present chapter merely points to a wider context of German speculation in the seventeenth century about the general *structure* of language and language's analogies to other organized thought processes and expressions of the mind. Kircher assures Kuhlmann that a *cista*, or mechanized coordinator of all tabulated definitions, will be able to relate parallel tracks in all forms of language — i.e., writing, music, mathematics, etc. — and has such immediate application as in cryptography ("occultos animi conceptûs communicare" [*ED* 14]). Though never worked out, the Kircherian *polygraphia* resembles the Leibnizian *characteristica universalis*, or reduction to calculable signs and use of signs in logical operations, in order to investigate phenomena of any type.[14] Thus, not surprisingly, Leibniz' quest for a *scientia generalis* is reflected, with regard to language, in his probing of the relationships underlying natural languages, hypothetical and actually concocted artificial languages, such evolving abstract, yet real codes as music and mathematics, and a possible general or rational language. In a leap which links him with today's structural anthropologists, Leibniz does not doubt that organic, "irregular" forms on varying levels of complexity partake of the same profound logic which underlies all life and derive from the pre-established harmony of the universe. The gap between a rationalistic and an organic view of language — i.e., between Leibniz and Humboldt — only appears wide if we superimpose this distinction on an essentially continuous development of German linguistics, contrary to the very sense of Leibniz' rejection of Descartes and Locke.[15]

Though few commentators mention Kircher in a positive way in this regard, the Jesuit polyhistor illustrates the existence of a German *scientific* tendency and capacity to entertain vitalistic concepts of nature, while exploring the possibility of generative forms in logic and language. Probably influenced by Paracelsus, Kircher believed in the presence of a goal-oriented force in natural processes, and in the collaboration of external and internal factors of development.[16] His *Arca Noë* (published 1675) posited that not all later known species were present in the Arc, but many developed out of the original primal types on board after their dispersal from it. These were the *primaevae species* from which all later actual ones come *realiter*, as the *semen universale* manifests itself variously, becoming *semen particulare*. Epigenesis, or growth of higher out of lower forms, takes place, but no genuine new formation, insofar as the *vis plastica* merely realizes stages of ontogenesis. In a medical treatise on the plague, *Scrutinium Physico-Medicum* (1658), Kircher suggested that tiny organisms which were probably only detectable with an excellent microscope carried infection from sick to healthy persons; his idea was so novel, that it was ignored.

But we can recognize the analogous thrust in Leibniz' concept of meaningful aggregate entities on all levels of complexity, all as monads partaking of the primal forming which has issued out of the essential laws of nature. The Leibnizian parallelism of the spritual and material creation, deriving from their preestablished harmony, is a worthy replacement for the Böhmean parallelism of organic and dialectic process (*Ausgeburt* and *Auswickelung*). The confused Böhmean drama of incarnation gives way to the rational order of evolutionary law. Interestingly, Leibniz' view of the interrelation of corporeal and psychological "perceptions" making up the total person admits a kind of direction which can be largely unconscious, as well as cumulative, without implying any lack of self-determination. Instead, the facts of biological evolution and historical experience indicate that the human being realizes a preformed capacity to acquire and integrate further unconscious and conscious experience. This proposition adumbrates not just the Kantian categories and modes of perception (time, space, causality, mathematics, logic), but also the Humboldtian preformed capacity (language).[17]

Kircher's and Leibniz' shared interest in the linguistic interrelation of corporeal and psychological factors, or of reality and mind, amounts to more than an epochal affinity. Kircher painstakingly compared the writing systems of the Egyptians, Chinese, and Aztecs in *Oedipus Aegyptiacus* in order to find the vestiges and determine the rules of a possible primeval picture language. In the *Erquickstunden* and elsewhere, Harsdörffer had popularized the more limited question whether the European alphabets derived via the Hebrew and Phoenician from a more ancient pictorial imagination. As Walker points out, Leibniz eventually thought that Chinese characters might derive from the hexagrams of the *I Ching*, in which he detected a system of binary numbers, and that, if Europeans once grasped these secrets, they could invent a special international language for intellectuals and communicate effectively with Chinese savants. In their intense consideration of the relationship between *verbum* and *res*, Kircher and Leibniz are spiritual forebears of modern scholars who search for anthropological and cultural data inherent in language and texts, regarded as documents, and of such eminent philologists in the Freudian group and "Wort-und-Sache" movement as the late Hans Sperber.

Though the letters to Kuhlmann do not elaborate in sufficient detail, Kircher's wish to define the basic operations of all languages (speech, music, logic, etc.) and relate them to a calculable key resembles Leibniz' thinking, insofar as Kircher's "method" supposedly will enable us to correlate and codify language; on an immediate practical level, it supposedly already permits us to teach such arts as musical composition and safe communication of the "hidden concepts of the spirit." Furthermore, Kircher is convinced that, in order to learn to manipulate a *cista* or write in a universal language, the operator need be accquainted with just one established code, his own native language. It is precisely in that sense he sums up his "*Polygraphia*, sive Artificium linguarum, quo cum omnibus totius Mundi populis, & linguis unusquisque, licet non alia, quàm materna lingua instructus correspondere posse demonstratur..." (*ED* 47). [*Poly-*

graphy, or the Theory and Art of languages, by which, as I show, anyone, no matter if he has never learned any but his native tongue, can correspond with all the people and languages of the whole world.] Implicitly, primal and sufficient logic resides in each tongue.[18]

For Kuhlmann, the primal utterance survives to greater degree in actual vestiges of an ancient organic unity of meaning and sound. Because of its deeper Japhethic roots, German still possesses the sacred qualities attributable to Adamic speech, and vibrates as a fountainhead of infinite potential. Nonetheless, albeit more corrupted, other languages all deriving from this ancient source, share in the same overall potential. An organically attached, time-bound medium, language for Kuhlmann is also an innate capacity to grasp and express a hypothetical infinity. Metaphorically, the potential of language is located for Kuhlmann in its veiled numerological correspondences; these directly link language to sacred mysteries. Attracted principally to the suggestion of numerological revelations in Kircher's treatment of language as a code, Kuhlmann missed the scientific implications. But his version of the survival in mankind of some immediate guidance inherent in language remains an intriguing religious counterpart to the early scientific delineation of a preformed or deep structure in the human mind.

Notes

1   The best general treatment of this phase in the poet's development is by Walter Dietze, *Quirinus Kuhlmann, Ketzer und Poet: Versuch einer monographischen Darstellung von Leben und Werk* (Berlin, 1963), pp. 82-100. I have discussed Kuhlmann's broader interest in an *ars combinatoria* und linguistic theory in *German Baroque Poetry* (New York, 1971), pp. 136-145.
2   Faber du Faur, No. 1317; references to the *Epistolae duae* will be by page number after the abbreviation *ED*. References to the *Kühlpsalter* will be by poem and line number (or strophe) from the critical edition by Robert I. Beare in Neudrucke deutscher Literaturwerke, N.F. 3 und 4 (Tübungen: Niemeyer, 1971). Translations from the original Latin are by the author, who wishes to thank Gene M. O'Grady for checking them for accuracy. Kircher's voluminous writings are being made more acessible by the forthcoming critical edition *Opera Omnia* by Olaf Hein and Helmut Kastl and

published by Edizioni del Mondo (Wiesbaden and Rome, 1974 ff.). A recent general treatment of the variety of the savant's interests, including language, is Joscelyn Godwin, *Athanasius Kircher: A Renaissance Man and the Quest for Lost Knowledge* (London, 1979). Concerning his influence on writers, see John Fletcher, "Kircher und die deutsche Literatur," in *Universale Bildung im Barock: Der Gelehrte Athanasius Kircher, eine Ausstellung* [...], ed. by Reinhard Dieterle et al. (Rastatt and Karlsruhe, 1981), pp. 31-39.

3 In ch. 3 of his unpublished dissertation "Das lyrische Werk Quirinus Kuhlmanns: Interpretationen zu seiner rhetorischen Struktur" (Rice University, 1970), Klaus K.L. Neuendorf examines this early impact of Kircher on Kuhlmann's development of a poetic "Wechselkunst," but does not cite the exchange of letters which intervenes after the *Neubegeisterter Böhme* and before the *Funffzehn Gesänge* (1677), the nucleus of the later opening book of the *Kühlpsalter*. Begun in Jena in 1670, following his "illumination," the *Funffzehn Gesänge* were being written during the same period; songs six and seven are dated in the year 1674. Neuendorf judges that Kuhlmann failed to appreciate the sense or potential of a combinatory art and, spellbound by contemporary ideas, was sidetracked into superficial formalistic playing with rhetorical elements. Kuhlmann's struggle for command over and power through language is deemed to degenerate into mechanistic tendencies which reflect his emergent fanatical strain. Neuendorf's antipathy for the manneristic excesses he finds leads him to negate the possible literalness in Kuhlmann's unorthodox statements or illogical constructs. For example, regarding the equation of scriptural insight with the knowledge gained by Adam and Eve through sin: "Diese zweifelhaften Aussagen sind nicht der Ausdruck der oft an der Grenze zur Blasphemie spielenden mystischen Denkens, sondern treten nur als Folge der übersteigerten Bildlichkeit auf" (p. 31).

4 I am conscious of the difficulty of isolating the elements which − whether or not largely in yet unresolved relationship internally in Kircher's encyclopedic work − correspond to the modern terms "structural" and "generative." Herbert Ernst Brekle's article "Die Idee einer generativen Grammatik in Leibnizens Fragmenten zur Logik" and Marcelo Dascal's corrective commentary "About the Idea of a Generative Grammar in Leibniz" (*Studia leibnitziana*, 3 [1971], 140-149 and 272-290) illustrate the problem of distinguishing the relative significance of the "analytic" (structural) versus "synthetic" (generative) approach even in the considerably more clarified stage of Leibniz' linguistic theorizing. The chapter "Zur Discussion der analytischen Urteilstheorie in der gegenwärtigen Philosophie" in Winfried Lenders' *Die analytische Begriffs- und Urteilstheorie von G.W. Leibniz und Chr. Wolff* (Hildesheim, 1971) examines the affinity between the modern views of "deep structure," innate "linguistic competence," and "generative grammar" (Chomsky, Quine, Katz et. al.), and Leibniz' theory of the coincidence of subject and predicate, logical relationships of sentence

elements, meaning and its structuring as immanent contents of consciousness, etc.; no barrier is descerned between Leibniz' rationalism and ontological view. As a stimulus to further research, I posit tentatively the existence in Kircher of a cruder, yet analogous dichotomization between the urge, on the one hand, to "formulate 'discovery procedures' for the establishment of the rules of particular grammars on the basis of attested utterances" (J. Lyons, *Introduction to Theoretical Linguistics* [London, 1968, p. 157]), with strong pedagogical hopes and stress on "communication"; and, on the other hand, the reductionist principle of arriving at the most adequate and satisfying explanation for all phenomena, one which overcomes the "ad-hocness" or "arbitrariness" of language while emphasizing its creative, expressive aspects as a carrier of information that derives from its own intrinsic rules.

5   In his excellent book *The Ancient Theology: Studies in Christian Platonism from the Fifteenth to the Eighteenth Century* (London, 1972), D.P. Walker concentrates on France and England and makes only brief mention of Kircher's and Leibniz' deep involvement in the comparative study of religion and culture in his chapter "Late Seventeenth-Century France — Jesuits in China." Besides a replacement for Max Wundt's book on *Die deutsche Schulmetaphysik des 17. Jahrhunderts* (Tübingen, 1939), a comprehensive study of German philosophic and literary parallels in stages of the tradition of an "ancient theology" is sorely needed.

6   *Delitiae Mathematicae et Physicae: Der Philosophischen und Mathematischen Erquickstunden Dritter Theil* (1653), p. 36.

7   *Erquickstunden Dritter Theil*, p. 37:
Der hochberühmte Ath. Kircherus weiset noch ein anderes Geheimnis in diesem Buchstaben/ und saget/ daß er eine Vorbildung deß Ab- und Zunehmens alles Weltwesens.

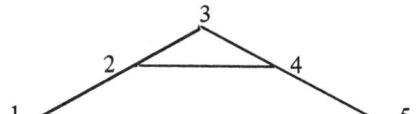

Von 1 in 2/ von 2 in 3 reichet das Wachstum/ dann fället es von 3 in 4/ von 4 in 5/ und dieses Ab- und Zunehmen wird miteinander durch 2 und 4 gleichständig verbunden. Diese Gestalt haben auch die Pyramides, Flamm- oder Spitzseulen.

In other words, the A evinces *in nuce* the same dialectic patterning as the entire cosmic and developmental drama from beginning to end; among other things, the I equates with unity of being and creation, the 2 with duplicity and manifoldness but also prefiguration and prophecy, the 3 with the turning and climax in Christ's agony, the 4 with postfiguration and fulfillment, the 5 with apocalypse but also Man's redemption in the world's catastrophe, as well as quintessential transfiguration of the elements. The A also mirrors the structure of the soul, the apex of which points to and touches heaven; like the pyramid, it signifies emblematically ascent, apotheosis, and return to origins.

8 *Erquickstunden Zweyter Theil* (1651), pp. 513ff. The Kühlpsalter responds to contemporary suggestions that, as Harsdörffer noted (p. 516):

Die XXIV. Buchstaben im Abc. können nach Lawrenbergii
Rechnung verwechselt werden
620448307827051883

Nach Puteani Rechnung:
620448017332394393600000 mal.

Nach Heinrich von Etten Meinung:
620448593438860623360000 mal.

In his "V. Aufgabe Die gantze Teutsche Sprache auf einem Blätlein weisen, by means of his famous "Fünffacher Denkring der Teutschen Sprache," Harsdörffer so arranged 48 prefixes, 60 beginning and 'rhyme" letters, 12 medial letters, 120 final letters, and 24 suffixes that anyone could dial German words, commanding all roots or "einsylbige Stammwörter," inflections, and rhyme-endings, forming further words from roots with the addition of particles, and also creating purely potential "blinde oder deutungslose Wörter" (pp. 516 ff.). As Wolfgang Kayser noted in his still important study, *Die Klangmalerei bei Harsdörffer: Ein Beitrag zur Geschichte der Literatur, Poetik und Sprachgeschichte der Barockzeit* (1932; 2. unver. Aufl., Göttingen, 1962), p. 185 n., with regard to the combinatory language wheel: "Diese Praxis ist unmittelbar aus der Kabbala übernommen. Harsd. konnte es in dem *Oedipus Aegyptiacus*, II, S. 471, Rom 1653, des berühmten Jesuiten Athan. Kircherus finden." Also still valuable is Paul Hankamer's study, *Die Sprache, ihr Begriff und ihre Deutung im 16. und 17. Jahrhundert: Ein Beitrag zur Frage der literarhistorischen Gliederung des Zeitraums* (1927; Nachdr. Hildesheim, 1965), especially the last two chs., "Grammatik, Philologie und Sprachphilosophie" and "Mystik und Naturphilosophie," dealing with the pronounced ontological tendency in German thought from Paracelsus and Böhme to Leibniz.

9 As summed up with Harsdörffer's usual caution in the *Erquickstunden* (Vol. III, p. 42): "Besagter Becanus wil auch behaubten/ daß die Nachkommen Japhets/ von welchen die Teutschen herstammen/ bey der Babylonischen Sprach-verwirrung nicht gewesen/ weil sie lang bevor ihre Mitternächtische Länder in Besitz gebracht/ wie hiervon ausführlich zu lesen *Specim. Philolg. Germ. Disq.* III. § 5.6.7." Harsdörffer remained similarly reserved with regard to a realist versus nominalist view of a possible universal language: "Weren die Wörter von Natur/ so müsten sie von jedem natürlicher Weise ohne Be[k]lemung/ verstanden werden/ und solches were die durchgehende und langgesuchte allgemeine Haubtsprache" (p. 40). Hankamer, *Die Sprache*, pp. 117-122, explains the Nuremberg principle of musical imitation of the operations of the Logos in nature through "tonal poems" and Harsdörf-

fer's inner distance from the thesis of a "Natursprache." This has been displaced by the sense of language's magic as an instrument for man's participation in cosmic "playing." The idea of the special civilizatory mission of the Japhethic stock was popularized by the French linguist and Orientalist Guillaume Postel (1510-1581), who initially focussed on the French as destined agents of renovation, then switched to the Germans as inheritors of Noah when he deemed the French had failed to lead a world reformation. The idea that Germanic had escaped the worst or was exempted in the Biblical confusion of tongues was picked up with chauvinist satisfaction in Britain, too. In *A Restitution of Decayed Intelligence: in antiquities. Concerning the most noble, and renowned English Nation* (1605, 1634), Richard Verstegan praises "the Teutonicke unto this day the ground of our speech" which reaches back to Babel, but will not go so far as Becanus who claimed it was Adamic, and is in fact sensitive to the fact the English tongue "is more swarued from the originall Teutonicke than the other languages thereon depending." Verstegan is in a long line of purists who admonish against rampant borrowing from the Romance languages and Latin. The distinguished Welsh linguist John Davies, in *Antiquae Linguae Britannicae Rudimenta* (1621), uses the same theory of a Japhethic branch of languages to argue the primary role of Celtic and the great civilizatory contribution of the Celts to Europe. The case for Celtic is reinstated in the eighteenth century by Rowland Jones in *The Origin of Languages and Nations* (1764) and by James Parsons in *Remains of Japhet: Being Historical Inquiries into the Affinity and Origin of the European Languages* (1767). Jones declares "there seems to be no room to doubt its being the first speech of mankind," and Parsons asserts "the confusion and dispersion did not affect any of the issue of *Japhet* or *Shem*." The movement toward a secular explanation of the diversity of languages, albeit originating in a rudimentary common pristine tongue, can be found in works such as Joseph Priestly, *A Course of Lectures on the Theory of Language and Universal Grammar* (1762), which carries further the general direction represented by Comenius and Wilkins in the seventeenth century.

10 Michael Hall treats the musical principles of structure in Nuremberg writing in his unpublished paper, "Aspiring to 'The State of Song': Klaj and the Nürnberg Lyric" (State University of New York at Birminghamton, 1973); pp. 82 ff. deal with the characteristic internal rhyming and superfluity of rhyme. As evidence of this tendency coming to the fore at certain moments in Kuhlmann, I would point to the virtual incantation in his introduction to Book III of the *Kühlpsalter* when he speaks of *"Geschicht- Licht- und Geticht-Christen"* (vol. I, p. 94) and develops his concept with musical variations such as "GetrichtChristen, deren Gott der *Pabst, Apap. Babel und Fabel*" (p. 96).

11 The classical early study of Leibniz' search for an artifical universal language is given in *La Logique de Leibniz* (Paris, 1901) by Louis Courturat,

who also edited the important sources. *Opuscules et fragments inédits de Leibniz* (Paris, 1903; Nachdr., Hildesheim, 1961). Earlier investigation in Germany, such as August Schmarsow's critical study and edition, *Leibniz und Schottelius: Die unvorgreiflichen Gedanken* (Strassburg, 1877), tended to concentrate more on Leibniz' praise of his native language, and somewhat less on his elaborate etymological study of its roots, discovery of the Indoeuropean family, and interest in such proponents of German's preeminence as the nature philosophers and mystics, including Böhme and Kuhlmann. The best representative of efforts to round out the fuller picture is Sigrid von der Schulenburg in *Leibniz als Sprachforscher* (written ca. 1929-39; publ., Frankfurt a.M., 1973); her ch., "Verwandtschaft der Sprachen und Völker" (pp. 68-114), is unexcelled in its presentation of his gradual conversion of the "Japhethic" and "Celto-Scythian" theories into the grander schematization of language groups very close to our modern view. In his article "The Languages of the World: A Classification by Gottfried Wilhelm Leibniz," in *Studies in Germanic Languages and Literatures: In Memory of Fred O. Nolte* (St. Louis, 1963), John T. Watermann arrives independently at similar conclusions. Further useful studies of the interrelatedness of Leibniz' interest in natural and abstract languages are: Günther Patzig, "Leibniz, Frege und die sogenannte 'lingua characteristica universalis'," and Hans Aarsleff, "The Study and Use of Etymology in Leibniz," *Studia Leibnitiana Supplementa*, 3 (1969), 103-112 and 173-189; Hans Burckhardt, "Anmerkungen zur Logik, Ontologie und Semantik bei Leibniz," *Studia Leibnitiana*, 6 (1974), 49-68; see also note 4. Other treatments of interest include: Angele Curras Rabade, "Consideraciones sobre la lengua universal leibniziana." *Anales del Seminario de Metafísica* (Madrid, 1970), pp. 7-39; Beate Dreike, "Der Einfluß von Leibniz' Philosophie auf Herders Naturauffassung" (Diss. Bonn, 1971); Renate Elisabeth Nuerner, "Gottfried Wilhelm Leibniz' Collectanea Etymologica: Ein Beitrag zur Geschichte der Etymologie" (Diss. University of Southern California, 1971); Albert Heinekamp, "Ars characteristica und natürliche Sprache bei Leibniz," *Tijdschrift filos.*, 34 (1972), 446-488.

12 *Journal of Warburg and Courtauld Institutes*, 36 (1972), 294-307.
13 In "Leibniz on Innate Ideas and the Early Reactions to the Publication of the *Nouveaux Essais* (1765)," *Journal of the History of Philosophy*, 12 (1974), 437-454. Giorgio Tonelli examines the origins of Leibniz' "innatism" in relation both to Locke and Descartes and to German philosophic tendencies of the earlier seventeenth century (including such stimuli for Kuhlmann as the pansophists and Kircher), and shows how misinterpretations delayed reception of the full import of his psychological and epistemological views in the eighteenth century, even for a "dissenter" to the empirical mentality of the age such as Herder (p. 452 f.); Leibniz' influence on the Kantian upheaval of 1769 probably was enabled in combination with the interest in Crusius' analogous doctrine.

14 As my earlier essay was going to press, an important comprehensive work on the Western philosophy of language by George Steiner, *After Babel: Aspects of Language and Translation* (New York and London, 1975) placed the German development from Leibniz to Humboldt and the Romantics in the larger European context (*vide* especially pp. 73-88). Besides showing the indebtedness of modern linguistics to that tradition, Steiner touches on the seventeenth-century interest in creating an international auxiliary language, a scientific "universal character" susceptible of mathematical manipulation, and a "true universal semantic" based on language's deep structure which manifests itself in such figures as Comenius, Kircher, and Leibniz variously (*vide* expecially pp. 198-205).

15 Eugenio Coseriu's treatment of Leibniz and Wilhelm von Humbodt as the pivotal figures in Part I of *Die Geschichte der Sprachphilosophie von der Antike bis zur Gegenwart* (Stuttgart, 1969), pp. 149-162, is consistent in its negative assessment of Leibniz' interest in devising a manageable system of signs for a universal language as an error recurrent since "R. Llull bis zu den falschen Universalien des heutigen Transformationalismus" (p. 149). Leibniz' awareness that language is not a completed, given naming of the possible, but consists of actual species of speech with their particular social-cultural existence and unrealized potential, supposedly goes against the purpose of his own *ars characteristica universalis*. In the same vein, Coseriu denies resemblance between the modern concept of deep structure and Humboldt's concept of "Sprachschöpfung" or reshaping from within, as the "inner form" continues to manifest distinct cultural characteristics of a particular language. F.H. Huberti raises this issue more productively in his article "Leibnizens Sprachverständnis, unter besonderer Berücksichtigung des III. Buches der Neuen Untersuchungen über den Verstand", *Wirkendes Wort*, 16 (1966), 361-375, when he asks whether there actually is a genuine conflict between Leibniz' early wish for a *characteristica generalis* and later sense of the organic vitality and sensual qualities of language. Modern theories of language are deemed to work out basic propositions at which Leibniz arrived by ontological postulation because he had to oppose the arbitrariness implicit in Locke's view of the individual user of language. Belief in a pre-established harmony entails as corollary that not only rational, abstract constructs, but also the developmental irregularities of natural languages reflect an underlying logic. This grasp of language as a structure of relations derives, in Huberti's opinion, directly from the youthful inspiration recorded in Leibniz' *De arte combinatoria* (1666). In his article "Point de vue: Leibniz und die These vom Weltbild der Sprache," *Zeitschrift für Deutsches Altertum und Deutsche Literatur*, 98 (1969), 216-240, Günther Heintz also affirms the relevance of Leibniz' cultivation of his German mother tongue, construction of a language of signs, and ontological approach to language. The judgment that, via Kant and Herder, Humboldt first provided a cure for Leibniz' lack of system leaves out of account the

typically "metalinguistic" stamp of Leibniz' thought. But this should not confuse us with regard to his theory of language. In fact, Leibniz is Humboldt's forerunner, because he attributes an inner character to language which parallels the subjective freedom of the monad; the individuality of an entire people is reflected in the cumulative experience of their means of communication. For Leibniz, too, a language amounts to a cultural history and world view. Leroy E. Loemker, *Struggle for Synthesis: The Seventeenth-Century Background of Leibniz' Synthesis of Order and Freedom* (Cambridge, Mass. 1972), p. 179, also relates Leibniz' search for a perfect or ideal language to his ontological sense: "Language itself is thus to be understood as possessing its own harmony, reflecting the general cultural order, and in a limited way the unity of all order. It has been pointed out that Leibniz' remarkable studies in comparative linguistics were inspired by his conviction that the universal harmony demands that there be a continuous evolution of forms and structures among all the languages of the earth."

16 I am heavily indebted for my summary of Kircher's biological theories in this paragraph to the monograph by Joseph Gutmann, *Athanasius Kircher (1602-1680) und das Schöpfungs- und Entwicklungsproblem* (Fulda, 1938).

17 Leibniz' contribution to the discovery of the unconscious is examined in the light of Freudian, Jungian, and post-Romantic psychology by Hans Ganz, *Das Unbewußte bei Leibniz in Beziehung zu modernen Theorien* (Zürich, Leipzig, 1917). In *"Sein" und "Geschehen" bei Leibniz, unter besonderer Berücksichtigung seiner Philosophie der organischen Wirklichkeit* (Munich, 1929), Anton Fischer demonstrates how, in conceiving of the existence of meaningful aggregate and evolving entities on all levels of complexity, Leibniz was also capable of understanding the existence of both an "inborn" and a therewith integratable "acquired" unconscious (p. 70 f.), as the larger part of the "perceiving" and "representing" continuum of the mind (p. 65). In the larger unity of the mind, this unconscious gradually shades into the focused conscious (p. 72).

The chapter "Nisi Ipse Intellectus" in Herbert Wildon Carr's *Leibniz* (Boston, 1929) discusses Leibniz as the first modern philosopher to assert clearly that the whole mind is active and constructive, that reality does not consist of things, but is the realization of possibilities, and that the world process is a complex spiritual development out of immanent potential. Anna Theresa Tymieniecka treats as interconnected Leibniz' psychological views, including the role of the unconscious (Part I, ch. 2), and the principle of the creative "organic continuity of nature" (Part II, Ch. 2) in *Leibniz' Cosmological Synthesis* (Assen, 1964).

18 Professor Gerhard Strasser kindly called to my attention an analysis of "Athanasius Kircher's Universal Polygraph" by George E. McCracken in *Isis*, 39, (1948), 215-228. McCracken concentrates on the system of "secret" writing proposed by Kircher in which Latin functions as the standard, i.e.,

sole simultaneously encode-decode language. McCracken mentions briefly kernel notions of a universal language which suggest a more sophisticated approach to structural analysis by Kircher; however, since Kircher never developed these, it is difficult to evaluate their full import apart from his immediate interest in coordinating sets of natural languages by means of a natural "code". I also wish to call attention to the excellent treatment of the quest for a universal language in seventeenth-century Europe in ch. 7 of Paolo Rossi, *Clavis Universalis: Arti mnemoniche e logica combinatoria da Lullo a Leibniz* (Milano-Napoli, 1960). Michel Serres, *Le système de Leibniz et ses modèles mathématiques*, 2 vols. (Paris, 1968), has elaborated the significance of Leibniz' polysystemic approach as ancestral to contemporary thinking in terms of codes. After my earlier essay had gone to press, the fascinating monograph by John Neubauer, *Symbolismus und symbolische Logik: Die Idee der ars combinatoria in der Entwicklung der modernen Dichtung* (Munich, 1978), became available, showing the relevance of Leibnizian thinking for literature, especially in new forms mediated by Romanticism. I have commented on his work in *Modern Language Notes*, 94 (1979), 1231-1237. The essay "Primal Utterance" was originally scheduled for appearance in 1975, but the unexpected and regretted death of Dr. Heinrich Gottwald, publisher of the Böhlau-Verlag, began an unfortunate delay which kept the paper locked up, with others, for some four years beyond the date of submission. Otherwise it would have come out simultaneously with George Steiner's *After Babel: Aspects of Language and Translation* (New York, 1975), with which, as I was delighted to learn, it was in sympathetic attunement through a mutual interest in late Renaissance linguistic speculation.

The Lords Prayer.

[text in Wilkins's philosophical language script]

— According to John Wilkins, *An Essay towards a Real Character, and a Philosophical Language* (1668)

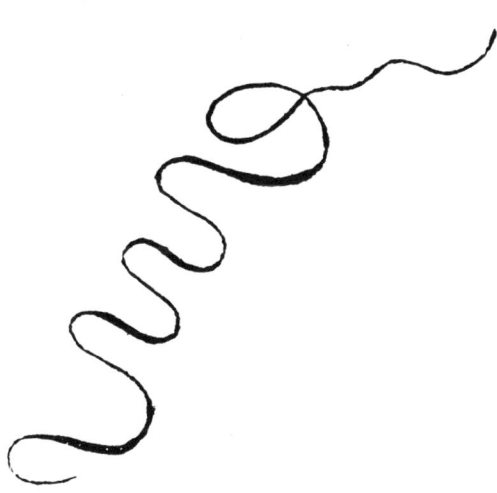

— Trim on freedom, *Tristram Shandy*, IX, iv (1767)

5. SCIENTIFIC DISCOURSE AND POSTMODERNITY: FRANCIS BACON AND THE EMPIRICAL BIRTH OF "REVISION"

Good faith demands that broad speculations about culture be so labeled. Admittedly, this chapter speculates about matters which may seem at best tenuously related: on the one hand, the emergence of scientific discourse, its influence, and its originally anti-traditionalist program in the Anglo-American world; on the other hand, the revaluative, transformational, and apocalyptic thought of Postmodernism. My purpose is not to erect a grandiose thesis, such as that repeated lapses of cultural memory enable us "unconsciously" to imitate an earlier key set of ideas and strategies vis-à-vis our own tradition. Yet, since "reformation" and "renaissance" were long ago elevated as guiding concepts of Anglo-American culture, the process of change may well have required eventually that we forget we are repeating a pattern, in order to forestall a genuine rebellion against the sustaining "myth" of transformation itself. For example, resistance to further questioning of the epochal transformation of culture soon appeared in Protestantism, which from the start developed its own conservative strains. Moreover, if to some extent today we merely imagine we are rejecting and superseding a heritage (which, paradoxically enough, is characterized by "progress"), then it follows that when the logic of our denial of tenacious paradigms does indeed conduct to antinomian or nihilistic obliteration of imposed imperatives and inherited traits, such incidents of extremism, too, may fit the overall historical pattern.

William Spanos cogently expresses a ruling Postmodern bias when he endorses a sweeping deconstruction of culture in his paper on "Breaking the Circle: Hermeneutics as Dis-closure":

> despite the alternations between its idealistic and realistic manifestations — and the significant exceptions to its binary structure — the Western literary tradition from the classical Greeks to Proust, Joyce, Yeats, and Eliot has been by and large, and increasingly, a metaphysical or logocentric tradition motivated by the Will to Power over existence.[1]

"Willful objectification of the 'mystery' " and "spatialization of the temporality of being" threaten suffocation and petrification, whereas

> destruction or deconstruction of the Western literary heritage ... promises the paradoxically liberating double retrieval (*Widerholen*). I mean the discovering not only of texts "buried" in and by the hardened tradition (i.e., the "meaning" for us in the present), but also of a stance before the Western literary tradition, especially as it has been formulated by the ontotheological New Critics and Structuralists, that opens up the possibility of a perpetually new — a postModern or an authentically modern — literary history, a history that, in focusing on dis-closure, both validates the inexhaustibility of literary texts (i.e., literary history as mis-reading) and commits literature to the difficult larger task of "overcoming metaphysics" — a history, in other words, that puts literature at the service of being rather than being at the service of literature.[2]

That is certainly an admirable program in its aim, but it raises momentous issues about the way in which our discovery of the "mystery" may or may not, as experience, flow and rechannel itself in myriad courses through the contingencies of language, memory, culture, history.[3]

Therefore, if I concentrate on only one set of symptomatic terms in the above passage, it is to address the general bias (and not necessarily to dispute specific points, such as the well-taken critique of most structuralist and semiotic approaches). "Liberating double retrieval," "a perpetually new ... literary history," and " 'overcoming metaphysics' " strike me as reformulations of several sacrosanct tenets of "our" culture supposedly under scrutiny and attack. While it is true that Spanos, drawing nourishment from thinkers such as Heidegger, avoids (pseudo-)scientific, and prefers philosophic, expressions, this momentarily distracts attention from what is fundamentally the restatement of a persistent binary relationship to existence. M.H. Abrams and others have shown that the progressive secularization of Western thought since the Renaissance has involved not just the reformulation of religious ideas "within the prevailing two-term system of subject and object" but also the assimilative poetization of the triumphant natural sciences in the eighteenth and nineteenth centuries.[4] The Romantics, too, had high hopes for a "perpetually new" poetry, which would simultaneously "overcome" and thereby redeem or "retrieve" the moribund past, as well as "liberate" existence as "becoming." Hence Postmodern propositions haunt me like ghostly echoes which cannot be disentangled from other ancestral contexts, those spectral families hardly banished into the recesses of memory — as into the dictionary and history book. Must I join them (ahead of wish) and drag with me into oblivion the corpse of the language and culture I did *not* invent, in order to help unclutter and unfetter Being? Yes; if I accept the most extreme conclusion deriving from Lord Bacon's veiled declaration that, as of the Renaissance, being in possession of a vocabulary — man's inherited burden — constitutes the gravity of Original Sin. Speech, even speech concerning the inauthenticity of speech, prevaricates meanwhile.

Perhaps my recalcitrant admission that I believe I have already rejected *earlier* versions of redemption by or as some radical break in consciousness only brands me as a hardened reifier and spatializer, an unbeliever lacking the amazing grace to be reborn in the spirit. Others may call this predicament a paradox. I merely report that even my alienation from my own culture strikes me as "typical"; it has resulted from my assiduous deconstruction of its myths and pretenses. I learned this ability from preceding European anatomizers; it isn't very difficult any more. So when I deconstruct Postmodern habits of mind, I sense I am co-imitating the Postmodernists' imitation of the very ancestors to whom — quite rightly — they impute the elaboration of the crucial ideas which underlie Modernity. In this respect, Postmodernism constitutes another gyre in the *circulus vitiosus* within which Western "identity" twists and turns to avoid ceasing to be what it is. Since Postmodernism strikes me as paradigmatic of recapitulation, thus subtly conservative, a release from the reality of the contemporary world, I am not surprised that a considerable segment of the Postmodern camp waits with millenarian excitement in the penumbra of an oncoming (requisite) Apocalypse. Rather than question the thematics of Decadence inherited from *fin-de-siècle* literature, Postmodern theoreticians merely repeat a favorite negative version of the cliché of a purgatorial revaluation of values — including their own. That proposition is mildly reflected in the title of Ihab Hassan's essay "Beyond a Theory of Literature: Intimation of Apocalypse?" Yet, like most theoreticians, Hassan can only set up lists of authors now "in," the approach to whose works is not facilitated or understood by older theoreticians. We are offered a few symptomatic terms, such as "non-telic," but Hassan soon has recourse to tired nineteenth-century notions of disappearance and silence when he hierophantically invokes the Postmodern prophets of apocalpyse and rebirth (Kierkegaard, Heidegger, Norman O. Brown, D.H. Lawrence).[5] Postmodernists now busily deconstruct Modernity, their immediate Babel and Babylon, with their own epochal jargon, zealous to break out of the intractable morass which encumbers existence.

The mainstay of Modernity *and* Postmodernity *is* imitation of scientific discourse, the mature habit of demystification, of deconstruction and reconstruction. The intrusion of science into art already seemed oppressively evident in Positivism a century ago, and half a century ago some observers saw further baleful omens in the reconstructive approach to culture and myth practiced by important Modernists. For example, reviewing *Ulysses* in the *Freeman* (July 19, 1922), Mary G. Colum noted:

> The alarming thing about "Ulysses" is very different [from the charge of obscenity]; it is that it shows the amazing inroads that science is making on literature. Mr. Joyce's book is of as much interest as science as it is as literature; in some parts it is of purely scientific and non-artistic interest. It seems to me a real and not a fantastic fear that science will oust literature althogether as a part of human expression; and from that point of view "Ulysses" is a dangerous indication...[6]

Contrary to expectations, perhaps, American criticism did not abandon the all-embracing pretenses of Modernist literature when theoreticians started turning away from the representative microcosm of the "verbal icon"; rather, by supposed or prophesied acts of total revaluation, the theoreticians arrogated to themselves the aura of "wholeness". René Wellek has astutely sensed that, in rejecting the "art" of literature, "recent criticism — and not only criticism in America — looks constantly elsewhere, wants to become sociology, politics, philosophy, theology and even mystical illumination."[7] Allan Rodway has detected an analogous expansionism in the British turning from New Criticism, but in my view he misjudges the metacritical mimicry of scientific discourse by equating it in some cases with actual science: "Moreover this sort of work seems scientific. Indeed it often is scientific, and that is why, as theorists in rival categories were to point out, it is not strictly literary criticism but metacriticism: a specialised form of sociology or psychology, history, biography or anthropology."[8] Nonetheless, the metacritical drive of Postmodern criticism reveals itself in forms as virulent as the Romantic climax.

When Postmodern theoreticians turn against spatialization of consciousness and extol a liberated art of time, two things tend to occur in critical practice. By deconstruction adherent critics alter slightly the literary and critical canon, shifting our attention to the latest qualifications for inner right(eous)ness. By reconstruction they also circle back to the primary "rebirth" experience of Romanticism and, before that, of the Renaissance and Reformation, when the dynamics of time were discovered[9] and time relationships, which shape entire bodies of discourse, were made into the chief subject of the emergent super-discourse after 1600. Now joyfully (Rabelais), now perplexedly (Donne), European intellect — having taken apart the Medieval system — considered culture in its totality, under the rubric of stages of history, as an educational happening, a redemptive becoming. Henceforth, each new extremely difficult passage, progressively adjusting to the traumatic recognition of the unmanageable products of prolific Western thought, could eventually be interpreted as postfiguration of the initial break: "just" another dissociation of sensibility.[10]

Before discriminating major post-Renaissance directions of Western rationalism (Descartes' radical doubting, Leibniz' ontological optimism, etc.), most cultural historians can more or less agree that all modes have focused initially on these propositions:
- (A) the existence of a plethora of cultural data, often seemingly contradictory, at times ludicrous, nonsensical;
- (B) the need for a critical assessment and arrangement of such data;
- (C) the advisability of devising a "method"
    - (1) to increase exponentially the capacity of the mind to sort and store,

(2) to avoid the past pitfalls and errors of the mind, which are deplorably evidenced in the cultural record,
(3) to create and expand certain knowledge.

The above amounts essentially to the empiricist program.

Spanos, too, indicts in particular the Cartesian quest for "certainty"; with the advent of the Romantic and Modern period, Hegelian dialectics, Symbolist-Imagist iconicity, and Nietzschean Will to Power provide not so much responses to the metaphysical aggression which has elaborated the positivistic "world picture," as omens of its end. Spanos prophesies that the ontotheological relay team of Plato, Aquinas, Descartes, Leibniz, and Hegel will not be able to hand on the baton (or as Bacon would say, the "torch").[11] It is curious how insistent the apocalyptic tone is in Postmodern pronouncements; the only other comparisons — aside from the immediately antecedent Schopenhauerian and Spenglerian pessimism underlying Modernism — are the expectations and dejections of the Romantics at the time of the French Revolution, or of the liberal and radical Protestants in the earlier seventeenth century.[12] In startling contrast, with the prospect of a triumph of rationalism on the threshold of the Enlightenment, when Leibniz looked at the multiplicity of forms of being as a flowing dynamics of energies, he saw their composite vector as a meaningful happening in time. His time-consciousness tended to make him delight in "accidents," surface phenomena, because his craving was to understand the invisible "rules" shaping the phenomena. For Leibniz, the intervening use of "artificial memory" and instrumental systems of abstractions (combinatory art, calculus) implied nothing "wrong" with earthly givens; rather, it portended a qualitative surge in spiritual evolution through the discovery of "method." The Leibnizian ecstasy is to believe confidently that the middle state of muddle and confusion is being overcome; man spirals onto a new plane and can reinstate his Adamic hopes, because he can render a critique of the mind's contents and even of the mind's operations. Thus with "control" over itself, the mind is promised a new start, virtually unlimited potential — a glorious prospect.[13]

Though Bacon and Descartes, in contrast, earlier approached the "results" of past mental life (human history) with grave suspicion about the operations as well as products of the mind, their critiques, too, had as their constructive aim a radical, qualitative break in consciousness and the eventual attainment of a comparable "certainty." And since American education has been so extensively colored by the empiricist bias, I shall concentrate on the Baconian complex to illustrate the longer-range implications of scientific discourse for all discourse. The most fundamental point is that scientific discourse set out programmatically to subordinate and even to swallow poetic discourse. Bacon converts the pattern of the Fall and Apocalypse into a historical vision of the contest between entrapment in degenerative cycles and breaking out of the "circle" (*Works* IV, 52, 383) into "continuation and further progression" (IV, 449) of a linear temporal pathway.[14] With the Puritan millenarians he shared his specific belief that a major cycle had turned and that in the midst of epochal disorder a providential momentum was building for a redemptive alteration of the mind. The evidence consisted, among other things, in the regeneration of Reformation hopes, the irreversible impact of printing and its attendant intellectual renascence, the actual new achievements in the pure sciences, and the literal expansion of civilizatory scope through exploration and colonization of the globe. The promise existed that men could permanently cease "wandering round and round as in a labyrinth" (IV, 81) by engaging in an ostensible act of cultural humiliation, abjuring the fantastic constructs and vagaries of their philosophic and religious heritages. Beyond revising the Renaissance principle of *docta ignorantia* whereby scholasticism and medieval discourse generally had been undermined, Becon now espouses an aggressive deconstruction which must include even his own mental life. By the radical new start from a zero position, the inductive method will permit the mind to "arrive at a knowledge of causes in which it can rest" (IV, 32), that is, to regain on a higher plane the lost Adamic state of the final "sabbath" (IV, 33; VII, 221). Guibbory notes:

> Paradoxically, however, the forward advance of knowledge is really a return to the original state of wisdom before the Fall. The linear path of progress which Bacon substitutes for the cycles of the past will actually complete the circle of mankind's history by leading man to the end of redemption which touches the prelapsarian state of bliss where the circle began.[15]

Milton grandiloquently translated the Baconian anthropological approach into poetic terms in *Paradise Lost* and *Regained*, as well as in his treatises on education and freedom of expression. But the most persistent post-Baconian tendency was the pseudo-scientific curbing of language out of suspicion about its insidious powers and, since natural language was seemingly unmanageable, the search for a substitute for language. Both compulsions are symptomatic of the rationalist attempt to escape from the intractable web of contingency. The Renaissance and Reformation rejection of scholastic values as tottering edifices of words intensifies into a concerted drive for a new discourse when Bacon suspects the schoolmen's books reveal that, if the mind works only "upon itself, as the spider worketh his web, then it is endless, and brings forth indeed cobwebs of learning, admirable for the fineness of thread and work, but of no substance or profit" (III, 285-86). The story is well known: Locke extends Bacon's distrust of "idols of the human mind" (IV, 51) into an unrelenting epistemological *Essay Concerning Human Understanding*, and taking the hint jocoseriously, Sterne eventually exhibits the mysterious dilemma of identity as circumscription in a hermeneutic circle. In my view, when Bacon says "Circular motion is interminable, and for its own sake" (V, 478), he expresses the fundamental ill ease which surfaces again so powerfully in Existentialism and in Postmodern literary theorizing.

James Stephens has traced the stages in which Bacon attempted to unfold his program for science and was forced to make adjustments based on the hard realities of communicating his elitist goals.[16] Though accepting the need for "one method for the cultivation, another for the invention, of knowledge" (IV, 42), Bacon was concerned that the newly reconstituted tradition — Renaissance learning — was oriented to rhetoric for its own sake rather than for delivery of pertinent modern knowledge. Stephens seconds Karl R. Wallace in deeming Bacon's contribution to reside in the application of Renaissance psychology to the communication process on behalf of a new progressive learning. In the long run, rhetoric had to be pressed into service appropriately, since an effective style was required to recommend reason and understanding to the imagination. In Bacon's attack on that refractory faculty, "which may at pleasure make unlawful matches and divorces of things" (*De augmentis scientiarum*, II, 13), we can detect the inroads of the late Renaissance dissociation of sensibility. Though art must play a role in skillful management of the various components of an audience, words remain suspect through their association with inherited errors and as sources of potential erring. Among ways to offset the danger posed by language, Bacon uses the aphoristic approach, representing fragments of knowledge and stimulating the intelligent reader to contribute extensions and conclusions, hence to discover. Similarly, the acroamatic approach seeks "by obscurity of delivery to exclude the vulgar from the secrets of knowledge."

Both approaches give scope to Bacon's emblematic proclivity. Since words are but "symbols of notions," yet embroil humankind in intractable muddles, he is fascinated by hieroglyphs, ideograms, characters, and gestures, because these suggest the possibility of an alternative universal language of pictures or signs:

> Moreover it is now well known that in China and the provinces of the furthest East there are in use at this day certain *real characters*, not nominal; characters, I mean, which represent neither letters nor words, but things and notions; insomuch that a number of nations whose languages are altogether different, but who agree in the use of such characters... communicate with each other in writing; to such an extent indeed that any book written in characters of this kind can be read off by each nation in their own language.
>
> The Notes of Things then which carry a signification without the help or intervention of words, are of two kinds: one *ex congruo*, where the note has some congruity with the notion, the other *ad placitum*, where it is adopted and agreed upon at pleasure. Of the former kind are Hieroglyphics and Gestures; of the latter the Real Characters...Gestures are as transitory as Hieroglyphics. For as uttered words fly away, but written words stand, so Hieroglyphics expressed in gestures pass, but expressed in pictures remain. (*De augmentis scientiarum*, IV, 1)

When Bacon resorts to mythmaking in the *New Atlantis* to lend moral authority to science as successor to man's earlier religious heritage, hieroglyphic reduction of "intellectual conceptions to sensible images" (*De augmentis*, V,5) obviates any affront or exposure to vulgar (mis-)understanding; and at the same time, the elitist code does not compromise the revolutionary role of science as true religion.

For the scientist as intellectual hero is compelled "to sweep away all theories and common notions" (*Aphorisms*, XCVII), sows "for future ages the seeds of a purer truth" (*Aphorisms*, CXVI), and would "let the human race recover that right over human nature which belongs to it by divine bequest" (*Aphorisms*, CXXIX).

The Postmodern bias against the older "image," against closed self-referential expression, seems to me be one of the many latter-day step-children of Baconian empiricism. Hence, for example, since the Imagist Ezra Pound was ever striving after an authentic "objective correlative" or the equivalent of Chinese ideograms in poetry, it amounts to sibling rivalry to attack Pound's "hieroglyphs" as unwittingly captive of their own terms, rather than as a deliberate means to restore language to a proper role. Postmodern "deconstruction" and "reconstruction" does, nonetheless, pursue another branch of the iconoclastic Baconian impulse to overcome "tainted and corrupted" learning enshrined in language, to topple "idols of the mind," dogmas which work an "enchantment from progress." Bacon's anti-book orientation is based on the supposition that words maintain false images cast by the human mind as a distorting "enchanted glass" — the theme which his contemporary Cervantes vigorously pursued in the *Quixote*. Though Bacon "rescues" the revered ancient philosophy with its colorful symbols and myths, he does so only to exploit it as a resource to recruit the special elite. Bacon's rationalist myth-making serves in the final analysis (like Cervantes' indirect rescue of romance?) as a means to replace tenacious old structures and convert the finest minds to science, the difficult "second Scripture." Bacon judges that even such carefully cultivated "literate experience" will remain inferior to the direct interpretation of nature, but he recognizes that it is a necessary channel and that only by passage through it can men be led to an awareness and overcoming of its limits. We can speak of the superiority complex of Western intellectuals who, since Bacon, take pride in their capacity to play with terms which — in varying degrees of openness or aggression — they are debunking and dismantling. It is a game from which the vast slave population (i.e., ordinary users of language as a repertory of commonplaces) are excluded.

The difficulty with this attitude becomes apparent as soon as we consider the divergence which indeed set in between science, promoting the search for new codes liberated from the past, and art, beholden to the contingent media of expression whether it will or not. With the invention of the calculus at the end of the seventeenth century, a threshold was crossed in the drive to elaborate a notational system which could engender virtually unlimited growth for mathematical language. It became not only possible but highly attractive to shift from qualitative (language-oriented) to a quantifiable (sign-oriented) examination of things, once mathematics had attained to its own complex, satisfying symbolism. The desire for the order, power, and purity epitomized in the liberated hard sciences gradually penetrated other realms, and in my view it has continued to fire the redemptive and apocalyptic aspirations of many sectors of the literary world down to the present. Poetic experiments to push language in the direction of a calculus and to release its potential as a primal code through the *ars combinatoria* and other "logics" were already being undertaken in the seventeenth century. In certain respects, Joyce continued to experiment with ways to reconcile rhetoric and logic in a polyphonic code and tested the limits for a natural language. But such reconcilements with or exaggerated hopes for natural language have been matched by an almost unbroken post-Renaissance tradition of suspicion and even hatred of language. Since language is doomed to remain incommensurate (except for a few anti-Baconians), the need to use it can be regarded as demeaning servitude or spiritual martyrdom, as Rimbaud, Hofmannsthal, and others have discovered in a less humorous vein than Sterne.[17]

Richard F. Jones has demonstrated how the Baconian prejudice against language was widely endorsed by the scientific community, who eventually helped bring about a stylistic reformation of English in the seventeenth century.[18] Their "aversion and contempt for the empty study of words" (Boyle) often goes hand in hand with antipathy for the older Humanist cultivation of languages for the sake of the heritages transmitted in them. The leading educational philosophers for the Puritans, notably Comenius and Dury, opposed the study of the classics as a pursuit lacking intrinsic value. Instead, the time-robbing acquisition of languages should be subordinate "unto Arts and Sciences," because in themselves languages "are worth nothing towards the advancement of our Happiness." The extent to which contemporary American rejection of language training still mimics the thought of our Puritan forebears bears witness to the spellbinding appeal of the new superdiscourse of science. Not satisfied with deconstructing the human past and scrapping it almost wholly as outmoded, the scientific coteries of the Puritans and Royal Society wanted to deconstruct language itself as an unreliable instrument, and to reconstruct a linguistic counterpart for the natural philosophy of the age, on the grounds that the consideration of the truth of ideas could not proceed without strictly controlled definitions.[19] The scientists' call for a plain language, stripped of superfluous adornments, purged of ambiguity, eventually found its counterpart in the attack on rhetoric in the pulpit as betokening corrupt habits or fanaticism.[20] By the close of the century, theological seriousness of purpose, too, came to be closely associated with ascendant neoclassical traits; and rehabilitations of figurative language increasingly rested on the virtues of less vulnerable primary sources such as the Bible, "true" eloquence close to the primal experience of the race.

The even more radical attempt to replace natural language with a "real character" gained impetus when Comenius in *The Way of Light* (1641) reconsidered Bacon's speculation in *The Advancement of Learning* (1605) about Chinese ideograms as one model for a symbolic code – though with unfortunate defects.[21] To help restore harmony to the "commonwealth of humanity" and mobilize the "innate Principles" of "knowing, willing, and achieving" rooted in "Human General Intelligence," Commenius proposed it was first paramount to overcome the powerful obstacle "which consists in the multitude, the variety, the confusion of language." This means finally the establishment of "a language absolutely new, absolutely easy, absolutely rational, in brief a pansophic language, the universal carrier of light." The ecumenical ambition and linguistic correlates of Comenius and Hartlib appear to underlie directly the elaborate treatises on pure, rational discourse by Dalgarno and Wilkins. In the *Ars signorum vulgo character universalis et lingua philosophica* (1661), Dalgarno begins, like the Lullian-Ramian encyclopedist Alsted, the German Calvinist mentor of Comenius, by postulating seventeen — later twenty-three — classes of irreducible ideas and by beginning every word in a primary class with the same letter as an unmistakable sign. Further modifications and subdivisions are marked by second, third, and subsequent letters, so that an adequately large vocabulary of artificial objective words can be generated by further application of this *ars combinatoria*. In a similar vein, Wilkins' *Essay towards a Real Character and a Philosophical Language* (1668) presented to the Royal Society an incredibly detailed, encyclopedic analysis of all categories of things, processes, and relations for conceptualizing matters mundane or divine. Next he offered a rationalistic anatomy of "natural grammar" and assigned to every structural function in the grammar a written mark or character; by combination and modification, every nuance of an objective discourse could be represented ideogrammatically. People of various nations would thus be able to "communicate by a *Real Character*, which shall be legible in all [natural] Languages," because it can be "made *effable*," i.e., read as phonemes "in a distinct Language."[22] In addition, Wilkins constructed a tentative example of an international "Philosophical Language" which could be uttered as composed sounds, even though the words were generated artificially, as in the case of the exclusively ideogrammatic parallel, "Real Character."

Soon after entering Oxford in 1661, the young Newton, in the wake of Dalgarno and others, was sketching his own project for a universal language based on an alphabetic shorthand.[23] The evidence is abundant that the British scientific mind was intrigued by the possibility of bringing the use of language and the formulation of metaphysical and theological insights into conformity with mathematically rigorous empiricism. The urge to "reify" thought is disguised since the trend of such reductionism is to create manipulable abstractions, a cipher of neutral, pure signs; in the beginning, the crusade against older, language-bound "metaphor," "emblems," "conceits," etc., lends the appearance of an escape from the trammels of a confused "pictorial" imagination, the residual habits of archaic fallen man. As already mentioned, the phase of quantifying all phenomena set in not just with Newton's theory of universal gravitation but also with his invention of the calculus, whose notational system liberated mathematical signs as a self-generative, self-correcting code. Yet, as is well known, Newton still clung fervently to his belief in divine revelation and redemption.[24]

The example of Newton cautions us against assuming that fundamental Protestant (hence late Christian) aspirations were simply displaced relentlessly by science. Rather, it strengthens the suspicion that Anglo-American empiricism absorbed and furthered the deeper drives of the millenarian Baconians. The Puritan stress on reform; their cult of education; doctrine of hard work; desire to rebuild lost Eden through scientific, technological control over nature; and their ecumenical program for the eventual restoration of fallen humankind became elements of a generally accepted mission for Western science *and* civilization. As Webster has argued, it was the Puritan eschatological vision which spurred them to the cultivation of science. Furthermore, the radical Protestant speculation about the creation of an elitist confraternity — Bacon's House of Solomon, Comenius' and Boyle's "invisible college," etc. — began to be realized on a practical level by the establishment of the Royal Society. On the Continent, the early parallel, especially among German Calvinists, was the Rosicrucian notion of an "Invisible College."[25] We tend to forget the importance of the interconnected webbing of *illuminati* movements in Western nations during the surge of pre-Revolutionary science, industrialization, and capitalism because so many features seem too bizarre to pertain to the formation of modern elitist sentiments. But the history of "secret" societies shows the relatively greater early success of Masonism in Protestant, and notably Calvinist, areas and its appeal especially to liberal (and often nominal) Catholics as a channel for associating with Enlightenment forces; and the theosophical and pansophical contribution to Masonic and Rosicrucian lore has been thoroughly documented.[26] If our memory of these links needs refreshing, we can engage in an intensive review with Hans Castorp under the tutelage of Settembrini in *The Magic Mountain*.

My point here is that the modern surface world dominated by the "pure" signs of scientific discourse rests on the elitist "secret" discourse which once was being actively pursued against the perceived monstrously deforming forces of human nature, against the voices of unauthentic authorities and institutions. The conviction in the efficacy of scientific discourse flourished when the fusion of Protestant craving for a radical transformation and of Humanist gnostic yearnings occurred. The latter d r i v e s , expressed through magic-mystical, hermetic-occult pursuits, provided a rich soil in which conviction in the efficacy of "purified" scientific discourse flourished.

I have recollected how, in the Hesperidean branch, the new discourse was accompanied by an ever intensifying skepticism about natural language and the operation of the mind, reflected in the culture's patchwork "vocabulary." Rationalist epistemological theory remained adamant in its zeal to debunk the mind, to grasp its archaic procedures, to dispel its obscurities, to control its waywardness. Perhaps the supreme monument to this attack on mendacious (i.e., natural) discourse by a contemporary of Newton was Locke's celebrated *Essay on Human Understanding*. In the Eastern branch, however, the new discourse took an altogether different approach to the vexatious evidence of some identity between structures of language and operations of mind.

The "linguistic model," which underlies a variety of approaches to literature, other arts, and culture generally, has acquired particular refinements by many hands. But, simplifying the larger history of this model, we can say the notion that methodological linkages between several subjects can be established because they can all be treated as *languages*, i.e., codes, results in large measure from the line of thinking traceable from Leibniz over Humboldt to today's structural linguists (Chomsky et al.) and anthropologists (Levi-Strauss et al.) and the literary formalists related to them. (Certain extreme formalists will probably dismiss the foregoing statement as an irrelevant "genetic" explanation for what now "is"; diacritical knowledge has small worth to those more interested in schematizing coordinates in a synchronic slice of life to detect the "grammar" imbedded in their specimen.) Leibniz was among the first to see that innatist views of natural languages — as having had a common (Adamic) origin, but having evolved over time in territorial and ethnic environments, subject to sometimes complex conditions, and working out their own grammars and vocabularies in a series of "accidents" —

promised more than convenient compatibility with the religious tradition of the dispersion of tongues after Babel. He recognized that the "accidents" displayed an actual organic continuum and that through and in human languages nature expressed possibilities, the manifold collective devising, acquiring, conflating, altering of codes which anthropologists can study as "cultures," "myths," "interchange," and so forth. Whereas a medieval realist theory threatened to convert humanity into a frightening collection of speakers of ideolects in loosely overlapping groups because it failed to explain the actual enormous diversity of tongues and peoples which the Renaissance savants, explorers, colonizers, and missionaries had (re-)discovered, nominalism *and* innatism in combination provided a more satisfactory key.

Leibniz grasped the proposition that the fundamental capacity which characterized a "human" being was the inborn ability to acquire and use "a" — that is, any — language. He conceived of the rules of languages as a deep structure in the mind resulting from earlier stages of evolution which eventually led to the point where, with this common genetic heritage established, "humanness" appeared biologically as an inherent attribute of each human monad. The activity of receiving, using, imperceptibly altering one — or with education or cultural experience more than one — code as utterance (in thoughts, spoken words, or recorded speech) was from that juncture the most significant kind of participation with other monads in shaping complicated levels of human symbiosis known as society, culture, religion, etc. Leibniz' thinking evidences the advanced Protestant consciousness of language and culture but it bears symptomatic resemblance to advanced Catholic theorizing such as that by Athanasius Kircher. Crucial for both as a point of convergence of ideas is their early obsession with the possibility of a "combinatory art." The dream of an *ars combinatoria* continued the Renaissance drive for control over all the profuse data with which the renewed civilization had to cope; and largely from it, as I have noted above, sprang the key Enlightenment concepts of a philosophic *methodus* and mathematical *calculus*. Thus, looking backwards from Kircher and Leibniz, we can discern among their superseded common ancestors Ramus and other sixteenth-century speculators about a "method" which would permit mechanistic manipulation of fundamental categories of definition and eventually of entire "codes." The first efforts, then, involved a fusion of the laws of rhetorical analysis and synthesis with the laws of logic.

The Lullian-Ramian project was to identify the universal fundamentals in a hierarchy of concepts, to arrange these in tables as signs, and to work toward solutions of difficult problems through permutations and combinations of alphabetic algorithms. Kircher believed, moreover, that ultimately it would be possible to *invent* totally new concepts by generating them from the initially established ones, so that the valid underlying structure would yield further "sentences" or complicated combinations which conformed to the abstract code. The earlier Renaissance search had been for "artificial memory," some means of mnemonic control of the recoverable repertory of knowledge, which had already proven to be enormous and still growing; in fact, the decline of the Dark and Middle Ages could be and was described largely as actual loss of vast treasures, a slowdown and shutdown of considerable extents of the human mind. Beyond mnemonic control by means of hierarchically organized encyclopedias, the later Renaissance search turned more aggressively to the expansion of the conceivable repertory literally through creation of ideas, to self-sustaining scientific "invention" (and not mere rhetorical *inventio*) as a new form of discourse. Kircher proposed, but never carried out, the construction of a *cista* ("box") in which all the perfected extant *tabellae* would be coordinated so as to permit combinatory crossing on various axes from framework to framework of values: a forerunner of the modern computer with memory storage. Kircher not only believed that such a device would produce new propositions but vaunted that by means of it eventually even "children and idiots" could operatively manipulate the various "languages" – natural tongues, musical composition, mathematical procedures, painting, etc. Several decades later, toward the end of his life, Leibniz advanced the similar view that, in effect, various bodies of theory and practice – arts and sciences – are semiotic systems living out of their own evolved rules and that these systems are analogous to the natural spoken languages.

Indeed, Leibniz was groping for the profoundest level of deep structure, the irreducible logic of the mind that would explain the universal grammar which is capable of generating particular sentences in any natural language, mathematical thought, musical expression, etc. He hoped to abstract from all these operations a "general" or "universal" language, a supercode reducible to notation in terms of which other codes could be scrutinized. Like Comenius, he also yearned to anticipate the ecumenical confraternity of expanding enlightenment by furthering the creation of an artificial, rational language for international communication. This language he understood variously in relation to sound, mathematical thought, and signs. According to his ideal, it could be expressed in numbers, spoken in phonemes, composed as abstract music, or written as ideograms (once more, as Bacon mused, after the supposed model of Chinese) — alternately or simultaneously. Leibniz suggested that there was a European family of languages which had evolved from some archaic unity — in a rough outline genially corresponding to today's picture of the several branches as reconstructed by etymological philologists and comparative grammarians. In Rome, Kircher sought to schematize the mythological complexes of several great cultures, including the Egyptian and the Greco-Roman, and coordinated their features in patterns to which Biblical and Christian lore could be compared as supposed governing form; however, his abstraction of common underlying structure amounted to a beginning of a new branch of scientific discourse: the anthropological study of comparative religion. In the case of both "Protestant" Leibniz and "Catholic" Kircher, we note the powerful fascination for representation by visual signifiers, a search to discover the pictorial base in primal layers of known languages as well as in more complicated formulations from later layers. The theory that the alphabets of the Mediterranean basin had evolved from pictorial signs, the perception of nominal roots as being the metaphoric heart of conceptual terms, the interest in Egyptian hieroglyphs and Chinese ideograms as a possible emblematic code — these and similar notions shared by such savants belong to a complex which deeply marked the poetry, drama, and fiction of their age and its successors. The practices of "spatialization" are rooted in their investigation and application of pictorialism.

By the foregoing I do not mean to imply that imitation of scientific discourse could or should be avoided in contemporary writing or criticism. Quite to the contrary, my skepticism is two-edged. I share the view which Donald Davie advances that a lack of historical awareness of the vast assimilation of scientific terms, which had subsequently lost their metaphoric vividness, prompted the standard charge that the atmosphere of the mechanistic, quantifying Newtonian age was inimical to poetry, even though, contradictorily, critics deemed the influence of the Royal Academy beneficial to English prose.[27] After the Romantics, literary history largely failed to distinguish between creative scientists themselves, with whom poets shared much vocabulary, and philosophers commenting on what scientists appeared to be doing. Yet the philological evidence tends to show that, simultaneously, eighteenth-century literary use of terms from the natural sciences helped support Lockean assumptions in ethics and psychology and in turn was stimulated by the philosophers acting as middlemen. The new vocabulary also appeared in the language of satirical and comic writers — such as Berkeley, Pope, and Swift — who opposed the whole materialist trend. One general result of the adoption of new scientific terms into common usage was the initial awareness that many elevated words used for centuries had been formed earlier in the same way; thus both these older and also the newer terms (e.g., "gravitation," "profound") could be and were deflated by humorists. As in the time of Rabelais, at a moment when language seemed to be changing too rapidly, writers had to consider the relative value of stablizing the process versus benefiting from its fluidity, since in fact the scientists were one of their most fruitful sources of new words or new senses for old words. Davie is convinced that thorough investigations by historical semanticists into terms like "spirit" will reveal the extent to which the earlier eighteenth century clung to metaphors bridging disparate realms; "the distinction which we make between the scientific and the moral was unnecessary, positively unwanted."[28] Once chemistry had freed itself from physics as a separate discipline, the Romantics turned to it as a natural science which could be an ally against the mechanistic view of things and source of revisionary metaphors — whence yet another wave of vocabulary. So we ought not to be surprised that actual or pseudo-sciences today (compare alchemy and chemistry in the Renaissance) still affect literary discourse as deeply as they do.

But there are curious contradictions — *not* paradoxes — in the pervasive Postmodern attempt to stake a moral claim for the deconstructive labors of those who battle the power of the "image," take apart and expose in all nakedness extant metaphoric systems, etc. In contrast to the Elizabethans, Davie argues, the Augustans had become more eclectic in deriving metaphors from virtually any source; Augustan metaphors, because they are just figures of speech, can thus refer to several incompatible world pictures: "Here is certainly a contraction, not in the field of metaphor, but in man's notion of its validity" — probably furthered more by philosophers of science than by scientists themselves.[29] Strangely, some Postmodern critics nonetheless act as if the most extreme Romantic wishdream of a magical key or a Modernist iconic poem represents the normative conditioning delusion embodied in (somehow not yet debunked) poetic language and constructs today; rather than acknowledging the extreme nominalistic pluralism of our own age. The same critics can demand a radical rebeginning, a new holistic vision which mysteriously follows what amounts to purgation, even though it is evident the new vision may not last long, of course, if another deconstructor arrives on the scene with his iconoclast's hammer in hand and quickly once more reduces all to fragments of *dead* (already pre-deconstructed) vocabulary out of which his predecessor has temporarily constructed a poetic utterance. The zeal to smash another's idol and to heap up piles of rubble as one's own transitory monument indeed seems to be the trademark of many a critic today. These traits might be termed the Postmodern panic.

A less deprecatory view of today's fashionable mutual deconstructing can be gained from Meyer's discussion "Concerning the Sciences, the Arts — AND the Humanities" in the inaugural issue of *Critical Inquiry*.[30] According to Meyer, artists tried to devise propositional programs in the early twentieth century out of the mistaken belief that science meant novelty and that it was sufficient to achieve the limited duration of scientific propositions. Meyer, reverting cautiously to the New Critical stance that a work of art is a "fabricated microcosm," argues that the truer analogy is between the single work of art and the collective body of practices and theories characterizing science.[31] Although ideas in a work of art lose their strangeness with time, as does a new scientific theory, its unique pattern never wholly does; for there is no supercession in works of art, neither confirmation nor disconfirmation of "truth." The credibility of works of art is corroborated by general human experience and their content can thus have some active impact on our concept of human behavior, no matter how unlikely the generic or epochal features may appear to the overly rationalistic observer of a later era; hence the survival of "classics" over centuries and millenia. Like Davie, Meyer recognizes that scientific theories can furnish matter for esthetic delight once they are registered phenomena in the cultural world. But the model of natural language is more applicable to art because men use and understand the medium without explanation, and each enjoys the personally variant possibility of a gradualistic increase and refinement of appreciation. Acquired rules and vocabulary of a language are first presumed to be in the minds of others on a tacit intersubjective basis, rather than discovered as conceptual knowledge. Beyond the finding that art like language is broadly characterized by "synthesis" and science by "analysis," Meyer expatiates on the impediments to any general psychological explanation of audience experience and reception. I must pass over his interesting comments on the methodological challenge of qualifying our approach to fit the nature of each distinct medium (fiction, painting, music, etc.), as well as on the practical nullity of discovering the behavioral neurobiological explanation for particular instances of artistic creation and reception. The important point is that, meanwhile, criticism, too, remains a kind of art. Inductive taxonomies comparing features of style do not lead to successively better hypotheses for the reason that the principles of organization of works of art alter from age to age and culture to culture (even on the same hierarchical level of structure, as well as in the articulation of variables). Only by adducing *ad hoc* propositions can the critic deal with actual cases. Despite all our attempts to identify generic modes and structures, the categories run up against limits imposed by the intrusion of unexpected associations (conflation), reversal or adaptation of function, etc., in actual works; and rhetorical systems persist mainly on the grammatical, not the semantic, level.

Returning an instant to Bacon, it is instructive to note that for him

> the art of Memory is built upon two intentions: Prenotion and Emblem.... By prenotion I mean a kind of cutting off of infinity of search. For when a man desires to recall anything into his memory, if he have no prenotion or perception of what he seeks, he seeks and strives and beats about hither and thither as if in infinite space. But if he have some certain prenotion, this infinity is at once cut off, and the memory ranges in a narrower compass. (*De augmentis*, V, 5)

When facing the hermeneutic problem of initiating direction, though he suspects the human mind of inveterate habits of self-deception, Bacon momentarily concedes human dependence on an intuitive step. But he does not devote himself to investigating, for their possible positive implications, the internal operations of the mind which permit us to possess a prior basis of knowledge or the creative will.[32] Stephens points out that Bacon simply admits that "no man can give a just account of how he came to that knowledge which he hath received" (*Valerius terminus*, cap. 18); Bacon assumes that a hermeneutic directedness permits the search for valid axioms and counsels intermediate rests for stock-taking so that the written form of the new philosophy will not contradictorily defeat its own goal.[33] Today we can cite Wittgenstein among extreme exponents of confidence in language as the valid, determining matrix of thought; the attribution of crucial ontological dimensions to language has flourished, as mentioned, in the line from Leibniz over Humboldt to the innatists in contemporary linguistics. Of course, Bacon propounds his psychology of discovery without the benefit of later Romantic perceptions of the fragment as a jagged nexus, a puzzle piece suggesting the total context; when Bacon uses the fragment to stimulate a sense of the total context within which a scientist works, he does not embark on questions which offer strong clues for alternatives to a sensationalist theory of the mind. Sensationalism followed comfortably the British materialist penchant. In essence, then, Postmodern antipathy to Symbolism, Imagism, etc., because these supposedly give readers a false sense of unity and completion, is a shadowy descendant of Baconian dislike of rhetorical system such as represented by Ciceronian elegance. The traditional Anglo-American habit is to drift into loathing the familiar furniture of the mind and to feel great satisfaction in clearing out the clutter — and refurnishing in a newer chic fashion. The mould of fashion is what philosophers say about science, directly or indirectly.

Meyer proposes, as a corrective to our misunderstanding of the role of science, that "Nature, Human Behavior, and Works of Art are antecedent to the theories explaining them."[34] Not only are theories in the Humanities still necessarily "plural" and "discrete," but further works of art can be affected by theories (e.g., Freudian notions in Surrealism), whereas in the realm of science there is no feedback from successive theories to phenomena of nature. The physical laws have always been operative in nature; however, the "composition" of church architecture, for example, has varied in startling ways over the centuries. Furthermore, Meyer holds that only the humanist-theorist can aspire to emulate the scientist, while the critic resembles, on the one hand, the historian, and on the other, various performers. The critic deals with a plethora of "texts" (events, documents), usually in relation to a larger body of "context" (traditions, codes); he interprets the "text" to some extent as a musician does a musical score. The contrast between "political science" and the "art of politics," between "medical science" and the "practice" or "art of medicine," etc., applies to the relationship between theorist and critic. The latter deals not just with general principles and typological analysis but with the non-recurring interaction of variables and idiosyncratic details which mark the work of art as a unique entity. The physician treats an actual person at an actual moment, just as the politician considers the given body politic and the critic speaks about the actual work of art. Applying Meyer's idea to the seeming paradox of Postmodern deconstruction-reconstruction, I see in this drive to remake our vision the supreme value traditionally attributed to *new* synthesis in the West. However, today the value often is asserted through (at times fanatical) denial of older syntheses, which are mistakenly regarded not simply as cultural givens, available vocabulary, but as wicked determinants and inhibitors.

That would be all well and good if, as Davie points out, it reflected merely the age-old eagerness of poets to embrace new vocabulary and renew their idiom — which is their primary objective, after all. Tough-minded historians might dismiss the Postmodern yearning for an apocalyptic cleansing as another amusing spectacle of absurd objectives. But some could take it more seriously as another symptom of deep malaise in the intellectual community of the so-called "developed" world. If the very culture is widely resented by disaffected intellectuals as repressive and muddled, this condition sometimes seems to resemble the grim rejecting mood of many factions in the Reformation era. The moral spleen, the thirst for justification, the iconoclastic itch may well derive from a profound religious need the satisfaction of which our scientific age has, to some extent, stifled. But, ironically, the righteous fervor in much Postmodern commentary strikes me as negatively imitative of scientific discourse in its early Baconian moment; for when empiricism took over the iconoclastic function of radical Protestantism, our world of "progress" and "revision" was born.

The most accelerated rejection of the humanistic revision of Christian values, bringing the savage denunciation of Enlightenment norms and Kantian objective categories, appears with startling clarity in the post-Romantic work of Max Stirner, often regarded as the spiritual forerunner of the most extreme atheistic existentialism. For Stirner, Western Humanism and Rationalism were a fraud, as was Hegelianism and all attempts to rescue German Idealism. This anarchic nihilist declared Man as well as God to be dead and (to the chagrin of Karl Marx) already denounced Socialism-Communism as a resuscitation of the unholy church which always assumes power on the pretext of knowing the good, but then through power programmatically oppresses actual — that is, transitory, mortal, creative — existence. In *The Ego and Its Own*, Stirner "posited [himself] on nothing," engaged in a radical devaluation of all values, and hurled a revolutionary challenge at the structure of the world as otherness.[35] Though his quest for a complete revaluation starting from the irreducible Cartesian datum of his own existence may strike many modern readers as "paradoxically" tainted by gnostic passion, Stirner in fact typifies a broad class of Western thinkers who experience the worst repercussions of the late Renaissance "dissociation of sensibility," a trauma which was already indelibly marked by gnostic sentiments at the start of the Renaissance. From Pascal to Sartre, we can trace the features of a modernized Western gnosticism, which in its latest guise today goes under the name of existentialism.

Hans Jonas has identified the symptomatic resemblances of our latter-day cosmic terror as that of aliens who are compelled, by their recognition of estrangement, to live in a ceaseless dynamics of realization. Supposedly, rest in the joy and certainty of a perceived reality no longer is conceivable.[36] Whereas earlier gnostic dualism at least pictured man heroically reclaiming his birthright against an antagonistic, anti-divine nature, existentialism reflects the total depreciation of nature, which (as a negative result of continuing scientific discourse) has become, or been unmasked as, indifferent toward man. The Pascalian thinking reed — crushed by a blind universe, no longer feeling kinship with a cosmic order but rather regarding himself as cast into prison — is still unable, now as post-Christian "unhoused" man, to repair the ruins of ancient cosmic piety and repossess the therewith linked ethics of classical civilization. Nietzsche saw that nihilism could spring from the devaluation of the interim highest values, if this process were finally interpreted as the collapse of the possibility of obligatory values. In the citadel of reason, Sartre reinstated the antinomian argument of the gnostics that, since there is no sign of a transcendent, man must regard himself as abandoned and reclaim his freedom, making himself his own project. Pneumatic man is beyond good and evil and creates in the intensely temporal mode of the Heideggerian "moment," with no real rest or place in the present since acceptance may merely be a masked relapse or brings the danger of entrapment in degeneracy (*Verfallenheit*).

The Platonic contemplation of immutable divine order (*theoria*), the beholding of eternal objects in relation to which human experience in time can be placed (as Dante still understood this), has, since antiquity, lost its status virtually in parallel with the deanthropomorphization of nature. According to Postmodern thought, the Renaissance program of epochal renewal, the Reformation recharting of course toward the goal of universal salvation, and in turn even the

Enlightenment secular doctrine of perfectibility and the Romantic revisions thereof have been replaced by the permanent eschatological tension of crisis: the commitment to constant futurity. One of the main charges Postmodern thinkers have leveled against Modernism is that (because of or despite its apocalyptic awareness) it tried to gather, codify, exhibit, and thereby rescue, in some necessarily transmuted consciousness, the complete Western heritage. But now, the Modernist tendency to iconize and reify all relationships has been denounced as often as the word Liberty was printed in the era of the American and French revolutions. In my view, however, major exponents of Postmodern literary theorizing, once more exhibiting a resurgence of gnostic forces in Western civilization, again conceive of life under the classically gnostic metaphoric notions of forlornness and dread. Though the tenacious concept of "homesickness" is no longer stressed in an environment of atheism, the existential notion of authenticity reinstates the gnostic concept of the "noise of the world," the confusing discourse of blinded captives and of unworthy laws, to which the spirit responds by "awakening." The ancient gnostics regarded man's spirit (*pneuma*) as caught in a falling or sinking which resulted from his "being-cast-into-the-world" (Heidegger's *Geworfenheit*, Pascal's "Cast into the infinite immensity of spaces of which I am ignorant, and which know me not, I am frightened"). The feeling of an absolute rift "between man and that in which he finds himself lodged – the world" was and again is primary (compare Heidegger's *Riss*). Against the mindlessness of a creation based on ignorance and passion, the gnostic rebel projects himself by a radical revaluation of otherness – which in today's terms ostensibly includes the entire Western heritage as inhibitory "noise." (Of course, existentialism is just more such "noise" to anti-gnostics.)

An even more negative assessment of Postmodern literary concepts results if we regard them as one bundle of many gnostic symptoms in the larger context of contemporary cultural and political thought and apply a critique based on Volume IV of Erich Voegelin's monumental study *Order and History*.[37] Voegelin renders a qualitative judgment of the two principal modes of understanding fashioned by Near Eastern, Mediterranean, and European civilization in antiquity: the *noetic* illumination (whose highest standard was achieved by Plato) and the *pneumatic* (whose epitome was St. Paul in the train of the prophets). In the several centuries leading to the formation and then collapse of the Roman Empire, ancient philosophy had to cope with a series of imposed traumatic redirectings of the impulse to create an ecumenic totality, the justification for which was the purported need to subsume diverse cultures under a mediating order. The great transition in antiquity was from culturally self-contained older empires with their complete cosmological system (Egypt) to universalistic empires which gradually rationalized "concupiscential" drives through an expansion of the mythological horizon in order to accommodate imperialist ambitions (Alexander to Augustus). In the Judaeo-Christian line of religious development, the disappointment over the lack of congruence — between spiritual aspirations for an ecumene on the plane of real time in history and the use and acquisition of power ostensibly to bring order — was another confirmation of "disorder." Given the special Jewish sense of the "chosen" people displaced in history, Paul definitively transferred expectations of eventual fulfillment of order to a transcendental plane. Achievement of a universal plan would proceed in a different realm than that of time, since the elect suffered and were manifestly impotent on earth; the Judaeo-Christian kingdom of God replaced the Greco-Roman pagan vision of ecumenical empire. Thus the tension between imperfect time and perfect eternity was intensely experienced, and generations of late pagan and early Christian thinkers began to elaborate that sense of another in-between kind of time which partakes of eternity and lends order to temporality — a kind of time which has a structure marked by cardinal points or turnings (*kairoi*) and directedness toward an ending (*apokalypsis*). This shaped the Western view of time processes and made the laws of time into the significant factor, the medium of experience underlying Western realist mimesis — the subject Erich Auerbach has examined. As Frank Kermode has shown, it deeply informed the Western idea of the special realm of "fiction."

The craving for a super-construct which would overcome real disorder in human affairs has never died. It was central in the thinking of liberal and radical Protestants in the late Renaissance when, after the disappointment in the failure of the Reformation and out of the trauma of bitter civil war, they reconstituted their faith in a radical break in consciousness. It was apparent in the ecumenical vision of Romantics such as Novalis who were reacting to the disappointments and trauma attendant upon the French Revolution (e.g., in *Christianity or Europe*). It thrives in the ecumenic-imperialist dogmas of a communist world revolution in the twentieth century. Voegelin characterizes the latter as a virulent focus of gnostic forces because, after several millenia, the main thrust of gnostic "rebellion" remains the destructive hatred of "what is," and the method of self-validation for adherents is largely through a disguised nihilistic attack on life and nature, though it also often enough occurs openly. Real humaneness is postponed puritanically on behalf of an hypostatized future. Like Jonas, Voegelin views the problem of the twentieth century as analogous to (*not* identical with) that of antiquity. Vast masses of disturbed peoples, to a great extent consisting of hordes of uprooted barbarians imploding into or from lower layers within the "developed" world, seeth with resentment. Gnostic attitudes encourage rage by the displaced against a supposed "system" which denies real satisfaction yet fails to achieve order in compensation. Modern gnostics foster readiness to follow a variety of ecumenical crusades. Since Napoleon's refurbishing of the hallowed imperial symbols, tailored into an explicit costume for the French Revolution as a unifying complex, we have had our fill of fascistic and totalitarian appeals by modernizers who wish to shortcut in their imitation or overwhelming of the developed countries.

In Voegelin's analysis, the confusion of the twentieth century reflects, then, the attempt at evasion of our ineluctable involvement in reality. He points to the age-old awareness of man's being grounded in the cosmos, yet of man's necessary moving from this ground toward "God"; consciousness of this motion (which entails the "separation" of individuation) has from the beginning constituted and still constitutes the inner basis of the human psyche. Seeking to become regrounded, man senses himself to be in a distressful in-between state (Plato's *metaxy*), even though his condition is the natural cause of his particular identity as a creature. The danger to man arises not from being "in-between," but from falsifications of his situation which exacerbate it without leading to any further peak moments of "illumination." Gnosticism is perverse insofar as it encourages the hypostatizing of constructs which seem to offer redemption, and thus induces human beings to pursue concupiscential goals — crimes and aggression — against all the *evidence* of history respecting the true nature of imperialist motives and imperialist exploitation of religious cravings and symbolism.

I, too, sense in much of Postmodern discussion the undertow of rechanneled religious hysteria which extensively pervaded Romantic metaphysical and social speculation and radical Humanist and Protestant ideas before that. Nietzsche's suspicions against the religious mentality as the fountainhead of nihilism seem not so farfetched, even if — as René Girard believes — Nietzschean fulminations, too, are tainted as an act of mimetic struggle with Europe's "shadow" and are provoked out of envy toward genuinely creative personality.[38] Postmodern existentialist criticism assails Modernism for having in effect hypostatized the organizing scheme of modern consciousness and the whole repertory of cultural possessions; this drive to control everything in an iconic construct supposedly subverts authentic being, which should be a constant "becoming." Even though Modernism pretends to bring everything pertaining to time process into co-presence, most extremely in the Symbolist "perfection" of a work of art, the literary habit of "spatialization" falsifies the temporal dimensions of life. But from my perspective, Postmodernism in turn indulges in another variation of the gnostic escapism described by Voegelin, because in its zealous reversal of values Postmodernism hypostatizes the basis of self-experience of the psyche, declares the process of discovering motion out of the ground to be the effective producer of values and creator of the future, and elevates "becoming" (confuses it) as equivalent to *real* temporal process in its vast wholeness. The rebellion against discovered groundedness takes its most immediate expression in the aggressive desire to dismantle "history," to deconstruct the encumbering paradigms and traditions and understandings and evolved relationships of the extant, complex, real, and contingent world. The gnostic analogue is battling the inimical "archons." On the pretext of an absolute "reconstruction" from *zero*, the Postmodern mind as *pancrator* thus arrogates to itself the stature of a transmundane godhead. With few distinguished exceptions, Postmodernism bypasses the tedious pathway of considering the minutiae of science, that unpleasant involvement in contingency. (A deeper artistic involvement with scientific lore and the mysteriously heavy plethora of details can, however, be illustrated by writers such as Pynchon.)

But Postmodernity will not and perhaps cannot dispense with the formal trappings of scientific discourse; thus this ruling discourse pervades even our critical efforts to grasp "authenticity" and participate in a fruitful art. Someday — doubtless in the lifetime of many present readers — mention of Postmodern ideas will evoke nostalgia, because they will be part of memory of what has passed in a series of events closely related to Modernism.[39]

Notes

1. William V. Spanos, "Breaking the Circle: Hermeneutics as Dis-closure," *boundary 2*, 5 (Winter 1977), 435.
2. "Breaking the Circle," p. 446.
3. In an excellent overview of contemporary theories of "The Hermeneutic Circle and the Art of Interpretation," *Comparative Literature*, 24 (1972), 97-117, Wallace Martin points out that the intense late twentieth-century discussion of hermeneutics was rekindled from German Romantic pronouncements, notably Schleiermacher's. Wallace eventually undermines the notion of a "hermeneutic circle" and favors a rational, objective, but antipositivistic structuralism like Barthes's (pp. 110-17), which acknowledges that literary interpretation is "historically contingent" because it is profoundly conditioned by "a critic's world view" (whether adequate or inadequate) and that "literature exists only in temporal movement" (uses of language by various others and ourselves). Literature can "shatter the individual languages we impose on other features of our world," and a work of art guides us toward a point of view, as we encounter it, much as does "ordinary" living speech. A humorous approach to these issues was taken by the philosopher Jacques Derrida in his two books published in 1967, *De la Grammatologie* and *L'Écriture et la différence*, which roguishly reversed the hierarchy of Western terms since Plato. Instead of privileging "voice" (logic, reason, truth, presence, etc.), Derrida accepts the external signifier, Writing, as extant. Presence is always marked by some

kind of event, by difference and deferral (Derrida's term *différance*); instead of achieving a synthesis of event and structure, we only see each instance from some perspective as a product in an unfolding production of differences. Intertextuality is self-parasitical. Every utterance in language exhibits "traces" of prior entities; the possibility of meaning something is effectively already "inscribed" in the ongoing Writing. In *Les Mots et les choses* (1966) and *L'Archéologie du savoir* (1969), the philosopher Michel Foucault has proposed that we dig into the philological data of texts to detect the stratification of encodings and the hidden "grammars" ruling various moments of history. In *Metahistory: The Historical Imagination in Nineteenth-Century Europe* (1973) and *Tropics of Discourse* (1978), Hayden White proposes that the writing of history is shaped by dominant tropes just as much as are literature and criticism; since in his view every kind of discourse is a kind of figuration, he analyzes visions of history in the post-Viconian tropological and generic terms used by literary theoreticians. The shift from structuralism to deconstruction is marked by works such as Paul De Man's influential *Blindness and Insight: Essays in the Rhetoric of Contemporary Criticism* (1971), exposing the figural shaping and rhetorical strategies of the observor of discourse who is actually caught up in the play of forces of the matter he seeks to describe or master. Since even the deconstructionist must inevitably unmask himself as an accomplice in the processes of discourse, deconstruction is itself always provisional, implicitly inadequate, prone to displacement.

4 Meyer Howard Abrams, *Natural Supernaturalism: Tradition and Revolution in Romantic Literature* (New York, 1971), p. 13.

5 Ihab Hassan, "Beyond a Theory of Literature: Intimations of Apocalypse?" in *Comparative Literature: Matter and Method*, ed. A. Owen Aldridge (Urbana, 1969), pp. 25-35. Norman O. Brown's influence as a latter-day prophet surged following his Phi Beta Kappa address at Columbia University (May 31, 1960), published, with introductory commentary by Benjamin Nelson, under the title "Apocalypse: The Place of Mystery in the Life of the Mind," *Harper's*, May 1961, pp. 46-49. This address — which invokes Emerson's — exhibits many key motifs symptomatic of a traditional Anglo-American malaise: "mystic academies" and "disclosure" versus mechanistic, democratized learning; "ideogram" versus "alphabet" (routinized language); liberating "imagination" versus the tyranny of "books"; Dionysus (or an apocalyptic Christianity) versus normalized Christ. Like the Modernists, Brown finds the roots of dilemma in the late Renaissance crisis of dissociation: "Read again the controversies of the seventeenth century and discover our choice: we are either in an age of miracles, says Hobbes, miracles with authentic fresh revelations; or else we are in an age of reasoning from already received Scripture" (p. 49b). In my view, Brown typifies the (often historically blind) love-hate relationship toward the givens of culture and human nature when he echoes the programmatic call of early British science

to overturn the deadening weight of Scripture; and thus his opposition to "scientific method" as the "attempt to democratize knowledge" is a standard confusion, because he mimics the elitism of the first radical Protestant empiricists.

6 Cited by Herbert Gorman, *James Joyce*, 2nd ed. (New York, 1948), p. 299.
7 René Wellek, "Philosophy and Postwar American Criticism," in *Comparative Literature: Matter and Method*, p. 23. Wellek recognizes that the "new motif of American criticism in recent years is Existentialism" (p. 21) but finds that critics today tend to use literature "only as a vehicle for ideas" — in the words of Karl Shapiro, for " 'culture criticism or theology, ill concealed' " (p. 23).
8 Allan Rodway, "Crosscurrents in Contemporary English Criticism," in *Comparative Literature: Matter and Method*, p. 54. Rodway lists the ruling fallacies in non-stylistic modes of British criticism as the "historicist, personalist, romantic, biographical, or intentionalist and effective" (p. 57) and notes the rise of a "linguistic fallacy" (p. 58), i.e., structuralism.
9 Among works demonstrating the significance of this development, special mention should be made of Herschel Baker, *The Race of Time: Three Lectures on Renaissance Historiography* (Toronto, 1967), and Ricardo J. Quinones, *The Renaissance Discovery of Time* (Cambridge Mass., 1972).
10 On the epochal interrelation of new metaphysics and science with literary revaluation and trauma in the late Renaissance, consult Hiram Haydn, *The Counter-Renaissance* (New York, 1950).
11 "Breaking the Circle," p. 437.
12 The importance of millenarian excitation for the breakthrough of scientific d i s c o u r s e and empiricism in Britain is convincingly and thoroughly documented by Charles Webster in *The Intellectual Revolution of the Seventeenth Century* (London and Boston, 1974), and *The Great Instauration: Science, Medicine and Reform 1626-1660* (London, 1975). Illustrative of links to radical Protestants on the continent, who desired a sure "method" and encyclopedic control, is the German Calvinist John Henry Alsted, treated in ch. 3 of *Puritans, the Millennium and the Future of Israel: Puritan Eschatology 1600-1660*, ed. Peter Toon (Cambridge and London, 1970).
13 For bibliography on Leibniz' contribution to psychology (concept of the unconscious, evolution of mind), linguistics (deep structure), and cultural anthropology (ontological basis of systems of signs), consult my article "Primal Utterance: Observations on Kuhlmann's Correspondence with Kircher, in View of Leibniz' Theories," in *Wege der Worte: Festschrift für Wolfgang Fleischhauer* (Köln, 1978), pp. 27-46. On the search for a universal medium of discourse, consult D.P. Walker, "Leibniz and Language," *Journal of the Warburg and Courtauld Institutes*, 35 (1972), 294-307.
14 The statements by Bacon interpolated in this paragraph are cited from Achsah Guibbory's excellent treatment of "Francis Bacon's View of History: The Cycles of Error and the Progress of Truth," *Journal of English and*

Germanic Philology, 74 (July 1975), 336-50. Like Guibbory, I will continue to cite from *The Works of Francis Bacon*, 14 vols., ed. James Spedding, Robert L. Ellis, and Douglas D. Heath (London 1857-74; facsimile rpt. Stuttgart, 1963), but will refer by title to chief works already conveniently subdivided by Bacon.

15 "Francis Bacon's View of History", p. 348. Brian Vickers' study of *Francis Bacon and Renaissance Prose* (Cambridge, 1968) is still indispensible for a primarily *literary* understanding of Bacon's style and its rhetorical structures. Since Bacon's impact clearly was not that of a scientific theorist or experimentalist, but that of an exponent of "method" who caught the imagination of his age, Vickers scrutinizes his habits of organizing a diverse range of writings and speeches for characteristic features; when one bridges the supposedly separate categories of Bacon's political, legal, literary, and "scientific" works, one discovers that rhetorical structurings, such as *partitio*, are central to the latter, too, and may well explain why they were received with respect. Contrary to Stephens, Vickers (ch. 3) does not assume that Bacon's main reason for using the aphorism is to conduct a psychological strategy. Rather, in the Renaissance, the aphorism already enjoyed special status, being associated with authoritative statement of laws and principles; and Bacon, essentially a creative writer, regarded it as one of several means at his disposal, though he recognized it was especially suited for the initial stages of guiding superior minds, as well as for avoiding the snares of faulty systems.

16 James Stephens, *Francis Bacon and the Style of Science* (Chicago and London, 1975).

17 The German Modernist confrontation with the "imperative" or problem of silence — and notably Hugo von Hofmannsthal's "Letter" of Lord Chandos to Francis Bacon ("Ein Brief" [1902]) — is explored in Oskar Seidlin's essay "The Shroud of Silence," in *Essays in German and Comparative Literature* (Chapel Hill, 1961).

18 Jones examines the epochal shift, mightily furthered by the natural alliance of the Puritan and scientific elites, in "Science and Language in England of the Mid-Seventeenth Century," *Journal of English and Germanic Philology*, 31 (1932), 315-31, and "Science and English Prose Style in the Third Quarter of the Seventeenth Century," *PMLA*, 45 (1930), 977-1009.

19 The educational program of the Puritan intellectual leaders and their ties with advanced Protestant thought on the continent are examined by G.H. Turnbull in his study of *Hartlib, Dury and Comenius* (Liverpool-London, 1947). These same connections are also treated in chs. 6 and 7 of Paoli Rossi, *Clavis universalis: arti mnemoniche e logica combinatoria da Lullo a Leibniz* (Milano-Napoli, 1960), within the fuller European context of a reconstituted global vision of the "drama" of history, modern rationalist encyclopedism and illuministic pansophism, and the search for a reliable "method," as well as for a universal language and real character.

20 The impact of science and rationalist philosophy is convincingly demonstated in Richard F. Jones's study of "The Attack on Pulpit Eloquence in the Restoration: An Episode in the Development of the Neo-Classical Standard for Prose," *Journal of English and Germanic Philology*, 30 (1931), 188-217.
21 See Benjamin DeMott, "Comenius and the Real Character in England," *PMLA*, 70 (1955), 1068-81; the interpolated wordings in translation from Comenius' *Via Lucis* are cited by DeMott.
22 John Wilkins, *An Essay towards a Real Character and a Philosophical Language*, fascimile ed. (Menston, England, 1968), p. 385.
23 See Ralph W.V. Elliot, "Isaac Newton's 'Of an Universal Language,' " *Modern Language Review*, 52 (1957), 1-17.
24 On Newton's theological views and the essential correspondence between divine and scientific truth for him, consult especially Frank E. Manuel, *The Religion of Isaac Newton* (Oxford, 1974). Newton's cultural anthropological speculations on the evolution and corruption of religious and metaphysical knowledge since remote antiquity can be more fully appreciated against the background presented in D.P. Walker's study, *The Ancient Theology: Studies in Christian Platonism from the Fifteenth to the Eighteenth Century* (London, 1972).
25 In *The Rosicrucian Enlightenment* (London and Boston, 1972), Frances Yates examines seventeenth-century British-German cultural relations and affinities, and relevant French and Italian sentiment, which help explain the favorable climate for Protestant acceptance of a scientific elite and furtherance of the Royal Society. A condensed version of her findings is given in her review-essay on Webster's study *The Great Instauration: Science, Medicine, and Reform 1626-1660*, appearing under the title "Science, Salvation, and the Cabala," *New York Review of Books*, May 27, 1976, pp. 27-29.
26 On British-German-Italian connections in particular, as well as the neo-mythic theme of a Salomonic "temple" and heritage among European *illuminati*, consult Karl R.H. Frick, *Licht und Finsternis: Gnostisch-theosophische und freimauerisch-okkulte Geheimgesellschaften bis an die Wende zum 20. Jahrhundert, Teil 1: Ursprünge und Anfänge* (Graz, 1975).
27 Donald Davie, *The Language of Science and the Language of Literature, 1700-1740* (London and New York, 1963).
28 *The Language of Science*, p. 59.
29 *The Language of Science*, p. 85.
30 Leonard B. Meyer, "Concerning the Sciences, the Arts — AND the Humanities," *Critical Inquiry*, 1 (1974), 163-217.
31 "Concerning the Sciences," p. 182.
32 Bacon's two "intentions" bear a rough resemblance to Descartes' two "acts" of the mind, "intuition" and "deduction," as described under Rule III of *Rules for the Direction of the Mind (Philosophical Essays*, trans. and ed.

Laurence J. Lafleur [Indianapolis, 1964]), e.g.:
> We can therefore distinguish an intuition of the mind from certain deduction by the fact that in the latter we perceive a movement or a certain succession of thought, while we do not in the former; and furthermore, because present evidence is not necessary to the latter, as it is to intuition, but rather, in a certain measure, it derives its certainty from memory. From this it follows that certain propositions which are immediately derived from first principles can be said to be known in different ways, now by intuition, now by deduction. But the first principles themselves are known only by intuition, while, on the other hand, ultimate conclusions are known only by deduction. (p. 155)

Though beginning confidently from the irreducible primal intuition of existence as a mind, Descartes — like Bacon — encounters language as a peril: "Now I am truly astonished when I consider [how weak my mind is and] how apt I am to fall into error. For even though I consider all this in my mind without speaking, still words impede me, and I am nearly deceived by the terms of ordinary language" (*Second Meditation*, p. 89).

33 Stephens recognizes (pp. 69 ff.) that a rational art of "memory" necessarily is useful to the reformer Bacon because this faculty is associated with history, whose unrealized resources must be mobilized for a radical change of course; but he emphasizes that, for Bacon, "rhetoric" plays no significant role in the process of discovery. This crucial question is also explored by Frances Yates in *The Art of Memory* (Chicago, 1966), pp. 370-73, and by Paolo Rossi in *Francis Bacon: From Magic to Science*, trans. Sacha Rabinovitch (Chicago, 1968), pp. 207-14. Perhaps because Bacon emphasizes such a grand leap or breaking out of cultural captivity, he largely satisfies his own libertarian-redemptive impulse and so does not become obsessed with hermeneutic circularity as a repetitive problem on a lesser scale. Once underway, the pilgrim mind (as represented by the scientific elite) makes its gradualistic progress out of and beyond the labyrinth, over waystations of concretized findings (emblematic formulations of discovery). See also Wallace Martin's "The Hermeneutic Circle and the Art of Interpretation."

34 "Concerning the Sciences," p. 203.

35 Stirner (1806-1856), who has had a significant impact on the Anglo-American anarchist and nihilist streams, is the subject of an excellent recent monograph by R.W.K. Paterson, *The Nihilistic Egoist Max Stirner* (London and New York, 1971). A more accurate translation of Stirner's *Der Einzige und sein Eigentum* would be *The Solitary (or Singular) and His Property* (or *Ownness*); actually, Stirner proposed that identity is absolute as an "open (or manifest) phrase," whereas concept or name is "a contentless word" ("offenbare – Phrase," "das inhaltsleere Wort"; *Kleinere Schriften*, ed. John Henry Mackay [Berlin, 1898], p. 115). Stirner accepts the void he becomes in order actually to be:
> Im *Einzigen* kehrt selbst der Eigner in sein schöpferisches Nichts zurück,

aus welchem er geboren wird. ... Stell' ich auf Mich, den E i n z i g e n , m e i n e Sache, dann steht sie auf dem Vergänglichen, dem sterblichen Schöpfer seiner, der sich selbst verzehrt, und ich darf sagen: Ich hab' mein Sach' auf Nichts gestellt. (*Der Einzige und sein Eigentum*, ed. Ahlrich Meyer [Stuttgart, 1972], p. 199.)

In the singular (sole one), the owner himself returns into his creative nothingness, out of which he is born.... If I posit Myself, the singular, my thing, then it rests on the transitory, the mortal creator of himself, who consumes himself, and I may say: I've posited my thing (affair) on nothing.

36 See Jonas' brilliant "Epilogue: Gnosticism, Existentialism, and Nihilism" in his book *The Gnostic Religion: The Message of the Alien God and the Beginnings of Christianity*, 2nd. rev. ed. (Boston, 1963).

37 Erich Voegelin, *The Ecumenic Age*, Vol. IV of *Order and History* (Baton Rouge, 1974).

38 Girard demotes Nietzsche in spiritual contrast to Wagner and Dostoevsky in "Superman in the Underground: Stategies of Madness — Nietzsche, Wagner, and Dostoevsky," *MLN*, 91 (1976), 1161-85. Despite Nietzsche's boast to kill the dead law, supposedly he slips into a competitive love-hate relationship characteristic of Western intellectuals; his "vision is turned into one of the countless inverted ethical Manicheanisms that the contemporary world produces in such abundance" (p. 1170).

39 I would exclude the apparently "different" thinker Heidegger from my assessment of the closeness of Modern and Postmodern ideas were it not for the fact he continuously transcribes paradigms worked out by Hölderlin — thus furthering the ontological developmental myth which Hölderlin, as well as Hegel and Schelling, imbibed from the same secularized theosophical-pansophical fountains of radical Protestantism. Heidegger describes the Renaissance shift beyond the medieval *argumentum ex verbo* and *argumentum ex re* (words from the correlative Book of Nature) to empirical gradualistic revision in his essay "The Age of the World View" (trans. Marjorie Grene, *boundary 2*, 4 [Winter 1976], 341-55). He observes astutely how, once permeated by the spirit of science, even "history as research projects and objectifies the past" (p. 346), and how having and elaborating a world-view characterizes the imitative humanistic disciplines. As man becomes increasingly subject and world concomitantly object (representational product, conquered picture, etc.), "the modern age races to the fulfillment of its nature with a velocity unknown to its participants" (p. 353); however, deeper reflection on the uniqueness of the historical moment "sets the man of the future in that in-between area, in which he belongs to being and yet remains a stranger to the existent" (p. 354). To me this sounds like merely another gyre of the revisionary Western mind, too in love with the pattern "in-betweenness" and "transformation" to overcome the mythic spell. If Voegelin is right, the most depressing "sameness" of our condition is the age-old inability to resist the misdirected craving for justification and meaning which springs from the tension so poignantly addressed by Heidegger.

6. THE REBEL IN SEVENTEENTH-CENTURY TRAGEDY

Concluding his essay, *Zur Genealogie der Moral* (1887), Friedrich Nietzsche asserts that European man turns to ascetic idealism in order to rescue his *will*; that, paradoxically, his self-hate remains at least a form of volition; and that he would rather choose the void as his purpose than be void of purpose.[1] These remarks, closing full-circle the matter of evolution of "bad conscience" in place of vital pride, cast considerable light on Nietzsche's rather compact, but brilliant summary of a classical ideal in opposition to degenerative "Christianity." He pays tribute to our race's golden age of heroism in Greece and Rome, and traces its decline over the intermediate conflict between the Renaissance, with its resurgence of ancient values, and the Reformation, a movement of "resentment" that restored the church. The last flickering of "political nobleness" then occurs in the French seventeenth and eighteenth centuries, but is smothered by the tide of democratization with the advent of the French Revolution.[2]

Apart from the merits of Nietzsche's thesis of a permanent polarity in history, one can recognize that the fierce, exalted, vital, and often spiteful figures of pre-Racinian drama certainly fit his depiction of *his* "classical" ideal (*G.M.*, I, xvi). The baroque age in France evinces a particularly aristocratic conception of the "poor player" in the theater of life. So many absolutes vie in the seventeenth century for acceptance as definitions of man, that man can choose to be almost anything, and may even crave to experience the conflict of extremes, no matter how contradictory, such as fanatic faith and scornful negation, sensual pride and adamant reason, brutal self-interest and total sacrifice, frenetic calculation and disenchanted insight into the illusory nature of the game. Indeed, although many a critic has attempted to impose a unifying concept upon the multifarious Age of the Theater, from Shakespeare to Racine, when man's theatricality was itself of paramount significance, the results have been inevitably too narrow.[3] For there appear on stage not only martyrs, but also puzzling antiheroes; the scene is overarched not only by divine province, ruling a world under the seal of theodicy, but also by arcane fate; not only is reason upheld as the supreme attribute of humanity, but unreason often is the engrossing spectacle or the pulse of a play's action; and not only do certain protagonists stand for, and subordinate themselves to, a recognized divine order, but others dare challenge it. Thus if we turn our attention to a few of the important *rebellions*, it is not to advance an explanatory thesis for seventeenth-century drama, so much as to indicate the scope of a new kind of intransigent individualism on the European stage alongside the conventional confessions of faith. Plays of un-Christian defiance and denial foreshadow traits of a later species of European heroism: the willful stance of secular champions of liberty. And the gradual sentimentalization of the antihero, observable throughout the seventeenth century, heralds the problematic rebel-heroes of Schiller and Alfieri.

Fascination with the stereotyped antihero is the first step in a long process of transference of emotional commitment. As seventeenth-century playwrights explore the problems of "guilt" and "conscience," they also expand our comprehension of the inner mind of "negative" figures. By lending various positive attributes to the antagonists in God's world, such as bravery, magnanimity, tender feelings and the like, seventeenth-century dramas show a steady shift of sympathies toward worldly action rather than pious passivity in religious suffering. The entrance of a new demonic persona into tragedy, no longer in direct juxtaposition to God as in mediaeval plays, but in magnificent isolation, marks – I believe – a watershed. Joost van den Vondel's masterpiece *Lucifer* (publ. 1654) represents in the drama what Milton's *Paradise Lost* does in the epic. That favorite subject of the times, a great Fall, connects the antagonist of God with all the princes who are cast down by fortune and are objects of our pity, though more importantly frightening examples. Not only is Vondel's Lucifer tragic because he *becomes* before our very eyes the arch-enemy and demon, but also because he possesses all the dark lustre of an embattled aristocratic heart. We are horrified by our knowledge that, by responding out of pride in his crisis of conscience and consciousness, Lucifer — a glorious angel — will plummet into his eternal role as lord of Hell. But we sense a genuine thrill before the spectacle of the necessity of prideful answer to any challenge which impinges on such princely glory. The larger encompassing subject of the play is the sacred mystery of humanity's creation, and the terrifying realization of Adam's *parallel* fall, which is reported to the heavenly host; however, the promise of divine mercy is developed throughout in the various councils and discussions, so that man's hope of redemption blunts the urgency of this issue on stage. The case of Lucifer is, however, unfolded with considerable attention and tension. The cast of characters consists of angels only and all events, though occurring in heaven, take place far from the seat of God, of whom we learn also only by report. "Lucifer and He are not confronting each other 'physically' and as on equal level, as they did in the parallelistic economy of the medieval drama. The present arrangement enables the poet to attribute to the protagonist of his play all the scope Lucifer requires as a Baroque hero without dwarfing his dimensions next to the infinite greatness of God."[4]

So mysteriously attributable to the laws of the universe is Lucifer's hubris, that we cannot speak of "sins" in his case, as we might about Marlowe's *Tragical History of Doctor Faustus* (publ. 1604). Faustus, for all his prideful urge toward experience and knowledge, is still fundamentally terrestrial, an aspirant to rebellion, but not a titan. Nevertheless, his "inability" to repent genuinely, in the depths of the heart, is more than just a Christian example of tragic deformation of a soul that, given Faustus' genius, could have soared close to the divine. Although Marlowe has Faustus express heart-rending awareness of his ineffectuality in prayer, his protagonist also represents the intellectual elan of the humanists — an inexorable force, a new absolute challenging the old. The point that Faust *dared* to act as he did may be somewhat blunted by his near paralysis in waiting for the dreaded moment of retribution. But his performance of a willful compact that must entail dire consequences is symptomatic of *provocation*, an important trait in seventeenth-century heroes generally. Faustus' waiting for repercussions is not so atypical, if we think of the many plays on "the other side," where a martyr only submits quietly to God's will *after* he noisily excites the world against himself. (Of course, in most martyr dramas, the victim attracts the world's violence and enmity just by existing.) Religious consciousness supposedly brings "real" freedom, although the "victim" deliberately chooses death. Choice entails, nevertheless, an irrational posture by many martyrs, whose proud attitude is thinly veiled in humble formulations. Corneille's aggressive Polyeucte (1643), for example, bridges the gap between the customary passive martyr and active hero. As a result of conversion, Polyeucte desecrates a pagan temple and provokes retribution. Not deterred by any consideration, not even by a genuine love, he exhibits berserk traits of iconoclastic absolutism – and seventeenth-century heroism. Decision, commitment to an absolute, elevate the hero. He demonstrates his strength of will, his authority, the glory of his role, by becoming free without regrets and by preferring immolation to spiritual abasement. Polyeucte, the noble Christian, reminds one of the arrogant *libertins* who sometimes committed outrages upon Christian worship in France. If, however, a protaganist of heroic spite chooses "nothingness" – permanence in death, rather than earthly emptiness – this choice involves a new issue. A defiant exit, not just edifying stoic resignation, more clearly belongs to activist theater.

The argument that, without reference to ultimate, usually Christian values, the heroic attitude of the seventeenth century loses its ethical substance and becomes mere pathos, is not convincing. It is only an indirect way of proclaiming that European tragedy *should* be rooted in Christian sentiments, but does not gainsay the fact that a definite theatrics of "martyrdom" exists which *is* capable of isolation. The stoic pose shades into perplexing self-assertion, when we find antiheroes who know how to die magnificently, worldly activists who can maintain their spirited attitude in the jaws of extinction. Such insistence on one's own nobility – despite or even because of the absence of any other higher value than one's role in the mysterious play of time – characterizes Savinien Cyrano de Bergerac's play, *La Mort d'Agrippine* (1633). The conspirators Séjanus and Agrippine not only do not recognize the emperor's claims to "divine" status, which the play shows clearly to be based on realities of power, but even yearn to topple him just to prove their own mettle. Each for his own reasons thinks it glorious to assassinate him and be "virtuous" (i.e., "manly"), albeit as supreme criminals. Séjanus is an anarchic nihilist who rebels without compunction and without fear of the catastrophe which might shake the greater world. He is also a freethinker who scorns everything having to do with religion, for example, the "omens" reported by Livilla in Act II, sc. iv. The political world of the Roman court in Cyrano's play is devoid of any ethical structure outside of the absolute convictions of personal worth that a character either truly possesses or lacks.[5] This inner certainty is the only guarantee, and from it springs therefore an entire system of value: radical individualism.

For in fact, Séjanus, the "noblest" in sentiments in a cruel game of *Realpolitik*, is an atheist. He recognizes no deputed god in Caesar, nor any Supreme Being presiding over the affairs of man; only man himself exists, to win or lose, according to his own determination, in the eyes of the only judge – his own conscience. Even Agrippine, as embittered as she is in her frenetic and intricate plotting for revenge, must stand amazed before the revelation of Séjanus' unshakable, sublime arrogance. When trapped, Séjanus scorns fear of death and embraces "nothingness" as his final gesture of defiance, even dares to pun:

> J'ai beau plonger mon âme et mes regards funèbres
> Dans ce vaste néant et ces longues ténèbres,
> J'y rencontre partout un état sans douleur
> Qui n'élève à mon front ni trouble ni terreur;
> Car, puisque l'on ne reste, après ce grand passage,
> Que le songe léger d'une légère image,
> Et que le coup fatal ne fait ni mal ni bien;
> Vivant, parce qu'on est; mort, parce qu'on n'est rien:
> Pourquoi perdre à regret la lumière reçue,
> Qu'on ne peut regretter, après qu'elle est perdue?
> Pensez-vous m'étonner par ce faible moyen,
> Par l'horreur du tableau d'un être qui n'est rien?
> Non, quand ma mort au Ciel luirait dans un Comète,
> Elle me trouvera dans une ferme assiette:
> Sur celle des Catons je m'en vais enrichir,
> Et, si vous en doutez, venez me voir mourir.
> Marchez, Gardes!
>
> (Act V, scene vii)

That violent pride cannot be misunderstood in the eighteenth-century sense of "moral" or "humane." It both shocked and thrilled the public in seventeenth-century France.[6]

La Mort d'Agrippine is, on the surface, a story of insane pride and vengeance. As widow of the great Germanicus, Agrippine lives and breathes political ambition; her sense of rank is inseparable from her personality; and, because in the course of Rome's internecine struggles, with her husband's murder and her decline from power, her dignity has been outraged, she must exact some terrible repayment to right the balance, failing to gain supreme authority. Her absolute claims match the amorality of the system over which Tibère holds sway as absolute despot; her motto is bloodcurdling: "Périsse l'Univers, pourvu que je me venge!" (IV, iii). By using Séjanus, whom she considers the assassin of Germanicus, as a tool to undo Tibère, and then eliminating him too, Agrippine hopes to achieve a double stroke. Her sister Livilla shares the family spite; mortified by Séjanus' apparent attachment to Agrippine, she promises to fatigue him with her presence even in Hades (V, ii). Yet the fury of these women pales in comparison with the cold, hard deliberation of Séjanus. A man of "low" estate who creates his own worth, while tearing down the false statue of established authority, Séjanus is a total skeptic. On the one hand he debunks:

> Mon nom seroit au rang des Héros qu'on renomme
> Si mes prédécesseurs avoient saccagé Rome...
> (II,iv)

On the other hand he asserts his "equality" with the best:

> Mais moi je rétrograde aux cabanes de Rome,
> Et depuis Séjanus jusques au premier homme;
> Là n'étant point borné du nombre ni du chois
> Pour quatre Dictateurs j'y recontre cent Rois.
> (II,iv)

He would actually be satisfied to die "Sous le pompeux débris d'un Trône renversé" to prove he is no slave, and pales before nothing Térentius can name that is odious or awesome, mocking even the Gods.

Séjanus sees one possible "positive" outcome of regicide:

> De courage et d'esprit cette trame est tissuë:
> Si César massacré, quelques nouveaux Titans
> Elevés par mon crime au Trône où je prétens,
> Songent à s'emparer du pouvoir Monarchique,
> J'appellerai pour lors le peuple en République
> Et je lui ferai voir que par des coups si grans
> Rome n'a point perdu, mais changé ses Tyrans.
> (II,iv)

Térentius, however, is of the opinion that Rome cannot exist under such leadership:

> Tu connais cependant que Rome est Monarchique,
> Qu'elle ne peut durer dans l'Aristocratique.
> (II,iv)

Séjanus the rebel instinctively introduces an *aristocratic* conception into his world, the principle of freedom. It is his loathing for slave mentality which makes him fret under the oppressive atmosphere of imperial Rome. For him, the Republic suggests the change that is needed. Perhaps Cyrano here expresses the sentiment of those Frenchmen who, essentially, would approve the rebellion of the nobles during the Fronde. In contrast to absolute rule, with its debasing reduction of all to the will of one, a commonwealth permits greater scope for individual aristocracy. In England, a balance of political power was finally achieved by 1680 which allowed a gradual formation of a parliamentarian "republic" (constitutional monarchy); in France, royal power triumphed and an absolutistic centralized state developed. Séjanus' is not the only dramatic voice speaking for *liberty* in the age of despots, as we shall point out.

But it is important to distinguish the *libertarianism* in Cyrano from affirmations of law or justice which only appear to be "rebellion." For example, in Lope de Vega's *Peribañez y el Comendador de Ocaña* (publ. 1614), the peasant's assertion of personal honor in killing his aggressive master actually is tried before the king in the final scene. Peribañez' defense emphasizes his pride in himself as a true Spaniard, "untainted" though of low estate, and his stature within the ranks of his own class; his plea opens thus:

> Yo soy un hombre
> aunque de villana casta,
> limpio de sangre, y jamás
> de hebrea o mora manchada.
> Fuí el mejor de mis iguales ...
> (III, xxvii)

In dying, the guilty Comendador has already repentently acknowledged the rightness of Peribañez' protection of family; the king too must recognize that "Esto justicia se llama." Peribañez action is interpreted as the law of the land. His manliness is a model. Granted, Lope doubtless is holding up a mirror for Spain to see her legal countenance as it should ideally appear; nonetheless, the "breach" of order proves actually to affirm, and is finally integrated into, the total structure of the kingdom. Lope's *Fuenteovejuna* (publ. 1619) similarly depicts the uprising of an entire village against its evil Comendador and his lackeys. When the royal commission of judges attempts to determine the culprit in this apparent outrage against authority, no one, though many are tortured, will betray his fellows, but all answer uniformly the name of their village, "Fuenteovejuna." Again, the king accepts "popular opinion" in the light of evolving law and pardons the desperate measures taken by an ideally magnanimous public. The village explicitly appeals to a concept of national order above local despotism by having already taken as its new emblem the royal coat of arms, the symbol of its political purpose:

> Señor, tuyos ser queremos.
> Rey nuestro eres natural,
> y con título de tal
> ya tus armas puesto habemos.
> Esperamos tu clemencia ...
> (III, xiii)

Fuenteovejuna is therefore a celebration of the triumph of justice; it is for its own times and circumstances a play about the establishment of valid authority, as Schiller's *Wilhelm Tell* is for the period of the American and French Revolutions.

The relationship between universal "order" and heroism is quite different in Daniel Casper von Lohenstein's *Epicharis* (1665). Though Epicharis represents the noblest aspirations of mankind and demonstrates unimpeachable courage, she is nonetheless a rebel against the highest instance of established authority, again the emperor. Because Epicharis cannot avoid the issue of liberty, she must struggle against the spiritual enslavement of an entire epoch, against an irreversible historical process. Thus she is doomed to become a political martyr. With its series of grisly prison scenes, the play *Epicharis* occupies somewhat a middle ground between the drama of edification and the drama of terror. While it derives from the Christian-Stoic tradition, its heroine is not only persevering, but filled with revolutionary fervor. Only when physically compelled does she suffer passively, for she equates slavery with cowardice and debasement and insists that freedom must be expressed. Loyal to a secular ideal, the state of individual liberty which the lost Republic once stood for, Epicharis connects the historical decline of freedom with the actual loss of human dignity. She undertakes to restore a whole people's surrendered nobility by transforming the Romans again into heroes. Epicharis may appeal like a religious martyr beyond corrupt earthly authority to a higher judgment, but her court is specifically terrestrial, the opinion of *history*; unlike the religious martyr, Epicharis promotes her ideal violently. The true stoic in the drama, Seneca, is unsullied by direct participation in the affairs of the conspiracy. Though disenchanted with the world, he watches nonetheless sympathetically, as an ideal inner spectator, how she uses dubious instruments — her corrupt fellows — for a good purpose.

Because her unfree contemporaries are unequal to the task, Epicharis must fail. For, in effect, she serves an ideal which exists only in men's minds, in memory, a phantom of time. She presumes to direct the course of history, to alter the order to be which the choruses treat — namely, Rome's inevitable decadence under the Empire:

> Rom ist das Bilt / die Freyheit war das Gold/
> Itzt aber ist in Eisen es gewandelt.
> (IV, 689-690)[7]

If Epicharis fails to restore the Republic, or the lost golden age of freedom, she triumphs spiritually as a herald of greatness of soul, the nobility which degenerate mankind craves. In the confrontation Nero-Epicharis and in the oppressive torture scenes Lohenstein shows an *historically* verified gradation of humanity from magnanimity to abject baseness.[8] This total testing of the reputed élite of a people reveals why, collectively, humanity is enslaved, while the ideal lives on in isolated heroes. Since the heroine's struggle is against intrinsic degrading forces in human nature with its corollary political organization, man — as best represented through Epicharis — seems tragically committed to the moral quest for his own nobility.

Lohenstein speaks continually of a remote, arcane, evolutionary will which he calls Fate (Verhängnis) and which is manifested in the laws of the real world. He implies — by omission — no direct religious authorship for the world, such as Providence. Instead, necessary failure on behalf of an ideal evokes problematic pathos, for human suffering *per se* has become his actual subject. That is why, even when so certain of their glory, Lohenstein's characters can sound hysterical in their affirmation of permanence through renown. Except for Lohenstein's first play (written at age fifteen), all his protagonists embrace suicide as a way to fix, guarantee their roles. Their response to the encroachment of the world is more desperate than in Christian plays about patient resignation. And because Lohenstein's source is history, he acknowledges no dramatic authority which may mitigate his portrayal of the perverse world. Heedless of propriety, as it governs his contemporary Racine, he amends almost nothing; with Renaissance, Elizabethan "coldness," he parades ghastly crimes and facts before us. Eighteenth-century critics were outraged that Lohenstein also placed erotic criminals in positions of crisis usually occupied by sympathetic martyrs. He appeared to ignore moral considerations and imply that man's urge to struggle is in itself noble, but that man is fundamentally incapable of overcoming the limitations of his role, while being all too painfully conscious of his condition. When the polyhistor Lohenstein turns toward psychology, he seems to subordinate philosophic and religious tenets as no more than "other" interesting facts in a grander picture. Until the ultimate facts are known, the sublime aspirations of mankind — including the urge for freedom of conscience — will remain puzzling and ambiguous. The critics of the Enlightenment, who wanted not an absolute, ruthless reason, but a humane, moral reason, complained both that Lohenstein was "irrational" and that his cynical "rationalism" destroyed the religious drama.

Lohenstein's antiheroines have many traits in common with the obsessed and ambitious creatures of post-Elizabethan drama, the notorious "politic brains" who fascinate us with their experience of guilt and evil. Frequently these Machiavellians also share traits with the tender sufferers of nascent sentimentalism. Examination of conscience had become generally a "secular" matter in the seventeenth century. We note, for example, that while John Webster's play, *The Duchess of Malfi*, is horrific and pessimistic, it never denies the importance of conscience, a humanizing force. Even the villain, Bosola, though twisted in his pride, can sympathize with his own victim, a martyr to her heart. We admire her brave constancy in maintaining inner rights and obligations. Bosola too, as her revenger, ultimately seeks to serve this attractive beauty of soul, however perverted his method, and his urge represents a labyrinthine groping toward the light. A prevailing rationalistic pessimism in the earlier seventeenth century yields eventually to a firming hope in the powers of human nature, an emotional shift roughly to be equated with the contrast between the position of Thomas Hobbes (1588-1679) and John Locke (1632-1704). Evolving doctrines of natural law consistently held that man must exercise control through reason. However, the scope of the reasonable was enlarged, until eighteenth-century thinkers could include most emotions, if only they appeared to be at least indirectly moral, i.e., humanizing. But, before the emotions could assert their full rights in sentimental literature, these rights had to be won. If many seventeenth-century plays seem "confused" on the issue, it may sometimes be that they are simply less smug about the emotions — even those which later are celebrated as "good." The upper boundary of the Baroque drama of rebellion is marked by plays which glorify the *beaux sentiments* of noble souls but evince a gloomy negativism.

The conflict between the "heart" and tyrannical reason receives its best treatment in Thomas Otway's *Venice Preserved; or, a Plot*

Discovered (1682). It shows the irreconcilability of personal interests and political realities. It also shows how questionable is man's compulsion for nobility, self-esteem, honor. The moral significance of human motivations is even more problematic because one can no longer clearly distinguish who are the villains or what is the exact role of society in good and evil. As in Lohenstein's *Epicharis* (1665), Otway "cynically" shows that a political conspiracy is nothing more nor less than the composite of its individual conspirators, whose motives in *Venice Preserved* range from mercenary ambition to vanity, idleness, and revenge. Far less potent are noble desires, such as to set society in order, obtain justice, etc. The society under attack from "within" is itself manifestly unhealthy or "unnatural," in the eighteenth-century sense. The government is based on harsh realities of economic, military, and personal power, and accordingly the corruption which power permits itself is rampant. The controlling oligarchy of the Senate is not a moral institution either in composition or in practice, though a few worthy men are in it. Both ties of blood and rival passions, such as for the favors of the courtesan Aquilina, link the two groups, the "libertines" and the "rulers." The former as fomenters of "rebellion," the latter as advocates of "order" represent a political tension that is reflected also in individuals. The unhappy and largely unthinking mass of Venetian humanity is caught between its dependence on forms and its suppressed urge for liberty.

The play through its rebels questions whether one is obligated to defend the structure; but it also asks whether one has the right to commit any act which will necessarily injure innocents sheltered under the state. Motivated to rebel by his sense of wounded honor and need for dignity, Jaffeir nevertheless capitulates finally to the entreaties of his wife, Belvidera, who begs him to save the citizens from an inevitable bloodbath. He saves the state, including its corrupt leadership, mistakenly hoping to redeem himself by a "moral" gesture in the heart of his wife. But his betrayal of the plot leads to an agonized crisis of conscience. First, he suffers the pain of realizing that he has, by "free" choice, demeaned himself in the eyes of the passionate, wayward, forlorn soldier, Pierre, the only person whom he really admires. Second, he discovers that his action has not gained the sought-after security, while it has destroyed the possibility of working toward the cause, however nihilistc, of rebellion. And third, he falls prey to a tormenting sense of guilt toward himself, as a *man*, who somehow failed to assert himself, i.e., his absolute liberty. He must accept a broken existence in a false world that contrasts with the resolute defiance of his betrayed friend. The latter needs to manifest his character as something irreducible. Although a criminal, Pierre possesses true dignity; his human worth is unmistakable, for he is free in spirit. His nobility fits the tradition of libertinism — anarchic self-consciousness. Despite everything negative, he upholds two cardinal values: "constancy" (to one's principle, be it oneself) and "freedom." Jaffeir responds to Pierre's example in extremity with an irrational counter-gesture of manhood, helping his friend to a final triumph of spite by stabbing him before he can be broken on the wheel, then stabbing himself.

Although Belvidera's conscience originally inspires her to prevent her husband from sullying himself in rebellion, she experiences overwhelming remorse for having led him onto the pathway of self-effacement and, as a repercussion, to tragic immolation. She perishes in despair by her own hand; this is a moment of deeper expiation. But the dubious order of the state continues, as if it is the necessary expression of man's perverse unhappiness. The stoic gesture of suicide is now sentimentalized to convey the pathos of the broken heart. Yet the act of dying is also the gesture of a self-glorifying radical individualism. Pierre's scornful rejection of the friar's attempts to convert him on the scaffold and his exultant laughter when, dying, he cheats "justice" (Act V, sc. iii) make his position unmistakable. Lohenstein's Epicharis, though not a "libertine" in the doctrinaire sense, dies similarly by her own gesture — with a touch of mad gloating. The pose of rebellion and the libertarian emotion link these two figures formally. Pierre is both free-thinking and frankly free-living, which latter trait links him also with libertinism in the tradition of Don Juan, the brain-child of the seventeenth century (Tirso de Molina, *El Burlador de Sevilla y convidado de piedra*, 1630). Pierre's frankness and basic loyalty are, however, also signs of nascent belief in natural love. Concerning the wider import of libertinism, Oscar Mandel summarizes: "From the carefully untheoretical hedonism of Renaissance Spain and Italy to the programmed license of the conscious atheist there is only a step, which Don Juan was to take with the first breath of freedom."[9] The late seventeenth century could sentimentalize the absolute claim of love, canceling all other considerations, as, for example, Dryden does in *All for Love; or, the World Well Lost* (1678). But Otway is deeper; his characters lose what is very real and important.

These notes on Cyrano, Lohenstein, and Otway examine only a few of the intertwined strands in the development of the seventeenth-century rebel from satanic antagonist to sentimental villain. Long after the Baroque rebel has been "humanized," the traits of his resentful titanism live on. Luficeric personality and "dark" heroism are important subjects in the drama of the Storm-and-Stress period, and finally, in the Romantic era as a whole. The poets rediscover tragedy in the Dionysian depths rather than on the well-defined surface of "pure humanity," which is frozen in statuesque affirmation. Alfred de Musset's *Lorenzaccio*, depicting Lorenzo's agonized quest for purity through rebellion and his tragic insight into his own inexorable corruption, is but one of numerous plays that open this new chapter.

Notes

1 *Werke,* ed. Karl Schlechta (Munich, 1955), II, 900.
2 *Ibid.,* II, 796.
3 This critique is more applicable to French criticism, which has persisted in excluding from view "nonclassical" traits, but also to German criticism which focuses too exclusively on "ethical" substance. But extensive new investigation of seventeenth-century drama, first by German and now by French scholars, is correcting such overemphasis. I would point to comparative studies such as the distinguished collection of essays, *Le Théâtre tragique* ed. Jean Jacquot (Paris, 1962), and Heinz Kinderman's monumental *Theatergeschichte Europas,* III and IV (Salzburg (1959-61), which aim to do justice to the rich variety of seventeenth-century drama.
4 Hugo Bekker, "Vondel's *Lucifer*: An Inquiry Into Its Structure," *MLR,* 59 (1964), 434.
5 Jacques Morel notes in his essay, "Les Criminels de Rotrou en face de leurs

actes," *Le Théâtre tragique* (Paris, 1962), a "theater of adventure" that is non-Racinian, free of all "constraining tradition" (p. 225), whose anti-heroes arouse "admiration" because of their "criminal grandeur" (p. 225); "ils possèdent aux yeux des contemporains de Richelieu et de Mazarin d'indiscutables vertus: ils sont grands par leur volonté lucide dans le mal, par leur courage devant la mort...en même temps ils sont des monstres, auxquels il est impossible de pardonner...une famille d'élus à rebours, marqués d'un sceau divin mais séparés par leur crimes du reste de l'humanité" (p. 232). I would agree with, and widen the application of Morel's conclusion: "Les grands Saints et les grands criminels ont, dans ce théâtre, la même trempe" (p. 237).

6 (*Euvres comiques, galantes et littéraires de Cyrano de Bergerac*, ed. P.-L. Jacob (Paris, n.d.), from which I quote Cyrano's text, reproduces the famous anecdote of Tallement des Réaux (p. 396): "Un fou, nommé Cyrano, fit une Pièce de théâtre intitulée la Mort d'Agrippine, où Séjanus disait des choses horribles contre les Dieux. La pièce était un pur galimatias. Sercy, qui l'imprima, dit à Bois-Robert, qu'il avait vendu l'impression en moins de rien. Je m'en étonne, dit Bois-Robert. — Ah Monsieur, reprit le libraire, il y a de belles impiétés."

7 *Römische Trauerspiele*, ed. Günther Just (Stuttgart, 1955).

8 Erik Lunding, *Das schlesische Kunstdrama* (Copenhagen, 1940), pp. 119 ff., also sees great merit in *Epicharis* as a drama of conspiracy in which the author is elevated above his subject ironically.

9 *The Theatre of Don Juan* (Lincoln, 1963), p. 43.

7. TIME AND ETERNITY IN ANDREAS GRYPHIUS' *CATHARINA VON GEORGIEN**

Der Fürsten Regeln sind sehr frembd
vnd schwer zu fassen. (V.169)[1]

"The rulebook for princes is most strange and difficult to grasp." These cynical words which the Persian vezier, Seinelcan, utters in Act V of *Catharina von Georgien oder Bewehrte Beständigkeit* [*Catherine of Georgia, or Proven Constancy*] (1647) serve here as an epigraph to remind us of a very important trait in Gryphius' world picture: the high profile of a new breed of men who take political behavior for granted as a reality with its own logic. Imanculi, having unwillingly carried out the royal death order against Catharina, discovers too late that Shah Abbas (Chach Abas) has meanwhile given in to Russian diplomatic pressure. To evade personal expiation for the outrage, the ruler accuses his servant of the capital crime; and the more skilled Machiavellian survivalist, Seinelcan, is quick with a word of counsel and consolation for the misfortunate courtier. With such details Gryphius too, for all his conservatism, bears witness in bitter earnest to the rediscovery of the state as the Renaissance had conjured it up. Though the Silesian poet tends to experience the harshness of history mainly as an ethical provocation, he unwaveringly studies the characteristics of dangerous convictions and errors of his own age. Born in the year of Shakespeare's and Cervantes' death, he is the most important initiator of a native high dramatic art in the Renaissance tradition. His works for the German stage depict multifarious political phenomena with genuine nuances for the first time. This ensemble of new creations — one need only think of the antagonists, Michel Balbus, Chah Abas, the Cromwellians, and Laetus, in the four major tragedies — signals the dawn of a modern consciousness in the German theater.

All the same, some accents in Gryphius' treatment of a political crisis can easily be missed, because our idea of the German historical drama remains caught up in a terminology handed down since Romanticism. Even Friedrich Sengle draws a distinction between the Baroque, when the poet "had completely honorable intentions" of historical fidelity in using evidence, although it might appear to us that he is attempting "to veil the unhistorical nature of the whole enterprise by his particular reference to facts," and the Enlightenment, which by its humane optimism about history prepared the way for the philosophy of history of the Goethean age and thereby for a "genuine historical drama." Sengle notes a certain panoramic way of looking at the world in the late Baroque and also, as a consequence of a "loss of ethos," especially in the case of Lohenstein, an understanding for "the laws governing the course of history as a realm unto themselves." But he will not concede full credit to this earlier, different approach to history, because

> in every instance what is involved are instructive examples from the political sphere, not the past in its own singularity. And so to some it may appear a matter of indifference whether the playwright selects his materials from the remotest past or from contemporary history. [...] In this kind of history there is no concept of intrinsic substance, no organic idea.[2]

But let us take for granted that it is an unrewarding enterprise to try to apply criteria from a history of ideas dependent on organicist metaphors, in order to reach judgments about Gryphius who saw historical events according to a salvational typology that found expression in emblematic imagery. Once we recognize the nature of such inhibiting critical vocabulary, it no longer is so surprising that Gryphius' *Catharina von Georgien,* in contrast to the *Leo Arminius, Carolus Stuardus*, and *Papinian*, has hitherto won scant recognition as historical drama. Another unjustifiable constriction of the field of investigation flows from our ingrained habit of relegating the nowadays less well-known occurrences in the East (Byzantium, Persia, etc.) to a category of lesser historical interest, as against "significant" happenings of the past in the West (England, Rome, etc.) In any case, in our century the *Catharina* strikes readers as being a "pure" example of universal themes of the Baroque in lyrical concentration.

Such a reading may well contradict the sense of the famous foreword to *Leo Arminius* (1646), Gryphius' first independent effort as a playwright, in which he announces *Catharina*, too, as a dramatic subject. In the earlier work, Emperor Leo's insight into the profounder obligations of an earthly ruler and the paralyzing power of his conscience bring about political ruin. During the holiest night of the year and all time, on the feast of the rebirth of the light, at Christmas, the usurpor Leo is toppled by the manic, ambitious, scornful upstart Michel. The tension with which this crucial turning-point is replete certainly satisfies our longing for "dramatic" conflict. In the *Catharina* (1647), however, our attention is diverted from the contents to the language. Somehow Gryphius overcomes the anguished, even morose irony of the situation in *Leo*, an irony closely tied to the themeatics of his paradoxical Christmas songs, without any loss of poetic intensity. Although the play *Catharina* is based on a contemporary incident, not a saint's story, scholarship used to assign it on general principle to the religious theater. It seemed to be a novel and model creation still proximate to to the Gryphian translations of the Dutch playwright, Joost van den Vondel's somber biblical tragedy, *De Gebroeder (The Gibeonites)*, and the French Jesuit Nicholas Causin's Latin martyr drama of the Roman noblewoman, *Felicitas (Saint Felicity)*.[3]

But because more recent scholarship has centered on the question of Gryphius' "unique" position as the first great dramatist in German in the age of the theater, his *Catharina von Georgien* too has been reclaiming its historical dimensions. In a basic treatise published in 1936, Helmut Kappler attempted a fresh clarification of the epochal concepts (transitoriness, fate, constancy, etc.) in Gryphius' works.[4] Most notably P.B. Wessels has sought to apply such constructive initiatives in a newer essay on "Das Geschichtsbild im Trauerspiel *Catharina von Georgien*," but does not advance beyond the older findings that history in Gryphius serves "merely as a representative paradigm," "as an occurence of transitoriness," etc.[5] It took a broader formuatlion of issues for a more fertile scholarship to emerge. One direction was represented by exegetes like Walter Benjamin and Erik Lunding who strove to bring Gryphius into closer proximity to Lohenstein within the capacious framework of European drama being opened up mainly by comparative studies in the earlier twentieth century, but who, in the process, overestimated the modernity of some thematic details.⁶ Another direction has been represented by scholars like Hans-Jürgen Schings and Janifer G. Stackhouse who attempt a more precise characterization of the artistic statement of Gryphius' tragedies exclusively on the basis of a Christian system of values.⁷ Occupying the middleground between these positions, researchers like Clemens Heselhaus and Elida Maria Szarota have indeed gone about interpreting the *Catharina* as a martyr play, but have paid attention to its problematic, as well as self-evident, aspects (e.g., the repeatedly discussed emblematic structure).⁸ They realize that the supposedly obligatory Baroque framework can turn into a prisonhouse of context, if one simply dismisses all other literary knowledge and perspectives acquired since Gryphius' times.

Szarota's bold thesis that the situation of Georgia mirrors primarily that of Silesia rather than of Germany as a whole may or may not hold up. All the same, her view of the play as "political drama" offers important starting points for a revaluation of Gryphius' artistic attitude toward the historical realm.⁹ Szarota connects the play's Stoic-Christian themes of the freedom and preservation of the self with Gryphius' persistent effort to bridge the opposition of time and eternity; *constantia* is the "existential" linch-pin. Moreover, Catharina's assertion of the "free spirit" gives expression to an "inner rebellion," a revolt "against the violence being done her conscience, her faith, her country, her son, her person" — here we might add: revolt against the ceaselessly recurrent danger and travail of temporality accepted as history's fundamental law in the mid-seventeenth century.¹⁰ Szarota even claims that the author's angry protest is displaced onto secondary figures, "Gryphius' rebellion against God breaking through the surface over and over, — a rebellion which, to be sure, he mutes and quells in himself."¹¹

That fits with Gryphius' intense feeling for legality as a highly principled lawyer; therefore, that perhaps also undergirds his struggle to comprehend in *Leo Arminius*, his concept of legitimacy and order in *Carolus Stuardus*, and his celebration of divine justice in *Papinian*. Janifer Stackhouse has thoroughly documented the poet's legal views and, what's more, his extraordinary erudition and faithfulness to his sources in the case of *Carolus Stuardus*.¹² In a more daring analysis,

M.S. South regards the author of *Leo Arminius* as an ironist tormented in his beginnings to the point of despair and even heresy, ready out of misery to cast doubt on man's salvation; only in the transcending figural portrayals of Catharina, Carolus, and Papinianus does he decisively pull back from the abyss of horror.[13] Even if we defer the question whether Gryphius later simplified or revoked such an insight into the world as the immanent, hopeless entanglement of imperfection, we can see that the menacing reality of political life is still a determinant of existence in the *Catharina*.

For "all [her] admiration for Gryphius," Szarota nonetheless faults "the undifferentiated and formulaic quality of [the play's] characters, [...] the as it were linear style of composition, [...] the weak construction despite all," in comparison with Corneille's presentation of complicated modern individuals in *Polyeucte*.[14] But, as is well-known, because Gryphius disapproved of Corneille's approach, I think we can use this observation to investigate more exactly the form-will evidenced in the structure of *Catharina*. Corneille's martyr play presents more than an exemplary story of profound religious change in antiquity. The conversion of the important Armenian Prince Polyeucte leads to more than a collision of paganism and Christianity on the island of Mytilene in the Roman Empire. On account of his love and sense of responsibility, Polyeutce as husband experiences the conflict of opposed forces and duties. These also afflict his wife Pauline in the most intense fashion when, after many years, still loving him in her heart, she remeets Sévère, who has arrived as minister plenipotentiary. The constancy, resolution, and generosity of this celebrated fieldmarshall and imperial counsellor incarnate primarily the ideal not of a Roman, but of a modern nobility. Understanding for genuine promptings of the heart enables the statesman to intervene with the Emperor in favor of the general manifestation of largeness of soul in the new Christian movement, once he has found himself compelled to pay sympathetic hommage to the mutual self-sacrifice of the couple. It is especially in the noble, shrewd antagonist Sévère, who reflects on the welfare of the peoples in the Empire, that poetically Corneille succeeds in gathering the strands of a complexity which the late Renaissance recognized in the world process; while the drama as a whole achieves this by tracing the already accomplished development of Christianity back to its earliest roots in the setting of Roman civilization. That is, the multifaceted dramatic conflict veils contemporary traits, putting primary layers of the French cultural heritage on display in antiquarian guise for better recognition. At this remote dramatic showplace of antiquity, Polyeucte can carry out his iconoclastic aggression against the "old divinities," yet reinstate hierarchical fulfillment of duty, and in the process attain the certainty of a human being as sovereign actor, and rest on his accomplishments in proud superiority, without shaking the primacy of reason.

In contrast, the *Catharina* is based on a contemporary subject. Gryphius exploits the extensive documentation of involved events in the national history of Georgia and its neighbors which he found in Claude Malingre Sieur de Saint-Lazare's *Histoires Tragiques de nostre Temps* (1635).[15] Apparently because Gryphius needed to tighten the broadly depicted materials so as to concentrate with dramatic tension on the final moments in the heroine's exemplary life, and because he wanted to transpose her story to suit Protestant sentiments, the source was not mentioned, quite contrary to his habitual practice. It is therefore especially significant how he treats the opposition Catherine of Georgia/Shah Abbas. The Persian King appears in the play as a monarch who has immediately fallen in love with his august prisoner (a motif connected with political deception in the source) and who, being plunged into dangerous vacillation by his passion, makes his regime's international game of intrigue all the more tangled. At first he tries to conquer the Christian princess personally and is even ready to elevate her as his spouse. Temporarily he concedes to a direct threat of war by the great power Russia, promises to release the queen, but does not keep his word, and attempts once again to break her unflinching resistance. In order at last to be rid of the Christian princess, because this passion seems to be undermining the security of the Persian state, the crafty vezier Seinelcan manages to steer the king into satisfying in the grizzliest manner this love which so easily turns into a craving for revenge.

The course and motivations of the principle events have a different look in the source used by Gryphius. According to Saint-Lazare, it is quite suddenly, after many years, that Shah Abbas reaches the decision to retry disaster-laden seduction and menace. His tardily invented love is just one more ruse out of his bag of tricks as a malicious *Realpolitiker*; his objective is to obviate possible consequences of a diplomatic entreaty which Crown Prince Tamaras is in a position to undertake only in the eighth year of Catharina's captivity. The passionate love interest to which Gryphius grants entire scenes is invented out of the sexual humiliation whereby, the source mentions, Shan Abbas much earlier let other members of the royal house of Georgia taste their political abasement. The French historian had already pre-formed the story according to traditional Christian views, yet Gryphius placed the conflict at the very heart of his play as if he felt compelled to endow it with a universal significance that would fittingly illuminate the role of the foreign queen as a heroine in the toils of the chaos of history.

We should speak of an obsession with history in the case of the *Catharina*, especially since the poet himself underscores his reshaping of the attested facts in a cogent preface on the "Content of the Tragedy":

Catharine, Königin von Georgien in Armenien/ nach dem Sie ruhmwürdigst ihr Königreich wider den grossen König in Persen zu vnterschiedenen malen beschützet/ jhres Schwehers vnd Ehegemahls Tod gerochen/ vnd endlich von dem König auß Persen mit vnüberwindlicher Macht vberfallen/ hat Sie sich in eigner Person in das feindliche Läger begeben/ vmb Frieden zu bitten: Alda sie stracks in gefängliche Hafft genommen/ nach Schiras der Persischen Hoffstadt verschicket. Vnd von dem verliebten Könige verwahret worden. An welchem Ortt nach etlicher Zeit/ als Sie dem in vnkeusche Liebe entbrandten Könige die Ehe abgeschlagen/ vnd bey Christi Bekändtnüß verharret; Sie/ (vnangesehen sich viel vmb jhre Freyheit/ vnd zuförderst deß Reußnischen Großfürsten Gesandter höchlich bemühet/) die erschreckliche Marter der glüenden Zangen standhafftig außgestanden vnd jhr jammervolles Leben voll freudiger Geduld/ auff dem Holtzstoß vollendet. Der gantze Verlauff jhres Lebens wird weitläuffiger erzehlet von jhr selbst in der dritten Abhandelung vnd was dem anhangend/ von dem Armenischen Gesandten/ in dem Sechsten Auffzuge der ersten Abhandelung. (p. 134)

[Catharina, Queen of Georgia in Armenia, after having most praiseworthily protected her kingdom at various times against the great king in Persia, having avenged her brother-in-law's and royal husband's deaths, and finally having been fallen upon with invincible power out of Persia by the king,

175

betook herself in her own person to the enemy camp to plead for peace: where she was straightway placed under arrest as prisoner, and sent to the city of Shiraz, to the Persian court. And was guarded by the enamoured king. At which place, after some time, when she had rejected marriage to the king, who was aflame with unchaste love, and had persisted in confessing Christ — and irrespective of the fact many, and foremost among them the Russian Archprince's ambassador, had troubled themselves exceedingly for her freedom — she withstood the terrible torment of the redhot tongs and brought her wretched existence to a conclusion at the stake, filled with joyous patience. The whole course of her life is narrated more extensively by herself and, in an annex to that telling, by the Armenian ambassador in scene six of act one.]

The first longer sentence summarizes the most important stages of Catharina's heroic life with a rapidity imitating the vortex of the time's happenings; and, after indication of the place of action and the conflict ("At which place, after some time [...]), it conducts us *in medias res* and directly to the catastrophe ("to a conclusion"). The inexactness of the phrase "after some time" and the repeated characterization of a Shah Abbas "enamoured from the first moment" and still "aflame" reflect the poetic falsification of the source. In reality, Catharina pined eight years in exile before Shah Abbas — apparently only for political reasons — directed his vengeful attention to her. Also distinctive is the dropping of the fact that Catharina accepted a Catholic priest, and specifically a Portuguese Augustinian, as confessor — which the source interprets as her conversion from the schismatic-heretical Greek Orthodox to the Roman confession. Just as in *Leo Arminius* Gryphius deliberately forgets the emperor's involvement in the iconoclasm dispute, so he generalizes Catharina's Christianity and, for poetic if not confessional reasons, he paints the originally Greek Orthodox queen in Lutheran Protestant hues. In contrast, the final shorter sentence evidences Gryphius' lively interest in the historical facts he was concerned not to omit. Moreover, this sentence gives a compact, more precise rendition of the epochal experience behind the drama hinted at in the first sentence ("The whole course of her life is narrated more extensively [...]"). These statements summarize not only the dramatic process of the tragic protagonist's isolation, but also the central theme of internalization, inwardness as overcoming of time.

A remarkable result of this shaping, from a twentieth-century standpoint, is that Shah Abbas, the ruler caught in his passion, gains in significance and becomes a "complex" personality on the plane of the dramatic and historical present, while Queen Catharina, in political and cultural captivity, in the final analysis plays more a "ceremonial" role. These categories which Herbert Lindenberger applies in the framework of European theater resemble Northrop Frye's distinction of "mimetic" as against "spectacular" forms.[16] The main concern of the martyr in Barock drama is proving himself and thereby rescuing the integrity of his culture. In general, so far as regards plotline, the inner preparation for a martyr's death is "untheatrical," and, in a certain respect, the realized self-satisfaction, as an overcoming of temporality, is manifestly "anti-historical." As the genres of the martyr and tyrant plays are closely related, the particular accentuation of the conflict is important. A tyrant too can, in a given case, play only a "ceremonial" role without "mimetic" effectiveness for the stage; that does not, however, impair the core effect, namely the public's joy at his fall, the overcoming of the barbarism he embodies. In *Catharina von Georgien*, Shah Abbas is an active monarch who entangles himself in a dangerous affair and whose human insufficiency is enacted. In contrast, like Calderon's constant Prince Ferdinand, Catharina once used to play a leading role in the state. By rendering judgment on this past, maintaining sympathetic interest in the fate of her people, and fusing both regal cares and personal longing for redemption in her thoughts, she becomes an intellectual model, she *is* a kind of consciousness. Catharina has the "ceremonial" function of the voice of conscience, not the "complex" role of a power-wielder who makes decisions in the thick of history. She embodies the legitimate aspirations of a people, their chained spiritual force and rights, that is, a historical potential. Catharina's suffering is pregnant with meaning, symbolizing, on the one hand, the fundamental situation of every soul, its imprisonment in time, and on the other hand, the whole complex of impeded civilizing values. All of that comes about without the queen "acting" before our eyes; she only needs to endure.

We glimpse confirmation of the deeper sense of Catharina's and Shah Abbas' reciprocal captivity in the closing scene as if in an emblematic-operatic *Gesamtkunstwerk* erected in a Baroque church, that is, in a masterful abbreviation of the play. In the flowing light the transfigured queen ascends in glory to heaven, at her feet cringes and whimpers the king already suffering hell's fire. To this exit out of the terrestial into the eternal there corresponds at the start of the tragedy the entrance into history as alienation and endagerment. In the play's construction, therefore, the epic retardation until the queen's appearance in act one amounts dramatically to drawing near the focal point of all temporal relationships in her consciousness. Lasting some nine pages, the series of scenes – the preface spoken by "Eternity" (I.i), the envoys of the Christian world, Demetrius and Procopius, who penetrate with their mission into the danger zone (I.ii), and Salome, who represents the human interests and needs of the queen as alter ego under neoclassical norms (I.iii) – leads us into the interior (I.iv, v) where all the lines of the time-eternity tension converge in a perspectivism that yet is sober in comparison to the play's close. A nine-page-long narrative scene (I.vi) then interweaves the present and memory, introduces world happenings into the passive sphere of the martyr, and in so doing reveals not only the background of the struggle by a Christian culture on a forward post surrounded by enemies and inwardly in disarray, but also its authentic soul in Catharina's spiritual strength.

As mentioned, Gryphius repeats and expands the bewildering historical details in Act III; initially Catharina broods over the events and relationships in grand outline in her first speech, a monologue (I.iv). After loss of her own parents she had become the wife of the Crown Prince of Georgia and born him a son, Tamaras, who was compelled to live as a hostage at the Persian court with his uncle Constantin. Constantin converted to Islam, betrayed his family, and fanned the flames of civil war with his treacherous invasion of Georgia. After having killed the king (his father) and crown prince (his brother) at a deceptive peace banquet, he attempted in vain to marry his sister-in-law, Catharina. In the midst of acts of violence, poisonings, assassinations, and massacres, Catharina had no choice but to assume charge and defend her land as head of state. We learn through the subsequent dialogue with the two Russians (I.vi) that despite a change of situation Georgia still is under constant pressure.

Her relation, the Georgian Prince Meurab, also converted after the cruelest abasement (Shah Abbas among other things had dishonored Meurab's wife and daughter before his very eyes). Presumed to be a broken slave, for long years Meurab served the Persian throne, but did so only in order to be able to protect his people and avenge himself. When, at last appointed viceroy of Georgia by his Persian overlord, he discovered that Abbas secretly was planning the final extermination of the Christian nobility, he mounted a successful resistance. With this surprising turn Meurab began a movement against Islam like that the Spaniards had already completed in their long national crusade ("Der Rach erhitzter Grimm hat als die Flamme pflegt/ Auß gantz Iberien das Vnkraut außgefegt," I.vi, 647 f. ["Vengence in torrid rage has as the flame is wont/ Swept this rank growth out of all Iberia"]). In the meanwhile he has brought Tamaras to the throne and has been conducting a complicated policy to assure Georgia the support of Russia and to play the Islamic great powers, Persia and Turkey, off against each other. Catharina now learns these newest particulars of the latest events from the envoys.

So we are prepared for the encounter of Catharina and Abbas in the last scene of Act I as simultaneously a representative confrontation of two ways and concepts of life in an almost apocalyptic situation. The imagery of conflagration and decay in the "Chorus of the Captive Virgins" underscores this. In the brief second Act, Gryphius examines the other "interior" (II.i, iii), which Shah Abbas and his two shadows embody, – the vezier Seinelcan, who champions *ratio status* with Machiavellian hardness, and the fearful, ineffectually softhearted official Imanculi. The king has to act correctly in the eyes of world opinion and acknowledge Catharina's dignity so as to buy the desired peace with Russia, the most important Christian great power (II.ii). A merely external propriety rules in the international sphere. But how little it avails the Christians to count on the word of a ruler of different faith is attested by the "Chorus of princes strangled by Shah Abbas," who beseech the "Judge of this world" for justice and vengence. The poet attempts to formulate a poetic response to this fervent demand for God's verdict, a sign of His caring. Gryphius' interpretation of Catharina's ultimate victory *in morte* furnishes the answer.[17]

The highpoint of the tragedy is reached in the eleven-page-long, second narrative scene (III.i) to which Gryphius gives special mention in his foreword. The Russian ambassador and Catharina meet, and hope for a genuine liberation seems to exist. Thus exactly in the middle of the play we learn not of thwarted, but of effective freedom as heroic activity in a treacherous world, of the fight for dignity and right that has conferred such high rank on Catharina. "Da war Georgien recht zwischen Thür und Angel" (III.i, 89) ["Georgia was caught there between hammer and anvil"], as the envoy expresses it, between the two Islamic nations, Persia and Turkey; and Catharina had correctly understood the situation. She succeeded in luring the traitor Constantin into a trap, but Abbas had immediately hatched a new ploy. The hostage Tamaras was sent home as a pretended token of peace. Since Catharina's son loved the same princess who was about to marry his cousin Alovassa, the latter being under Turkish protection, Abbas hoped to instigate a quarrel between the princes that would weaken both branches of the Christian house. With the objective of simultaneously inducing Alovassa's defection from his ally Turkey, Abbas secretly encouraged him to kill his rival Tamaras and promised to stand by with aid. Luckily the cousins discovered the deception and formed a compact in common with Turkey. Abbas now took up arms to force Georgia back under a Persian protectorate. It was at that juncture Catharina, as head of state, went to the Persian camp under shield of truce to conclude a peace and avoid a bloodbath. Because (as narrated in the first act) Alovassa had meanwhile been poisoned, the queen had left her son behind. This foresight proved to be the correct measure, Abbas treacherously taking her prisoner.

The recounting of these happenings throws a clear light on the significance of her role, since she has acted worthily as chief of state on past occasions. On this occasion too she shows her "greatness of mind" as queen, for we see her masterful ability in analyzing the complex web of political connections and events. The capacities that become visible in her correspond to the urgency of her nation's crisis. Contrarily, the all-consuming, lurid fires of transitoriness leap up again as an immediate peril; the Persian monarch's lyrical effusions (III.ii) and his vacillating command to Imanculi (III.ii) set in motion an ironic fulfillment of the ambiguous promise of an imminent return home held out early in the play. Given the Persian ruler's murderous decision, the repetition of the theme of "des Heimzugs Anfang" ["beginning the journey home"] in the naively joyous, second "Chorus of the Captive Virgins" deepens the sorrow and anger of the audience over the queen's powerlessness.

In answer, her lonely voice sets forth the importance of conscience in the defense of "Freiheit/ Herd und Kirch" ["freedom, hearth, and church"] in the great monologue of the fourth act (IV.i). The principle of self-mastery triumphs through Catharina's constancy (IV.ii). Imanculi's arguments for compliance are rejected in a model lesson on Christian fundamentals (IV.iii). Catharina's lyrical prayer for strength and fulfillment of her yearning (IV.iv) is an important component of the already beginning ritual sacrifice which is to elevate the theater as an instrument of sacred truth. The party of innocence is confronted by crass worldly despotism. As soon as "the grim judge with soldiers and executioners" appears bodily before "Catharina and Salome with all the ladies in waiting," a moment takes shape on stage that has been represented by countless painters over the centuries: holy martyrdom, the suffering of a true believer annointed for death. The "Chorus of the Virtues, of Death, and of Love" explicates the higher sense of the powers Death and Love which Catharina has interrelated and affirmed in her meditations; powers which Shah Abbas senses, through his encounter with Catharina, only indirectly and inadequately in impure mortal fashion — and to which he succumbs in the final analysis through grief, loss, madness.

In the classical messenger scene opening act five, Cassandra reports the cruel torment; and then the tortured body of Catharina, still living, is exposed to view for the last time (V.iii). The forces contending in Shah Abbas appear in tumult, until the news of her death plunges him into selfish anxiety over the consequences (V.iii). And the Russian ambassador's indignation over this act of violence and provocation immediately lends the sorrow over loss of "the flower of womanhood" a far-ranging international political significance (V.iv). Her case proves "im Angesicht der Völker stets und frey; Daß weder Redligkeit noch Trew in Persen sey" ["in the face of all peoples constant and free, there is neither honesty nor trust in Persia"] (V.231 f.). The express condemnation of Persian barbarity is implicitly a preliminary to claims for reparation and a break with Russia; possibly a crusade by the Europeans, as the failure of Seinelcan's further diplomatic manoeuvres betrays (V.v). In Gryphius' interpretation of the conflict, Persian culture lacks genuine understanding of humane values; whereas, despite all its dissention, confusion, and disorder, "Christian" civilization produces a Catharina, a Tamaras, and other champions of a future triumph of the soul. Catharina's terse prophecy of Shah Abbas' demise (V.431-40) is a poetic abbreviation of the favorite themes of apotheosis and justification in the Baroque theater — the fuller version is the Iberian reconquest of Ceuta in the postlude of Calderon's *El prĭncipe constante*, which is led personally by the ghost of the martyred Ferdinand.[18]

The question of the ruler's legitimacy may no longer be central today in the shaping of a historical subject, but it was decisive for Gryphius. It is therefore important not to confuse the poet's conscious irony on this point with the ambiguity that manifests itself in the further course of literary development. Yet, besides the traditional explanation of the ideological context for Gryphius, the modern critic and scholar feels obligated to indicate the direction implicit in some aspects of his message. For example, no reader today, observing Gryphius' "interest" in Shah Abbas, can simply ignore the fact of the gradual rise of the antihero in European drama since the late Renaissance, or discount the presence of the age's gloomy insights into the *Realpolitik* and Machiavellian intrigues of the state, and other similar contexts. Just the proportions of Gryphius' negative thematics and negative role-creation make us more sensitive today to the scope of his portrayal of the dangerous figures and to the creative potential residing therein.[19]

In the seventeenth century, medieval salvational history transformed itself irrevocably into a secular universal history that finally embraced all quarters of the globe. For example, in Lohenstein's polyhistoric novel *Arminius*, the thought and behavior of constituent sectors of contemporary European civilization are compared with attributes of almost every known culture of antiquity and modernity (among others, with Egypt, Persia, China). But what does Gryphius make of the exotic strands called Georgia and Persia, "present-day" fragments of a considerably enlarged world history? The opponent roles are so closely reciprocal in Baroque drama that tyrant and martyr plays share essentially the same contents. It is just that the tyrant play stresses the collapse or exposure of the moral emptiness of a seemingly absolute ruler or of a corrupt system he embodies. As in Racine's *Athalie*, the ethically superior party can even attack the tyrant and bring about his fall through a plot. Or the attack supported by the martyr hero can misfire as in Lohenstein's *Epicharis*. The generic balance generally shifts from tyrant to martyr drama as soon as, for whatever reasons, the standardbearer of a religion, ethic, or state form no longer can act, as is the case at the start of Gryphius' *Papinianus* und immediately after the reported iconoclastic outbreak in Corneille's *Polyeucte* (where there is no tyrant in the narrow sense, but only the apparatus of an imperial order in decline). In the usual framework of the martyr play the tyrant becomes an aggressive antagonist who brings about the hero's fall through intrigue.

The fact Shah Abbas is surrounded by only a few courtiers is typical in this respect. Gryphius is still operating within neoclassical constraints by using a minimum of representative figures. In contrast, he moves farther toward Baroque encyclopedic fullness when he portrays the role of a larger coalition of political parties and religious movements as the collective adversary in *Carolus Stuardus* (1649). Though of consequence in the interpolated narrations, the traditional element of a conspiracy or cabal is otherwise rather limited in *Catharina von Georgien*, apart from Seinelcan's influence at court. The absence of a rescue is not the result of the wrecking of a grand, intricate plot, as in Lohenstein's *Epicharis*. Catharina's isolation in the midst of an alien culture contributes much, however, to the poetic magnification of her case; and as already noted, drawing the international events into the queen's intimate circle shifts the emphasis to her ceremonial performance in time. She makes visible the Christian understanding of history; in her reflections, she represents the prized "greatness of mind" of the authentic European; the play is a ritual testing.

Therefore, the great world panorama recedes behind the "Gedächtnüß nur verschwundner Libligkeit" ["memory only of charms now fled"] (I, 316). Although Gryphius takes care in exploiting his source fully, he really diverts our attention here to the power of speech in the high expiatory victim, untouched by the real power of the tyrant; and our ears as modern readers are also attuned to the all-too-human counter-voice of the smashed victimizer. While the martyr is liberating herself from the chains of the historical condition, her soberly ecstatic dying evidences traits which mark her — in the Hegelian sense — as a "world-historic" individual. On the one hand, she must escape the oppression of existence in order to affirm and realize her own principle, "freedom": "[...] ist nur der Traum zu war/ Doch diß Gesichte macht die Hülff jhr offenbar/ Die Freyheit rufft vns heim!" ["(...) be the dream but too true/ Yet this vision makes manifest: help comes, Freedom summons us home!"] (I.v. 355 f.). On the other hand, she bolsters the earthly force of this principle by her action and example; as her country's sovereign she was indispensible to the defense of the endangered real state, of the home, of "freedom" in the terrestial realm. She unites in herself the paradox of the European striving for freedom; without "freedom," existence is in the final analysis worth little or nothing in the West. In the way that history serves as a kind of theater for making Catharina's heroic force visible, so her ascension, as presented on stage, imparts the feeling of human sublimity — we experience the distinction between high and low. By means of this ritual, viewers of Gryphius' day might enjoy the confirmation of Catharina's, that is, their own cultural essence and destiny, which the poet consciously and carefully generalizes. With Catharina they have a share in definite values as Christians and Europeans.

One of these values is the above discussed experience of the distinction between the inner world of heart, mind, and soul and the outer world of history as temporality. But if we scrutinize this contrast more closely, that means Gryphius, too, knows the pleasure of chosing a role and conjures for us the fact of having and playing roles in the tides of time. An object of critical attention since Benjamin's important work, perhaps the greatest discovery of the age of the theater was this new awareness. History *is* drama in the seventeenth century; but, at the same time, one is liberated from it as one awakes from a dream. Time-conditioned roles thrust themselves upon humanity in the theater of the world; but to the extent the martyr or hero remoulds time from within and masters the role, he compels us to accept *his* interpretation of his own existence directly or indirectly. In a meaning-laden passage in the first act, Catharina narrates a dream in which she is bleeding under the weight of her crown, but finds she is wearing in its place "Verdorrte Rosen-Aest" ["Withered rose branches"] wound about her forehead; and a strange man attacks her, until, awakening from her faint and without being afraid, she discovers Shah Abbas in splendid attire at her feet (I, 323-352). The just received news of Tamaras' reconquest of their homeland is at first misinterpreted as the sense of this dream, and Catharina's trust in God's providence promotes a "false" hope, which the nervousness over these palpably intuitive omens mutes. The aesthetic quality of Catharina's vision naturally evokes a reaction like that peculiar to the Catholic cult of the saints.[20] The charged symbols and splendor point toward her extraordinary election, and her concept of herself as "Gottes Magd" ["God's handmaiden"] (I, 460) intensifies this impression. The ethical perspective of older historical drama generically requires elements of the fabulous or a "higher reality" which enable the hero to transcend the terrestial realm of history. Through these the poet calls attention to the limits of history — otherwise (as many Renaissance poets, especially the great English playwrights, were already fearing in the wake of Machiavelli) history would be a self-determining force containing sufficient justification in itself. The process which illuminates the "laws" of history and the "hierarchy" of being in Catharina's case is her victory over life's dream and her realization of the inner vision. Her martyr's fate is characterized by a typical upwards directed movement, a gradation which is intended to lift the spectator's consciousness. That also explains why "disillusionment" in Gryphius' *Catharina* has a positive effect, that is, conveys an edifying religious experience, whereas "disillusionment" of the nineteenth-century variety, e.g., in Büchner, works negatively as disappointment in a realm of life that is limited to itself and is thus our terminal reference.

Presenting family relationships as a microcosm of the state in question was a favorite poetic means of magnification in the Baroque. As such details were available in Gryphius' source, his approach was especially appropriate in the instance of a less familiar personality from the periphery of Europe. The national history is turned into a personal drama, and we experience the chaos of crises immediately as a family affair, as also is the case to a certain degree in *Carolus Stuardus* and *Papinianus*. This intertwining of the sufferings of a people and their ruler still springs from the theory of the "two bodies" of the ruler. According to this doctrine derived from the Middle Ages, the sovereign's power inheres in his office, and not in his vulnerable creaturely person; both "bodies" nonetheless are united in one human being.[21] The drama *Catharina von Georgien* thus has the character of a lyrical meditation on the quality and constitution of power; it shows how Shah Abbas fails to learn self-mastery, whereas despite all burdens and mortal vulnerability the title heroine is capable of preparing inwardly for the most extreme demands imposed by her historical role and of upholding the dignity of her office. Although *her* drama is to be seen as a *translatio* from worldly to divine plane, in the worldly-historical realm this transposition validates the legitimate power based on the superiority of genuine Christian being.

Why then does Shah Abbas have the last word in the play? It is not enough to say his word is mortal, whereas Catharina's final lines are immortal in Gryphius' view. Even if we grasp the division into Shah Abbas, Seinelcan, and Imanculi, in line with French neoclassical treatment, as a critical analysis of "Persian" being, we cannot easily get around the fact the final scene peaks in a portrayal of human decrepitude and nothingness. Gryphius is able, as some great poets are, to fashion evil-doers with exceptional acuteness and intensity – for example, the above-mentioned inexorable egotism of the political adventurers Balbus in *Leo Arminius* and Laetus in *Papinianus*, and the ideological fanaticism of the party of the regicides in *Carolus Stuardus* – and to make them viable dramatic figures alongside the protagonists. We learn the full extent of Shah Abbas' malicious, hard political aggressiveness through Christian eyes and hence must acknowledge him as a dramatically adequate counterpart. Racine's "monstre naissant" Nero in *Britannicus* fascinates us although we hate him for his crimes. Likewise, a deeper human stirring finally is glimpsed in the defeated monster Shah

Abbas. Though too late and doomed to fail, it endows him with a certain sentimental rank as a son of earth — and thus with an undeniable complexity. Regret and admiration contend in him, until completely consumed by Catharina's light he collapses with the abashed cry, "fire" (V, 408).

The Persian can appear to be the really tragic figure to a modern public, because he knows that he must love Catharina, his victim, even beyond her death — and remain forever inexorably conscious of his own self-killing and chastisement. In an age which celebrated the Petrarchan-Orphic theme of inextinguishable passion in numberless poems as well as in the newly developed dramatic-lyrical genre of opera, that comes as no surprise. But, then, should we — can we today — read Shah Abbas' approximately one hundred passionate lines only as an attention-getting, ultimate, ironic unmasking of his "alien" (un-Christian) nature? Or does the intensity of his adoration of what he neither is nor could be conceal yearning, loss, a deeper music which the Baroque poet believed he disdained but found it was impossible wholly to repress?

As a consequence of Catharina's captivity, the internal political history of Georgia — which is thematically related to the contemporary basic problem for Great Britain: civil war and the danger of an illegitimate succession to the throne — is drawn into a wider circle of world history. The clash of diammetrically opposed concepts of the state in *Carolus Stuardus* takes place in *Catharina von Georgien* on the level of the juxtaposition of enimical states. Shah Abbas suffers moral defeat because he is incapable of distinguishing between the false lure of his feelings and the public aspect of his office, because as servant of his people he is incapable of renouncing what is inexpedient for their welfare. In this respect Shah Abbas is branded as unfit for his his high office, when he "bests" Catharina. Both she and King Charles "win" by being executed. Although Shah Abbas' failure prompts the surmise he must sink sooner or later, in his wavering and in his severity he nonetheless resembles Massanisa at the crossroads, the even more complex figure in Lohenstein's *Sophonisbe* (1680), an ascendant ruler who finally chooses *power* and forgoes normal human bliss for a historical-political aim. Shah Abbas remains aimless in time after having, as an instrument of "inconstancy," prepared the way into eternity for his epitome of happiness, Queen Catharina. And precisely in the moment of irremediable loss a new human image becomes visible in his words: the image of the human being who exists *only* in time's toils.[22]

Notes

* I have translated the essay "Time and Eternity in Andreas Gryphius' *Catharina von Georgien*" from my original German version ("Andreas Gryphius' *Catharina von Georgien* als Geschichtsdrama") expressly for the present volume, with the objective of helping to widen access to this area that is still poorly known outside of Germanist circles in the English-speaking world. Gryphius has been included in versions of conference papers on the German Baroque which I have been invited to give at the University of Texas in Austin (1971), at the convention of the North East Modern Language Association in Boston (1973), at the Comparative Literature Symposium of Florida State University in Tallahassee (1973), at the Universities of Manchester and Reading in England (1979), and to the Division on Drama at the convention of the Modern Language Association in Los Angeles (1982).

1 *Catharina von Georgien*, Act V, line 169. References to Gryphius' play will henceforth be cited by capital or lower-case roman numeral for Act and scene, and by arabic numeral for line in an Act (or page number), from vol. III of the *Trauerspiele*, ed. by Hugh Powell, which is the same as vol. VI of the *Gesamtausgabe der deutschsprachigen Werke*, ed. by Marian Szyrocki and Hugh Powell [*Neudrucke deutscher Literaturwerke*, n.s., 15] (Tübingen, 1966). All translations from the play and from critical commentary on Gryphius are my own.

2 Friedrich Sengle, *Das historische Drama in Deutschland: Geschichte eines literarischen Mythos*, 2nd ed. (Stuttgart, 1969), pp. 11-15. (The first edition was titled: *Das deutsche Geschichtsdrama* [Stuttgart, 1952]). On the taletell Romantic keyword in Sengle's phrase, "die Vergangenheit in ihrer Eigentümlichkeit" ["the past in its own singularity"], see Wolfgang Fleischhauer, "*Eigentümlichkeit*: Ein Beitrag zur Wortgeschichte," in *Herkommen und Erneuerung: Essays für Oskar Seidlin*, ed. by Gerald Gillespie and Edgar Lohner (Tübingen, 1976), pp. 56-63.

3 Powell, *Trauerspiele* III, p. vii.

4 Helmut Kappler, *Der barocke Geschichtsbegriff bei Andreas Gryphius* (Frankfurt, 1936).

5   P.B. Wessels, *Das Geschichtsbild im Trauerspiel "Catharina von Georgien" des A. Gryphius* (s'Hertogenbosch, 1960), pp. 12, 17.
6   Walter Benjamin in his influential book, *Ursprung des deutschen Trauerspiels* (Berlin, 1928); Erik Lunding in *Das schlesische Kunstdrama* (Copenhagen, 1940).
7   Hans-Jürgen Schings has focused on the *Catharina* and *Papinianus* in two notable contributions to the volume, *Die Dramen des Andreas Gryphius: Eine Sammlung von Einzelinterpretationen*, ed. by Gerhard Kaiser (stuttgart, 1968). Janifer Gerl Stackhouse has investigated the literary sources and backgrounds of the major tragedies in her book, *The Constructive Art of Gryphius' Historical Tragedies* (Berne, 1986).
8   Clemens Heselhaus, "Gryphius' *Catharina von Georgien*," in *Das deutsche Drama*, ed. by Benno von Wiese (Düsseldorf, 1958); Elida Maria Szarota's ch. "Gryphius' *Catharina von Georgien*," in *Künstler, Grübler und Rebellen: Studien zum europäischen Märtyrerdrama des 17. Jahrhunderts* (Berne and Munich, 1967).
9   Szarota, *Künstler, Grübler und Rebellen*, p. 210. She also points out Friedrich-Wilhelm Wentzlaff-Eggebert's opinion that the parts of the tragedy *Catharina* which seem least dramatic "should be understood in their full significance touching the state and politics." (Cf. Wentzlaff-Eggebert, "Die deutsche Barocktragödie: Zur Funktion von 'Glaube' und 'Vernunft' im Drama des 17. Jahrhunderts," in *Formkräfte der deutschen Dichtung: Vom Barock bis zur Gegenwart* [Göttingen, 1963], p. 8). — Szarota repeats the thesis of parallels in Silesia's history as a buffer state in ampler detail in her book, *Geschichte, Politik und Gesellschaft im Drama des 17. Jahrhunderts* (Berne and Munich, 1976), pp. 130-135.
10 Szarota, *Künstler, Grübler und Rebellen*, p. 201.
11 Szarota, *Künstler, Grübler und Rebellen*, p. 215.
12 Janifer Gerl Stackhouse, "Gryphius' Proclamation of *Recht* in *Ermordete Majestät*: A Source and Text Analysis" (Diss. Harvard University, 1973). — In contrast, Kappler unconvincingly asserts in *Der barocke Geschichtsbegriff* that values in Gryphius are only surface motives ("Anlässe" [p. 42]).
13 M.S. South, "*Leo Arminius* oder die Häresie des Andreas Gryphius: Überlegungen zur figuralen Parallelstruktur," *Zeitschrift für deutsche Philologie*, 94 (1975), 161-182.
14 Szarota, *Künstler, Grübler und Rebellen*, p. 214.
15 The text of his main source (mentioned by Gryphius in his *Leichenabdankungen*) is reproduced in full in E. Susini's discussion of this find, "Documents inédits: Claude Malingre, Sieur de Saint-Lazare, et son histoire de Catharine de Georgie," *Études Germaniques*, 23 (1968), 37-53. Susini believes Gryphius could also have become more closely acquainted with the story during his visit to Rome in 1646 through the report *Delle conditioni de Abbas Re di Persia* by Pietro della Valle, a friend of Athanasius Kircher.
16 Herbert Lindenberger, *Historical Drama: The Relation of Literature and*

Reality (Chicago, 1975); Northrop Frye, "Specific Forms of Drama," in *Anatomy of Criticism* (Princeton, 1957), pp. 282-293. Regrettably, Lindenberger confines himself mainly to English, French, and Spanish drama after the Renaissance and, except for fleeting mention of Gryphius and Lohenstein (based on Benjamin), ignores German drama before Lessing.

17 I am in agreement with Szarota's conclusion that Catharina does not transcend just by a passive *imitatio Christi* and *sola fide*, but becomes a vessel of meaning through tenacious "frommes Handeln" ["pious action"], consistently fulfills her historical mission, and only after reaching that matured stature overcomes as a ruler of double attributes, both as a combatant and as a sufferer (*Geschichte, Politik und Gesellschaft*, pp. 66-72).

18 Schings rightly polemicizes (*Die Dramen des Andreas Gryphius*, p. 71 f.) against Heselhaus' opinion that the final scene is "incomptabile with the martyr tragedy of religious style" because uttered here are "words of vengeance which neither sound very Christian, nor fit Catharina's earlier patient and serene manner" (Heselhaus, "Gryphius' *Catharina von Georgien*," p. 77). Wessels too rejects this oversimplification (*Das Geschichtsbild*, p. 13 f.). Schings stresses, moreover, the way the "apocalyptic and eschatological ending" of the tragedy points back to its beginning and directs our gaze toward a "perspectival vanishing point." Schings also consistently examines the problem of political history (pp. 44 ff.) which "for as long as one can remember [has given] some cause for puzzlement" and contradicts "all principles of economy and strict functionality of parts in the dramatic structure," "[...] as these had become obligatory since Lessing. Gryphius drags the pre-history into the dramatic present in three batches that are monstrously thorough and, besides, oddly placed. And to top the superfluity, not even overlaps are avoided." Indeed, "[...] even though the vicissitudes of Catharina and the Georgian royal house may be conveyed in full detail without gaps, all the same the contours [...] remain unsharp, the names and events swallow one another, the particulars are lost in a uniformly pulsating wave of chaos that heaps horror upon horror. But perhaps that is exactly the intention of those history reports," which "[...] in their pathetic compaction adequately characterize the chaos of the historical world [...]."

19 Nonetheless, from such structural premises Schings regrettably does not draw the conclusion that the special arrangement of Shah Abbas' role as counter-exponent of history lends him, too, more than negligible dimensions which outlast the obvious content in Gryphius' statement and are brought out as latent form in the play. When it is a matter of Shah Abbas and the passions, Schings leaves aside the possibility of a meticulous search for evidence of the work's intentionality and repositions himself on the plane of "doctrine," for example (*Die Dramen des Andreas Gryphius*, p. 58): "Cast in the matrix of Christian tradition and stamped by the experience of *vanitas*, Gryphius' understanding and treatment of the earthly

passions in the tragedy is unambiguous and pejorative throughout. That distinguishes him and the rigorous, almost ascetic ethic of his tragedy in principle a priori from the modern dramaturgy of a Shakespeare or Racine, but also from his successor Lohenstein — and makes talk of the 'tragic' Shah feeble." However, Wentzlaff-Eggebert sees the overlappings and the gradualism in the development from Gryphius over Lohenstein to German Classicism: "What is later designated as 'heroic spirit' in German Classicism has its starting point in these Baroque tragedies" ("Die deutsche Barocktragödie," p. 17).

20 Szarota pertinently remarks: "By virtue of the fact the plot is centered on Catharina and Shah Abbas and Meurab's deeds are only reported (I, 479-716 and III, 381-392), the politically highly interesting role of Meurab, whose national consciousness awakens in the final hour so as to rescue Georgia from demise at the hand of the Shah's vassals, drifts into the background. This seriously diminishes the play's political effect. Meurab was more suited than all others to be the national hero of Georgia." For Szarota the greater interest in the queen's role can be explained in part by her tragedy symbolizing the historical situation of Silesia (*Geschichte, Politik und Gesellschaft*, p. 130). I regard the Protestantizing of the Catholic ground-form, rather, to prove its aesthetic attractiveness which as a dramatist Gryphius is unwilling to forgo. In my estimation, Meruab's heroic dissimulation (likewise his real success as defender of his homeland) comes quite close to the ideal of political prudence which Lohenstein argues in his novel *Arminius*. Gryphius has to acknowledge Meurab and feels it is legitimate to admire him as a peripheral figure. But because Meurab possesses a dark side imposed by fate's decree, he is far too "complex" to be suitable as a "pure" martyr; no matter what, in contrast to a rueful Leo Arminius, he simply does not give up.

21 Cf. Ernst H. Kantorowicz, *The King's Two Bodies: A Study in Mediaeval Political Theology* (Princeton, 1957).

22 The legitimacy of distinguishing between the two levels — the authorial message and the creative act of composition produced by the artist — can be illustrated through a comparison of the case of Bertolt Brecht. Like Gryphius, Brecht is a spokesman of certain doctrinaire views and is equivalent to a medieval preacher, rather than a modern person, in his simplifying interpretation of history. A liturgical-taxonomic rendition of the ideological contents of his plays, even if we make reference to Brecht's critical and propogandistic comments, will still not suffice to explain the structure of the plays in the context of twentieth-century drama. Cf. Lindenberger with regard to Brecht and "the larger historical patterns whose presence we recognize outside the [ideological] framework of a play" (*Historical Drama*, p. 137 f.)

8. LOHENSTEIN'S *EPICHARIS:* THE PLAY OF THE BEAUTIFUL LOSER

> Der blinde Simson bringt sich spielend in das Grab;
> Und unsre kurtze Zeit ist nichts als ein Getichte.

These lines (241-242) from the famous dedicatory poem prefacing the *Sophinisbe* (pp. 244ff.) have all the savor of that ironic ambivalence which we associate with Lohenstein as a ponderer of the records of humanity.[1] But this may be another way of saying that the playwright indeed had the poetic capacity to express wonder over the puzzling spectacle of defeat and collapse. For is it always the "good" who win in his plays; and is the final gesture of the "blind" hero less admirable — less necessary in a higher scheme of values in Lohenstein's work — than the success of the vile? This question does not seem to have greatly concerned interpreters who find satisfaction in a moralistic reductionism derived from some particular aspect of Lohenstein's larger view. But fewer critics today brandish some truistic formula such as that "reason" is superior to "passion" and then quickly assign to two camps the "good" and "bad" players of a living moment of Lohensteinian history. Fortunately, recent research into pre-Enlightenment features of his thought offers cautions and safeguards against an unduly limited sense of the authorial plane, intentionality, and dramaturgical structure. We have been amply warned about the principles of "occultation," "perspectivism," and "searching doubt."[2] The recent interest in Lohenstein's use of prudentialist ideas, notably those of Gracián and Saavedra Fajardo, has also markedly deepened critical awareness of his complexity.[3] Yet, in some respects, the prudentialist phrases have been read as indices for a more sophisticated reductionism. The newer temptation to simplify assumes the form of deciding that the final level of guidance for viewer or reader of the plays is, variously, choral, annotational, intertextual, contextual, and so forth.[4] In essence, the reductionist approach requires us to believe that some particular aspect or level in the works cancels out enormous areas of artistic interests, portrayed subjects, and ingenious "contradictions."

The nature of the issue can be gauged by asking ourselves what constitutes "success" versus "failure" in a Lohenstein play, even if we take prudentialist undertones into consideration. Such nuances are unmistakably associated with his involved concept of "rational gamesmanship" ("vernüftig spielen," So, p. 247, line 102). The preface to the *Sophonisbe* presents man as the creature who plays and dissembles ("Wer niemals thöricht spielt/ die Klugheit oft verstellt/ Aus Thorheit Vortheil macht/ ist Meister in der Welt," lines 107-108). Since Lohenstein himself draws the comparison to his art ("Ich liefer nur ein Spiel," line 19), we must remain on guard against facile reconstructions of his authorial capacity exclusively in terms of a political apology. I propose to examine as an illustrative case Lohenstein's interpretation of the story of the virgin Epicharis, a pagan "loser" who in her zeal to topple Nero technically possesses greater purity than the shorn playboy-hero Samson does in his opposition to the Philistines, until his final act of expiation (Judges, 16). Since the "winner" Nero is so obviously villainous as antagonist to the title heroine Epicharis, the problem of esteem generically for a "winner" can be clarified by looking at an antagonist whom previous Lohenstein scholarship has tended to regard as a model figure: Augustus.[5] I have discussed elsewhere the reasons why the emperor-ascendant, a consummate Machiavellian, though the epitome of the triumphant Roman political ethos, is not "intended as a moralistic explanation of success because he is both the darling of fate and shrewder."[6] In this regard, Elida Maria Szarota has arrived at similar conclusions.[7] Her analysis, indicating why we should read Augustus as a figure who, though fascinating as an imperialist mastermind, is anything but unequivocally idealized by the playwright, permits me to compress my introductory contrast. A fuller discussion of Augustus would require an excursus into Lohenstein's second published play, the *Cleopatra* (1661; second version 1680). It must suffice here to reiterate that I find more convincing Joerg Juretzka's approach to the tensions in the *Cleopatra* as resulting from the discrepancy between the traditional association of the Roman Imperium with order, stability, and an era of peace, and the actual moment of history portrayed, when Rome is the warring enslaver of the world and its own people and Augustus, maneouvring toward supreme power, is the heart and core of the anti-libertarian tendency.[8]

Of course, it should not be automatically excluded that, when composing the *Cleopatra*, Lohenstein might have been working with quite different concepts and feelings. The Romans who intrude into Egypt in the *Cleopatra* would not have to be ambiguous a priori — nor would Augustus by necessity have to represent, among other things, a frightening instance of menace, the scarcely contained disorder in history, the transitory order bought visibly at a tragic price in the play. The revelation of Augustus' faults and crimes in the novel does not change the fact that he is the child of fortune, the right person in the right place at the right time for succession to supreme power — one of the important opening themes (*Arminius*, I. i. 6a et seq.).[9] Lohenstein evokes the idea of Providence as sponsor ("Alleine wo Gott und das Verhängnüs etwas vergrössern wil [...]," I.i. 6b), even though he immediately proceeds to introduce the budding resistance of part of the world Rome oppresses ("Unter diesem Joche schmachtete die Welt und Deutschland," I.i. 7b). We could, accordingly, separate the aspersions cast on Augustus in the *Arminius* from the glittering picture of the world conqueror who in the *Cleopatra* (V. 741ff.) ceremonially communes with the memory of Alexander. We would ignore the charges that Augustus sought to carry out impure designs on Asblaste; that is, that this paragon of Roman order was tempted to commit in a stealthy fashion the transgression which Nero later blatantly commits against Rubria in the *Agrippina* (II. Reyen), before his further crimes in the *Epicharis*. Furthermore, we would regard as unrelated the fact that the conquering Romans, who had been partly fooled by Augustus, had played along with the manipulator, or had failed to grasp the impact on Rome and to resist in the *Cleopatra*, were the not-all-so-remote ancestors of the undermined, spiritless, and cynical Romans in the play *Epicharis*. Their last flickering of political will in the Pontine conspiracy ends in the dungeon. As in a Baroque painting employing the technique of *lux in tenebris*, only the radiance of Epicharis shines there in the somber ambience of disillusionment.

A girl of manly character replaces the Roman archetype, the Horace, Coriolanus, etc. But, strangely, there is no trumph or reward for the heroine in the ordinary sense. If Lohenstein had "approved" of Roman behavior and development at large in the first version of *Cleopatra* but then, however abruptly, a few years later converted them into dubious and villainous inhabitants of an antiheroic world, for some reason he did not in parallel cancel out the Roman way as the prevailing force in subsequent history. Of course, he could not do so without violence to the established record. All the same, older scholarship sometimes interpreted the defective course of Western history, so scrupulously observed by Lohenstein in his plays, to reflect adversely on his own moral character. And it is not difficult to understand why his meticulous anatomy of the failure by the Romans themselves to reverse Roman history in the *Epicharis* would irritate critical sensibility in our era, when many would gladly believe some permanent reversal of the forces which shape history has been guaranteed. Some critics may prefer to read back from Lohenstein's *Arminius* into the *Epicharis* certain above-mentioned, more positive sentiments to lift the terror of history the younger writer perceived at an earlier experimental moment. Be that as it may, the text of his play only grants Epicharis the opportunity to proclaim her own lasting fame, Nero's lasting infamy (V. iv. 732) — an outcome which the audience itself indirectly corroborates by its interest in returning to the spectacle of Rome. But on the dramatic plane of time, despite Epicharis' exalted political convictions and innate nobility, she is defeated in the real world and appears to be manifestly out of tune with history.

Supposing further that Lohenstein actually embraced the concept of a providential preparation for the role of Leopold — that he regarded that prefigurative function of rulership as the highest guiding principle, and not first and foremost as a given social and political reality of his own century — then we might even conclude that we ought to swallow the martyrdom of Epicharis and find some prudentialist consolation in the survival of Nero, a criminal monster. Just such a conclusion is argued with intelligence by Aikin in Ch. 6. Though Aikin believes that Lohenstein is probing the traditional concepts of divine providence, punishment for decadence, and the perfection of virtue through challenge, etc., by examining a nadir in human affairs, she acknowledges the troubling "ambiguity" of Epicharis' active quest for freedom and status as a "martyr." I disagree with Aikin's interpretation that "As Epicharis finds Rome unready for *der Freyheit Gold*, so Lohenstein seems to find it unready for the form of government of the empire practiced in his own day [Wahlkönigtum]" (p. 186). Since Epicharis' major compromise, directly resulting from her attempt to involve her contemporaries, is to accept as interim solution an elective monarchy, then it is precisely the ironic parallel to the "elective" imperial system which would link the decadent Romans spiritually to Lohenstein's contemporary world of the (in fact quite decayed and fragmented) "Holy" Roman Empire, but would separate Epicharis from its normative despotism to the extent that in her heart she remains a staunch Republican.

As Jean-Marie Valentin has shown, the preceptors of the Catholic school in Sion, capital of the Valais, were able to take over the play *Epicharis* from the Lutheran school stage virtually unchanged and, by a few clever touches, reinterpret Lohenstein's title figure in 1710 as wickedly inspired, perverse in her tenacity, and rightly punished![10] In their production the Stoic Seneca is consistently praised for resisting the evil appeal and sticking to his principles at supreme personal cost; Nero's barbarism is muted by suppression of Seneca's actual death scene. Lohenstein dwells on this favorite subject of the late Renaissance with the same intensity as Monteverdi in *L'incoronazione di Poppea*. Because these particular Catholic educators wanted to uphold the principle of the divine right of kings, they lent a drastic sense to Nero's survival as the dubious established authority. And it is easy enough to see why the noble portrayal of Seneca by Lohenstein or of Papinian by Gryphius could offer solid material for like-minded conservatives – Lutheran or Catholic. But it is intriguing that the Sion revisor, Pellissier, sought to reduce her perseverance to physical courage and had to work against her intrinsic stature in Lohenstein's version by modifying terms which suggested her martyrdom for the Republican cause. The new title, *Coniuratio Punita, Das Ist Die in ihrem bösen Vorhaben abgestraffte Epicharis*, shifts the entire emphasis to the downfall of vain ambition. Below I shall return to the discovery by Bernhard Asmuth that, *inter alia*,

Lohenstein wrote the *Epicharis* in some measure of tacit artistic rivalry with Tristan L'Hermite, because a comparison of two versions of the same story, one by a major and controversial French playwright, offers even more illuminating glimpses into authorial procedures and intent.[11]

If the natural audience response today is to favor and admire "punished" Epicharis, it is difficult to imagine that the seventeenth-century audience could easily withhold at least grudging admiration. This would generally be truer in the case of Protestants in an urban environment such as that of Breslau with its cross-currents and advanced pansophical and liberal strains of thought, though Gryphius, had he lived another year, would probably have found her heroism to be very problematic from his own irenic, conservative point of view. But even Gryphius had already provided a bridge by showing, in his final play *Papinian*, how an idealistic pagan figure could be accommodated. Thus those who came to a reading or viewing armed with contrary rationalizations would scarcely be inclined unfavorably toward Epicharis, since rejection of her on the grounds of some technical claim to allegiance by Nero would go against an audience's generic expectations based on martyr stories, as well as experiential and cultural instincts. One could nonetheless argue that today we find scant consolation in Epicharis' defeat simply because we lack the broad seventeenth-century perspective on martyrdom, which frequently involved accepting an irreconcilable conflict between ethical imperatives and wordly power. But if Epicharis is providentially defeated, does that mean a significant sector of Lohenstein's audience actually shared her ideals and fervor, at least transposed into their own terms, and valued these beyond the hypothetical "highest" referent (Leopold as successor to Nero)? Or, going even further, does it mean a seventeenth-century audience could enjoy the form of a martyrdom as a value in itself divorced from "acceptable" ethical substance? In a tug of war between Tacitean gloom and recondite prudentialist *desengaño*, does Lohenstein regard Epicharis' strivings and sufferings just as a magnificent gesture, but without profound immediate linkage to the spiritual course of humankind or applicability in history?

These questions raise the issue to what extent we may legitimately interpret the play also as a psychological and sociological statement which has some lasting validity beyond the immediate framework of psychological and sociological theories of the late seventeenth century, since, after all, the playwright obviously arrived at his own artistic synthesis in the process of sorting out the already available explanations. These represent some of the *données* of his cultural vocabulary, not his own mind necessarily. I believe that appreciation of Epicharis' new way of "losing" can be enhanced by the testing out of categories which derive from wholly modern standpoints. For example, the approach to Lohenstein's plays as documents of social criticism has been outlined sympathetically by Johannes Klein;[12] and Winfried Weier has rather convincingly described the shift in Lohenstein's works to a secular "mixed" character, whose autonomous being expresses itself in a flow of psychic and erotic energy.[13]

Klein is little surprised by the obvious "contradiction" in the plays between Lohenstein's keen analysis of the dehumanizing pressures in an age of despotism on the one hand, and his expression of cultural hopes attached to the revered tradition of a universal order under the Reich on the other. But such meditating on a grand European and Western polity, which naturally summons the aspiration that the nominally surviving Empire fulfill its civilizing mandate, does not — in Klein's view — blunt Lohenstein's basically anti-absolutistic concepts of law and right. Instead "das Innerweltliche, Irdische" overwhelms the choral framework of eternal values inherited from Gryphius, because Lohenstein is an observer without illusions, demonically sensitized to the contemporary meaning of social and political perversion in the Roman era, capable of radical exposure of the inhuman in humanity, but also anticipating the reconstruction of humane ideals by the German Enlightenment and Classical dramatists. According to Klein, Lohenstein's fascination for the essence of womanhood reflects *inter alia* a search for alternatives to tyranny, statism, imperialism. Through the "superwoman", as contrast to the Caesarian prince, he elaborates the existence of a psychological core demanding outlet and scope; however, the erotic energies of Lohenstein's heroines can find no satisfaction in the turmoil and treachery of their actual world. Struggle against disorder in history tragically leads into repressive control and colossal corruption under the

Roman aegis. This is, of course, a major theme of the *Arminius* in its opening statements. How far the obsession with the collapse of Rome could be secularized from the Renaissance through the Enlightenment is majestically evident with the appearance of the first volume of Edward Gibbon's *The Decline and Fall of the Roman Empire* in 1776; and how rapidly the long-range secular tendency of this obsession actually became rooted in early modern times is appreciated in Part III of Jacob Burckhardt's *Die Zivilisation der Renaissance in Italien*, published in 1860. Since Lohenstein was reading Machiavelli along with other theoreticians at the time of composing the *Epicharis* (e.g., in an annotation to IV. 459 on the preferability of death with fame, he cites both Machiavelli and Matthieu), we cannot discount the presence also of earlier Renaissance layers of thought about Rome nor presume that these are obliteratingly overridden by later conservative Christian revisionists who had the objective of co-opting Machiavellian theory and its more secular derivatives. And in the pattern of the triumph of a (Roman) this-worldly, disciplined state over older cultures (Egyptian, Carthaginian) in which political and religious life were connected, Klein senses Lohenstein has mirrored "die Aufsaugung des Kirchenprinzips durch den Absolutismus" – an unpalatable and frustrating reality for most orthodox Lutherans after interminable religious and civil warfare. The Reformation had borne strange fruit, and a wide variety of Protestant visionaries were convinced that a further enlightenment had to follow and transform backslidden Europe.[14]

The complex manner in which Lohenstein could nevertheless reconcile his somber historical awareness with his essentially positive view of Protestantism is evidenced in the *Arminius*. For now I would like to continue from Klein's observation that Lohenstein was not so much a pessimist as a depictor of the dark realities of the state, and never inwardly on the side of Caesarian power. This is certainly clear in the case of Epicharis, because the playwright took care to upgrade her social status from freed slave to noblewoman and thereby endow her with Opitzian qualifications for a tragic role, by borrowing much of her heroicized aura from the lengthier portrayal in Desmarets' romance *Ariane* and compacting it (I. 113ff.), but also retaining the useful ambiguity of the romanesque account prior to the generic happy ending and disclosure (which Lohenstein jettisons whole, because he reverts to the tragic potential of the serious historical account by Tacitus et al.). In my view, Aikin misunderstands the adaption of romanesque characterization and plot elements by Lohenstein when she interprets that Epicharis' revelations of her long-standing hatred of Nero may reveal suspect drives, "a more selfish motive than she pretends" (p. 186). Tristan and Lohenstein convert the figure from romance so as to retain her mystique, yet meet the requirements of historical veracity. Lohenstein also lends her a familiar attribute of the martyr-saint, when he exhibits her unmistakable chastity; in fact, Epicharis helps bring on disaster for her cause because she is pure and, out of personal integrity, will not give in to the sexual advances of Proculus who then betrays the conspiracy. And yet, as her cause, she upholds the superiority of the Republican ethos, an earlier standard of moral strength corrupted by Caesarism. Perhaps most telling is the negative depiction of Seneca in the paired Neronian play *Agrippina*. As Klein says (pp. 240ff.), Lohenstein demonstrates how this Stoic sage so revered by Renaissance Europe, a man capable of profound insights, is in the *Agrippina* also capable of covering up and going along with heinous crime on high; how he compromises in the enervating atmosphere of the court — only to become himself the victim of despotic arbitrariness in the *Epicharis*. Lohenstein does more than sardonically condemn this model, he also reveals the historical laws which permit tyrannies to thrive on fear, as the good are driven into isolation and finally withdraw into an interior world of ideal purity. From the *Agrippina* to the *Epicharis*, Seneca traces a fall and reascent, and, in the latter play, Lohenstein pays tribute to his regained spiritual stature in the act of dying, which remains almost the only means available in the kind of world Seneca knows.

Epicharis never concedes to any authority her right to act, that is, the assertion and exercise of her principle: freedom. Curiously, the Roman tragedies — Lohenstein's most pointed indictments of absolutism — carry no direct diplomatic dedication to the Hapsburgs.[15] If in these plays he felt with special intensity the dilemma of the corruption of power, or also was reacting positively to his own experience and knowledge of Republican concepts and social vitality in the Netherlands, Switzerland, or elsewhere, he could not have chosen a better standard-bearer. Since Epicharis' classical standard of virtue antedates Caesarism, the Republican cause assumes the general function of representing the primal impulses of mankind, our lost dignity (which the Renaissance had proclaimed), the course from which we were deflected (a connection which radical Protestants would appreciate), a taste of the prelapsaran soundness of being. But as Weier convincingly argues, Lohenstein definitively modernizes the tragic protagonist by viewing him as a "monadenhaft[es] Kraftzentrum", propelled by "Ichgefühl" rather than by transcendental ideas (p. 534). Thus perseverance on behalf of a principle, even in the case of his "purest" heroine Epicharis, involves a realization of personal "identity" so that martyrdom is regrounded in an immanent arena of history. *Constantia* comes to mean being faithful to the deeper cravings of one's own spirit, and in the case of Epicharis that includes feeling bitter hatred for Nero, preferring death with honor over any concession, once actual revenge is excluded. Her extremism seems to be a special form of "energy" erupting through the paralyzing constraints of Roman corruption. Another kind of resistance in Lohenstein's plays (notably the African) springs from the psychic reality of love, which exhibits its own constancy under threat by ambition and power. In Weier's terms, "[...] die 'Freiheit' des 'Geistes' [bei Lohenstein] ist die aus der rein immanenten Schwungkraft souveränen Geistes resultierende Energie, die genau wie jene Freiheit der Gedanken [bei Gryphius] zwar constantia begründet, aber im Unterschied dazu allein aus sich selbst schafft und daher Ursache und Zweck zugleich ist" (p. 527).

Self-actualization, the release of the deeper identity, the insistence on bringing about the mind's desire mean that the Lohenstein protagonist does not just hold out, with eyes directed to a higher order, but spites the contrary forces of time, faces real pain and misfortune (Weier, p. 538). Moving from Lohenstein's "antiheroines" Agrippina, Cleopatra, and Sophonisbe to the less problematic feminine roles of Epicharis, Isabella, and Ambre does not mean leaving the political arena. Rather, attention is shifted from active ruler figures to persons who, affected by dire decisions of rulers, seek to mobilize power through other traditional channels in response. Even Lohenstein's youthful work in Gryphius' shadow, *Ibrahim Bassa* (1653), is not a martyr play about religious faith. Rather, the protagonists believe in the absolute mandate of their hearts, whereas the antagonists will not or cannot recognize the validity of any pattern of conduct other than *raison d'état*. Prodded by scheming courtiers, the jealous sultan regards the lovers as traitors when they escape and then appeal to the sanctity of their personal commitment. Paradoxically, though they uphold the idea of earthly felicity (an idea which gains revolutionary vigor in the eighteenth century!), Ibrahim's stoic death means the extinction of the self which would enjoy; and it is on account of the impossibility of denying love and in order to fulfill it that he acts in such a way as to provoke retribution. In this sense, their story is indeed a tragedy of human rights crushed by the state, so that it is appropriate for man and wife to speak of their sentimental loyalty in the tones of a Gryphian victim. Their deeper identities depend on their sharing certain sentiments. Ibrahim sees dying for love as a final glow of real experience, an ecstatic release (V. 7-12). But he never rejects as meaningless his own political past, at various levels including the office of vizier, and is anxious about leaving Isabella alone amid enemies, when in a turn of power their envy and malice strike him down. Isabella is able, however, to perpetuate their love in sublimated form by setting out to publish the crimes of Soliman in Europe and stir a cultural crusade. Thus the play really demonstrates the polarization of mankind into the camps of humanity and barbarism.

The lovers in *Ibrahim Bassa* mirror the purity of their sentiments in each other. This matter of the possession of an image (*Bild*) which functions as a soul is central in most of Lohenstein's plays. Twenty years later, in the mature drama *Ibrahim Sultan*, Lohenstein's awareness of the Turkish realm as the incarnation of base tyranny, and everything inimical to the ideals of European civilization, is more somber; the sultan's bestial lust vividly exhibits the dangerous nature of this truly antiheroic empire. In the following chapter on "Dream and Calculus in European Baroque Drama," I shall consider the very different approach which Tristan takes to the characters of Osman and the unnamed "Mufti's daughter" and can dispense with such a comparison for the present purposes.¹⁶ In Lohenstein's version of the story, the pious Mohammedan Ambre in *Ibrahim Sultan* does not fix her gaze on any sexual partner but on the inner picture of God which she treasures, because this spiritual light constitutes for her her very being. In contrast, the sultan desires to posses her, because — in his own words — he needs a soul and craves the glow which emanates from her, unique in his court where sensualism, intrigue, and turmoil reign. Raped by her vengeful monarch, defiled Ambre summons the Turkish nobles and shames them into rebellion by her suicide. Her greatness of spirit can inspire a rejuvenating change in the government at this tragic price, but the nature of the Turkish state remains fundamentally unaltered. Death symbolically cleanes her of besmirchment and permanently safeguards her role — just as it did that of the Roman heroine Lucretia. The *dramatis personae* in the Turkish world who assert an ethic of humane standards or commitment exemplify how Lohenstein strove to develop a concept of personal integrity. The problem of loss of self arises as soon as a noble figure is placed under constraint to deny his own inner image; and in the case of rulers who have lost any worthy concept of self, the unstable tormentor manifests powerful symptoms of alienation from his own humanity.

Although this sterner concept of identity derives in general from the Christian-Platonic hierarchical view of created life, according to which the intellect is mankind's highest attribute, the mind is no longer necessarily divorced from action. In *Epicharis*, Lohenstein deliberately explores two basic pathways for the fulfillment of his inner image by a protagonist in a degenerate world: heroic rebellion, and stoic passivity. These two roles also distinguish two fundamental attitudes about responsibility for social institutions in contrast to total default and acquiescence.¹⁷ We witness the formation and collapse of a conspiracy against the tyrant Nero, a turning point in the development of a once great people. The setting ("Der Schauplatz stellet für ein verbrenntes Hauß und Garten") is the period following Nero's outrageous caprice in burning his own capital city. In the opening scene of Act I, the first speakers depict a Rome in ruin, destroyed by the same forces which undermined Carthage, Babylon, and Troy, all victims of the power of time. This despairing picture —

"Dis sind der Zeiten Früchte. Sie bauen heute was/ und morgen wirds zu nichte" (I, 7f.) — could be from a Gryphian sonnet. In Tristan's terse play, the action begins with Sabine (Sabina Poppaea), rid of Agrippina and Octavia as rivals, now traducing Nero to fear and therefore purge his preceptor Seneca.[18] Act I focuses upon the peril for the wearied philosopher, whom guilt-ridden Nero ambiguously commands to stay at court as a needed spiritual shield (sc. ii). Act II shifts to the conspiracy, with a reluctant Piso (sc. i) joining Rufus, Scevinus, and Lucius, but the freed woman Epicharis (sc. ii) emerging spontaneously *in medias res* as the inspirational leader, who draws an extended comparison between the conflagration of Troy, the disaster for their heroic ancestors, and the shameful depredations of the "monster" Nero. Lohenstein not only tacitly ennobles his heroine, he concentrates immediately and in far greater detail on her leadership and principles, as well as on the particular motivations of other plotters. His Epicharis does accept the inalterable fact of defeat for earlier civilizations, but she refuses to attribute their fall simply to the process of temporality. Rather she states that man is responsible for himself:

> Wir heucheln unser Schuld. Der ungeheure Blitz
> Der so viel äschert ein/ wird in den schwartzen Hertzen
> Der Sterblichen gezeugt. Der Brand/ den wir beschmertzen
> Kommt vom Verhängnüs nicht/ er rührt nicht ungefähr/
> Nein/ von der Mißethat des grimmen Blutthunds her. (I, 26-30)

Thus she accuses the Romans of moral failure and cowardice and calls upon them to regain their ancient condition as a race of heroes, an appeal which is indissolubly tied with her goal of restoring the Republic. Epicharis' conviction springs from her intense faith in the reality of being free, and she has corresponding character traits — control over misleading affects, resolution in crisis, physical courage under torture. She epitomizes the indomitable player who dares to seize the occasion, to ride the treacherous wave of fortune, knowing that boldness is allied to virtue and magnanimity (I, 465ff.).

Yet we spectators shudder in our admiration, for the course of events moves inexorably against her. And indeed, the first chorus *Des Geschreys und der Wahrsager* (I, 769ff.) states outright that, though Rome is falling apart, "Doch wird der Fürst beschirmt" (790). The choral augury (799-804) can be read analogically — in typical seventeenth-century fashion — as a reference to the eventual renewal of Rome in the Holy Roman Empire (first tercet), as well as to the abortive political pains to bring forth a new government (first and second tercets):

> Die Deutung kan nicht fehln
> Rom mühet sich zu erwehln
> Ein neues Haupt der Erden.
> Doch der Verhängnüs-Schluß
> Macht: Daß solch Ratschlag muß
> Kund und Kräbsgängig werden.

I posit that this all-too-readily deciphered "double" sense is itself in turn doubly ambiguous. Lohenstein could rely on conservative Catholics and Lutherans to read such proper sentiments into the pagan oracle. That predictable response automatically cloaked his work with a desirable immunity from the charge of depicting what it depicts: *lèse majesté*. But as we have seen, an actual attempt to milk the play for conservative propaganda in Sion required considerable tampering. When we arrive at the second chorus *Der Klugheit; Des Gelückes/ Der Zeit/ Der Verhängnüßes* (II, 473ff.), we have to strain exceedingly if we peer into the ominous shadows which engulf the operations of Fate for some glimpse of the hidden analogy, Providence. It is as if Lohenstein, himself overpowered by the mystery of the past, dares to bring his Christian audience up against the ungraspable law for which the analogy is but a poor copy — rather than the reverse, merely providing a murky copy. It is true that we hear familiar prudentialist terminology; however, even the highest and most promising category, *Klugheit*, cannot avail, though combined with pre-eminent virtues, against a decree of Fate, so that these terms ambivalently stimulate us. Called in question are not merely the subordinate categories of time and circumstance conditioning the moment in which the human actor must formulate his response; also the spiritual resources, human ingenuity (*Witz*) and shrewdness (*Scharf-Sinnigkeit*), all levels of prudential foresight collapse. For as Fate tells us (542-545):

>   Der Klugheit Spigel weißt: Daß er von Glase sey
>   Wenn ihn mein Zepter trifft. Und wenn mein Auge blitzt
>   Springts Glückes gläsern Ball/ der Zeit Chrystall entzwey.

If *Verhängnis* is an arcane, ultimate context in which the activity of every *persona* is enmeshed, while both Fortune and Time on the one hand, and Cleverness on the other, are only subordinate factors in a "game" already subject to Fate (578), then it is very difficult to believe that Lohenstein intended to render a moral judgment against Epicharis on the grounds of her failure.

Whether and to what extent a traditional moralizing interpretation is also adequate for Lohenstein's other plays is a question which can, for now, be left moot. But a few general remarks are in order regarding the as yet inadequate picture of Lohenstein's particular kind of Protestantism; scholarship in this area certainly needs to be refined, and when it is, the results may well induce critical modifications in the interpretation of the plays. Although I reject a foreshortened portrait of Lohenstein as a prudentialist who is presumed to mean Providence in a somewhat reflexive, orthodox Lutheran manner, tinged by late Renaissance Catholic thought, whenever he says Fate, I also deem inaccurate the more extreme opposite conclusion that he had completely veered from the Christian context into some virtually godless existential scrutiny of human affairs. This latter view was argued intelligently — and for the most part productively for purposes of analyzing the specifics of plays — by Lunding in 1940: "Gott ist für Lohenstein nur insofern wahrnehmbar, als er mit dem Intellekt erreichbar ist" [...]; "Die Tatsache allein, daß das Göttliche bei Lohenstein zum Kuriosen entwertet wird, zeigt die tiefe Kluft zwischen ihm und Gryphius."[19] Lunding's thesis that the collapse of the traditional apparatus of religious drama, beginning with Gryphius, already posed the possibility of an accelerating drift toward "Nihilismus" (p. 40), recurs some two decades later in a carefully modified form in Verhofstadt's thorough and stimulating monograph as the thesis of the disintegration of an older world view and revitalization of the components of vastly expanded knowledge.[20] My own position in this regard began to change, starting with my paper "Cosmic Vision in Lohenstein's Poetry," *Neophilologus*, 53 (1969), 413-422. The wide range of Protestant thought across

Northern Europe — especially in the Netherlands and England, but also in Germany — provides ample evidence of liberal and radical directions which were fostered under the outward tokens of tradition, to wit: the development of confidence in a rational purpose behind history, hope in a providential breakthrough in the cosmic plan, and belief in the efficacy of exploration, discovery, and empirical science as the vouchsafed instrumentalities of a new dispensation. The process of secularization often involved the construction of concepts which appeared derivative from and compatible with accepted ideas — ordinarily as a natural step in the generation of new terms, sometimes as a deliberate strategy which obviated the problems of conflict. The latter seems more probable in the case of Lohenstein, who combines a political-social shrewdness and a craving to elaborate his own encyclopedic frameworks, containers which highly condition their contents. This subject, too, exceeds the scope of the present chapter and must regrettably be postponed.[21]

Here I am concerned to demonstrate not only that Epicharis' "failure" could stir admiration, at least in the eyes of her contemporaries depicted in the play, but that Lohenstein presents no grounds for dismissing that admiration as wicked or ill-conceived, even though Epicharis lifts her hand defiantly against the predecessor of Leopold and, unwittingly, in opposition to a decree of "Providence" (as soon as we transcribe Fate in prudentialist terms). Far from being traditional, the *Epicharis* bears all the marks of a highly experimental and precocious phase in the playwright's creative development. He takes up a well-defined subject matter that could easily be converted into a standard typological portrayal of misguided rebellion. Instead, the particular political crisis presented in the drama assumes the character of a testing for the variegated humanity which Lohenstein studies as participants in the historical process. We are allowed to observe how the individual weaknesses of the conspirators undermine Epicharis' purpose and many seemingly strong men buckle under duress, while she is proven in the fire. This collective unmasking, disillusionment, and degradation of humankind is a complex analysis of the reasons for the race's general enslavement, without denying the validity of the exceptional person.

The passive ethic of the other idealized figure of the drama, Seneca, an internal commentator, competent to appreciate Epicharis' "divine spirit" (V, 48), is a contrasting foil. He has taken mental refuge in a transcendental principle of righteousness which makes him immune to every sort of threat, including that of malicious defamation through state propaganda. From his lofty vantage, even an attack upon his public image cannot really damage him any more than the gods are hurt if men break their images and lay waste their temples:

> Ja/ wie die Götter selbst nichts schmertzliches empfinden/
> Wenn man ihr Bild zerbricht/ die Tempel äschert ein:
> So/ weil die Weisen ja auf Erden Götter seyn
> Und Geister über Sonn und Sternen in sich nehren/
> Kan Unfall zwar den Leib ihr bloßes Bild verzehren/
> Nichts aber Irrdisches dem Geiste Schaden thun. (V, 56-61)

In exploring the bases of identity, Lohenstein sought to discern the formal patterns underlying the phenomena of human will. It is instructive to contrast Lohenstein's with Tristan's portrayal of Seneca since, as Bernhard Asmuth has shown, both playwrights had as a major common source the romance version of the philosopher's involvement with the conspirators in Desmarets' *Ariane*.[22] In Tristan's play, the ardent Republican Epicharis realizes that only Seneca possesses the moral stature to persuade the populace of the rightness of the action being plotted (*MS* II. iii. 566-576). She has her lover-elect Lucain approach him, while she listens in hiding. This situation closely parallels the intimate sounding out of Seneca by Lucain, who is expressly designated as his nephew, in the *Ariane*; and Tristan repeats in essence (*MS* II. iv) the same reasoning by Seneca why as Nero's mentor he cannot participate, also the same warnings about the weak elements and personalities in the conspiracy, with the advice the coup be executed with all deliberate speed. Just before her sudden arrest by Procule (II, v), Epicharis excuses Seneca's "weakness" as honorably motivated (II, v), but does not react to his parting words. In these, Tristan swiftly introduces a new theme which offsets the effect of the Stoic's ambivalent withdrawal. Seneca is attracted in his final hours toward a novel teaching, recently carried to Rome, and of course the audience alone knows its name:

SENEQUE
Aussi bien i'ay promis d'aller voir cette nuict
Vn vieux Cilicien aux bonnes moeurs instruit,
Vn Prophete nouueau dont la doctrine pure
Ne tient rien de Platon, ne tient rien d'Epicure,
Et s'esloignant du mal, veut introduire au iour
Vne loy de respect, de justice & d'amour.
Ie te veux faire part de ses auis idelles.

LUCAIN
I'ai trop d'auersion pour les sectes nouuelles.

By suggesting that Seneca will be direcly influenced by St. Paul, Tristan imbues the sage's death *in extremis* with Christian overtones. His disdain for earthly affairs acquires a special sanction, which offers some satisfaction to the more religious members of the French public.

Reducing Lucanus to a quite marginal role, Lohenstein simultaneously omits any close family linkage between Seneca and the Republican core. The relationship becomes entirely societal and philosophical. As the conspiratorial party discusses possible moves in the opening scene of the *Epicharis*, the fact emerges that absent Piso has already been working on Seneca (I. i. 353ff.), and Piso's ally Natalis sets off to arrange at home a confidential interview with Seneca on which they can eavesdrop.[23] Misgivings about Piso's character and suspicions that he may simply be aiming to replace Nero on the throne surface in scene ii. Stemming the defeatism of Scevinus and others, Epicharis rejects merely finding another ruler, such as morally suspect Piso, insists on the restoration of self-government for Rome, but accepts the interim compromise solution of elevating Rome's worthiest citizen Seneca to the throne. Thus Seneca's arguments are elicited early in the play (I. iii) in response to the urgings of the uncertain Natalis and the more resolute Sulpitius Asper. Not only does Lohenstein shift the moment forward, so that it furnishes one of the immediate factors to which Epicharis must react as the inspirational leader; he also does not offer – and if Tristan's treatment figures large in his total literary awareness of the subject, he deliberately avoids lending – special sanction to Seneca as a proto-Christian figure. Moreover, Lohenstein's own annotations reveal his awareness of the ideas of the radical Protestant John Milton in formulating the principles of justifiable rebellion against a sovereign. As in Desmarets' *Ariane* and Tristan's *La mort de Sènéque*, here too in Lohenstein's version, Seneca indicates his sympathy and counsels haste, even though he chooses to stand aside. But Epicharis hears this with a larger circle of plotters gathered round her than in Tristan's version, so it is on her instant management of the situation and the dynamics of revolutionary leadership of the social elite that Lohenstein focuses (I. iv).

In accord with French classical norms, Tristan divides the subject of Seneca's death into two parts. First there is the scene of spiritual preparation by Seneca, aided by his wife Pauline, because the philosopher expects to be put to the test of torture and resolves to expire steadfastly, avoiding betrayal of anybody, yet hopes posterity will absolve him of any blame for the disorder of his times (*MS* V. i. 1503ff.). The suicide command arriving from the emperor precipitates the decision by Pauline to die with her husband. But the actual bloodletting and Seneca's magisterial composure exiting from the world are narrated by the Centurion in a messenger scene (V. iv) which closes the drama, so that our attention like Nero's apprehension is oriented to the supreme Stoic gesture. But it has been transmuted into martyrdom, since Seneca speaks mysteriously of the teaching by the man from Tharsus, of a "Dieu Liberateur" who has ravished his soul (V. iv. 1834ff.). Since Lohenstein's treatment of Seneca's exit is so expansive (V. i.), there can be no mistaking that he omits such a Christian reference. One of Seneca's first statements pays tribute to Epicharis and associates her courage with his principles (V. i. 8). He then launches into a broad philosophic and historical analysis of his own times, with the example of Socrates as our fixed standard and reference (V. i. 43). The fall of classical models such as Socrates and Cato, or inversely, the rise of Caesarian tyranny, amounts always to the same thing, to the demise of freedom: "Ja mit ihm leget sich die Freiheit in sein Grab" (V. i. 86). The unmitigated indictment of Neronian Rome, the yearning for release from its vanity, the determination to finish in consonance with his own teachings are grandiloquently expressed; nonetheless, ironically, Seneca must struggle against the elevated love of Pauline and finally acquiesces in her wish to die with him. Then Lohenstein actually stages the grim, often sardonic, event: Seneca has to go to some effort to snuff out his own life. But his communion is with his classical pagan model: "Ich sehe Socraten mir diesen Kelch zutrincken" (V. i. 411). His offering is to "Erlöser Jupiter" (437), a quotation deriving from another case in antiquity, as the annotation indicates. Nothing prevents us from reading such references as typological analogues for Christ and God the Father; however, it is clear that Lohenstein's interest is so riveted on the historical data and on Seneca's own historical consciousness that the kind of intellectual work we in turn must engage in, if we draw such parallels, conditions the overall impact of the play. Our recognition of the Socratic paradigm occurs in combination with witnessing the audacious presentation of the grisly dungeon scenes, as well as Seneca's protracted dying. These features mark Lohenstein, at least in this phase of creativity, as a daring combinatory experimentalist whose mind could enter unpredictable avenues.

Tristan, too, presents an adamant Epicharis who tells Nero to his face that the attempt against him is laudable and legitimate:

> Ie te hay comme vn Monstre abismé dans le crime,
> Et treuue que ta mort est vn coup legitime. (MS V. iii. 1743f.)

But, again for reasons of decorum, she is delivered into the hands of inhuman executioners to die off stage and simply disappears from view, ceding place to the spectacle of Seneca. I believe we must take seriously the inversion of this order by Lohenstein (whether or not he was reacting artistically to Tristan in particular). Both playwrights overturn the romanesque "escape" of the heroic Epicharis from the clutches of the police, when in the *Ariane* the Pisan conspiracy is betrayed and crushed. There the generically appropriate solution is that the world presumes Epicharis has expired gallantly, whereas she has actually meanwhile been smuggled out of prison after the start of the interrogation, torture, and widening discovery of complicity. As noted, Tristan even reverses her romanesque rank as a noble, though this permits him to imply an intrinsic qualitative standard since she can instruct Nero on how to die well (*MS* V. iii. 1750). All the same, the Roman patrician supersedes her by rank and reputation, whereas Lohenstein precisely places Epicharis' last breath as the capstone. The Silesian playwright devotes a final scene to the lower depths of the state, its dungeons, where a duel of will takes place between two concepts of insanity. Nero and Sabina seek to impose their view of the rightness of power and the madness of opposition, while Epicharis refuses to buckle and turns her definition upon them. Who is the "victor" in this contest between oppressor and resister, if Epicharis correctly concludes, "Itzt wandelt Tyranney sich erst in Aberwitz" (V. iii. 698), and Neronian rule slips irrevocably into the abyss of the "non-human"?

Unmistakably, the contest is also between two concepts of human governance. Tigillinus, chief operative of the police state, specifically invokes the doctrine of the divine right of rulers, the untouchable majesty of a sovereign and state authority:

> [...] Die Fürsten sind geweiht.
> Zu Göttern dieser Welt/ für die die Sternen kämpffen;
> Und dich dünckts Heyligthumb so große Sonnen dämpfen/
> Für derer Strahlen dir solt Aug und Licht vergehen? (V. 542-545)

Explicitly, the assertion is that Fate, represented by the order of the stars, supports the earthly divinity, the ruler, which will prove to be the case in the immediate situation. Against the mystique of rulership, Epicharis asserts natural law and natural aristocracy, dignity based on merit, the fallibility and corruption of power, and the decacy of legitimacy merely inherited:

> In wie viel Fürsten steckt ein knechtisches Gemütte?
> Hof-Heuchler/ Henckers-knecht; Ja tausend Sclaven sind
> Viel edler/ als ihr Herr. Er bleib ein Helden-Kind
> Ich eines Grichen Magd! Ist mir der Weg verschrencket
> Zur Tugend: ihm zur Schmach? Die Kraft des Stammes sencket
> Sich in den Propffern ab. (V. 548-553)

Ironically, her argument also applies to the Romans at large; so that, in historical terms, their decay deprives her of the opportunity of living in a world where virtuous men exist with the strength to govern themselves, deprives her of adequate contemporaries in sufficient number. Caesarism reflects the collapse of a people, not a worthy pathway. Epicharis and her closest companions are an anachronism because they possess the vision and capacity of freedom. In this sense we may then, indeed, speak of Epicharis' "blindness". Her tragic flaw consists in still believing, contrary to the evidence, some of which she herself has adduced, that the liberation of society from oppression is a necessary, attainable enterprise.

As Epicharis sees the curtain falling, she appeals to the verdict of history — that is, to us, the spectators of time. Acting as *juge d'instruction*, Lohenstein lays out the documents and evidence before us; he has it from a variety of first- and second-hand sources, including more credible witnesses such as the great historian Tacitus. The final act of the play exhibits Nero, who continues the Caesarian arrogation of power, in the process of responding to Epicharis' sincere challenge to despotism. The main activity of the state, we learn at this juncture, is not just the ruthless extirpation of the dissenters and would-be reformers. The state is also busy covering up its crimes, burying its victims and faking the meaning of their suffering, as soon as the exercise of terror no longer serves its purpose. As a political thinker, Epicharis understands this activity. Thus when the intensity of the political pressures causing the rebellion manifest themselves in the dungeon and anxious Nero tries to adjust, by pardoning broken conspirators, Epicharis deliberately does what she can to spoil his management of the denouement. Finally, her only remaining card is defiance through suicide. We can measure the significance which Nero attaches to her pronouncements by his closing instructions. Henchmen are rewarded, the army and populace are mollified with gifts, ceremonial obliteration of the rebels and public thanksgiving are scheduled. The propaganda arm of the state is to entrance the city and world "mit tausend Freuden-Zeichen" as the corpses are flushed down the Tiber (V. iii. 738ff.). We hear the prince, who thinks he is having the last word, speak the very commands which are intended to shield him from the light of the mind and the judgment of history.

To sketch the full picture of political degeneracy and misdirection in the *Epicharis* exceeds the limits of this probe into the austere "beauty" of the title heroine; however, that total revelation must be regarded as one of the several conventional frameworks within which Lohenstein exhibits her particular being as a reality. The phenomenon Epicharis provokes more questions than it answers in an age of princely despotism in Europe after devastating internecine warfare, only suspended by the settlement of 1648. We can formulate questions with some reasonable relationship to the inferences which more urbane readers of Lohenstein's age might draw. For example, if Nero will eventually have to submit to the judgment of history, will not all rulers and peoples also in due course be examined before the bar of maturing or matured human reason — in works of art comparable to the *Epicharis*, or in other appropriate forums in a future age? In contrast to the failure and punishment of Epicharis, are not the rewards of the surviving system of tyranny typically earned by the betrayer (Milchius) and torturer (Tigillinus)? And even though most spectators would describe them as morally ugly, is it not the fact that successful evil is not anachronistic? As Asmuth has pointed out (p. 69f.), Lohenstein was conscious in the dedication to Baron Otto von Nostitz of reinterpreting the Tacitean label *libertina mulier* as *libertina sed illustris mulier*. Characteristic of Lohenstein's treatment throughout the play is a provocative ambiguity regarding Epicharis' social rank, but this is part of a pattern of ambivalence which includes Nero, too. His is "ein knechtisches Gemütte" (V. iii. 548), though draped in purple; while she, "eines Grichen Magd" (V. iii. 551), undertakes magnanimous actions, because she has remained "ohne Freyheit frey" (I. i. 109). Lohenstein prefers not to resolve the suspicions raised in detail by Proculus that Epicharis is in fact of high birth:

> Die raue Schal umbschleust der Diamanten Licht/
> Ein knechtisch Kleid vielmal das edelste Geblütte.
> Die Tugend und Gestalt ist von so grosser Gütte/
> Sie saget Glück und Zeit es hertzhafft ins Gesicht:
> Es ist Epicharis aus knechtschem Stamme nicht. (II. i. 34-38)

The playwright allows baser personages to sense she is a "noble soul" (II. i. 43) and even to propose the rightful primacy of natural aristocracy: "Nun urtheil: Ob mit Fug durch Satzung man verstößet Was die Natur pflantzt ein?" (II. i. 52f.). The many references in the opening scene to the elegant companions of her recounted past, drawn from the *Ariane*, have already conditioned the internal audience of discontented Romans, as well as readers or spectators, to surmise her high origins.

The opening scene is also laden with allusions to theatrical performances and life as theater in antiquity, frequently borrowed whole from the romance. Epicharis clearly envisions her struggle against Nero as a dramatic contest which will gain her renown:

> Des Ruhms verspritzte Blutt
> Für allgemeine Ruh ist eine Purpur-Flutt
> Daraus die Tugend uns/ die wir großmütig sterben
> Und lachen Feind und Tod/ muß Ehren-Fahnen färben
> Die Welt und Nachwelt rühmt. (I. i. 85-89)

She invites the Romans to assume the roles of heroes with her (I. i. 90ff.). Her protracted masquerade as a man has been necessitated in response to constant Neronian oppression witnessed by her (I. i. 234 and 250). These are legitimate counter-measures to the masquerade and fraudulence of power (I. i. 314) and balance out the treacherous inversion of values incarnate in figures such as Proculus, "Der von der Zung ein Mann/ ein Weib ist in der That" (I. i. 342). Recognition of the duplicity in the world does not detract from Epicharis' stature in the eyes of the demoralized Romans; her grasp on this situation only corroborates for them that she has a bold intellect. But in dramatic terms, Epicharis' ability to see the profound deception and corruption which she opposes is directly proportional to her tragic blindness as an actress on the world stage — a player presuming to elaborate a role which in general has passed from the scene. Thus the performance of this role brings increasing isolation of the *agon*, finally a splendid aloneness as the element which the particular society is expelling.

The dramatic process of *desengaño*, of exposure of human abasement in Rome, amounts at the same time for the audience to an experience of the withdrawal, retreat, shrinkage into an internal repository of the values which Epicharis treasures but which history has in the meanwhile repressed. Ostensibly, the dangerous aspirations of beautiful Epicharis are safely contained by the example of the failure to make them prevail again. Even the doctrine of a providential decree can be invoked for traditionalist minds (as Lohenstein realizes), and is cited in the choruses, a proper burial shroud which appears to assure that the threat to despotic government is dead — just a beautiful memory shriveled up into the stories of untoward events in ancient Rome. In that setting tyranny drives decent humanity into extreme forms of behavior for preservation of the good. Epicharis understands the motivation of Seneca facing final disappointment as unsuccessful teacher of Nero, the eventual monster who holds sway over a degenerated society. Even given his gesture of reciprocal understanding of her purpose, Seneca's retreat into inner purity exhibits, however, the paralysis of virtue engulfed by evil. And Epicharis reverses the direction of the moral imperative by storming the citadel of a corrupt state — through her political thought, through active resistance, and though checked, through attempted use of force. When Lohenstein implicitly indicts those aspects of his own age which reflect the unfreedom of Rome, he also indirectly posits the splendor of an Epicharis who tries to act on such an indictment. Thereby the playwright demonstrates the applicability of principles to the real world of history. Conscience is not solely a secret core into which noble impulses contract as refuge, it is also the source from which new forces of redemption may flow.[24]

If, metaphorically, we equate the social corruption and moral paralysis of Rome with "blindness", this collective state of the body politic does not exclude the presence of light or vision within — discoverable through the special human beings like Epicharis who function on behalf of the human spirit. In his *Second Defense of the English People* (1654), John Milton, become blind, dwells on the symbolic inversion of role which this condition has often traditionally figured. Before taking up again the reasons why he endorsed the execution of the king and introduction of the Commonwealth, he reflects:

> It is blasphemous to believe that God is jealous of truth, that he does not wish it spread freely among mankind. Not, then, because of any wrongdoing does it appear that this prophet (Phineus), so zealous in instructing the human race, and that many of the philosophers as well, were blind.

In his drama *Samson Agonistes*, Milton immortalizes the captive hero, blinded, in whom the inner strength resurges for the affirmative action of bringing down the temple upon the vile Philistines, though it cost his own life. The passionate actor, "Der blinde Simson bringt sich spielend in das Grab," Lohenstein notes. Against the burst of light, which floods out in the passing "poem" of time, we can assert the errors, failure, blindness, and suicide as grounds to impugn the heroic personality. Instead of seeing Epicharis in dramatic context as the actual and attested bearer of light, we can cast aspersions on her foolish resistance to encroaching monumental gloom.

I am not advancing a substitute doctrine, but positing traits which are shared by spiritual affinity across sectarian frontiers. The reversal of values presented in the contrast of the freethinking "slave" and despotic, dehumanized "emperor" who survives him while under "Heaven's" sponsorship belongs to the mass of paradoxes in Lohenstein's plays which scholarship cannot adequately address so long as it ignores the liberal Protestant heritage, accessible to him, and overvalues certain Catholic and conservative Protestant elements, impinging on the crossroads of Silesia. Nor are all the impulses from "Catholic" nations uniformly or necessarily conservative or reactionary. Criticism can understand how a Milton travelled to the heart of Counter-Reformation Europe and returned to England quite ready and able to support the concept of a Commonwealth (not to mention the repercussions of his visit to the silenced Galileo!). Lohenstein, too, deserves a more sensitive hearing when in his dramaturgy he travels back and forth in time and spirit between the ancient and modern, but also recognizes his precise historical situation as a Protestant in the middle of Europe. I suggest further that his polyhistorism masks attitudes intersecting those of the latitudinarian and radical Protestants who turned to the expansion of the sciences and to the empirical reconstruction of knowledge as the supreme task of "modernity." The play *Epicharis* may well reveal, at least in the period relatively still close to Lohenstein's visit in the Netherlands, his serious consideration of some of the liberal political correlatives: the possibility of a social contract based in nature, but fulfilling man's birthright of freedom. If confidence in the course of human affairs took root slowly and finally matured in the *Arminius* for

Lohenstein, his earlier insight into the ineluctable necessity for the failure of freedom and for "compromise" would render his *Epicharis* a genuine tragedy.

Even if, on one level, Lohenstein could have rationalized his dramatic *opera* as forming together an orchestrated set of inquiries which plumbed the dark side of theodicy, and even if his final tendency might have been a gnostic exultation in the power of the human spirit to triumph over the false and confusing (as in his panegyric to Gryphius), the play *Epicharis* takes place at a moment when man's divine *pneuma* seems to be utterly engulfed. The only pathway for the almost extinguished spirit is rebellion against the corrupt principle of actual rulership (cf. the archons in gnostic teaching). Thus the *Epicharis* may well embody one of the most revealing instances of a struggle between the dread-resolving concept of theodicy and the age-old self-glorifying gnostic rebellion – a struggle which ended in the later fusion of these forces in the Enlightenment doctrine of perfectibility. The late Klaus Günther Just has meditated on the creative shaping of a new vision, which emerges from older modes, in a sensitive essay entitled "Allegorik oder Symbolik? Zur Figuration der Trauerspiele Lohensteins."[25] And in my above-mentioned essay on "The Function of Myth in Lohenstein's *Arminius*", I have suggested that – instead of applying just the limited reading of Prometheus as a Noah, and thus also a Christ figuration – it is possible to ponder his "story," as experienced by Zeno, for its symbolic patterning in its own right. Besides the possible hermetic-alchemical hints, Prometheus can readily be understood as an expression of gnostic principles, even though it is a fateful and necessary inclination of the creation which buries his genius in the ruins of time, and there occurs no direct confrontation between an embodiment of the *demiourgos* (Nero) and the exemplar of *pneuma* (Epicharis) such as we witness in the far more extreme situation of the *Epicharis*. In the case of Prometheus, we indeed still witness something of the inexorable indifference of a cosmos in which the true godhead is remote and sought after by divine intellect in a world of confusion (various corrupt religions and philosophies); however, the countervailing symbolism of interconnectedness and a great chain of being helps redirect gnostic pride toward the goal of overcoming the world through the erection of a new edifice of certainty (through science).[26]

Two thirds of a century separate the confident denunciation of the rottenness of the state by Epicharis from the dream-like searching opposition by Prince Hamlet, whom we today still regard as the archetype of modern consciousness. When Hamlet is dying, he asks the loyal Horatio to "report me and my cause aright to the unsatisfied" *(Hamlet,* V. ii. 338f.) — a task which has challenged poets and scholars down to the present. Epicharis proclaims her own triumph through the verdict of history (*Epicharis*, V. iii. 725-732), and current debate seems to be turning more and more to the question how to resolve the conflict between supposed imperatives of social and political thought of Lohenstein's age and the thrust of that postponed verdict.[27] Did Lohenstein, in *Epicharis*, "see" beyond the seventeenth century, however dimly, to a time when a comprehensive verdict could be arrived at in open court? As we fashion our own sense of the present value of the play, we may be able to agree at least that it portrays a final stand against the corruption of power. Although she uses dubious instruments out of desperation, Epicharis is absolved like Prince Hamlet because, in his words, she too ultimately decides, against her times:

> [...] let not ever
> The soul of Nero enter this firm bosom. (*Hamlet*, III. ii. 387f.)

Notes

1 References to the plays will be by act and line, or by page number, in the respective volumes of the critical editions prepared by Klaus Günther Just, *Türkische Trauerspiele, Römische Trauerspiele*, and *Afrikanische Trauerspiele* (Stuttgart, 1953-1957) [Bibliothek des Literarischen Vereins in Stuttgart, Nos. 292-294]; whenever required for clarity, titles will be cited in abbreviation. The essay "Lohenstein's *Epicharis*: The Play of the Beautiful Loser" was first prepared in a shorter German version entitled "Der Sieg des absolutistischen Hofes: Politische Fragwürdigkeiten in Lohensteins *Epicharis*" for the joint congress of the Wolfenbütteler Arbeitskreis für Renaissance-Forschung and Internationaler Arbeitskreis für Barockliteratur, held in 1979,

and was there read in absentia. This shorter version was tried out in English, under the title "The Triumph of Despotism: Lohenstein's Questioning Answer on Politics in *Epicharis*," at the meeting of the Philological Association of the Pacific Coast at Stanford in 1981.

2 The components of this general direction emerged in a cluster of virtually simultaneous monographs assessing the artist's objectives in the light of his late work: Elida Maria Szarota, *Lohensteins Arminius als Zeitroman: Sichtweisen des Spätbarock* (Bern/München, 1970); Gerhard Spellerberg, *Verhängnis und Geschichte; Untersuchungen zu den Trauerspielen und dem "Arminius"-Roman Daniel Caspers von Lohenstein* (Bad Homburg/Berlin/ Zürich, 1970); Dieter Kafitz, *Lohensteins "Arminius": Disputatorisches Verfahren und Lehrgehalt in einem Roman zwischen Barock und Aufklärung* (Stuttgart, 1970); and Bernhard Asmuth, *Lohenstein und Tacitus: Eine quellenkritische Interpretation der Nero-Tragödien und des "Arminius"-Romans* (Stuttgart, 1971). I have discussed these in some detail, respectively, in: *JEGP*, 70 (1971), 502-507; *JEGP*, 71 (1972), 413-418; *Germanistik*, 12 (1971), 96-97; and *Daphnis*, 1 (1972), 223-228. Whenever it is clear from the context, a subsequent reference to an already cited critical work will henceforth be given by page number, after the author's name if required, in parentheses.

3 Though already noted by the authors cited in note 2, this subject has enjoyed a more exhaustive exploration in the monograph by Karl-Heinz Mulagk, *Phänomene des politischen Menschen im 17. Jahrhundert: Propädeutische Studien zum Werk Lohensteins unter besonderer Berücksichtigung Diego Saavedra Fajardos und Baltasar Graciáns* (Berlin, 1973). I have discussed Mulagk's findings in *JEGP*, 75 (1976), 259-264.

4 For example, the monograph by Rudolf Furrer, *Vernunft und Leidenschaft in der Erstfassung des Trauerspiels "Cleopatra" von Daniel Casper von Lohenstein* (Zürich, 1970) serves to illustrate the attempt to construe the choruses as an ultimate determinant of meaning, and so subordinate all details to a narrow allegorical purpose derived from the choruses: "Die Interpretation eines jeden barocken Trauerspiels hat demnach die Aufgabe, die Auslegefunktion der Reyen im Ganzen des Dramas einsichtig werden zu lassen" (p. 90).

5 Augustus is still regarded thus in ch. 7 of Judith Popovich Aikin's monograph *The Mission of Rome in the Dramas of Daniel Casper von Lohenstein: Historical Tragedy as Prophecy and Polemic* (Stuttgart, 1976). Aikin stresses the prefigurative and typological nuances of Augustus' role in a teleological plan of history, making him into an almost depersonalized embodiment of goodness and generosity, and glossing over as mere lapses and concessions some cardinal examples of his extraordinary Machiavellian cunning (pp. 226ff.), whereas she conversely renders wholly negative the struggle by others to survive against him: "Political freedom, then, although meaningful to Lohenstein and Silesia, as well as to Antonius and Cleopatra, is a

blind motif in this drama. It reveals itself to be a product of false pride and desire for power, and a *superbia*-like resistance to destiny" (p. 221).
6 *Daniel Casper von Lohenstein's Historical Tragedies* (Columbus, 1965), p. 93.
7 *Geschichte, Politik und Gesellschaft im Drama des 17. Jahrhunderts* (Bern/ München, 1976), pp. 157-165). I have discussed Szarota's views in more detail in *German Quarterly*, 51 (1978), 505-510.
8 *Zur Dramatik Daniel Caspers von Lohenstein: "Cleopatra" 1661 und 1680* (Meisenheim am Glan, 1976), p. 140. See my review of this monograph and other work on Lohenstein in *Argenis*, 2 (1978), 377-382.
9 The derogatory information is duly indexed by the original editors of the two-volume polyhistoric novel. Consult the heading "Augustus" in the index at the end of the second volume in the facsimile reprint of *Großmüthiger Feldherr Arminius* [...], edited by Elida Maria Szarota (Bern, 1973) [= Nachdrucke deutscher Literatur des 17. Jahrhunderts, 5], e.g. *Verliebet sich in die Asblaste, I. viii. 1188. a. seq.; Urtheil über seine Tugenden und Laster. I. viii. 1202. a.; Sein Hochmuth zieht benachbarten Völckern allerhand Unglück zu.* II. i. 70. b.]
10 "Une représentation inconnue de *L'Epicharis* de Lohenstein (Sion, 1710)," *Etudes Germaniques*, 24 (1969), 242-248.
11 See Asmuth's detailed analysis of the relationship in *Lohenstein und Tacitus*, Ch. 3, "Die französischen Quellen der *Epicharis*". I include Tristan as a significant playwright in my comparative essay on "Dream and Calculus in European Baroque Drama," in *Studi in onore di Aurelio Zanco* (Pisa, 1977). Less convincing is the thesis of possible artistic indebtedness to Guilliam van Nieuwelandt, advanced by Peter Skrine, "A Flemish Model for the Tragedies of Lohenstein," *Modern Language Review*, 61 (1966), 64-70.
12 "Die Gesellschaftskritik im Drama Lohensteins," *Archiv für Sozialgeschichte*, 5 (1965), 227-244.
13 "Duldender Glaube und tätige Vernunft in der Barocktragödie," *Zeitschrift für deutsche Philologie*, 85 (1966), 501-542.
14 The nature of advanced Protestant ideas is examined in great detail in the case of Britian by Charles Webster, *The Great Instauration: Science, Medicine, and Reform 1626-1660* (London, 1975), and the impact of numerous figures also significant in German territories is considered; regrettably, no book of comparable scope exists in the case of Germany.
15 The first edition "A1" of 1665 is without a dedication. A later (?) issue "A2", using the same printing stock as "A1", has an added dedication to Baron Otto von Nostitz (described by Just in his edition of *Epicharis*, p. 149f.), which is probably the same as that in edition "B" of 1685 (reprinted by Just, pp. 295-296). This contains the expected, requisite statement of the contrast between Nero's barbaric turpitude and Leopold's clemency ruling over a happier people, e.g.: *Nostrum Carmen sub clementissimo*

INVICTISSIMI LEOPOLDI Imperio Neronis detestandam Saevitiam ridet (p. 295). The *Agrippina* is dedicated to Herzogin Louise von Liegnitz, Brieg und Wohlau as a contrasting exemplar of virtues (p. 12-13).

16   See note 11.
17   While Aikin's analysis of the theme of "moral freedom" and of "inverted relationships" in the play is very useful and to the point (p. 192), she omits reiterating the relevant fact established in the *Agrippina*, that Seneca is highly compromised by past acquiescence, when she discusses his kind of "free will" (p. 193). Epicharis' major acquiescence is to the halfhearted compromise needed by her contemporaries: electing an acceptable ruler — Piso and Seneca being the unworkable candidates! The mordant ironies in the *Epicharis* suggest to me that Aikin's definition of Epicharis' *superbia* as "a disdainful, proud, and willful heroine" (p. 200) indeed needs fresh consideration within a framework of reversal. It may answer *acedia*, well-reasoned moral sloth, in an age of defeatism.
18   References to *La mort de Sénèque* will be by act, scene, and through-numbered lines, and when required for clarity, following the abbreviation *MS*, from the critical edition *Le théâtre complet de Tristan L'Hermite*, edited by Claude K. Abraham, Jerome W. Schweitzer, and Jacqueline van Baelen (University, Alabama, 1975).
19   Erik Lunding, *Das schlesische Kunstdrama* (København, 1940), p. 91f.
20   Edward Verhofstadt, *Daniel Casper von Lohenstein: Untergehende Wertwelt und ästhetischer Illusionismus* (Brügge, 1964).
21   However, I have alluded to aspects of the advanced Protestant acceptance of science, as the means to repair the ruins of time since man's fall, in my paper, "The Function of Myth in Lohenstein's *Arminius:* The Case of Egypt and Prometheus," *Argenis*, 2 (1978), 187-228.
22   Gerhard Spellerberg pointed out the importance of Desmarets in an earlier article, "Eine unbeachtete Quelle zur *Epicharis* Daniel Caspers von Lohenstein," *Euphorion*, 61 (1967), 143-154.
23   In my view, Aikin mistakes this treatment of an established plot detail as a direct authorial brushstroke to characterize Epicharis' suspect motivation (p. 187); she also fails to distinguish the behavior of deceivers in the light of prudentialist and theatrical concepts of "deception" (*Verstellung*), the importance of which Asmuth and Mulagk show. See note 17.
24   I endorse Aikin's shrewd observation that "The lack of a final chorus may indicate the ambivalent result; instead of an ultimate answer, Lohenstein indicates that the dialectic must continue — in the audience, in the works of the theorists, and in history itself" (p. 201). But in that case, insofar as Europe continues in a direction antithetical to rebel Epicharis, or Epicharis does not symbolize "renewal" of pristine impulses, Aikin's conclusion that "Divine Providence thus receives its justification, even in one of the darkest periods of earthly history" (p. 202), is no longer self-evident if by "justifica-

tion" we mean merely the survival of the system (HRE). If the younger Lohenstein, in a remarkable exception, wanted or was unable to arrive at a "wrap-up" chorus for *Epicharis*, did this result from indecision or prudence (not saying what was on his mind)? Only his first play, *Ibrahim Bassa*, also lacks a final chorus, ending on the high and intense note of Isabelle's condemnation of Turkish despotism and proclamation of a cultural crusade.

25 *Antaios*, 10 (1968), 91-108.
26 On the pervasive influence of gnosticism and its intertwinings with Christianity, consult Hans Jonas, *The Gnostic Religion: The Message of the Alien God and the Beginnings of Christianity*, 2nd enl. ed. (Boston, 1963); and on the eruption of such currents in Lohenstein's era, consult Karl R. Frick, *Die Erleuchteten: Gnostisch-theosophische und alchemistisch-rosenkreutzerische Geheimgesellschaften bis zum Ende des 18. Jahrhunderts; Ein Beitrag zur Geistesgeschichte der Neuzeit* (Graz, 1973).
27 This direction emerges from the aggregate picture assembled by Wilfried Barner, Gerhard Spellerberg, Bernhard Asmuth, and Elida Maria Szarota in their notes on aspects of the play for *Die Welt des Daniel Casper von Lohenstein* (Köln, 1978), published as a "Begleitbuch" on the occasion of the première production of the *Epicharis* by Schauspiel Köln, January 8, 1978.

9. DREAM AND CALCULUS IN EUROPEAN BAROQUE DRAMA*

The drama of which I speak was conceived while Europe lay under a particular intellectual clime, or one might almost say, spell. If the Renaissance had rediscovered history, the intense preoccupation with time as contrastable moments and eras had led to a puzzling perspectivism, a capacity to meditate over the scenes of personal existence, to ironize over the vicissitudes of earthly affairs, to marshall seemingly incongruous, uncontrollable facts and forms with the power of wit. By the beginning of the seventeenth century, this capacity had contributed to the floration of the metaphor of the world theater − so well known in the works of Shakespeare, Bidermann, Rotrou, Calderón and others as to permit me to dispense with illustrations. I wish to recall, however, that this total system of ideas − that man was an actor, life a dream or vision, a script written by a mysterious authorship − not only lent generic self-awareness to the drama, but also provided it with a complete, consistent "methodology." Newer philosophical waves, such as the rebirth of Stoicism in the first decades of the seventeenth century, might sweep over the drama and affect the stance of martyrs and heroes. But, for great playwrights, story content was henceforth subordinate to the nature of all story as a dream-like process. Many famous early Baroque protagonists more openly share such authorial insight in the way, like Hamlet or Segismundo, they grope through the labyrinth of the action toward acceptance of a role or penetrate outward costume and show. By becoming at last simultaneously actors and spectators of themselves, they exemplify then "modern" consciousness.

Nevertheless, when I read a stereotype encyclopedist of the opening decades of the seventeenth century, I tend to feel that all bodes well for the rationalist ethos of Western civilization and that Romanticism may never actually occur with all its strange repercussions flowing from its belief in the individual creative personality *and* in an invisible, encompassing spiritual continuum. I even imagine that certain Baroque authors whom the Romantics revered, such as Cervantes and Shakespeare, perhaps will turn out never to have written their most haunting masterworks. Let me cite, by way of illustration, that prolific and optimistic John Henry Alsted in his *Theologia naturalis* (1615) and *Cursus Philosophici Encyclopaedia* (1620): "A person is a single intelligent being subsisting in itself."[1] This intelligent identity, as later in Descartes' view, is attached to a machine: "For the body is the instrument of the soul not only in good, but also in evil actions, which to be sure are organic. For only the soul produces inorganic actions."[2] Ideally, this highest and eternal aspect of man rules: "The rational soul, it follows, is that most august mistress and dictator whose potencies are two, intellect and will."[3] Fortunately, according to Alsted, our intellect, as transmission unit, is aware of certain innate principles — such as God and the moral imperative — and, therefore, the will can serve as the agency to effect its recognitions. Yet the person arrives wrapped in his or her finite machinery, the body, amid the inexorable movement of a happening, that is, time: "For the cosmos is nothing other than the clock of this universe which measures time and constitutes the parts thereof."[4] Describing how the human apparatus is linked to the larger machinery of Nature, Alsted cheerfully recommends that we read that Book emblematically and, unlike the astute anatomizer Donne, is not troubled by the world's sickness and decay. Alsted is symptomatic of a rival tendency in interpreting the emergence of the "modern" consciousness found in Baroque world theater; he continues the Ramian belief in the possibility of a "method" or "calculus" allowing a terrestrial expansion of the human mind. This interest in a combinatory art, which includes both analysis and synthesis, thus ultimately the invention of new propositions, wards off the negative inference that Renaissance discoveries have shattered all coherence. In *Clavis Artis Lullianae* (1633) he specifies that "method is an instrument for thinking" and that it is the creation of new categories which "is the work of reason, by which science increases."[5]

In general, late-Renaissance writers were tempted to elaborate a more rigid identification of the self with the mind. The revivified

Stoic attitude that the supreme good consisted of virtue alone, and that to secure virtue all passions must be thoroughly checked, found fertile ground, as the popularity of Lipsius' compilation *De Constantia* in the early seventeenth century shows. In combination, however, the puzzling sense of alienation from natural existence which such a dualism suggested, and the acuter awareness of the workings of time and decay of nature, also inspired an intenser feeling for the ego, the elusive and transitorily embodied entity conscious of itself and defined largely in terms of its mental property. While the Renaissance had regarded personality as central and had glorified subjective individualism, the Baroque age experienced the radical division of the self through reflection. Doubtless the supreme monument to this new preoccupation is Montaigne's lifelong effort to capture his own identity in the flux of time. We may regard his essays in the last decades of the sixteenth century as one natural outgrowth of the earlier humanist epistle, with its often rambling mixture of serious and incidental matters, recounted by a mind conscious of history, its blending of philosophic attitude, reportage, and biographical notes. As several critics have noted, Rembrandt's series of self-portraits forms an analogous attempt to understand the self through temporal perspectivism. Both great artists are fundamentally meditative, taking themselves as the theme, but gaining only glimpses of various masks, cross-sections of existence at disparate moments in the time process with all its metamorphoses. On the one hand, such a union of skeptical method and sentimentalization can be interpreted as a deepening of the Western concept of a permanent personal identity as a supreme value. But on the other hand, it can also be seen as an incursion behind the mask of person, an exposure of roles as ephemeral.

In Montaigne we already see the confluence of "dream" and "calculus" as modes of perception. Akin to his "passive" experimentalism is the "active" disillusionistic approach which Bacon takes to the human mind in the *Novum Organum* when he separates the "cultivation" from the "invention" of knowledge. Even after a thorough sorting out of the accumulated repertory, a debunking of misleading concepts no matter how venerable, and a separation of the realm of verifiable facts from that of mere opinion, thinking humanity cannot rest on its achievements. Wary of the deep-rooted habits and tricks of the mind, Bacon devises a method of "anticipation" of its further erring and resistance to a program of discovery of hard reality. He is even suspicious of language as a hodgepodge of entrenched misunderstandings and processes of imagination. By insisting on the need to measure and check the products of the mind, as a way to liberate the mind from its own dream states, Bacon recapitulates the development from Rabelais to Cervantes. To the Renaissance act of comparing and contrasting entire epochs and traditions as mental sets, that is, as "fictions" from which one could or did emerge, is now added the Baroque act of testing the processes of the mind and debunking its typical products, notably constructs of language. The mind by its own instrumentality turns to a critique and assessment of itself.

This proposition is all the more plausible when we note the parallel happening in the Baroque theater, where the play within a play, that is, the play as instrument for analyzing the nature of playing, is the ruling obsession. Paradoxically, the self-scrutinizing Baroque *theatrum mundi* brought about not only an intense discovery of ego, but also its exposure and conquest. In accord with its own principle of disillusionment, the world theater constantly reminds that the spectacle is indeed a play within play, a vision, a dream, a groping in the labyrinth. Such treatment of its own structures evinces, then, that widespread late-Renaissance manneristic tension when the art form, and with it its image of man, is mirrored in a regression to infinity. The irrepressible metaphysical occurrence entwined with the acceptance of modern science seems to be that, through a surge of visionary power, man splits permanently in self-reflection into both actor and spectator. The traditional religious use of a projected vision is still striking in 1678 in the famous opening of Bunyan's *Pilgrim's Progress:*

> As I walked through the wilderness of this world, I lighted on a certain place where was a den, and I laid me down in that place to sleep: and as I slept, I dreamed a dream. I dreamed, and behold I saw a man [...]

Appearing eleven years earlier, Milton's *Paradise Lost* exhibits the fuller impact both of Baroque perspectivism and theatricality, and of the expanded cosmological and developmental picture, on religious writing prior to the triumph of the *philosophes*. Having decided that the Reformation must be continuous, Milton cannot resist the idea that the mind is involved in a progressive self-realization and liberation; for him, too, all of human history thus becomes the unfolding of an age-old drama of consciousness. When we regard the "age of the theater" as bounded by two major breaking-points – a "dissociation of sensibility" in the late Renaissance (Eliot) and a pre-Enlightenment "crise de la conscience européenne" (Hazard) – our tendency is to forget that the drama itself was throughout in constant agitation over the deeper issues of the nature of human consciousness and found it very difficult to dispense with the metaphor complex of "dream" in favor of "calculus." If modern literature repeatedly drifts back to the thematics of "dream," the seventeenth-century "crisis" merits consideration as revelatory of a fundamental direction for Western civilization. The still somber Catholic-prudentialist, the more entrepreneurial Protestant-renovative, and the Enlightenment-liberal hope in human educability seem to reflect increasing trust in the "calculating" control of the mind over itself. However, the discovery of "dream" seems to have served not only as a stimulus for the devising of scientific control over the mind, but as a channel for, in, and of itself, as the essence of mind.

    I venture the following speculative meditation about spiritual affinities in reaction to the innumerable and unavoidable hints in Western literature since Sir William Jones and others called more detailed attention to the treasures of the Indian tradition. I hope to suggest another thread which may interlace with the two larger tangles, European late=Renaissance experience of "time" and "dream" processes, which scholarship has long been sorting out.[6] Schopenhauer's definition of tragedy as the highest genre which "objectifies the idea of Man" in Book III of *Die Welt als Wille und Vorstellung* (1819) is, beyond doubt, the pivotal formulation of an aesthetic seeking to harmonize Western concepts of disillusionment and tragic insight with Indian categories. Nevertheless, the usual questions Western critics still ask – to borrow Paul Goodman's terms are the „formal" and the "final."[7] That is, on the one hand, we wonder where this particular mode came from; and we discover isolated instances of the world theater as far back as the late Middle Ages in Europe, indeed in early Christian and ancient classical authors, as Curtius has traced in the section "Schaupsielmetaphern" in his still indispensable *Europäische Literatur und lateinisches Mittelalter* (1948).[8] Without other considerations being taken into account, though, it remains difficult to grasp why such an older nucleus would flare up so brilliantly in a certain era. For example, Heinz Otto Burger has amply documented the extent to which the idea of the world theater simultaneously took hold in Central Europe as well as in Spain, England, and France.[9] On the other hand, inquiring about the end or aim of such art, we tend to lapse into traditional allegorical interpretations based on Christian views as "normative"; this habit is naturally more pronounced in critics who, like Burger, are focusing on the Early Baroque as point of reference. Yet admittedly the modes of the world theater also have already served and still serve as a vehicle for other tenors — a fact which is made apparent in a broader comparative *and* diachronic study such as Robert J. Nelson's *Play within a Play*.[10]

But Goodman's "formal analytic" question, regarding what happens and how, liberates us to accept analogies which have no traditional genetic or final explanation. We feel authorized to search beneath the agitation of European thought in a period beset by world and civil war for synthesizing patterns which are widely shared, even though on the surface the authors in several nations attach their works to particular and variant cultural dictates. We can consider the proposition, as some Romantics began to sense, that if the earlier Baroque struggle to discriminate between appearance and reality was meaningful and many succeding generations experienced that meaning largely through the metaphoric structure of world theater, then visionary European drama of Shakespeare's day already shared with Hindu works like *Shakuntula* in certain universal traits of mind. In Vedantic philosophy, truth is observed simultaneously from the perspective of the world of appearances, where everything is relative and multiple, and from the perspective of the absolute, when reflection, duality, difference all resolve into the unity of Universal Being. Central to classical Sanskrit drama is the theory of *rasa*, the creation of a dispassionate delight in the minds of the audience who are enabled to look at the *lila* or play of life steadily and see it whole.[11] When the playwright strikes a correct balance among the eight stable sentiments of humanity codified by Hindu analysts, he evokes "a single, ineffable, transcendental joy," a fleeting experience of the divine.

For all his doubt, hesitation, and pessimism, Hamlet – in my view – ultimately glimpses such a harmony and can die resolute and satisfied. Indeed, his story bears striking thematic resemblances to the dramatic poem *Bhagavad-Gita*. Having tried all to reconcile his kinsmen, driven out of his kingdom by his uncle, beleaguered and outnumbered, with no choice but to wage war, the humane and noble Arjuna cannot act because of his moral scruples. Krishna appears to explain Arjuna's life role (*dharma*) as a princely leader and the inescapable duty to act in the world of relativity or appearance. On one level, Arjuna must fulfill his role even though it leads to suffering and guilt feelings; but on another level, Arjuna's concern is meaningless, because the entire phenomenal world is an illusion, a play in which human beings are the unwitting actors. The ghost is the supernatural agent who appears to Hamlet and incites him to action under the puzzling bonds of duty which cause conflict and apprehension. After agonized soul-searching like Arjuna's, Hamlet ineluctably becomes involved in the action of his destined role and resolves his dilemma. In addition, from the very start, despite errors, Hamlet evinces an ability to transcend the mere phenomenal world and, though to others a brooder and eccentric, responds intuitively to higher promptings of the play of life. Metaphorically, his sense of the world is closer to the work's poetic ambience than that of any other character.[12]

Elizabethan and post-Elizabethan drama boasts such a notable assortment of intellectual protagonists that we can readily arrange various configurations of wayward geniuses, cracked scholars, malcontents, and politic brains. But Hamlet assumes a lofty place among all cases for several reasons: as prince, he fuses the older archetypal royal role, proper "rulership" in all its senses, with the newly constituted Renaissance role of élite sensibility and learning. At the same time, from his hierarchical pinnacle, he reaches down with his intense personal grasp of "theater" to ennoble the newer Baroque role of the "actor," about which I will comment further below. He is also clearly related to the disturbed intellectuals who must find the way to set right again their dislocated world. These relationships alone suffice to recall that in Hamlet there converge so many primary types of late-Renaissance humanity that generations of critics have justifiably viewed him as the authentic, complex representative of late-Renaissance modernity.

Furthermore, the action of Hamlet's story fits the five stages of development recognized in Hindu drama. The desire to attain something (*arambba*) leads to an organized effort to achieve the goal (*prayatna*); then the possibility of success is admitted in relation to efforts and obstacles (*papti-sambhava*); and the felt certainty of success (*niyatapti*) is crowned by the actual attainment (*phalagama*). T.S. Eliot may paraphrase "Krishna, as when he admonished Arjuna/ On the field of battle" in "The Dry Salvages" (*Four Quartets*), but antipathetic to the Danish prince's secular recapitulation of Arjuna's perplexity, he opines in his essay on the play in 1919 — quite crosswise, in my opinion — that it is a failure because Hamlet cannot "objectify" the "feeling which he cannot understand." Hence his sallies of wit and half madness "are not part of a deliberate plan of dissimulation, but a form of emotional relief. In the character Hamlet it is the buffoonery of an emotion which can find no outlet in action; in the dramatist it is the buffoonery of an emotion which he cannot express in art."[13] This, however, cavalierly ignores Hamlet's traumatic self-association with the "fool" role, and thereby shuts off appreciation of the intersecting Renaissance literary traditions exploited by Shakespeare precisely for their relevance in conjunction. One illustration of the relevance of folly must suffice; the movement of Act II leading Hamlet to the idea of using a play as a device to catch the king corresponds to the emergence of an organized effort in Hindu dramaturgy. Thus, when Act III opens, Hamlet already has the king worrying "why he puts on this confusion, / Grating so harshly all his days of quiet / With turbulent and dangerous lunacy?"

I am sure also that Hispanists cock their ears at the terms "turbulence" and "confusion" — key principles of Golden Age drama espoused by Lope de Vega in his famous treatise in verse, *El arte nuevo de hacer comedias* (1609), and contained in the title speech by Segismundo ending Act II in Calderón's *La vida es sueño*. In the theory and practice of great Baroque playwrights, unlike later French classical and rationalistic structure generally, the rhythm of the play is not linear nor are its parts symmetrically balanced. Instead, the action steadily increases in pace and complexity, culminating in a fifth act or the finale of the third which assumes the virtual proportions of an independent play. We spiral upward toward the plane of the fifth act or finale in a labyrinthine manner which makes us *feel* the quality of involvement in time as a process, rather than a rational control as if we are overseeing a series of logical connections permitting only one line of development. Precisely *because* its reversals have the arbitrariness of dream or nightmare, and its line of development constantly emerges out of the profusion and turbulence of each successive moment or *occasio*, the Baroque play possesses the dynamics equivalent to Montaigne's *Essais* for exploring life in motion. The final security of the martyr, the certainty of the prince, the emergence out of tenebrae of the gleam of divine light, the sudden penetration into hidden realms — there are many arrivals on various levels of consciousness; but it is the arrival that counts.

This structure is evident in its most complicated form in the Baroque plays about the actor who, in the course of considering how to enact a role, discovers in the tension and flow of his own life the evolution of a spiritual identity. And in the Genesius and Philemon plays, for example, we witness reversals which simultaneously signal the emergence of spiritual forces of renewal in history. Whether for one man or for a world not yet awakened to Christianity, the profoundest movement of soul is conversion, the subject of Jacob Bidermann's *Philemon martyr* (ca. 1615), in which a figure of low estate, an actor, is led by divine grace onto a new pathway through his miming. Though Philemon is a mere proletarian pagan wastrel in the beginning, he possesses an imaginative flexibility that permits his heart to become a vessel of spiritual decision and inner change in his society. After many ambiguous exchanges of costume, feigned dreams, and comic confusion, the actor who is interrogated in place of the Christian leader upsets the Roman governor with a meaningful examination of discovered true identity. The governor is so vexed he sends for the actor Philemon who, with his wit, may chase away his bad humor; more confusion ensues when the onlookers applaud what they regard as a masterful performance by the detected Philemon; and next, the governor is angered thinking the mime transgresses the limits of good taste and blasphemes; but gradually they realize his earnest, which moreover inspires the timid Christian community to come into the open, despite the threatened punishment by the imperial authority. As the angels celebrate Philemon's triumph, we learn that the city is swinging to Christianity: the whole social body is discovering and confessing a new way of life.

The conversion of an actor was a gripping theme in European Baroque dramaturgy because it aptly expressed man's protean character as a roleplayer and the birth-pangs of consciousness. In Lope de Vega's *Lo fingido verdadero* (1618), the genial artist Ginés proclaims that an actor, in order genuinely to imitate nature, must possess in his own heart the imaginative capacity to be and suffer all roles. When a play Ginés devises, based on his own anxieties about his unrequited love, turns into tragic reality for him, he experiences absolute exhaustion and surrender. Out of this emptiness as a broken man, he then finds his way to Christianity through studying the role of a martyr assigned to him by Diocletian, persecutor of the new faith. Postulating how to play, Ginés discovers his deeper identity as a man who has undergone disillusionment and finally accepts actual martyrdom as an answer to his own life. In Jean Rotrou's *Le Véritable Saint-Genest* (publ. 1647), Genest believes similarly that a true artist must identify with his role, the earthly author with his own hero, as model, and thus he "loses" his own identity by studying the role of the contemporary martyr Adrien. Finally, however, Genest ceases to take mere human art seriously and fully attains the heroic plane of his imitated ideal Adrien; he simultaneously reaches the pinnacle of his acting when an angel dictates his role directly to him in the immediacy of faith and he translates it into the language of the stage. All the reversals and realizations of Rotrou's play are foreshadowed in the complex dream with which it opens and through the hidden irony in Genest's initial espousal of the eternal values of classical art in an aesthetic debate with Valérie and Dioclétien. When the play within the play is staged, we can actually see the conflict within

Genest which is couched in his dialogue on the opposition between the heavenly and earthly monarchies. The invisible and infinite intervenes here as protagonist principle in the temporal realm; while seemingly "permanent" authorities of the historical scene, unable fully to comprehend their actual roles, watch the drama which signals the reversal of their mandate, yet remain frozen in their attachments to role. They fail to become spectators of themselves as actors.

In most cases, hence, the phenomenal level of historical action is, metaphorically, an imprisonment, as Hamlet perceives (II, ii. 237-43):

> Hamlet: Denmark's a prison.
> Rosencrantz: Then the world is one.
> Hamlet: A goodly one, in which there are many confines, wards, and dungeons, Denmark being one o' the worst.
> Rosencrantz: We think not so, my lord.
> Hamlet: Why, then 'tis none to you, for there is nothing either good or bad but thinking makes it so. To me it is a prison.

In Calderón's *La vida es sueño*, getting out of prison is synonymous with arriving, through disillusionment, at insight into one's role. Virtually one line in ten of the play contains the verbs to see or to know or related forms. When Segismundo fails his first test and is returned as the unredeemed, self-styled "human monster" to the tower, he has at least grasped that "all people dream what they are, even though none of them realize it." Clotaldo's point, that even if Segismundo is dreaming, he will lose nothing by being good, eventually is fulfilled. In actual fact, the awakening of Segismundo leads to a higher restatement of his symbolic condition in the tower, before the education of his soul by the attractive light of Rosaura and other manifestations of divine principles. Segismundo never becomes absolutely free in the relative phenomenal world, however, in so far as each step of his learning process entangles him in restraints just as binding as his former chains. His ascension spiritually is interrelated to his acceptance of laws and duties as prince on the plane of relative truth, the battlefield of time. Segismundo discovers that the very world before his eyes may disappear, reappear, metamorphose, whereas only the attraction toward divine light is permanent and solely performance of obligations according to an accepted ethical code affords a limited means of expression of his attraction toward the elusive radiance. Though Segismundo's adherence to such a code will bring a spiritual peace more rewarding and less ephemeral than sensual indulgence or license, disillusionment here is associated by Calderón with radical sobriety. Nonetheless, I would deem this occurrence, the experience of purification, to be one kind of satisfactory transcendence. Who then is Segismundo — is his *only* a typically Western identity?

One may object that Segismundo is the protagonist in a highly lyrical and symbolic genre, peculiar to Catholic Spain and inextricably enmeshed in that culture's metaphysical and theological thinking, a genre whose lineaments A.A. Parker has so masterfully drawn; and this I readily admit.[14] However, as Rosaura first penetrates the play's realm and enters Segismundo's prison, the rocky defiles mark the edges of a dream, more than an imagined remote Poland. But does Hamlet then actually have a distinct specific identity, because his play's more proximate northern Protestant ambience makes Denmark seem just slightly more historical and tangible for us? I submit that what so distinguishes these great dramatic protagonists, so that they exist as "mythic" figures for us today, is their respective "southern" versus "northern" general experience of the nature of identity, rather than fixation in a role as specific temperamental, social, and historical types. Yet I do believe also that they represent, as well, the artistic insight into a lasting experience felt intensely since the Renaissance, though repeatedly suppressed. Even when they commit themselves, these princely exemplars experience the captivity in, and irreality of, identity. Their "awakening" countervails the ordinary sense of reality promoted by Western civilization, its basic code of "imitation" or "mirroring" expounded so ably by Auerbach in *Mimesis* (1946). And we thus find — in the period immediately following the vigorous outpouring of what (for want of a better term) I will call "pure" world theater — the direct application of its techniques and sense of life to some of the most puzzling and most exciting manifestations of individualistic extremism. It is as if, during the continuing "liberation" of individual existence from set roles in a previously fixed medieval order, the Age of the Theater resisted giving way to the Age of Reason, the metaphysics and psychology of "dream" to the abstract logic of "calculus."

In an earlier examination of "The Rebel in Seventeenth-Century Tragedy," I have already considered aspects of individualism; and inevitably the present essay touches again on certain features of that same literature.[15] But what I wish to sketch here briefly is the way in which the Early Baroque scrutiny of man's state tended, over a lengthy interim, to be superseded by a High Baroque "methodology," an approach in the drama that, by its strange closeness to rationalism, more disturbed than pleased the succeeding age with its yearning for the affirmation of beneficent natural law and its craving for clarity, simplicity, neatness, manageability in all things. Largely deriving from the eighteenth-century reaction, the persistent scholarly charge has been that, from about 1640 to 1680, many playwrights relativized values and indulged in manneristic toying with the newly developed elements of European drama. Critics smug in their Enlightenment faith and probity taught us to be suspicious of later seventeenth-century plays which, though they had manifestly broken old ideological ties, did not yet espouse an unambiguous future ruled by poetic justice but remained perversely interested in dark aspects of life. As devil's advocate, I propose to show instead that major High Baroque playwrights indeed experimented with the common "romantic" framework of drama of their day, but did so as a means to liberate themselves for "scientific" treatment of man according to the dictates of reason, unhampered *either* by older religious scruples *or* by a newer secular doctrine of perfectibility. The real temptation they probably knew was the attraction toward a method, not toward a complete world view.[16] The drama of romance, of the exotic, of primal conflicts transposed to mythology or remote settings furnished a neutral ground for testing out suppositions about man, the operation of rationally definable forces. By bridging romantic drama and world theater, — that is, by showing that these forces were masked under the phenomenological surface of events — High Baroque playwrights finally established history itself as the self-explanatory and absolute ambience of man.

Corneille's spirited first version of *L'illusion comique* (ca. 1635) marks a borderline, knowingly looking back at the Spanish thematics of the "actor," "enchantment," and "theater of theater," unknowingly also at the sublime Shakespearian "magician." Corneille's evocation of the "magic" of theater cannot be separated from an examination of the "miracles de l'art" (I. ii). Here, too, the ironic examination is inseparable from the spellbinding evocation of theatrical "magic." The playwright, subsumed in the magus Alcandre as demiurge,

> Grand Demon du sçavoir, de qui les doctes veilles
> Produisent chaque jour de nouvelles merveilles,

is everywhere at work in the "illusion" he conjures in varying scenes. While some "players" can laugh at projections of human feelings and predicaments (the verb *rire* permeates the text), others witness them with apprehension. But the tables can be turned from scene to scene, too, so that the freer "spectator" becomes the troubled "actor." And we begin to learn that release from states of mind and life situations corresponds to the concerned father Pridament's "awakening," when he realizes his son Clindor is acting in plays and not actually going through the conflicts witnessed. Clindor belongs to that socially dubious profession which has come to stand for the metaphysically ambiguous awareness of self. Underneath the imaginative playing, though, we glimpse the steady assertion of a distinctly secular, rational view of life. Just as Cervantes has debunked romance, so Rosine gives voice to the decidedly secular analysis of the uncheckable power of natural drives, in contrast to mere concepts such as virtue and honor (V.iv):

> Cesse de m'estourdir de ces noms odieux!
> N'as tu jamais appris que ces vaines chimeres
> Qui naissent aux cerveaux des maris et des meres,
> Ces vieux contes d'honneur, n'ont point d'impressions
> Qui puissent arrester les fortes passions?

When I assert that the train of great rationalist philosophers such as Ramus and Descartes prepared the ground for such a shift, I refer not to specific filiation but to ascendant habits of mind in Europe which also make their appearance as artistic methodology even in plays like Pierre Corneille's *Rodogune* (1644). Implicitly, the action — like a fairytale — takes place in the interior illumination of nightmare, surrounded by tenebrae. Today we can also pay tribute to the play's Freudian and Jungian patterns as basic statements. Simplifying the action, we see that the exponent of love and heart, Rodogune, faces Cléopâtre, exponent of hate and statecraft; or, transposed into "alien" terms of myth analysis, Venus Urania encounters Kali through the play's double set of mirrorings. The twin brothers Antiochus and Seleucus, who love each other deeply, as a reflected self, must cope with the gradual discovery of the perfidy of the Queen-Mother. She has already wed their treacherous uncle Antiochus, who himself has eventually been removed by her, and she has murdered in ambush their returning father Nicanor. Just as the father had fallen in love with Rodogune, the queen's opposite, so the twins do, too; and Cléopâtre schemes against a lasting challenge to her own power, power being all that she ultimately exists for. Of course, this situation permits the playwright to mask his abstractions as he dwells on the problematic anatomy of power which had fascinated Machiavelli and other theoreticians. But much more is involved when Cléopâtre, exercising her "hidden wrath" and the "secret of courts," strives to undermine trust and to manipulate the sentiments of others as mere pawns in her game. Reacting to their mother's design against Rodogune, the brothers separate into two distinct components of masculine idealism, one passive, one active; the first destined to be a murder victim, the second to prevail over evil. Thus the traditional romantic subject, a hopeless conflict of desire and duty, is no longer the central matter, so much as the sheer experience of "contradictions" that bids to paralyze and defeat the human mind. The dualism of the Cartesian world resounds in young Antiochus' speech to Rodogune which precipitates a resolution. It is a model of a new calculus of categories which the dialectic inherent in rationalistic dualism generates:

> Satisfaites vous-même à cette voix secrète
> Dont la vôtre envers nous daigne être l'interprète:
> Exécutez son ordre, et hâtez-vous sur moi
> De punir une reine et de venger un roi;
> Mais quitte par ma mort d'un devoir si sévère,

> Écoutez-en un autre en faveur de mon frère.
> De deux Princes unis à soupirer pour vous
> Prenez l'un pour victime et l'autre pour époux;
> Punissez un des fils des crimes de la mère,
> Mais payez l'autre aussi des services du père,
> Et laissez un exemple à la postérité
> Et de rigeur entière et d'entière équité.
> Quoi? n'écouterez-vous ni l'amour ni la haine?
>   (Act IV, sc. ii)

For all its traditional legalistic tone, such language throws into relief the underlying structure then bequeathed to neoclassical psychological drama such as Racine's. Out of the tension of antithesis, new categories are produced; and these in turn interact in an evolving logic which deepens our grasp of the original terms, indeed aim to cause wonder on recognition of their import. Such a calculus becomes even more evident when the given human equations are shown not in a static or remote "romantic" setting, but in a recognizable slice of history which pertains exemplarily to the greater story of Europe. As Jean Racine says proudly in his prefaces, his play *Britannicus* (1669) possesses verisimilitude because it is authoritatively documented, mainly in Tacitus. He also insists that history is a process, any juncture of which must be understood according to the precise development of factors; his Nero is specifically "un monstre naissant," tired of decent rulership, ready to eliminate rival or troublesome members of the family, and even loyal mentors. When, in Act II, scene ii, Nero lists what stands in his way ("Tout: Octavie, Agrippine, Burrhus, Sénèque, Rome entière, et trois ans de vertu"), we can at once fit the moment into a larger known pattern of the operation of natural laws in history. And thus the archetypal conflict of hate and statecraft versus love and trust in *Rodogune* is relocated in one of many specific historical variations recognized by the age.

Neronian tragedies by other exponents of seventeenth-century rationalistic realism demonstrate clearly the structural principle which Racine embraces. For example, Daniel Casper von Lohenstein's play *Agrippina* (1665) examines another precise intersection of the same flowing historical pattern, when Nero, now as full-blown tyrant, takes his final step over the edge of sanity through matricide. In an equally desperate attempt to regain control over the monster, Agrippina ventures incest. As the second chorus "prophesies" through the vision of a defiled Vestal priestess, such crime in the heart of Rome portends the collapse of a great civilization, another version of the story of Troy. Aeneas, we are reminded, transmitted the symbolic life-fire to a new, vigorous people, but as the flame gets out of control it threatens to corrupt and ruin them. With time, the inheritance from their ancestress Venus degenerates in the house of the Caesars, and, in parallel, in Rome. Lohenstein's play *Epicharis* (also 1665) treats the larger question of decline at a slightly later intersection where the doom overhanging Rome is fully confirmed by the purge of the philosopher Seneca along with the participants in the Pisan conspiracy. In the transformation of terms, the simplistic romantic pairing of an active and passive component of idealism in the twin brothers of Corneille's play *Rodogune* recurs in the particular historical moment for Rome treated by Lohenstein in the juxtaposition of Epicharis, fervent rebel, and Seneca, comprehending but adamant Stoic, co-equal martyrs in an antinomy of the modes by which man affirms his dignity. Seneca takes refuge in inner unassailable right, while Epicharis strives in vain to restore lost freedom, the nobility of Roman character fostered in the Republic; the antagonist of both figures is the inexorable inconstancy of human affairs, the corrosive power of time. Symptomatically, the mechanistic imagery of clockworks, applied to the insufficient scheming of the human brain, intrudes in the luxuriant vocabulary of *Agrippina* (e.g., V.ii, lines 161 ff.), out of tune with the technological realities of the historical moment, but consonant with the polyhistor's larger interest in suggesting the intricately spun web of cosmic and temporal processes in which life is caught up.

Some implications of Lohenstein's calculus of the logic of history are thrown in relief, if we compare his predecessor Tristan l'Hermite's *La mort de Sénèque* (1645), which treats the same moment when a paranoiac, sinister, and cunning despot crushes the conspiracy whose heart is likewise Epicharis. Whereas she indicts inner corruption, epitomized by Nero, and relates his burning of Rome to that of Troy, Seneca bitterly interprets the iron spell of the empire under Nero as "god's scourge to punish our past sins." All the time that Seneca, though sympathetic to the rebel cause, withdraws into his essentially religious posture of resignation, Epicharis toils to outcalculate the operation of recognized forces – continuing even under torture to do whatever she can to rescue the conspiracy. But, just as shown again in Lohenstein's play, the rebellion disintegrates from the inner logic of the spiritual condition of the Romans. The nominal leader Piso, falling apart under challenge, proclaims the debilitating slave consciousness in his lament that Rome's "evil Genius upholds tyranny." The world is taking up arms against Rome just when her nobles would do the same to avenge the world, but for some reason "Heaven has betrayed us by protecting crime." Tristan's hint that Seneca has received Christianity in his final moment is not necessarily just a concession to popular sentiment, but also primarily locates the whole action in the bigger pattern of the decline and fall of Rome which increasingly obsessed the late Renaissance. Eventually, as a complex example, the story of Rome came to inspire fear of a possible similar waning of "modern" Western civilization.

Though a freethinker himself, Tristan certainly alludes to the secret workings of Providence behind the events of the world theater, at least through Seneca. But Lohenstein remains ambiguous on this score in his Neronian dramas, and we hear only of Fate as the highest level of determination. Critics may argue, of course, that Lohenstein writes with ironically chilling accuracy from the gloom-shrouded perspective of the age depicted, when the world appeared to the Romans to be ruled by such an arcane will, not yet understood as Providence, but that he himself grasped Fate to be the earlier unenlightened perception of Providence. In Lohenstein's complete dramatic *oeuvre*, Rome is examined also in earlier phases of its ascendancy as an aggressive, disciplined state, and in several places we are allowed oracular glimpses of the rise and fall of empires on a colossal scale of time – quite in line with the Christian interpretation of the succession of mandate. Yet an exciting new idea is detectable in both Tristan and Lohenstein when they make a pagan rebel, in love with man's lost freedom, conspire mistakenly against the governance of our world – for Epicharis dares to define history in her own secular terms, dares to attempt to outwit the dictates of time. Here we have a second kind of calculus in the drama: the magnificent, but mostly futile, urge in man to liberate himself through the adamantine application of his own resources, guided by the light of the mind which is conscious first and foremost of its own necessary glory. When the playwrights begin to study the *calculations* of men, and to do so with unwavering gaze through permutation of rational categories or what I call a calculus in the drama, an intense irony arises from the simultaneity of structural levels.

The drama is loosened thereby from older ideological moorings; the relativization of values progresses; and eventually, out of the ethos of martyrdom and heroism, there emerges a formalistic tendency, the logical abstraction of patterns. The last play written by the religious dramatist Andreas Gryphius illustrates the epochal drift. In *Papinan* (1659) we witness the title figure's heroic perseverance, against threats of a despicable tyrant, in his assertion of the moral law which governs all. Though Papinian could seize control with broad support of constitutive elements of the Roman state, he refuses to sully himself by clutching the corrupting instruments of power and instead chooses to die on behalf of principle: the sanctity of law. Laelus, a politic brain, has counted on and promoted this turning in his elaborate, patient plotting to overthrow the emperor himself. Just a minor hesitation in grasping the moment, however, nullifies the calculations of a Machiavellian mastermind; and ironizing over himself, Laelus scornfully accepts death in a startling outbreak of pride when the final moment comes. It is as if Gryphius, for all his pious intent, cannot repress wonder over the sheer ecstasy of will, the experience of the quest for glory itself. Antiheroic Laelus is a shadow which strangely haunts the play, suggesting the existence in Europe of an entrenched new secular pattern that yields variable modes of self-assertion in the toils of history. Gryphius may hate it, but he is too clearsighted not to take cognizance of it.

To understand the newer sense of "awakening" in the absoluteness of the human condition, we must turn to the serious practitioners of a secular disillusioning or revelation who revise the inheritance from older world theater. For example, the metaphor of dream, opening Tristan's Turkish drama *Osman* (1646-47?), still dominates the action as thoroughly as in Calderón's *La vida es sueño*. But when the sultan's sister — apprehensive over the choice of means to save her brother — broods that the true may be wrapped in the false, and when he — realizing he has finally been replaced on the throne by his mad uncle — discovers himself in "a new labyrinth wherein my reason loseth itself," we recognize the psychological and political dimensions of such statements, totally without religious reference. The blindness out of which characters fail to awaken at all, or until too late, is the limitation imposed by human nature itself in its various particular instances. The sister's repressed jealous passion for her brother, the latter's mistaken pride, and other impulses motivate underground the decisions which, on the surface, at first appear to them quite otherwise occasioned. The historical events of a people are shown by Tristan to be inextricably woven from the interplay of internal, to large measure hidden, energies. In the long run, the splendid individual is impotent and isolated in the flux of time — yet tragically compelling. Osman vibrates with pure masculine élan, natural aristocracy, cultural pride. Feeling himself alone in Turkey, which he regards to be in decline, he wants to renew Islam in Egypt away from the debilitating influences of Constantinople and near-by alien Christianity; but he fears human contact when he summarily rejects the proud daughter of the Mufti. Not only is she his real equal in intensity of soul, and the right political match, but when scorned she rallies against him the jannissaries and other vested interests who fear his charisma and ideals. Osman asks too much of the human flesh, but dies (in Tristan's interpretation of the contemporary story) in glory before the gates of his own palace. In the aftermath, the daughter of the Mufti kills herself as the only way to eradicate the still living image of Osman, the best of his race. It is a terrifying eruption of the life-force, self-annihilating in its surge. So radical is the isolation of Tristan's major figures that Claude K. Abraham and Daniela Dalla Valle emphasize their "existential" inability or unwillingness to communicate with or understand one another.[17]

When Lohenstein treats the same subject in his *Ibrahim Sultan* (1673), reference to the dream-like quality of existence remains restrained until the eerie closing. Then we witness almost simultaneously the coronation of Ibrahim's infant son in the pomp and splendor of the palace above, as the state continues as an entity with its own life, and the strangulation of the madding father in the tenebrae of the dungeon, as the individual fallen man expires. Lohenstein, who knew Tristan's work, literally reverses the formula and, with cool formalistic logic, willfully achieves another transformation of the factors. It is a virtuoso exhibition by an artist who is fascinated by the possibility, the challenge, of bringing forth an experimental variation. Here Ibrahim is the decadent, whose failures as leader and corrupting example have dismayed the Turkish élite. He is a violent soulless monster, craving the radiance of Ambre, the pious daughter of the Mufti; and when she painstakingly refuses him on the grounds of a religious vocation, he rapes her and casts her out; but, converting disgrace into martyrdom by suicide, like Lucretia, Ambre inspires the nobles to rebel and restore order.

One further illustration from tragedy must suffice to mark the upper boundaries, in the 1680's, of a late Baroque sensibility which, without yet having surrendered the perspective of a world theater, increasingly focused on the rationale of history as its true subject matter. Thomas Otway's *Venice Preserved* provides a remarkable case of the relativizing effect of rationalism, applied merely as an instrument, and not yet harnessed to a reconstituted ethos. Clearly, neither the aims advocated by the republican revolutionaries, nor the doctrines maintained by the patrician establishment, explain the crisis. Just as little does the anarchism of a few or the confusion and timidity of the masses, or the political expertise of manipulators, or sexual need, familial instinct, or ego craving alone determine the relationships in the power structure or sentimental structure of the moment. Rather, all elements are operative, and Otway gives us no single anchor of belief beyond our awareness that we *are* indeed capable of seeing this complexity, and ambiguity, of existence in the act of choosing — whatever the choice. Although placing a very different critical construction on the play, Frank Warnke cogently describes this feature thus:[18]

> In *Venice Preserv'd*, for example, emotional attitudes, though projected with great power, do not manifest themselves as forces working on individual figures who are consistent mimeses of human beings. Jaffeir's love-honor conflict, for example, may be conceived of in two opposed ways: love for

> Belvidera versus honor toward Pierre, or love for Pierre versus honor toward Belvidera. The erotic focus of the play shifts between the ideally pure Belvidera and the courtesan Aquilina, the function of hero shifts between Jaffeir and Pierre, and the plot itself is presented in a thoroughly ambiguous way, as a murderous conspiracy and as a noble blow for freedom. *Venice Preserv'd* is not so much a drama, in the Renaissance or Baroque sense, as it is a dramatic fantasy on the series of subjectively obsessive themes.

In this same two-way formula, I see instead how the rational mind of the late Baroque hypnotically forces the human equations posited for it by the facts of nature, society, and history, and in its puzzlement and bedazzlement over them, forgets to suppress unpleasant discoveries which will badly clutter up the oncoming best of all possible worlds. Admittedly, such a lapse of censorship betrays a certain devious indulgence, which is evident especially in the nihilism of radically sentimentalized selves. Without certainty in a creed, only the personal code can remain, identity as be-all and end-all; when the older Christian sense of history is reasoned away by the disillusioning accomplishment of gaining a secular, rational view of it, we are thrown back again on the irreducible verities of the romantic drama of human types, and a circle closes.

But in the twentieth century we have little cause to speak of Otway or the tragedy of the morally yet unreconstructed High Baroque disrespectfully. From the midst of today's Theater of the Absurd and our pompously repetitious shattering of the "illusion" of an intervening rationalistic concept, we look back — if not with nostalgia, certainly over a gulf — at the pathway which once did lead out of the perils of "dream" into the supposed security of "calculus." Two instances of the new German potential at the end of the seventeenth century for shifting the grounds for the interpretation of life as theater will serve to illustrate the general European redefinition of "awakening" as the emergence into the light of a rational understanding of man. The preliminary step in the new direction is taken in the *Trauer-Spiel von dem Neapolitanischen Haupt-Rebellen Masaniello* (publ. 1688) by Christian Weise, based on the folk uprising of July, 1647, under the lead of a fisherman, Tommaso Agnello, to demand restoration by Charles V of Naple's freedom from taxes and imposts. This is the first German play with successful mass scenes and considerable attention to ordinary citizens of a state. The tragedy springs from the inherent presumption of a common man assuming authority and rank, that is, being tempted out of his own natural sphere. As in Bidermann's *Philemon*, but for quite different reasons, the motif of changing clothes is key. Masaniello commands his enemies, the monks and priests, to wear trousers so they cannot conceal weapons, and the politically astute archbishop permits this, knowing that the radical alteration of class appearances will eventually rebound against the rebel. In turn, he compels Masaniello to assume the splendid robe of office and symbolic sword in a ceremony in the cathedral to solemnize the treaty between the people and government. Though the fisherman wants to remove his incommensurate costume, he cannot accomplish the act, and his moment of triumph is therefore a turning point toward a fall. His fears of alienation from the folk and of megalomania ironically come true, although Weise motivates his madness also physiologically and sociologically as the effect of poison (V, ii, iii). Masaniello, who could not quit after "right" was restored, slips into the role of tyrant and is finally assassinated. A deeper identity emerges from Masaniello, and his acceptance of a costume for a particular role indicates the role's sinister latent effect. His transformation from honest fisherman to bad ruler is a personal tragedy. But it is also representative of a principle to which, over the deceptive pathway of violent opposition, man can fall prey: the corruption of power, one of many dangerous aspects of reality in the actual vicissitudes of history.

In Weise's *Ein wunderliches Schauspiel vom Niederlandischen Bauer* (publ. 1700), another version of a popular story to which Jakob Masen much earlier gave a final shape in Jesuit comedy (*Rusticus imperans*), the drunk peasant Mierten is put to bed in the palace of the Duke of Burgundy and treated as a visiting prince on awaking as a prank. Then, again drunk, he is dressed in his old clothes and laid in the same gutter, so that he holds the experience to have been a wonderful dream. The situation, of course, superficially resembles that of Segismundo in Calderón's *La vida es sueño*. Not a serious trial of an actual prince takes place, but rather the real class structure of the courtly society is inverted for amusement – the old trope of the topsey-turvy world. The drastic lesson of the

Spanish "dream" is accordingly mitigated. The beast comes out in Mierten, yet he remains a laughable, even likable, fellow. His logic is on an earthly plane; for example, after eating all he wants, he is annoyed when he cannot have his fill of women, too, at court (III,iv).

The wise chamberlain Robert draws a generous conclusion from this display of coarse appetite and uncouthness dressed in so splendid a costume:

> Wir sind alle Bauern; Doch welcher den Bauer im Hertzen verbergen kan/ dass er nicht an das Tage-Licht kommen kan/ der wird ein qualificirter Hofmann genennet. (IV, vi)
>
> [We are all peasants; but he who can conceal the peasant in his heart to prevent his coming into the light of day, he is called a qualified courtier.]

Mierten resembles Sancho Panza in possessing a certain natural honesty whose example is beneficial to higher minds, if rightly considered:

> Gnädigster Herr/ muss doch ein Mensch offmahls von unvernünfftigen Thieren was lernen/ warumb soll man sich allzeit eines Lehrmeisters schämen/ der gleich unter die vernünfftigen Menschen gezehlet wird [?].
>
> [Most gracious lord, since a person ofttimes must learn a bit from animals lacking reason, why should one persist in being ashamed of a tutor who is counted right among the beings possessing reason?]

These thoughts betray a mood of well-tempered reason, confidently interested in common sense and ordinary human nature. The hierarchy of seventeenth-century intellectual and social values is still tenuously intact, but we hear unmistakably the first notes of the Enlightenment. The human mind believes that it has or in the longer run can assert control over its dreaming.

Notes

*   Elements of "Dream and Calculus in European Baroque Drama" were first sketched in a paper entitled "European High Baroque Tragedy" given at the North East Modern Language Association convention held in Saratoga, N.Y. (1972).

1. Johannes Henricus Alstedius, *Cursus Philosophici Encyclopaedia Libris XXVII Complectens Universae Philosophiae methodum, serie praeceptorum, regularum & commentariorum perpetua* [...] *opera ac studio* (1620): "Persona est res singularis per se subsistens & intelligens" (column 161).
2. Alstedius, *Theologia naturalis exhibens augustissimam naturae scholam* [...] (1615): "Corpus enim est instrumentum animae non solum in bonis, sed etiam malis actionibus, quae quidem sunt organicae. Nam inorganicas sola anima producit" (p. 213).
3. *Theologia naturalis:* "*Anima rationalis*, domina illa & dictatrix augustissima, cuius potentiae duae sunt, intellectus & voluntas [...]" (p. 603).
4. The same term is used as for the ordinary clocks that are encountered in daily life in all towns and cities. *Theologia naturalis:* "Nam coelum nihil est aliud, quam huius universi horologium, quod metitur tempus ipsiusque partes constituit" (p. 295). In a dissertation (begun under my supervision prior to my moving to Stanford) on "The Unities of Time and Place in Sixteenth-Century Theater and Criticism" (SUNY-Binghamton, 1975), Dana S. Clarke has shown the close connection between a new time-awareness in the Italian urban setting of the ending fifteenth century and in the innovative Italian playwriting in the vernacular and in Latin of early Humanism. This time-structure incorporated in artistic practice antedates the effect of the rediscovery of Aristotle's *Poetics* and the waves of subsequent critical theorizing about the unities. Clarke considers Romance and English, but not German, literature.
5. *Clavis Artis Lullianae* (1633): "Methodus est instrumentum dianoeticum" (p. 75); "[multiplicatio] propositionum [...] est opus rationis, quo augetur scientia" (p. 83).
6. For instance: Ricardo J. Quinones, *The Renaissance Discovery of Time* (Cambridge, Mass., 1972); Manfred Weidhorn, *Dreams in Seventeenth Century English Literature* (The Hague, 1970).
7. Paul Goodman, *The Structure of Literature* (Chicago, 1954).
8. Ernst Robert Curtius, *European Literature and the Latin Middle Ages*, transl. Willard R. Trask (New York, 1953).
9. Heinz Otto Burger, *Dasein heißt eine Rolle spielen: Studien zur deutschen Literaturgeschichte* (Munich, 1963). In his article "Où situer la fin de la Renaissance dans l'histoire de la littérature française," in the volume *Littérature de la Renaissance à la lumière des recherches soviétiques et hongroises*, ed. by N.I. Balachov, T. Klaniczay, and A.D. Mikhailov (Budapest, 1978), 407-431, Yuri B. Vipper prefers the broader historical label "seventeenth century" for the post-Renaissance phase in its entirety, but he discerns a prolonged alternation, rivalry, and interplay of "classical" and "baroque" impulses, with a certain intermingling of realism (e.g., Sorel), within this framework from 1600 to 1660 in France, notably in the drama (e.g., Rotrou as pronouncedly "baroque"). Interestingly (pp. 423 ff.), Vipper resists the concept of a "counter-Renaissance" stream or of "mannerism" as a distinct

subperiod in the late 1500s, endorses Klaniczay's limitation of "mannerism" to the elite aesthetic sphere, and tries to bracket out Montaigne as a special case of survival of the Renaissance, neither Classical nor Baroque, while he sees the visionary passion of Agrippa d'Aubigné as decisively Baroque, and Milton as a newer variety of the dramatic approach characteristic of Baroque art. Tibor Klaniczay's exposition of "La théorie esthétique du maniérisme" is pp. 327-384 of this volume; also see his earlier sociological analysis, "La crise de la Renaissance et le maniérisme," *Acta Litteraria Academiae Scientiarum Hungaricae*, 13 (1971), 269-314. Both of these essays and other of his contributions on the Renaissance and Baroque have been gathered, in German translation, in *Renaissance und Manierismus: Zum Verhältnis von Gesellschaftsstruktur, Poetik und Stil* (Berlin, 1977).

10 Robert J. Nelson, *Play within a Play: The Dramatist's Conception of his Art: Shakespeare to Anouilh* (New Haven, 1958). More sweeping in its range is the later study by the German comparatist Manfred Schmeling, *Das Spiel im Spiel: Ein Beitrag zur Vergleichenden Literaturkritik* (Saarbrücken, 1977); see my review-essay in *Die Sprachkunst*, 10 (1979), 241-248. In the ch. on "Spectacle and the Language of Illusion" of his book *Toward Dramatic Illusion: Theatrical Technique and Meaning from Hardy to "Horace"* (New Haven, 1971), Timothy J. Reiss examines the split between Classicism and Baroque as two differing kinds of illusion the age tests out: the first creates apparent transparency of language and its coincidence with theme, as if "there is no action going on outside the language," whereas the second promotes "movement, color, and spectacle," recognition of illusion, the ambiguity of multiple interpretational possibilities, whereby "language becomes counterpoint to the action" (p. 148).

11 On the fundamental categories, see the Introduction to P. Lal, *Great Sanskrit Plays* (New York, 1957). For the detailed exposition of the subtleties of this tradition we are still indebted to the definitive work by Arthur B. Keith, *The Sanskrit Drama, in its Origin, Development. Theory and Practice* (Oxford, 1924).

12 In a unpublished seminar paper written under my direction at SUNY-Binghamton, Gail Sullivan has developed in some detail the "Vedantic" affinities in *Hamlet*.

13 Eliot's Hamlet essay has been incorporated in his collection, *Elizabethan Essays* (London, 1934), pp. 55-63.

14 Alexander A. Parker, "Towards a Definition of Calderonian Tragedy," *Bulletin of Hispanic Studies*, 39 (1963), 222-237.

15 *Comparative Literature*, 18 (1966), 324-336.

16 Cf. Timothy Reiss' emphasis of the way Rotrou's *Saint-Genest* and Corneille's *L'Illusion comique* involve the spectator in the conclusion to his book *Toward Dramatic Illusion*, and his sense of an analogy in the changing world view: "The development of the drama seems to reflect, in microcosm, the great shift from a dialectical mode of reasoning to an analytical one. During

this period, of course, a radical new approach to learning evolved under the auspices of Ramus and Descartes in France, and Bacon in England" (p. 180 f.).

17 Claude K. Abraham, *The Strangers: Tragic World of Tristan l'Hermite* (Gainesville, 1966); Daniela Dalla Valle, *Il teatro di Tristan l'Hermite* (Torino, 1964).

18 Frank J. Warnke, *Versions of Baroque* (New Haven, 1973), p. 203.

10. TRANSFORMATIONS OF THE FEMALE DELINGQUENT IN FICTION

1. The Iberian Pícara

Alexander Parker's use of "delinquent" in place of older "pícaro" or "rogue" acknowledges the need to repristinate our critical vocabulary for describing a genre after its originary impulses may have exhausted themselves.[1] If the literature of delinquency perhaps trumpeted the arrival of what in *La scienza nuova* (1723) Giambattista Vico termed the "demotic" age, then today's readers are situated well past the Renaissance stance of man between the angels and beasts, well past Hamlet and tragicomedy, and somewhere around the lower reaches of comedy and farce. In accelerating the slide down the mimetic scale proposed by Vico's follower Northrop Frye,[2] roguery should have pushed us out of the comforts of metaphor into the harsh particularities of metonomy. Be that as it may, I hope to illustrate how the glamorizing and sentimentalizing of lowerclass strivers after their rough start in early modern literature eventually gave way to trivialization of female criminality. In this sense, the notion of the exhaustion or disintegration of the picaresque genre is ambivalent if what we actually mean in the later twentieth century is that the underlying mythologeme is a widely lived and felt reality, something quite ordinary.

In fact, we encounter another major element besides crime in the Iberian core of the genre, and that is the culturally specific outsider status of the delinquent. There is good reason for the perennial scholarly debate whether the title figure of *La vida de Lazarillo de Tormes y de sus fortunas y adversidades* (1554) is the first *pícaro*, rather than merely a prototype, and whether the anonymous author should be presumed to be a *converso* intellectual, perhaps also an apostate.[3] To answer these questions is to measure the relative importance of the social crisis for the New Christians of

253

Jewish and Moorish ancestry after the national reunification of Spain, in comparison to the moral vision of the Counter-Reformation and Baroque, as the crucial precipitating factors for the literary genre. Our answer will also affect our view of the "original" and/or "significant" traits of the Iberian *pícara*. Why should the early female delinquent move on a horizontal plane through geocultural space, yet vertically through society and psychological crises, as Claudio Guillén has suggested?[4] Or did the roguess, as an inherently neo-medieval incarnation of greed, lust, and pride, remain a mere convention until the eighteenth century, her sinful drive furnishing chiefly a plot device, as Julio Rodríguez-Luis has argued?[5] Or did the Spanish *pícaras* exhibit the tension between the need to adjust to society and the urge to preserve inner freedom, which Horst and Ingrid Daemmrich find already characteristic of Lazarillo?[6]

Lazarillo's mother is a case in point. Her insignificant and precarious social status appears in her maiden name, plain Antona Pérez. Widowed, she moves to the university city of Salamanca to earn a living and there eventually takes up with the black groom Zaide, so that white Lazarillo gets a dark baby brother. Zaide is severely punished for stealing supplies and equipment, but the destitute mother once again manages to survive as a servant in an inn until she places Lazarillo with his first master, the blind beggar. The statements in chapter one, that Lazarillo's own natural father, a miller who short-weighted sacks, was accused of "ciertas sangrías malechas" ["certain ill-done bleedings"] and "pasdeció persecución por justicia" ["suffered persecution for righteousness' sake," cf. Matthew 5:10], are probably code phrases hinting at his own tainted blood, even though, in escaping from his situation, the father died as a muleteer in a campaign against the Moors. Lazarillo's proletarian origins are lowly and ambiguous. The author associates several themes: the desperate condition of the impoverished, their outlets through demeaning and illicit activities (notably prostitution for women), the links between low-caste Iberians and racially tainted, marginal elements of society. The ironic voice of Lazarillo constantly exposes the truth of the complicity of respected classes, such as the priesthood, in deceit and fraud. His very cynicism finally gains him a foothold in a society that is obsessed with honor and appearance.

The Catholic Baroque writer Francisco de Quevedo uses these established lowlife motifs for their symbolic value in his novel *La vida del Buscón llamado Don Pablos* (1626). By creating a first-person narrator who strives to convince us of his accurate reconstruction of memories and yet is split between his function as a character and his accrued ironic knowledge as a "writer," Quevedo gives a further distancing twist to the generic illusion of autobiographical realism; the inner ironies of the story are wrapped in Quevedo's outer authorial manipulation and his relation to the reader, the work, and Spanish society.[7] The need for a social niche and livelihood is inexorable, and the "Sharper's" family is very conscious of education and the arts as means whereby the desirable fiction of respectability may be achieved. Their striving is a perverse mockery of the Renaissance idea of man as the asserter of his own dignity. As Pablo's father, a thieving barber, proudly instructs him in Book I, ch. 1: "Hijo, esto de ser ladrón no es arte mecánica sino liberal" ["Son, the business of being a crook is not a mechanic but a liberal art"]. His mother Aldonza is related to persons with family names all based on those of saints, but hence clearly of tainted *converso* blood. Pablo, whose underworld argot is loaded with joke religious terms, remarks disingenuously: "Sospechábase en el pueblo que no era cristiana vieja" ["The twonspeople suspected her of not being an Old Christian"]. For reliques his mother has pieces of hangman's rope around her bed, and her rosary is made of the molars of dead people; thus it comes as no surprise that she is punished for witchcraft. The connection is an old one. Witches were closely associated with secret knowledge of forbidden sexual practices and services. Whereas the point of view of regular society is that it must protect itself against crimes and against moral and spiritual subversion, the underworld — colorfully represented in Pablos' account — struggles against that harsh repressive order and fears being caught either by secular authority or, far worse, by the dread Inquisition.

Our ingrained critical habit is to focus on shifts in the depiction of male delinquents around 1600. But the literary tradition of the *pícara* reaches back a full century earlier in Spain to Fernando de Rojas' narrative drama commonly called *La Celestina* after the dominant female criminal in it. The original version of sixteen acts was published in Burgos in 1499 under the title *Comedia de Calisto y Melibea* and it was expanded to twentytwo acts in the edition of 1514 under the appropriately modified title *Tragicomedia de Calisto y Melibea*. Though grown old, Celestina is still an energetic procuress who commands the loyalty of a string of whores. As we learn from her conversation with Pármeno in Act VII of the longer version, she herself had a model for the profession of go-between, purveyor of cosmetics, seller of charms, patcher of bodily defects and lost maidenheads, in her friend and his late mother Claudina. Celestina plays on this family bond in her attempt to reconcile Pármeno with Sempronio and to employ both lackeys for her schemes, which include helping their master, the lusty impetuous Calisto, in his love affair with Melibea. Celestina glories in her clandestine work that penetrates into the households of proper families and brings the passions to fruition. Yet while she is proud of her own criminal skills and success, she steers Pármeno away from the dangerous topic of his mother's punishment for witchcraft — a case in which Celestina was implicated but which has since been forgotten. Celestina's rebukes to the inexperienced Pármeno contain veiled warnings that seem to reflect the mentality of the persecuted New Christians. Eventually, Pármeno and Sempronio kill the proud woman in a heated quarrel over loot (XII). When Calisto soon after learns they have been summarily beheaded, he identifies emotionally with the ruffians and cannot desist from his own waywardness (XIII). His fall from the ladder during a tryst (XIX) and Melibea's suicide leap from the tower of her family's house (XX) complete the spectacle of passionate self-assertion that erupts at every level of society. The world of her father Pleberio, the grieving representative of social virtue and order, is effectively shattered (XXI). Florence Weinberg has interpreted Celestina as a negative archetypal figure, the Great Mother as Terrible Mother; the depiction of her witchlike snaring of others in the toils of sin thus accords with orthodox views of the ending fifteenth century, even if we perceive the results today as an existential crisis in Renaissance urban society.[8]

Another startling early or proto-picaresque story by a *converso* author is Francisco Delicado's *Retrato de la Lozana andaluza* (1528), set in the vibrant, but dangerous Rome of the early sixteenth century, the scene where the author actually composed it. It is written from the point of view of the expatriate colony of Iberian *conversos* in the corrupt Holy City, a relatively more tolerant refuge, who regard Spanish values with scepticism and hostility; and it incorporates in its ironic and pessimistic vision of humanity both their exile and the trauma of the barbaric sack perpetrated by the Spanish and Imperial troops in 1527. Delicado celebrates freedom, love, sex, wit, and vitality in a world whose vaunted higher values have been destroyed by the anointed authorities in charge. The central figures are the criminal Rampín and his friend and protectress Lozana ["Spirited"], whom the entire Roman *demimonde* admires for her beauty, grace, loyalty, and generosity, and who by natural endowments is better than her world. Delicado swathes his story of the fragile moments of joy and the search for lost "peace" in protective Erasmian ambiguities, but it is a secular response to the situation.

The stories of Celestina and Lozana demonstrate the important social factor of stigmatization. But we can also understand what is being "marked" by the particular stigma (here by *converso* status) as a larger field organized around polarities. These polarities can be conveniently labeled by a general mythological analogy as those of Hermes and Aphrodite and secondarily those of Dionysos and Demeter (the latter pair often present in parodic sacramental references). A third mythological identity of the *pícara*, especially if she is older, is that of the witch; the male counterpart is a demonic antihero or the devil, rather than the ordinary rogue.[9] The subsidence or shift of polar tensions in the standard male delinquent identities (Hermes/Dionysos) has its parallel in portrayals of the roguess (Aphrodite/Demeter). In this sense, the original "marking" of the *pícara* evolved into an independent signifier transponible to other cultures and transformable over the centuries. Christian authors could readily attack the *pícara's* sinfulness — her secret activities on behalf of the life-force — by situating her story in the same favorite narrative paradigm of "erring" which circumscribed the rogue.[10] This eventually was misperceived as a merely formal plot-element of serial, episodic construction.

The sense of a community somehow remains intact in Delicado, whereas Rojas exudes the alienation of a disturbed onlooker in the midst of dire existential errings. Rojas, too, was of a *converso* family and belonged to the humanist intelligentsia. His brooding vision of the self-destructive rage to live appeared not long after the publication of Sebastian Brant's *Narrenschiff* in Basel in 1494. The *Celestina* marks a problematic rupture with the past as clearly as do Brant's warnings, from his Catholic humanist standpoint, about disintegrative forces threatening European civilization. One of the most fascinating adaptations of the idea of an anti-society as a Ship of Fools is the frontispiece to the first edition (1605) of Francisco López de Úbeda's *La pícara Justina*, showing the "Nave de la vida picaresca" which, impelled by "Pleasure," drifts to sea down the "River of Forgetfulness" and toward "Disillusionment" in the "Port of Death." The picture is framed by objects associated with picaresque life, and it represents the obvious fundamental forces through the classical gods Bacchus, Ceres, Venus, and Cupid, as well as in the figures "Time" and "Idleness." Standing prominently amidships are Mother Celestina and her literary offspring Justina, dressed as a muse, while Guzmán de Alfarache sits on the prow as a beggar and in a rowboat the forerunner rogue Lazarillo tows the larger picaresque ship. Celestina's spectacles may allude to Quevedo, whose novel *El Buscón* may already have been circulating in an early manuscript version. In any case, the "Ship of Picaresque Life" clearly attributes to the Celestina story a significant role in the evolution of picaresque thematics. The Celestina type will recur everywhere in European literature, but like the ferocious Spanish warrior who is reduced to the Capitano in the *commedia dell'arte*, it is often assimilated as an unproblematic stock comic character. An example is the foul-mouthed, lustful old procuress Cyrilla in Andreas Gryphius' *Horribilicribrifax* (1663).

With the *Justina*, we are far from the existential anguish of the original *Celestina* or the somber naturalism of the *Lazarillo*. Úbeda, of *converso* background but well-connected with the royal court, treats his subject as a literary game for the amusement of the sophisticated who are entranced with the picaresque genre at the turn of the century.[11] His book is, among other things, a reply to and satire on the counterpoised picaresque adventures and moralizing digressions of Mateo Alemán's enormous two-part *Guzmán de*

Alfarache (1599, 1604). In his prolix confession, Guzmán — son of a Genoan usurer and a whore, then passed off as the illegitimate offspring of a Spanish nobleman — becomes a hardened criminal, yet also acquires a thorough formal education, and wanders about Europe in a worldly pilgrimage. Moving encyclopedically through every level of society, he indicts all aspects of the corrupting power of money, before he permanently repents. The range of scholarly opinion on Alemán (yet another author of *converso* background) is about as vast as his novel. He has been interpreted as sincerely upholding Counter-Reformation values or voicing an aristocratic protest against hurtful features of early capitalism, but he has also been viewed as the creator of an unreliable, existentially deformed narrator through whom the vicious reality of decadent Spanish culture is revealed.[12]

Whatever Aleman's true purpose, the *Justina* is transparently presented as a burlesque fiction and as a *roman-à-clef*, when its narrator, who is the daughter of lightfingered innkeepers and descended from entertainers, imitates the confessional mode of the *Guzmán*. The roguess' adventures take her from the "highlands" — historically, and now ironically, associated with the most ancient pure Christian blood — to various thinly disguised cities (Valladolid, Leon, Madrid), where activities of the court, the citizenry, and specific individuals are mocked. Úbeda assumes a satiric stance toward a nation heavily populated by impecunious and recent gentlefolk who loudly prate about honor but many of whom are fearful of close inspection of their family trees. At the same time, Úbeda exploits the attractions of the picaresque life, with its freedom of the open road and dismissal of the claims of honor. Justina exposes the details of her own impure origins on any pretext with a cheerfully insulting counter-logic to that of normal Spain. Through her purported discipleship under Celestina as a talented whore and thief, and through her wit, verbal ingenuity, and skill and zest for playacting, Úbeda aims to outbid Alemán. The genre is now a recognizable system loosened from the painful aspects of a lowerclass sociolect. Whereas Quevedo morally censures the wit and ingenuity of his Sharper as a moral blight on Spanish society, Justina's entertaining traits as an artist seem almost to outweigh her roguery in importance, and in this respect she anticipates the strange imperial jester who is the title figure of the anonymous *La vida y hechos de Estebanillo González, hombre de buen humor* (1646).¹³

In *La hija de Celestina* (1612), expanded as *La ingeniosa Elena* (1614), Alfonso Jerónimo de Salas Barbadillo, a friend of Cervantes, blends the formulae of the romance (*in medias res* beginning, interpolated recountings of past events, third-person narration, higher social level of success, etc.) and the story of the feminine confidence trickster. Barbadillo's rhetorical flourishes of moralizing and the requisite tragic ending to her guilty life obviously are not calculated to obliterate our sympathy for his beguiling, beautiful criminal as she makes her way in Toledo, Seville, and Madrid, but rather to excuse this clever antiheroic approximation of the seventeenth-century courtly novel. If the *Guzmán* represents the climax of the Counter-Reformation, new possibilities flow at once from a comic revisionary attitude toward it.

The tendency to sentimentalize the underdog makes its appearance almost simultaneously in Spain and France, as Richard Bjornson has demonstrated.¹⁴ For example, by conflating older romance and newer picaresque fiction, Charles Sorel's *Vraie histoire comique de Francion* (1622) and Paul Scarron's *Roman comique* (1649-57) humanize the aspirations of low-born characters and engage the sympathies of an expanding French urban readership. The novelist Scarron portrayed his chief protagonists, Destin and his fiancee Estoile, as likeable for their common sense and perseverance in a tawdry world of strolling players, sharpers, and ridiculous provincials. Similarly, Alonso de Castillo Solórzano's *La niña de los embustes, Teresa de Manzanares* (1632), even though it is narrated as an autobiography, replaces the straight linear plot with the romanesque twists and turns of the long adventure novel. *La garduña de Sevilla y anzuelo de las bolsas* (1642), Castillo's novel of the beautiful, ingenious, and indestructible swindler Rufina, abandons the picaresque first-person point of view for the more diverse third-person narration of romance. As the antiheroine moves from one successful strategm or duped husband to another, she often outwits criminals who are by far more unpalatable or, as a ruse, for gain, she poses in appealing social roles familiar from stories of love and honor, all of which has the effect of lending her the color of a heroine of romance in the eyes of the reader, too. Any moral point to the coopted picaresque genre is blunted by the compromise solution of allowing Rufina to settle down in an unfashionable retail business with the man she loves.

Although it may be significant in the depiction of some *pícaros*, serious moral reflection is not among the predominant traits of the Spanish *pícaras* of the sixteenth and early seventeenth century. What the female delinquents have in common are: a) their endowment with intelligence, wit, and physical charms in some blend: b) their descent from lower-class, criminal, and/or outcast families or dubious parentage; and c) early tutoring in dishonest practices by their elders or a Celestine-like guide. Their drive to escape from social misery and absurdity unfolds as a propensity to evil, expressed through deception, infidelity, ingratitude, treachery, vengefulness, cruelty, greed. The *pícara's* craving for freedom is seen in constant unrest, in frequent escapes and changes of household, job, occupation, name, spouse, or lover. The powerful eroticism of the earlier *pícaras* closer to the writing of the *Celestina* undergoes important modification by the time of *Don Quixote*. As we see in the case of Elena in *La hija de Celestina*, Teresa de Manzanares in *La niña de los embustes*, and Rufina in *La garduña de Sevilla*, erotic love is juxtaposed with or gives way to idealized love, and the language used by the antiheroine is upgraded to meet the stylistic demands of a socially more acceptable amorous code.[15]

2. The Female Delinquent in Northern Europe

What of the female delinquent in the Northern Baroque? Alexander Parker has argued that the morally serious variety of picaresque narration, such as upheld by Mateo Alemán and Francisco de Quevedo, reached its culmination in Hans Jacob Christoffel von Grimmelshausen's *Der Abenteuerliche Simplicissimus Teutsch* (1669).[16] The *Trutz Simplex: Oder Ausführliche und wunderseltzame Lebensbeschreibung Der Ertzbetrügerin und Landstörtzerin Courasche* (ca. 1670), one of several related books which Grimmelshausen wrote to capitalize on the popularity of *Simplicissimus*, deserves to be more widely known in its own right, too, and as more than just the source of Brecht's figure Mother Courage. The moral consciousness that Simplex ultimately affirms, and the sin-prone natural actor that he is in the theater of the world, both speak in the complex, multi-layered first-person voice of his "biography" from its very first words. Although Simplex grows richly endowed with experience and wisdom, the *Simplicissimus* is not a novel of education, but a symbolic pilgrimage toward conversion. In contrast, Grimmelshausen makes Courasche's first-person voice obsessive and hard. Even though she can stare unflinchingly at the horrors of the Thirty Years' War and her unvarnished account reveals things that should move and teach her readers, her heart excludes genuine moral scruples or regret. By standards of the Baroque world-theater, she is ultimately an obtuse observor of her own existential predicament. This single-minded roguess remains unrepentant to the last page, after recounting decades of monomaniacal self-assertion and her real enjoyment of the life of crime. Whereas Simplex desires to bequeath a spiritual message, her motive in dictating her memoires is explicitly to wreak revenge on Simplex, who angered her by slipping from her net in the Sauerbrunnen episode in *Simplicissimus* (Book V, ch. 6). Simplex' utterances, like his career, are freighted with an encyclopedic burden of variegated symbolism. Thus from a modern point of view, one result of Grimmelshausen's experimentation with an unredeemed, unrepentant picaresque voice in the *Courasche* is a more intense, coherent characterization of the antiheroine.

Otherwise, in general terms, Courasche can be categorized as the "Rufina" type. Obviously, the story-line of the *Courasche* employs numerous elements of romance, just as does the *Simplicissimus*. Not until chapter 10 does the vivacious, bold criminal learn that she is the illegitimate offspring of a Bohemian nobleman. But by then, as if by natural endowment, she already has perfected the art of playing the role of a romance heroine in order to cloak herself with respectability and snare suitors. Simplex' eventual discovery of his actual origins as the legitimate son of the hermit, a respected nobleman, logically reinforces his choice to imitate his father. Courasche, in contrast, resembles Guzmán and Rufina with respect to the ambiguous, mixed condition of being a noble bastard, born through illicit lust and pride. However, unlike Guzmán, Courasche is adamant to the end in her queenly pride; and unlike Rufina, she does not finally need a soft nest, normalized security, when her beauty fades. Courasche's rebellion is total insofar as in old age she prefers the freedom of lawlessness with the gypsies.

The young Courasche is drawn into the tumult and adventure of the war when she is disguised as a page to save her from pillaging troops. Thus begins her lifelong preference for wearing breeches (sometimes under a dress) and her series of marriages or affairs with captains, lieutenants, and, in the ebb of fortune, non-commissioned officers. The hazards of combat and her talents and appetites as a whore and confidence trickster keep Courasche in constant motion. Her activities shift back and forth between the army and various cities. Besides saying a great deal about her prowess in combat and her methods to dupe society and land solid marriage contracts, she frequently mentions her private monetary transactions as she traverses Europe. Chapters 14 to 21 form an interesting section, because after many personal and sexual triumphs Courasche is attracted to the lucrative sutler's trade, enters into a mock marriage with the corporal Springinsfeld allowing herself full license, and follows the army to Italy, a scene fascinating for Northern readers. (Springinsfeld, also a character in the *Simplicissimus*, tells about his own life, including the time with Courasche, in a later novel named for him [1670].) Besides provisioning the troops and serving drinks, Courasche gains from prostitution. The theme of insatiable greed, taking for the sake of taking, is so well-established that many late chapters turn into virtually separate tales with distinct subgeneric traits and symbolic rather than romanesque value. For example, chapter 17 is a contest of coarse scatological pranks in which she outdoes rival whores; 18 is the folktale of the servant imp in the bottle, whom the "fortunate" possessor soon wants to get rid of; 19 is a confidence game which leaves a respectable townswoman in a ridiculous situation because of her greed; 20, a comic robbery of jewel dealers, exhibits the increasing primacy of revenge even over greed as Courasche's motivation. The use of preshaped stories, such as the novella of the "pearquake" in 25, becomes more evident as the novel moves toward its conclusion and the fortunes of the antiheroine decline.

Having separated from Springinsfeld when the Italian phase of the war winds down, and having found scant opportunity for profit in Prague, Courasche tries to settle down to farming — but her choice is a farce. For she only perks up when she can pursue unsavory and illicit activities and when, in effect, she undermines the idyllic image of the country. At last, she contracts the feared "French disease" and goes to Sauerbrunnen for recuperation where the affair with Simplex occurs (ch. 24). Grimmelshausen saves as an enticement for the reader Courasche's arrival, finally, at the explanation of the trick she played on him by afterwards dropping her maid's illegitimate child on his doorstep as if it were the fruit of their own liaison. As significant as Courasche's anger is her barrenness. (In ch. 5 of *Springinsfeld*, Simplex in turn reveals Courasche's providential error, since the boy was indeed his son by the chambermaid; in ch. 7, he admonishes Springinsfeld not to curse Courasche, but pray for her.) The final reported phase of Courasche's life is her association with the gypsies and rapid rise to leadership as the wife of their chief (chs. 27, 28). Although doubtlessly Grimmelshausen intended this state to symbolize her permanent commitment to an abhorrent anti-society, it is difficult for modern readers not to admire her daring and hardiness. It is difficult to measure exactly how far we may "misread" by projecting onto her figure something of the glamour of freedom which was attributed to gypsies in late-eighteenth-century and Romantic literature. In any case, Grimmelshausen's irony is simple and direct when he lets Courasche convict herself through boastful injury to normal human society on the last page:

> Und eben deswegen habe ich mich mein Lebtag über nichts mehrers verwundert, als daß man uns in den Ländern geduldet, sintemal wir weder Gott noch den Menschen nichts nutzen noch zu dienen begehren, sondern uns nur mit Lügen, Betrügen und Stehlen genähret, beides zu Schaden des Landmanns als der großen Herren selbst, denen wir manches Stück Wild verzehren.
>
> [And that's why my whole life long I've been not more amazed by anything than that people tolerate us in their lands, since we desire to be of no use or service neither to God nor man, but have fed ourselves through lying, cheating, and stealing, to the hurt both of countryfolk and the great lords on whom we eat up a good deal of game.]

Grimmelshausen's serious affirmation of the law is unmistakable between the lines. Here there is no subtle double irony comparable to that in the conversation between Ricote the Moor and Sancho Panza in *Don Quixote*, II, ch. 54, when the highminded exile defends Spanish justice against his naive, less patriotic, pureblooded neighbor.

Grimmelshausen attained an unusual generic moment by combining the glamour borrowed from romance and the condemnation pronounced by the Spanish moralists. Daniel Defoe, in effect, more radically transformed the picaresque genre by paying elaborate attention to the sentimental life and moral predicaments of the roguess in *The Fortunes and Misfortunes of the Famous Moll Flanders* (1722). The dissenter Protestant Defoe, assuming the mask of editor in a Preface, claims that the story of lewdness and crime is not a novel or romance, but a "private history," an authentic life-drama which can morally instruct. The two parts of *Moll Flanders* are ostensibly based on actual memoires put together in 1683 by the seventy-year-old title figure after her second return to England from the American colonies. Because of the detailed examination of her early years in various households, Moll's narrating voice gives a confessional consistency to Part I that anticipates that of Samuel Richardson's sentimental epistolary novel *Pamela* (1740).

Moll's typical picaresque craving for the secure status of a gentlewoman is rooted in fatherless poverty and her lowly birth to a female felon in Newgate prison. This obscure background is symbolically foreshortened into the memory blank of her mysterious wanderings until the age of three with the "gypsies" (who may have been disguised lowlife actors and tricksters who used this convenient cover). However, in Defoe's narrative structure, once Moll gets a toehold as a foster child in Colchester, her continuous moralizing commentary begins to serve purposes other than psychological portraiture. Because her reflections relentlessly expose the problems of women under real economic and existential conditions, the story moves in the direction of the later social novel; for example, we enter into such forbidden precincts as the business of giving discreet shelter to unmarried mothers and pregnant whores, boarding out or even disposing of unwanted children, etc. And, through Moll's experience, Defoe seems to examine the altered nature of individual identity in a world where social roles can be manipulated artistically as a kind of theatrical performance, just as, increasingly, the habitual parts played in society can be redefined (bought or sold) in abstract monetary terms and have become commodity packages.[17] The frequent mention of specific prices and sums of money, credit, or tradable goods lends a realistic flavor to the theme that not beauty, love, or virtue counts, but only your financial means. After a certain distance into the book, it is no longer easy to distinguish her critique of her society from her rationalizations of her own conduct.

The earlier crises which Moll goes through in Part I constitute her education in the social typology of male and female roles. Moll perceives the attitudes of all whom she meets to be calibrated against the standard set by the comfortable bourgeoisie. With her liaisons and marriages, Moll progresses through a series of lessons as do the original *pícaros* with a series of masters, and it is from her delinquent's perspective that we see the drives, weaknesses, strengths, follies of various men, and the enormous scope of pretense and appearance in their lives, as well as in hers. According to the picaresque model of continual instability and moral erring, she has to recover after the loss or disappearance of each mate.

Although Moll becomes a firstrate actress in order to play the game well against the men and the society they rule, her own life reveals ironically that the principle of deception afflicts the consumate deceivers, too. Even nature seems to play confidence tricks. When she seeks a new life in Virginia, she discovers that her husband, the humane, likable plantation owner, is actually her own brother, and Defoe forces his readers to go through the agony of the choices faced by Moll. Back in England, Moll cannot bring herself to be hard enough toward her Lancashire husband who played a reciprocal confidence game on her in the equally mistaken hope of marrying into wealth. At the risk of spoiling her long-fought-for marriage to the clerk at the Bank of England, she intervenes to save the somewhat wild Lancashire gentleman from the charge of having committed robbery on the king's highway, because she feels real sympathy for him in his hapless parasitical state. Death and mischance can suddenly snatch away security, as when after a respite of five years she then loses the clerk whose financial solidity, which seemed like a bourgeois substitute for lost Eden, melts away and with it his will to live.

If, in Part I, the good husbands are like the elusive father she needs, she habitually calls "mother" the astute women, such as those in Bath and London, who give her pragmatic advice. Like her true mother whom she remeets in America and the *alter ego* nurse figure in romances, they always counsel self-interest. When young, Moll sells and resells herself to an available husband. She learns the hard way when old that if a poor woman refuses to be a servant, economic necessity will force her to theft or prostitution. Similarly, maternity is a travail or a tragedy, since the children must share the alienation of the mother, who is burdened by her surviving offspring or not infrequently must abandon them. Her natural feelings do not alter these harsh economic laws. Moll comes to realize she must rely on herself, and Defoe's deeper subject in Part II is her tenacious struggle for autonomy which ironically parodies the bourgeois attempt for salvation through effort. Since her second period in the colonies yields success and riches despite all obstacles, Defoe seems to be affirming a positive Protestant sense of individual worth, the ideal of renewal through a new kind of productive living away from the corrupt homeland. Her achievement is demonstrated in material terms, in contrast to the aristocratic Spanish ethos of a century earlier, and we easily recognize her natural superiority to her dependent Lancashire spouse.

Defoe appears to reshape the Catholic theme of the conversion of the rogue to fit the Puritan idea of election. He does not appear disturbed by the separation of economic behavior from religious sanctions when Moll "proves" herself through success; rather, he seems sympathetic toward the aspirations of the underclasses as something we should expect on the basis of natural law. However, the obvious ambiguity for modern readers is that Moll is *literally* "saved" by her proclaimed repentance experienced as an adult in Newgate. She has every reason to interpret deportation to America as a providential chance for rebirth, since a histrionic display of religious reform saves her from the gallows. After her conversion she shows no exceptional interest in religion and she never makes restitution of illgotten gains except as an investment in other castoffs transported to the New World. The application of the lessons she has learned brings prosperity and thereby a kind of respectability that substitutes for or enables piety.

Moll is aged 48 when, at the start of Part II, she compulsively slips into the riskiest acts of thievery, as if she is courting disaster and trying to provoke the world or God to take serious notice. But the loneliness of her existence in the criminal fringe of London also suggests a new capacity to participate in the metropolis as in a kind of theater, as if she is withdrawing even more from the immediate involvement in life characteristic of youth into a kingdom of the mind chacateristic of age. Her protean metamorphoses and disguises are remarkable. Moll's autonomy requires emotional detachment as an artist-voyeur, a refusal of commitment to any limited and limiting aspect of the passing scene. It is not a generic confusion on Defoe's part, but a new kind of complication he introduces, in portraying the traditional *pícara* who aspires to success not as a reprehensible sinner, but as if she is a vital person filled with the contradictions of a real personality. What is strange, however, is that Moll obsessively hides that personality and disowns any precise identity. Being a fraud and criminal finally allows her to present a safe, because practiced and false, face to the world. A major symbolic fact of the plotline is that the accidental release of her true name results in social disaster. Understandably, therefore, she makes privacy and concealment into the most important factors of her existence; and yet, this drive stands in glaring opposition to the act of "confession," which is what her memoires are all about.[18] One explanation may be that Defoe is exploring in *Moll Flanders*, as in *Robinson Crusoe*, the paradoxes and strangeness of extreme individualism, the ascendant values promoted by Renaissance Humanism and Protestantism, the puzzles of the autonomous self which eighteenth-century writers will scrutinize again and again.[19]

3. The Roguess in the Eighteenth and Nineteenth Centuries

Defoe's sentimentalization of the roguess in *Moll Flanders* harbingered an eventually far-reaching shift of attitudes. By closer attention to the mitigating social circumstances, some eighteenth-century authors relaxed the moral condemnation of female delinquents.[20] This gradual rehabilitation paralleled that enjoyed by the rogue and, as mentioned, appeared in France in the early seventeenth century in the novels of Sorel and Scarron. The eighteenth-century fondness for the female comic roles — for the lovely Columbine of the *commedia dell'arte*, for the pert serving-maids in Molière, Marivaux, Lessing, or Gozzi, for the sensible lower-middle-class types like Beaumarchais' Suzanne — no doubt helped broaden acceptance for criminal or tainted antiheroines, too. The subsidence of notable portrayals of the passions and transgressions of aristocratc women, such as those by Shakespeare, Corneille, Racine, and Lohenstein, left a gap that tended to be filled from below in an age of intensifying bourgeois rejection of despotism, the courtly world, and the "excesses" of late-Renaissance literature by and large. What occurred might be described as a gradual approximation toward the middle. Although eighteenth-century writers were depicting at least three socially distinct types of female criminals — the (sometimes "virtuous") protitute, the libertine, and the political *Machtweib* — these portrayals could overlap.

More obviously picaresque, despite the lack of any *converso* taint, is the antiheroine of the Abbé Prévost's *La véritable Histoire du Chevalier des Grieux et de Manon Lescaut* (1731). A new-style *femme fatale* from the lower orders of society, Manon captivates the morally weak nobleman and repeatedly drags him down into degradation and crime. Finally, having been transported as a felon to Louisiana, where Des Grieux follows her, Manon dies exhausted but purified by her sufferings. Whereas Defoe's Moll gets a practical fresh start in the New World in her quest for security and respectability, Prévost's Manon experiences the new sentimental equivalent of the delinquent's conversion. What Mary Magdalene was to the Baroque, the ultimately virtuous prostitute Manon becomes to the eighteenth century. She graduates into the sacrosanct equality of the martyrs of feeling. In an age which will challenge authority and hierarchy in the name of nature, both Manon and the fallen Des Grieux are among the tragic representatives of a "natural" aristocracy. It is clear that Prévost is spokesman for an ambivalent cause and situation. He reveals, especially through Des Grieux' lucid self-examinations, the pervasive corruption of the times. Yet Des Grieux explicitly champions the revolutionary idea of immediate earthly happiness against remote religious hope, overturning the restraints of the family, society, and morality and suffering the consequences.

In contrast, in Richardson's *Clarissa Harlowe* (1747-48), the title heroine, violated by the impulsive libertine Lovelace, meticulously resists all familial, societal, and natural pressures in order to maintain her own extreme moral position. In effect, by her refusal to compromise and marry the chastened, worshipful Lovelace, she forces him to follow her into the afterlife when she dies in the odor of sentimental sanctity. The most radical travesty on such moral heroines, epitomized in the works of Richardson, is made by the Marquis de Sade in the paired novels *La Nouvelle Justine, ou les Malheurs de la vertu* and *L'Histoire de Juliette, ou les Prospérités du vice* (1797). Even the names of the sisters in these books of picaresque pornography are probably meant as an ironic inversion, the first echoing that of the roguess Justine as well as Jean Jacques Rousseau's *La Nouvelle Héloïse*, the second calling to mind Shakespeare's tender Juliet. In any case, Justine is a parodic Clarissa who is ceaselessly punished, brutalized, and humiliated for her unreasonable refusal to cease being a victim and to join the libertine exploiters and desecraters. Diametrically opposite, Juliette learns the perversely rational, wholly unsentimental lesson of power from the criminals who wreak their will as an anti-society within the corrupt mendacious nations of Europe and she thrives as a greedy sexual terrorist. In the series of atrocities which constitute the Sadean narratives, we meet a host of other vicious women rebels such as the brigand chieftainess La Dubois, the ferocious lesbian Lady Clairwil, the calculating murderess Durand, the Princess Borghese, the Abbess Delbene, etc. Daughters of a rich Paris banker being educated at a fashionable convent, Justine and Juliette are precipitated into harsh reality and the effective status of the *picara* by the deaths of their suddenly bankrupted parents.[21] It is fundamental to Sade's black humor and his metaphysics and pathology of pleasure that Justine is forced continuously to experience the sexuality and absolute evil she denies, while Juliette, driven to assert the meaning of atheism and seeing the world from the monster's point of view, must obsessively war against the limits of nature and the social norms she rejects. Sade's thesis that genuine atheism entails absolute immorality goes right to the heart of the problem of radical individualism and the threat of alienation in the late eighteenth century. Virgil Nemoianu sees the writings of Sade as part of high Romanticism in France, as a visionary exploration of the autonomy of the self and the enactment of individual will.[22]

The grand alliance of the libertines in the Sadeian "Société des Amis du Crime" expands with lavish theatricality on the idea of a libertine subversion of normal society, a subject already treated in Pierre Choderlos de Laclos' *Les Liaisons dangereuses* (1782), where the threat is posed by a brilliant couple as the secret nucleus. Laclos' central figures are the aristocratic seducer Valmont and his criminal inspirer Madame de Merteuil who lucidly and cynically compare their illicit exploits and exchange views on the vulnerability of others and techniques for victimizing them. The epistolary novel serves to reveal how illusory is our notion of sharing language as a social instrument for intersubjective communication, when, in fact, Machiavellian seducers can analyze our personal style and manipulate codes of expression with ruthless logic.

In the slightly earlier novel *Jacques le Fataliste et son maître* (written in the 1770s, published in 1796), Denis Diderot has a fictive authorial persona "Moi" explicitly involve the "Reader" not only in the debate between freedom and determinism, but also in the problematics of interpreting the motives of participants in a society torn between the rival sentimental and libertine codes. We are invited to eavesdrop on the story of Madame de la Pommeraye and the Marquis des Arcis (Part 3), as the landlady at the inn recounts it in extensive detail to Jacques and his master — the internal audience constituting a miniature society which, among other things, embodies evident picaresque traits —, and we hear their reactions as the tale unfolds. This theater in theater, or fiction in fiction, induces us to venture a simple step of the imagination and to posit that we, too, could be *in* such a script, at one moment expressing ourselves as "subjects" or judging the open or hidden thoughts and behavior of others, and at another moment, being observed and assessed as analyzable "objects." The interpolation of the landlady's story about persons who fabricate stories within actual life for ulterior motives dizzyingly potentializes the ontological and hermeneutic mysteries of subjectivity for us.[23]

Having endangered her impeccable reputation in order to win the

271

libertine Marquis, La Pommeraye is infuriated at attaining at best only the sterile kind of relationship that Valmont and Merteuil develop in Laclos' novel. She seeks revenge with the adamantine determination of a Clarissa and the wicked cunning of a Juliette through an elaborate strategm to trick the Marquis into marrying a beautiful whore whom she sets up as a paragon of virtue and grace, a target worthy of his deceiving attentions. But the scheme backfires when the Marquis grows to love sincerely and even forgives La Pommeraye's unmasked hired agent who is manifestly a latter-day, tender-hearted *pícara*. In an ironic turn, both the former libertine and the desperate prostitute want to be good and reaffirm the basic instuitution of marriage, while La Pommeraye's doubly deceptive theater yields unexpected existential salvation for grievous sinners, and the bitter manipulator is condemned to the rationalist hell of isolation in herself.

This is certainly a new twist in the favorite older storyline of a strong prideful woman who attempts to manipulate, or disappointed, avenges herself on, a sometimes inherently weaker man. The attractive variety of such aristocratic adventuresses appears in Lessing's play *Emilia Galotti* in the jilted Countess Orsina who in Act IV fires the title heroine's father Odoardo up to the sticking point and provides the tragic dagger which he will use in Act V to rescue Emilia's honor rather than, as Orsina intended, dispatch the corrupt prince. Orsina descends from the passionate Baroque anti-heroines and has the operatic glamour we associate with the Queen of the Night in Mozart's *Zauberflöte*. In Schiller's *Don Carlos* (1787), this ancestry still peeks out from the sentimentalized role of the courtesan, the Princess of Eboli, the king's mistress. Through her grave miscalculation in seeking to revenge misprized love, she precipitates the doom of the prince and the innocent queen. Though springing from her own criminal conduct, the dire reversal of Eboli's fortune nonetheless wins her a place among the tragic victims. The fascinating schemer Adelheid von Walldorf in the Storm-and-Stress history play *Götz von Berlichingen* (1773) has the vaulting ambition, without the remorse, of a Lady Macbeth. Goethe daringly portrays her seduction and murder of both the knight Weislingen and his retainer Franz, when she raises her sights to the newly crowned young emperor Charles, and only the secret tribunal (Vehmgericht) can stop her. In opportunistically ignoring class boundaries, the unsentimental, political *Machtweib* Adelheid combines the deadly rationalism of the libertine and the sexual waywardness of the *pícara*.

These types persist in nineteenth-century literature, but also undergo important modifications and replacements. As her rival statue memorializes, the essentially innocent whore Violette represents the nonviable alternate pathway of nature, the lost paradise, and the "son's" incestuous relation toward the "mother" in Clemens Brentano's *Godwi, oder das steinerne Bild der Mutter* (1801-2). The libertine women (e.g., the free-thought, free-love advocates Molly and Countess G.) of Brentano's influential novel are reincarnated in Eichendorff's *Ahnung und Gegenwart* (1815) as the brilliant, flamboyant, dissolute "green huntress" Countess Romana, whose moral rebellion ends in suicide. Romana's story allegorizes the attraction to our origins and the attendant threat of alienation. For Eichendorff, rejection of Christianity and a dark hankering for submerged paganism are the historical-developmental parallel to psychological regression into the infantile and cultural descent into a lower state of nature. Out of these Romantic problematics, and the lure of the exotic and archaic, Prosper Mérimée distilled his novella *Carmen* (1845) which, through Georges Bizet's opera version (1852), would provide Modernist authors (e.g., Nietzsche, Joyce, Mann) with a stereotypic reference for the "life-force" or "will." Even the epigonal recapitulation of this figure in Wedekind's plays *Erdgeist* (1893) and *Die Büchse der Pandora* (1902) — woman as elemental, amoral, instinctive as against everything cerebral, artificial, and conventional in modern society — has entered the opera repertory through Berg's *Lulu* (1928-35).

The glory and cruelty of life is usually the common theme linking otherwise divergent approaches to the female delinquent in post-Romantic literature. William Thackeray's novel *Vanity Fair* (1847-48) achieves one of the last complex characterizations of the roguess in Becky Sharp, the clever, unscrupulous, and plucky daughter of a penniless artist and a French opera dancer. Despite the obvious damages to morality in winning her way into high society in Paris and London, she commands reader sympathies for her vitality.

Gustave Flaubert divides the lowerclass adventuresses into two basic types in *L'Éducation sentimentale* (1869). Rosanette represents the more generous and resilient proletarian woman of pleasure to whom there cling faded vestiges of the Renaissance and Rococo courtesan, whereas social rage and desperation take on a vampiristic cast in La Vatnaz, a vicious petit-bourgeois schemer, embittered radical, and intellectual hanger-on. Emile Zola's anti-heroine in *Nana* (1882) is a tyrannical Rosanette who wields her power as heedlessly as a Carmen.

The already rooted Gallic penchant for strong women may in good part explain the vogue of the Austrian novelist Leopold von Sacher-Masoch in France in the last quarter of the nineteenth century, but he also came on scene opportunely with the rise of the Decadents and Symbolists. In contrast to social deviants of the older picaresque milieux, we must distinguish the domineering, torture-inflicting Slavic women in Masochian tales as genuine cult figures, and not a few are explicitly depicted as queen-priestesses ruling over worshippers of the great mother in exotic enclaves within the Christian world. Auguste Villiers de l'Isle-Adam's Sara in the Decadent-Symbolist play *Axel* (1890), who rejects the monastic veil with contemptuous violence, only to join the equally rebellious hero in disdaining life's riches as incommensurate with their own sublimity, is one of the last major aristocratic female criminals who make their own law on aesthetic grounds.

Guy de Maupassant's novel *Bel-Ami* (1885) takes the harsher Naturalist view of the pervasive corruption of the Third Republic and rampant social climbing by aggressive and criminal underlings, the inheritors of the demoralized France after the critical turning-point of 1848 which Flaubert analyzed in *L'Education sentimentale*. Two kinds of women stand out, and win our grudging admiration or even our respect, for their capacity to survive under the double standard and against all the double dealing. Madame de Marelle is the shrewd, amoral aristocratic bohemian who never allows ordinary human feelings to disrupt her secret life of pleasure. Madeleine Forestier is the upward bound, resilient writer who has learned to work indirectly through the masculine power apparatus and to take calculated risks. It is clear that women who obey the dictates of religion, society, or feeling are victims or dupes in the modern world and that only carefully plotted crime pays. An alternate kind of liberation through a career that brings special fringe status is often depicted in the social novels of Realism. For example, in *Effi Briest* (1894), Fontane shows the possibility of redemption through art in the case of La Trippelli, who has shed her identity as the provincial Prussian named Trippell, and in contrast to Effi, rules deep emotion out of her disciplined theatrical existence. La Trippelli lives, in effect, a perpetual, but sanctioned picaresque existence, patronized by wealthy men and travelling about Europe for concerts.

Although the moral emphases might change, on a formalistic plane it was the performance of a series of illicit acts or clever tricks by a conscious outsider which gave generic consistency to the picaresque tale. Once her delinquent activities were absorbed into other narrative structures in the nineteenth-century — e.g., Naturalist examinations of the unsavory corners of contemporary life, detective stories, the social novel, etc. — the roguess tended to disappear as an independently significant figure in literature, although she lingered in the modern drama — e.g., as Mutter Wolfen in Hauptmann's thieves' comedy, *Der Biberpelz* (1893), and in Brecht's epic play of the Thirty Years' War, *Mutter Courage* (1941). But the principal abode of the roguess appears now to be in trivial literature: in the crime stories of the scheming climber epitomized already by Mary E. Braddon's Victorian novel *Lady Audley's Secret* (1862), and in historical romances epitomized by the twentieth-century American bestseller, *Forever Amber*, not to mention soap operas like *Dallas*.

The low ebb in the fortunes of the *pícara* tempts to speculation. Did Romantic glorification of the artist legitimate that important component in the more interesting freebooting adventuresses and displace the center of interest from crime to creativity — as we see, for example, in the justified self-assertion of the passionate La Tosca in Puccini's opera? Has the modern liberal-democatic world, by satisfying the material wants of the masses, yet steeping itself in antiheroic *ressentiment*, unlearned its older interest in the swashbuckling *pícara* who is out for success, because nowadays we encounter the sisters of La Vatnaz everywhere? Has our fascination for the female delinquent been replaced by a dull suspicion that out on the streets and in the hustings, under some universal curse of pathological crime, a female as well as male variety of nihilistic rage is seething, as Flaubert suggested? Or is our sense of a moral nadir and empty epigonal amusement over shady ladies the lull before some surprising release of redemptive aspirations? Byron already summarized in *Don Juan*, and G.B. Shaw has echoed the suggestion in *Man and Superman* (1903), that the scofflaw rake would now, after centuries of sinning, really like to escape from his own myth and join Mozart in heaven. Perhaps Defoe and Diderot will yet prove to have been prescient when, in the eighteenth century, they suggested that as an ultimate transformation the roguess, too, might finally want to be good.

Notes

* "Transformations of the Female Delinquent in Fiction" first appeared in German under the title "Pikara und Schelmin," in *Der deutsche Schelmenroman im europäischen Kontext: Rezeption, Interpretation, Bibliographie*, ed. by Gerhart Hoffmeister (Amsterdam, 1986). The present version is based on a paper which I originally prepared in English and presented at the University of Pennsylvania and at Peking University in 1985. The female delinquent was incorporated in several wider treatments of picaresque literature which I presented to the Third Annual Conference on Comparative Literature at the University of Minnesota, Minneapolis in 1975, for the Committee for the Arts at the University of California, Berkeley, and at the University of Pisa, Italy, in 1976.

1   Alexander A. Parker, *Literature and the Delinquent: The Picaresque Novel in Spain and Europe, 1599-1753* (Edinburgh, 1977), Preface.
2   Northrop Frye, *Anatomy of Criticism* (rpt. New York, 1969), defines "the clever, likeable, unprincipled *pícaro* of the picaresque novel" as a variety of sophisticated "low mimetic comedy" (p. 45), above which "high mimetic tragedy" occupies a "central position [...] balanced midway between godlike heroism and all-too-human irony" (p. 37).
3   The case for regarding Lazarillo only as a prototype, and Guzmán as the first authentic, complex *pícaro*, is put most forcefully from a Catholic humanist perspective by Parker in *Literature and the Delinquent*, chs. 1, "The Genesis of the Picaresque," and 2, "The Delinquent Emerges." Since Parker, the best comparative study covering, as Parker does, both male and female delinquents in Spain, France, Germany, and Britain, is Richard

Bjornson, *The Picaresque Hero in European Fiction* (Madison, 1977). One of the most helpful discriminations of the generic structures and history is the essay "Toward a Definition of the Picaresque" by Claudio Guillén, *Literature as System: Essays toward the Theory of Literary History* (Princeton, 1971), pp. 71-106; Guillén stresses outsider status, rather than specific social taint as characteristic in the early works.

4 Guillén, *Literature as System*, p. 84: "The *pícaro* in his odyssey moves horizontally through space and vertically through society [...]."

5 Julio Rodríguez-Luis, "*Pícaras*: The Modal Approach to the Picaresque," *Comparative Literature*, 31 (1979), 32-46.

6 Horst S. and Ingrid Daemmrich, *Wiederholte Spiegelungen: Themen und Motive in der Literatur* (Berne and Munich, 1978), in ch. 9, "Lebenskunst — Situationsanpassung."

7 Cf. Harry Sieber, "Apostrophes in the *Buscón*: An Approach to Quevedo's Narrative Technique," *MLN*, 83 (1968), 178-211.

8 Florence M. Weinberg, "Aspects of Symbolism in *La Celestina*," *MLN*, 86 (1971), pp. 136-153.

9 Cf. the mythological spectrum detected by Weinberg, "Aspects of Symbolism"; Celestina's implicit counterpart is the devil (p. 147). Annis Pratt et al. elaborate "Jungian" feminist categories in *Archetypal Patterns in Women's Fiction* (Bloomington, 1981). Although they do not consider the tradition of the *pícara*, they "see a relationship between the rise of women's fiction in the last several centuries and three interrelated repositories of archetypal materials: the Demeter/Kore and Ishtar/Tammuz rebirth narratives, the grail legends of the later Middle Ages, and the cluster of archetypal and ritual materials constituting the Craft of the Wise, or witchcraft"; their first (double) set and last set are more suggestive as factors in picaresque fiction.

10 I have treated this ground-figure in my essay "Erring and Wayfaring in Baroque Fiction: The World as Labyrinth and Garden," *Revue de Littérature Comparée*, 58 (1984), 277-299.

11 In his study *Pícaros y Picaresca: "La Pícara Justina"* (Madrid, 1969), Marcel Bataillon treats Úbeda's novel as evidencing "la parodia triunfante en la llamada 'época barroca' [...] un proceso de deformación y acabamiento de la herencia del Renacimiento" (p. 51).

12 In ch. 2, "The Soul's Dark Journey," of *The Myth of the Pícaro: Continuity and Transformation of the Picaresque Novel, 1554-1954* (Chapel Hill, 1979), Alexander Blackburn reviews the evolution of the debate and elaborates the psychological-existentialist grounds for a severe negative critique of the moral vision not only of the anonymous author of the *Lazarillo*, and even more so of Alemán and Quevedo, as failed.

13 On the distinctions between "decadent" Iberian and "serious" late picaresque fiction, see my article "Estebanillo and Simplex: Two Baroque Views of the Role-Playing Rogue in War, Crime, and Art (with an Excursus on Krull's Forebears)," *Canadian Review of Comparative Literature*, 9 (1982), 157-171.

14 E.g., on the effect of different social attitudes widespread in the readership north of the Pyrenees, see Bjornson, *The Picaresque Hero*, pp. 154 ff.
15 Cf. the findings of Pablo Javier Ronquillo, *Retrato de la pícara: La protagonista de la picaresca española del XVII* (Madrid, 1980).
16 Parker, *Literature and the Delinquent*, ch. 4: "Germany and the Thiry-Years War."
17 Cf. the section, "*Moll Flanders*: A Portrait of the Artist as Play-Actor," in David Marshall, "From Readers to Spectators: Theatricality in Eighteenth-Century Narratives" (Diss. Johns Hopkins, 1979), pp. 271-311.
18 Guillén, *Literature as System*, p. 92, connects the more general "distrust of all externals" and "exercise of dissimulation" in the Renaissance with the more specific case of the picaresque antihero as "a lonely spirit, or a dissembler, or a hypocrite."
19 I treat generic resemblances and changes between *Simplicissimus* and *Robinson Crusoe*, in the article, "Erring and Wayfaring in Baroque Fiction."
20 Symptomatic of completed passage to the social novel is the sympathetic treatment of a single woman of low station struggling for social and economic independence, e.g., in Fanny Burney's *The Wanderer, or Female Difficulties* (1814). The heroine Incognita is deemed "a female Robinson Crusoe" and her serial trials and struggles through five volumes are expressly related to the developmental theme of erring. In effect, despite all the indignities she suffers, Incognita dons the educational mantle previously worn by women of a higher social order in the sentimental *Bildungsroman* of the Enlightenment, e.g., in Christian F. Gellert's *Das Leben der schwedischen Gräfin von G.* (1746).
21 As Guillen, *Literature as System*, pp. 79 ff., points out, with the *Lazarillo*, we have "the first significant appearance of the myth of the orphan" that in some form or other lasts at least through the first two centuries of picaresque fiction. I believe that Sade exploits the picaresque theme of orphanhood to underscore the discovery that, because God is dead, parents too are dead as an institution with genuine social authority. The parallel during the French Revolution was that the king and queen, as national father and mother, were executed to make way for "liberty, fraternity, equality." While we can regard the acceptance of that drastic step as evidence of an Oedipal revenge by the long-suffering, still largely religious populace, it happens to coincide with the logic of the radical atheist viewpoint about authority. Sade can revel in orphanhood, since it is in fact tantamount to liberation of the subject (in both senses of the word).
22 Virgil Nemoianu, *The Taming of Romanticism: European Literature and the Age of Biedermeier* (Cambridge, Mass., and London, 1984), pp. 108-111.
23 On the linkage of varieties of "confessional" narration with the themes of marginality, outcast status, and the perils and wonders of subjectivity see my article, "Disembodied Voice, Disinherited Mind: Development in Pre-Romantic and Romantic Fiction," in *Proceedings of the Eighth Congress of ICLA* (Stuttgart, 1980), vol. I, pp. 479-486.

11. ESTEBANILLO AND SIMPLEX: TWO BAROQUE VIEWS OF THE ROLE-PLAYING ROGUE IN WAR, CRIME, AND ART (WITH AN EXCURSUS ON KRULL'S FOREBEARS)

No one has yet convincingly identified the protagonist who claims to be writing not just another picaresque fiction, but genuine autobiography in *La vida y hechos de Estebanillo González, hombre de buen humor*,[1] which first appeared in Antwerp, capital of the Spanish Lowlands, in 1646. Hans Jacob Christoffel von Grimmelshausen, the real-life experiencer behind the Cervantine masks swathing the first-person delinquent of *Der abenteuerliche Simplicissimus Teutsch*,[2] was identified only two centuries after the initial appearance of his novel at Mömpelgart in 1668. Scholarship has verified most of the historical background – geography, chronology, battles, major personages – in both works. In fact, one wonders whether during his camp-following and antics across Italy, Spain, France, the Lowlands, Germany, Austria, Poland, Russia, and elsewhere, the self-styled centaur, half Gallegan, half Roman, who is conscious of living to outstrip the extant picaresque masterworks, might have rubbed shoulders with the ubiquitous autodidact adventurer Grimmelshausen. Whether or not the still unverified Iberian and now known German witness to the disorders and calamities of the Thirty Years' War ever drank at the same inn or stood in opposing armies (e.g., at the battle of Nördlingen in September 1634), both fictions depict how a desperate underling finds his way as a professional fool in a mad world. But the difference is that, although Simplex engages in worse crimes, he rises to a loftier view of the folly of the age, transcending the role Estebanillo keeps, and reaffirming his destiny as the Christian fool.[3] Grimmelshausen succeeds in wedding this theme, a favorite in German literature since the reappearance of Wolfram's *Parzival* in print (1477), Sebastian Brant's *Narrenschiff* (1494), and Erasmus' *Encomium Moriae* (1509), with the theme of conversion from the mature Spanish picaresque genre.

Simplex' tale begins when war disrupts his boyhood in a peasant village and he flees to a brief refuge in the woods with a hermit, but then is drawn again into the tumult of the contending native and foreign armies and enters the Protestant encampment at Hanau, commanded by (the historical) James Ramsay, the Scotch colonel in the Swedish army, whom Grimmelshausen makes into the hero's as yet undisclosed uncle, the hermit's brother-in-law, for romanesque purposes. Simplex suffers abasement, being forced into the role of camp fool; gradually he learns deception, greed, and vanity; he pushes into the fighting ranks, furthers his ambition as an intrepid bandit, switches sides when fortune dictates, is carried across the face of Europe by turns of events, as well as explores all sectors of society. Estebanillo, an urban nobody driven by the standard craving for social status, not only gravitates toward the power network of the Empire, serving with the most cynical Falstaffian valor in moments of danger, but also eventually carries out high-level missions as an imperial courier. The novel about Simplex exhibits the grand architectonics of the Baroque world theater; its original five books suggest five acts in a drama of inversely mirrored worldly and spiritual progress. The added sixth book ('Continuatio'), in which the purported author dies in an even more remote hermitage on a desert island after having been lured back into motion, reexamines the fundamental paradigm of worldly inconstancy versus spiritual security. Simplex' misguided picaresque quest for status is transmuted in the ultimate confirmation of his higher birth, a resolution borrowed from older romances.[4] When, like his true father, he takes refuge in hermitage in Book V, Simplex' farewell to the world — lifted from the Spanish moralist Guevara — asserts the principle of salvation, the need for redemption expounded by Mateo Alemán in *Guzmán de Alfarache* (1599).[5]

In contrast, Estebanillo's clinging to the fringes of exalted circles brings no qualitative end to the serial repetition of his escapades. After various scrapes and adventures in southern Europe, even facing the Turks at sea, he gets caught up in the war in Germany. Like Courasche later, he becomes a provisioner off and on and also in other ways turns a quick profit riding the tide of universal madness. What is more striking is how he becomes the Imperial Fool, jester to such greats as the army commander Ottavio Piccolomini and Prince-

Cardinal Don Fernando, Philipp IV's brother, Governor of the Low Countries, thus bringing us into contact with the supreme tier of leaders from an underling's angle. Estebanillo's lucrative drunken fits and his terror during a theatrical menace of castration, perpetrated against him for amusement, strangely captures the nightmarish currents of the age. Like Perkeo, the later celebrated fool of Heidelberg, Estebanillo develops his vice of drunken clownery into a business and, not surprisingly, as his novel closes, he faces inexorable collapse. Hospitalized as a drunkard, he needs more desperately than ever the safe, soft niche he has sought to earn as buffoon to overlords. In a lowlife travesty of the abdication of the exhausted Emperor Charles V and his withdrawal into monastic peace, Estebanillo claims he is orphaned by the departure of so many regal personages from the scene and pleads to retire to a modest gambling casino in Naples. Whereas Simplex reverses the ending of the novel *Lazarillo de Tormes* (1555), in which after trying out the role of ecclesiastical servant as a con game, Lazarillo opts for a *marriage à trois* under the patronage of the archpriest, Estebanillo affirms the Lazarillian principle of the pension: social security, not salvation.

The opening paragraphs of *Simplicissimus* wittily contrast the inflated glory of princely origins like those in a romance with the banal reality of the country folk. In chapter 2, a brilliant parade of classic and poetic references maintains the ironic tension already inherent in the narrating voice of Simplex. On one level, he is a protagonist acting as if before our eyes; on another, he is the mature witness recollecting the pathway and commenting morally as in the Spanish genre. Although our attention may be riveted on the sudden ravaging of his village, the narrator, from the very first sentence on, tacitly informs us he has meanwhile acquired impressive learning. Beginning with *Lazarillo de Tormes*, the arrival at the role of writer is inherent in the social anxiety and self-consciousness of the speaking 'I' of the delinquent. But in *Simplicissimus*, we are constantly reminded of the fact that Simplex is an autodidact and author of considerable parts. Evidence of the literary prowess of Estebanillo is thrust upon us even before the main text of the novel. In a foreword, Estebanillo compares the twists and turns of his life to the labyrinth of Crete; in a second prologue in verse, he shows off his acquaintance with languages and names some eighty roles he played high and low. There is no mistaking he hopes to seize the attention of courtiers and rulers with his pyrotechnic punning, argot, Latin tags, Biblical and literary allusions, elegant vocabulary and colloquialisms colorfully commingled. Whereas Simplex has complex visions of the epochal criminality, Estebanillo remains heartless to the finish so that his quipping descriptions of barbarity acquire an hallucinatory character. Critics as diverse as Parker, Spadaccini, and Bjornson agree that Estebanillo epitomizes moral corruption and social degradation, a repugnant anomie that results from institutionalized degradation. It is not merely the lack of serious thought about moral, religious, and social issues that chills our blood, but the virtually total repression of feeling by the Imperial Fool and his dedication of this record of abasement to the highest élite.

Estebanillo's artist father, a painter and gambler, has transmitted to all his sons, like original sin, the familiar picaresque malady, "que fue ser hijodalgo, que es lo mismo que ser poeta; pues son pocos los que se escapan de una pobreza eterna o de una hambre perdurable" (I, 149). Because being a poet is equated with being a gentleman, art provides the opportunity to rise from proletarian depths. And so, besides instruction in roguery and inevitable entry into a more mundane apprenticeship to gain a living, Estebanillo is encouraged to educate himself, and somewhere along the way he has mastered the poetic idiom of Spain, for he is tireless in composing verses of praise, witty petitions, or amusements for the great. Quite in passing in chapter 10, we find out that it was only by virtue of knowing Latin that he could converse at the court in Poland. But the most bizarre feat accomplished by the aging rogue is his victory in the poetry contest in chapter 12. As so often, it all starts as a joke. Inspecting the forest of competing entries, Estebanillo realizes that they consist more of Greek prose than of Spanish verse. A student, asked about these "Hebrew or Chaldean mysteries," despairs of explaining them to him, "porque lo que de presente anadaba válido era el gongorizar con elegancia campanuda, de modo que pareciese mucho lo que no era nada y que no lo entendiese el autor que lo hiciese ni los curiosos que lo leyesen" (II, 472f). This critique accepted at face value by Estebanillo is framed, according to the point of view of the harsh "realist" writers of picaresque novels, as a description of Spanish culture toward the climactic breaking point of the Thirty Years' War. The elegant shell is hollowed out within; all parties strain to understand the highflown terms which no longer mean anything. Having watched a chum unpack flour, Estebanillo accepts the challenge to do something very recondite in the manner of Juan de la Encina and, over some wine, produces a hyperbolic and obscure sonnet that outstrips all established pomposity.

Estebanillo's flamboyance mocks that of Spanish letters, and when the academic judges proclaim him a "second Góngora," their tribute is a dubious honor. Instantly twenty different explications of his poem are ventured; he is celebrated because he is not understood. No wonder he leaves the "troupe of a thousand cultivated versifiers" for the more honest of mercenaries who at least know that bread — the subject of his recondite eloquence — is the core theme of all stunts and songs of the rogues tramping the king's highway. As merely one instance, the thrust of Estebanillo's travesty of Góngorism reinforces that of his whole book: the plea for bread. As the foreword claims, this is not merchandise for the market, but a gift to "princes and lords and persons of merit" to prompt their reciprocal support. Self-styled as "flor de la jacarandaina" in sentence one, Estebanillo lures us with generic bait; and he doubles the fiction by swearing in sentence two, "que no es la fingida de Guzmán de Alfarache, ni la fabulosa de Lazarillo de Tormes, ni la supuesta del Caballero de la Tenaza, sino una relación verdadera con parte presente y testigos de vista y contestes, que los nombro a todos para averiguación y prueba de mis sucesos, y el dónde, cómo y cuándo, sin carecer de otra cosa que de día, mes y año, y antes quito que no añado" (I, 133f.) However, in artistic terms, this fiction of "true" history, in contrast to the picaresque novels in vogue, actually results from Estebanillo structuring his existence by overt or tacit generic reference. He is as much captive to the conventions of roguery as Quixote is to the spirit and deeds of Amadis and other heroes of romance. He appeals to a contemporary audience who are presumed to understand the generic rules and appreciate his efforts to outstrip the existing models. Estebanillo exemplifies the national addiction to the literary drug — not a cure for the deep ills it palliates. His book exudes a manneristic decadence when the genre turns back upon itself self-hypnotically.

Simplex' multifaceted life has been so thoroughly analyzed by recent scholarship, and deservedly so, that I can concentrate here on a couple of salient distinctions.[6] It is clear that Simplex educates himself further under the tutelage of the Protestant pastors, of Herzbruder, and so forth, but also through assiduous reading to which there are numerous allusions. By the time Simplex, as the bold Huntsman, secretly plunders and capitvates the imagination of the region of Soest, he is *already* a published author and rather proud of his writings. However, no matter what he may yet derive from European literature, the deepest core of teaching remains the hermit's woodland school in the early chapters of Book I. The key composition in the novel *Simplicissimus* is thus the nightingale hymn which the hermit intones at midnight to ward off evil. It makes explicit thematically what has occurred in the innocent sounds of the shepherd's pipes in chapter 1: that the paramount function of art is to keep the spirit wakeful through the gloom of existence, to fend off the wolf, emblem of spiritual threat. At the pinnacle of worldly success in Book IV, Simplex moves through an exemplary labyrinth, the metropolis of Paris. He is soon a stage idol, known as the Beau Alman, who masterfully sings, in a foreign language he doesn't understand, words which make the ladies of the capital thrill. As the title of chapter 4 states, Simplex is inevitably drawn into the Venus-Berg, the secret edifice of big-city sin, to serve a lady of such august rank that it would be fatal for him to glimpse her face. When he eventually sneaks out of Paris with (so he first believes) a case of syphilis in token of subjection to Venus, his 'illease' over Parisian ways is unmistakable. It turns out that he has actually contracted mere chicken pox, and he later regards this children's disease as a secret instance of grace through chastisement, a reminder of innocent simplicity; the immediate irony, that the great lover is thus disfigured, is scarcely lost on the reader.

The stage triumph of Simplex savors of that strange ambivalence so characteristic of high moments in the novel. M.E. Schmid has convincingly identified the 1647 Paris production of Rossi and Buti's *Orfeo* reported in the *Gazette de France,* as the probable main source, among the plethora of Orpheus dramas and operas, for Grimmelshausen's invented literary episode experienced by Simplex from the perspective of chief performer.[7] In the opera, having begged Venus' aid to win Eurydice, whom death quickly claims, and having penetrated to Pluto and Proserpina in Hell, rewinning Eurydice only to lose her once more, Simplex commands the spectators with his dolor. Then the story takes a significant turn. Because Simplex-Orpheus forswears women in his grief, the Bacchantes strangle him and pitch him into the water. As any Jungian analyst would note, this is ambiguously the feminine element of the unconscious, also that of baptism. Beau Alman, his head alone sticking from a pit to be visible illusionistically on the surface but whom the operator of the stage dragon cannot locate to chew, is unable to restrain his smirking over the ridiculousness of the whole business. And the ladies of Paris take good note. Günther Weydt has shrewdly pointed out that, in converting the basic Adonis novella, then so popular in Europe, into this section of the novel, Grimmelshausen still retained and even sharpened the Venus allusions despite the shift from Adonis to Beau Alman for the male figure.[8] An important aspect of the expansion and deepening that occurs is the achievement of a Baroque perspectivism, a multifaceted referentiality in the novel equivalent to that familiar from complex Baroque dramas. For example, when Beau Alman, who will penetrate to the secret quarters of imperious women and participate in the underground rites of Paris (Venus-Berg) in an episode that shadows the widely read Adonis tale, is playing Orpheus and pleads for help to retrieve Eurydice, he prays to Venus. This montage technique of the layering and interconnecting of motifs produces a scenic conglomerate rife with ironizing about the nature, processes, and intentions of art. However, Weydt is interested principally in showing that the direct intermediary of the story materials for Grimmelshausen was not Bandello or a Romanic source, but his important contemporary, the Nürnberg writer Harsdörffer.

Otherwise Weydt might have gone beyond the casual suggestion that the opera and Venus-Berg episode in *Simplicissimus* seems to anticipate something of the tone of Thomas Mann's Esmeralda Hetaera thematics in *Doktor Faustus* and remarking on the scattered references to the former book in the latter. After having drawn a grim account of the evolution of German culture and of the sicknesses of modernism in his late work *Doktor Faustus*, during the composition of which he had been consulting Grimmelshausen, an author who had written satirically of an earlier collapse of decency and order, Mann sensed a profound craving to grasp meaningfulness in the bitterly compromised traits of the artist. Since the artist figure was linked, in his own mind, with the mythological complex of the hermetic, it should not be surprising that he would find correspondences and consolation in *Simplicissimus* in the long run, a book ostensibly narrated by a person who assumed a whole range of hermetic roles (thief, trickster, scribe, rhetorician, etc.), yet emerged spiritually 'saved' despite his encounters with demonic forces. Whether or not Grimmelshausen was hinting at an allegorical sense to the comic rituals in the Beau Alman passages, the elderly Thomas Mann doubtlessly took great interest in a number of hermetic patterns in the story of the survivor Simplex before and/or anew in *Felix Krull* — as the markings in his copy of the 1909 *Simplicissimus* edition reveal which can be dated roughly by age characteristics.[9] For instance, on finding, or rediscovering, that Simplex (i.e., Grimmelshausen, hidden behind elaborate authorial masks in the fashion of the *Quixote* and *Francion*) has just written a *Joseph* novel, Mann slashed a large exclamation point in the margin with uncharacteristic excitement. Of course, Mann expressly interpreted his own Joseph as a Hermes figure, but it would require a careful reexamination to determine whether Grimmelshausen was as clearly conscious of such a linkage with other manifest Hermes traits in *Simplicissimus*; nonetheless, the grounds for self-identification on the part of Mann are quite immediate. In addition, one of the alternate names for Grimmelshausen's hero, Simplex, possesses several qualities which Mann could associate with Felix: The names resemble each other phonemically through the similarity of their final syllable and ocularly through the crossover of vowels. Being bisyllabic, each can suggest the notion of the double, a direct implication in Grimmelshausen's novel ("duplex" and "duplicitas" as antipodes of "simplex" and "simplicitas"), as well as basic to Mann's thematics; both names are anchored metaphysically as positive states, and one can enable the other. The passage through the realm of earthly reality leads by role reversal or doubling in such a way for Simplex that, after being threatened with *duplicitas*, he comes full circle into a regained and heightened *simplicitas*. Whereas Mann conducts us toward, but not onto, the threshold where the youthful, lucky hero will, in formalistic analogy to the traditional *pícaros*, inevitably become disturbed, anxious, needing meaning – in short: ready to become a writer –, the person who has been setting down this confessional fiction and whose later perturbation of spirit is foreshadowed in the opening paragraph of the novel. The exemption, the "miracle" produced by the novel remaining a "fragment," is no accident: Mann never shows us the moment of reversal when Felix ("Infelix") would experience *infelicitas*.

Oskar Seidlin has shown that, in writing *Felix Krull*, Mann was continuously mindful of the picaresque tradition and of Cervantes.[10] When Felix is born by the banks of the Rhine to a family of dubious enterprise, there can be no question but that Mann offers, detail by detail, analogues for the start of the first Spanish rogue Lazarillo, by the river Tormes, the more obvious of many literary ancestors. In a subsequent study, Donald F. Nelson has demonstrated how thoroughly Mann informed his "satyrpiece" with symbolic meanings on the psychological and mythological levels as an exploration into his own identification with Hermes and the "archaic depths of the Jungian Collective Unconscious."[11] These appreciations of the *Bekenntnisse des Hochstaplers Felix Krull* are so instructive that I can point to them with the suggestion that we could add Grimmelshausen on both sides of the ledger; that is, we should evaluate Mann's response to *Simplicissimus* as an act of recognition not merely that the hermetic and picaresque were related, but that they had in fact been artistically joined by the seventeenth-century novelist. In the oft cited letter, dated February 18, 1941, in reaction to Kerényi's book *Das göttliche Kind*, Mann drew together the features of "hermetic" lack of unity of character and the picaresque in his own novels:

> Und den primitiven Mangel an 'Einheit der Person,' von dem Jung spricht, habe ich in den "Geschichten Jaakobs" ganz auf eigene Hand als humoristische Tatsache behandelt [...]. Die mythologische Figur, die mich jetzt notwen-

diger Weise mehr und mehr anzieht, und bei der ich wieder soviel Schönes in diesem Buche fand, ist der mondverbundene Hermes. Er spukte schon bisher da und dort durch die Joseph-Bücher; aber im letzten Bande, der den Helden als Staats-Geschäftsmann von reichlicher Durchtriebenheit zeigt, wechselt dieser aus der ursprünglichen Tammuz-Adonis-Rolle immer mehr in die eines Hermes hinüber. Seine Aktionen und Transaktionen sind moralisch-ästhetisch nicht gut anders zu vertreten, als im Sinne des göttlichen Schelmen-Romans.[12]

I would propose that the transformations of role undergone by Simplex cover many of the same mythological moments alluded to above by Mann and that, moreover, the containing framework of the *Simplicissimus* was the newer merged humoristic-picaresque manner of narration, one variety of which had appeared in the *Francion*.

Were we to take up once more the example which intrigued Weydt, the Beau Alman section, it would not be far-fetched to speculate that (regardless of Grimmelshausen's "conscious" purpose) Mann could have read the Venus-Berg happenings in *Simplicissimus* under Jungian tutelage and regarded the seventeenth-century book as a kind of pre-revelation. If so, Grimmelshausen would have confirmed and reinforced Mann in his own treatment of the story of the artist as a Hermes who interrelates with the Feminine, as a confederate of Venus, as the messenger who penetrates to the life-secret and survives bringing back his knowledge, even if in disguised symbolic form. According to Nelson, the closure of the novel *Felix Krull*, with Maria's exuberant cry 'Holé! Heho! Ahé!' should be read as a veiled reinactment of the ancient mysteries as the mercurial or hermetic mediator Krull passes from the daughter (Proserpina) to the mother (Demeter). "[...] in Senhora Kuckuck's embrace the end stage of transmutation is reached: the achievement of psychic wholeness through a union of the conscious and the unconscious."[13] Simplex' arrival in the bedchamber of the mysterious high and mighty masked lady would corroborate the occult sense of his penetration into the realm of death as Orpheus to resuscitate Eurydice; except, of course, that no modern rescue occurs by breaking off the story in the manner of *Felix Krull*. Grimmelshausen subtly manages to have things both ways in his own fashion. On the one hand, like Leverkühn in *Doktor Faustus*, Simplex retreats from the inner sanctum of the Feminine with a case of "venereal" disease; on the other, he wends his way toward "home" bearing the poxicratic scars of "childhood," after all.

Both *Estebanillo* and *Simplicissimus* contain such a plethora of allusions to the artist role that we can appreciate its problematical importance in these works quite without extrinsic evidence. Enjoying them naively, "as if" they were genuine autobiographies (which, of course, they are not), in no way excludes recognition of the ambivalent profile of their artist-narrators. Several scholarly hypotheses, however, can be adduced which, in trying to explain the unusual fusion of educative attainments and roguish career, lend support to the argument that each of the two seventeenth-century novelists was self-consciously using the comic tensions inherent in the apparent contradiction of high and low attributes. Marcel Bataillon has maintained that, in fact, two different personalities were amalgamated to create the strange conflict between Estebanillo's lowly and grotesque function as clown and his position of trust as diplomatic courier.[14] Certain realities of various far-removed power centers of Europe must, according to Bataillon, have been known to the actual author who, being directly connected with the Imperial headquarters in Brussels, wrote the chimerical biography not as a confession, but as entertainment for an in-group, in order to amuse and gain favor from his chief, the great generalissimo Piccolomini. Bataillon's candidate for the actual authorship is Captain Jerónimo de Bran, quartermaster to the Imperial forces, trusted agent of Piccolomini, acknowledged servant of the Emperor, lover of the arts, a Galician who was educated to write Italian, etc. From the existence of strikingly similar portraits of Estebanillo as rogue (for the novel) and of Bran as an elegant Imperial officer, both engraved by Lucas Vorsterman, Bataillon has ventured the conclusion that the frontispiece and many of the details of Estebanillo's missions were for the sake of mystification, hinting at the identity of the actual author. From the archival evidence of the existence of a Stefaniglio (the name is typical for a jester) in service to Piccolomini, it seems probable that such a person did exist whom the witty literatus Bran could have appropriated for an alter ego in his writings. If Bataillon's suggestive analysis is not totally wrong, it could be modified into the more sensational, but less probable hypothesis that Bran at some time assumed the disguise of a clown (perhaps an actual court fool) under the name Estebanillo. In any event, the lack of sarcastic verve toward the politically great and the ostentatious literariness of Estebanillo's approach to roguery would fit a personage who deliberately studied lowlife.[15]

But we know that assuming the point of view of a delinquent or fool constituted a major literary mode of the seventeenth century — not necessarily based on biographical reality. This factor is strikingly evident in the development of Grimmelshausen who, according to Manfred Koschlig, was deeply influenced by (the then still anonymous) Charles Sorel in the process of composing the *Simplicissimus* and thereafter in even greater measure.[16] Such connoisseurs of the seventeenth-century novel as Leibniz, who shared appreciation of *Simplicissimus* with the time's most sophisticated readers, regarded Sorel's *Francion* as a major achievement and model in Europe. Both the *Francion*, explicitly cited by Grimmelshausen (who had read the German edition of 1662), and the *Simplicissimus* are cast in the pseudo-confessional picaresque mode, but their wealth of disparate, often contradictory elements is unified by the constant sense that we are experiencing a fiction. Thus both have the stamp of real experiences, (auto-)biographical facts, and immediate historical context, while they succeed in bringing together high and low life by the fusion of diverse courtier roles and jester existence. A central preoccupation of the *Francoin* is with the behavior and mentality of a new European type, the self-proclaiming "artist," who frequently blends into the phantast and madman. The amusing aritifices and preposterous schemes and ambitions of this human type contribute to the larger goal of satirical exposure of social realities, as in the Jupiter episode of Book III of *Simplicissimus*. Grimmelshausen successfully combined the new style of fiction demonstrated by the *Francion* and other generic materials and impulses and he superimposed his own lived experiences on them.[17]

That is, *today* we know that a great many of the happenings in *Simplicissimus* feed on actual moments in the author's life, whereas much more derives demonstrably from his insatiable reading and powers of absorption as an autodidact. But this may mean that in a kind of modern naiveté we are pulling apart — and taking a different pleasure in dissecting — what was an accomplished fiction. Koschlig argues that, in terms of the seventeenth-century novel, Grimmelshausens's use of the *Francion* "manner" ("Manier") clearly signaled a new, highly appreciated approach in fiction, and that in his case the older Spanish picaresque models exercised a mainly indirect influence through this newer, more comprehensive approach. Key terms that recur throughout Grimmelshausen attest the relationship. The goal of "satirical" ("satyrisch") writing is "completeness" ("Vollkommenheit"), i.e., "truthfulness" ("Wahrhaftigkeit"), a modern disillusionistic verisimilitude that refuses to ignore the low, mean, deviant, ridiculous, criminal in human affairs; hence the reiterated rejection of the older chivalric, pastoral, etc., as mendacious and comic, because self-evidently preposterous. Whereas Sorel's aim is a complete illustration and survey unmasking his world, Grimmelshausen's religious orientation in *Simplicissimus* transmutes the social-critical amusement into an emblematic, symbol-laden tale. His later works then, according to Koschlig, loosen this religious tie and move toward a more utilitarian, rationalistic satire.

In Book V, Simplex penetrates beneath the Mummelsee on a fabulous voyage to the realm of the Sylphs, learning that all the waters are interconnected in the earth's depths and finding a utopian order to which that on the surface is a sorry contrast. It incorporates counterparts to all the races and nations of men. Demonstrating "vorwitzige Importunität," the intrepid explorer Simplex, in answer to the query of the Sylph King, lies about the behavior of the various classes of humanity; his glowing report is a sardonic topsey-turveyness reciprocal to the one he has just been privileged to discover. "[...] ich sehe wohl," says the King, "daß du ziemlich kurios bist" (p. 445). The double meaning of "kurios" is especially appropriate for the particular hermeticism of Baroque Simplex who as clown, thief, illusionist, and confidence man goes about discovering secrets just under the surface of things and, as masked writer, conveys his knowledge, which paradoxically includes the tenet of "Vorwitz," the dangerous legacy of the fall in Eden, "maßen wir noch alle an unsrer ersten Mutter Kuriosität zu däuen [verdauen] haben" (III, ch. 23, p. 296). It is the artist Simplex who, having just play-acted the descent to Hades as

Orpheus and about to be invited into the Venus-Berg, can speak with deprecating nonchalance about the occult sciences revealed to him: "[...] denn ich hatte aus Lust bei meinem Doktor schon perlutiern, resolviern, sublimiern, coaguliern, digeriern, calciniern, filtiern, und dergleichen unzählig viel alkühmistische Arbeit gelernet [...]" (IV, ch. 4, p. 313). Being the nephew of Schimmelpreester, Felix lives in other times and may less censoriously become privy to contemporary secrets. But when he dreams of evolution after the grand lecture by Professor Kuckuck on the train from Paris to Lisbon, he envisions himself in the magic transactional idiom of French as if Mann, consciously or unconsciously, echoes the Simplician-Christian term for the strange adventure of curiosity: "Voilà le voyageur curieux."

It may not be feasible to do more than speculate how the wars of religion led to widespread disillusionment about the purported ideological grounds of conflict and to new perceptions of realities such as the functioning of the modern state, and the nature of social roles; or how such perceptions influenced the evolution of the picaresque novel. But the two late works in that stream, *Estebanillo González* and *Simplicissimus* — and one could also cite the *Francion* — do exhibit an incontestable fact: the arrival at a significant fusion of the roles of the criminal, clown, and artist. It only makes sense that, by the mid-seventeenth century, we should hear in fiction the first-person voices of aggressively self-defining underdogs who — most often in vain — seek to reshape themselves through role-playing. The drive of the confidencemen and rogues to realize their fortune through theater exhibits the shadowy counterpart to the higher knowledge sought and gained by the sublime Prince Hamlet who, standing at the mid-point of the World Theater in European literary history, disillusionistically tested reality in a flowing series of theatrical meditations and experiments.[18] As the prefatory bragging about his acting by Estebanillo and the opening emblematic portrayal of Simplicissimus as a chimerical monster on the world-stage cannot fail to remind us, the rogue, in becoming self-conscious through and of art, finds his identity within the shifting pages of a bigger play in progress.

Notes

1 *La vida y hechos de Estebanillo González, hombre de buen humor, compuesto por él mesmo*, ed. Nicholas Spadaccini and Anthony N. Zahareas (Madrid, 1978), 2 vols. All future references are to this edition and are indicated in parentheses in the text. The present essay is based on papers given at the Renaissance Conference of Northern California held at Stanford in 1980, and at the convention of the Modern Language Association in New York in 1981.
2 Hans Jacob Christoffel von Grimmelshausen, *Der abenteuerliche Simplicissimus Teutsch*, ed. Alfred Kelletat (München, 1956). All future references are to this edition and are indicated in parentheses in the text.
3 From the perspective of a Catholic humanist, Alexander A. Parker contrasts the two figures in his excellent chapter 4 on "Germany and the Thirty-Years War" in *Literature and the Delinquent: The Picaresque Novel in Spain and Europe* 1599-1753 (Edinburgh, 1967) 75-98. Since Parker, the best comparative study is Richard Bjornson, *The Picaresque Hero in European Fiction* (Madison, 1977) 75-98. Also consult Bjornson's article, "Estebanillo González: The Clown's Other Face," *Hispania* 60 (1977) 436-42, and Nicholas Spadaccini, "History and Fiction: The Thirty Year's War in *Estebanillo González*," *Kentucky Romance Quarterly* 24 (1977) 373-87, and "*Estebanillo González* and the Nature of Picaresque 'Lives,'" *Comparative Literature* 30 (1978) 209-22.
4 In his chapter on 'Translations and Transitions,' in *The Picaresque Hero*, 139-65, Bjornson connects two important phenomena exhibited in Sorel's *Francion*, but does not directly suggest their applicability to Grimmelshausen's *Simplicissimus*: one is the loosening of hierarchical norms in the ideal social order under the pressure from the growing bourgeois reading public in France, who could enjoy the story of the ultimate success of a rogue who somehow maintained his sense of truth and identity (p. 154); the other is the use of a "romance pattern" to resolve the conflict between the inner aspirations of the protagonist and external appearances (p. 157).
5 In *Picaro – Landstörtzer – Simplicius: Studien zum niederen Roman in Spanien und Deutschland* (Darmstadt, 1972), Hans Gerd Rötzer posits that the changes introduced by Aegidius Albertinus in his German version of *Guzmán* (1615), Grimmelshausen's source, definitely fixed such an emphasis. Albertinus took apart the joined narrative levels of achieved awareness (*desengaño*) and experienced time (*engaño*) in Alemán and transposed them into a progressive linear structure in two parts, the latter consisting mainly of the enormous sermons of Guzmán as redeemed hermit. Hence Albertinus's "Gusman lebt nicht im Konflikt mit der Gesellschaft, sondern nur im Spannungsfeld zwischen Sünde und Gnade" (p. 96); and in turn, Grimmelshausen's Simplex must be seen as an "artificial" figure involved in a logical series of "representative" roles, and not as engaged in flight from the world,

but renunciation (p. 142f.). In contradiction to Parker's thesis of a conversion, awakening, and social reintegration on the part of the original Spanish Guzmán, Benito Brancaforte has proposed that the circular structure of *Guzmán de Alfarache* is "Sisyphean," ambiguous, and open-ended (Introduction to his edition in 2 vols. [Madrid, 1979] 1, 17-37). At their deepest level, his reflections are fraught with contradictions resembling the anxiety in so many modern confessional novels. In *Guzmán de Alfarache: The Unrepentant Narrator* (London, 1977) 37-42, 93-5, Joan Arias has argued that the protagonist is hostile and devious toward his readers and world. The contradictions between his pious rationalizations and driven behavior fit a basic existential pattern. He creates a false idealized identity and condemns the unavoidable evil of mankind only in order to excuse his own failures in life. Bjornson, however, sees at the root of the self-justification the special problems of the *conversos* and other underdogs: "Alemán displays a profound sympathy for the tragedy and pathos of those whose lives have been distorted by the society which hypocritically disdains them" (*The Picaresque Hero*, 65).

6   The Grimmelshausen critical renascence reached a new peak on the three-hundredth anniversary of his death, and fuller bibliography will be found in the listings of *Wolfenbütteler Barock-Nachrichten* 3-7 (1976-80). Consult the special memorial issues of the journals *Daphnis* 5 (1976) and *Argenis* 1 (1977).
7   Martin Erich Schmid, "Orpheus: Grimmelshausen – Anton Ulrich – Francesco Buti; die Quellen zum Pariser Opernkapitel im *Simplicissimus*," *Argenis* 1 (1977) 279-99.
8   See chapter 3, "Der motivgeschichtliche Probefall: 'Beau Alman' und seine Herkunft aus Harsdörffer und der romantischen Novellistik," in Weydt's *Nachahmung und Schöpfung im Barock: Studien um Grimmelshausen* (Bern, München, 1968) 47-58.
9   I am grateful to the Thomas-Mann-Archiv (Zürich) for the privilege of being able to examine Mann's personal copy; an analysis of the import of the markings exceeds the scope of the present chapter.
10 Oskar Seidlin, "Picaresque Elements in Thomas Mann's Work," *Modern Language Quarterly* 12 (1951) 183-200.
11 Donald F. Nelson, "Preface," in *Portrait of the Artist as Hermes: A Study of Myth and Psychology in Thomas Mann's "Felix Krull"* (Chapel Hill, 1971) [i].
12 *Thomas Mann – Karl Kerényi: Gespräch in Briefen* (Zürich, 1960), 98.
13 Nelson, *Portrait of the Artist as Hermes*, 106. I am indebted to Kurt Weinberg for pointing out in conversation that Lazarillo cries 'olé, olé' at the end of the first "Tratado." This famous wordplay (on the bullfight and the word "smell") occurs when the rogue gets his revenge on the blind man by inducing him to butt against a post: "¿Cómo? ¿y oliste la longaniza y no el poste? ¡Olé! ¡Olé!, le dije yo." I believe that Mann would readily

have picked up this exclamation as a "marker" for a hermetic *pícaro* because of the underground association with the archaic ritual of bullfighting.

14 Marcel Bataillon, "Estebanillo, González: bouffon 'pour rire,' " in *Studies in Spanish Literature of the Golden Age, Presented to Edward M. Wilson*, ed. R.O. Jones (London, 1973), pp. 25-44.

15 In the Introduction to their critical edition of *Vida y hechos*, Spadaccini and Zahareas do not find any convincing likeness between the two engravings (I, 27), but arrive at an essentially similar view of the generic results: "Poco cambiaría en cuanto a la composición de la obra: si un autor apócrifo dió a un pícaro inventado una dimensión histórica, un bufón auténtico dió a vida verdadera una dimensión ficticia o literaria" (I, 29).

16 See the section "Das Lob des *Francion* bei Grimmelshausen" in Koschlig's *Das Ingenium Grimmelshausens und das "Kollektiv": Studien zur Entstehungs- und Wirkungsgeschichte des Werkes* (München, 1977), pp. 45-89.

17 Spadaccini and Zahareas astutely note the telltale traits of melancholy beneath the professional "good humor" of the learned buffon (*Vida y hechos*, I, 45ff.); but they do not connect his pathetic strivings with the new generic type of the desperate or cracked intellectual-adventurer, familiar in the drama and novel of Europe throughout the seventeenth century, nor do they mention Sorel's *Francion* (1622) or Grimmelshausen's *Simplicissimus* (1668).

18 I have discussed the thematics of the World Theater as a persisting literary stimulus in my essay "Dream and Calculus in European Baroque Drama," in *Critical Dimensions: English, German, and Comparative Literature Essays in Honor of Aurelio Zanco* (Cuneo, 1978), pp. 181-200; and in a review article focused on "Manfred Schmeling, *Das Spiel im Spiel. Ein Beitrag zur Vergleichenden Literaturkritik* (Saarbrücken 1977)" in *Die Sprachkunst*, 10 (1979) 241-8.

12. ERRING AND WAYFARING IN BAROQUE FICTION: THE WORLD AS LABYRINTH AND GARDEN

The terms of the heading will sound obvious to those fascinated by the great age of exploration and colonization following Columbus' famous voyage; the literature of intrepid wayfaring, from Díaz del Castillo's story of the conquest of Mexico, or Camoens' global Portuguese epic, or Hakluyt's account of British sea adventure to Olearius' description of the Dano-German expedition to Persia, is so vast that it forbids citation[1]. In any case, the task here is to examine an independent, and a more or less constant, habit in fiction reaching into the anthropological novel of the Enlightenment: the portrayal of educational development as erring, as movement which more often than not gains its meaning in relation to the terrain traversed. While the Renaissance was expanding a rich literary tradition associated with the master-image of the "garden," it was also elaborating a newer tradition associated with that of the "labyrinth"; thus the further evolution of these poetic means provides important clues to the character of the literature of error of the successor Baroque age. Our departure point, then, is long after the moment when Dante had brought together in the *Divina Commedia* three crucial paradigms of quest and discovery — those of the journey or pilgrimage, of postlapsarian rediscovery of the innocent freedom of Eden through poetry, and of spiritual attainment of the City of God. Dante so reconstituted our sense of the world as fallen and labyrinthine that now the personal pathway of discovery could symbolize both the protagonist singer's mission and redemption, and also picture the past and future of the human race. We shall also move beyond the moment when Pico della Mirandola and other Renaissance savants began proclaiming a renewal of the quest for occult or magical keys to relate various bodies of religious beliefs and mythological lore. The term "labyrinth," as Gustav René Hocke has shown, established itself in an age awed by the challenge of coping with the new order of complexity posed in large measure by its own zeal for exploration and discovery[2]. In Hiram Haydn's view, the sixteenth century also evidenced a deep streak of skepticism concerning the power of the human mind to gain truth, and this furthered a tendency toward unsystematic and experimental empiricism, as well as toward gnostic, hermetic, and cabalistic occultism[3]. So if the garden — as Bartlett Giamatti has shown — had long been the master-image for both the fallen and the splendid order of creation, both human craving and human destiny, the labyrinth, too, from the beginning suggested both negative and positive senses of searching for efficacious knowledge or salvation through threatening or apparent confusion[4].

The Renaissance bequeathed to the Baroque four main types of educational and quester fiction pertinent to our topic: the lowlife struggle of the rogue, the story of bourgeois or courtly aspirants to a better life, the idealized contrast of a utopian society, and broader humoristic encyclopedism. The basic picaresque storyline is clear despite controversies over the exact stages in the rise of the literature of delinquency and its precise ideological allegiances[5]. The criminals in the forerunner dialogue play *La Celestina* (1494) all suffered violent deaths. The interpolated garden became the place for seduction with disastrous consequence, and the disorder of the urban world invaded the symbolic order of Pleberio's house. The prototype novel, *Lazarillo de Tormes* (1555), set the lasting picaresque mode of harsh disillusionism. The novel's first-person protagonist bore all the scars of a desperate outcast, who had arrived by traumatic trial and error at his compromise with deceit and statement of himself. Sometimes a rogue is a fallen member of a well-placed family, as is the later case of Alemán's *Guzmán de Alfarache*, but ordinarily he comes from the lower depths of society and schemes his way through the school of hard knocks or is straightway tutored in crime as the road to social security. Even though Quevedo added the layer of moral comment characterizing the Baroque stage of picaresque narration, he maintained the sordid origins and outcast traits for his Buscón.

It is also instructive to recall, in rough outline, some major features of that wholly different realm of the elegant Renaissance psychological romance[6]. Ariosto's *Orlando Furioso* (1516) treated education in general, as involving the persistent problems of man's natural condition, not as any specific engagement on the historical plane, even though the work's final moment — Orlando's emergence from madness and rout of the infidel — obviously satisfied the societal requirement for a high moral outcome. Ariosto, a gentle master of illusions, showed the knight Ruggiero falling into the role already tested by Astolfo on the island of Alcina. Spellbound and spiritually enervated by the lure of her garden, Ruggiero finally manages to rearm himself and escape the seductive magic. Eventually he discovers the contrasting realm of Ligistilla, maintained by genuine zeal and care; but, ironically, manly knights grow restless in this perfect garden of everlasting peace and must set out again to test themselves in the dangerous contests of existence. In short, Ariosto recognized that illusion is necessary to life; without motion there would be spiritual paralysis. In the *Fairie Queene* (1590), besides constant allusions to the political fate of England, Spenser examined the conflict between the values of this world and the next with subtle irony and the aim of discerning a proper order and balance which the virtues can obtain. We follow multiple instances of venturing forth, as various knights struggle against mutability and for permanence. In passage to a state of active temperance the hero first must avoid the shoals of despair which error interposes. For example, though the symbolically wandering island of Acrasia is only an imitation of the lost earthly paradise, its artifice fools even Guyon, the protagonist of the virtue of temperance in Spenser's psychomachia.

Spenser also specifically related the dangers of art, when it undermines and corrupts nature, to "lust, illusion, false values, magic, the implicit theme of pleasure overcoming duty and honor, passion overwhelming reason"[7]. There is a particularly Protestant slant in Spenser's exposure of the way language, too, becomes negative if rhetoric and imagination serve delusion and despair; it is man's self-deluding and perversion which in fact alters things and separates nature into good and bad versions. In the *Fairie Queene*, various gardens on the island stand for states of mind, false and parodistic Edens, culminating in the mentioned sterility, artifice, and death of Acrasia's Bower of Bliss, which pretends to abrogate time. In contrast, the symbolic garden of Venus and Adonis in the *Fairie Queene* exhibits positive nature, fecundity, and life, and embodies the reality of time; Venus as the "great mother" and Adonis as the "father of forms" incarnate the "image of the process."[8] Nature is the legitimate channel through which fallen man must work, restoring his senses to their proper role and status, in Spenser's Protestant view. But as Patricia Parker notes especially in regard to Book VI, "romance itself is a bower, charm, or region of wandering, an evasion, and yet one perhaps necessary to the life of poetry"; hence Spenser's "genuine ambivalence, what may be finally not a doubleness of vision but a doubleness of mind" about "both the desirability and the danger of delay or wandering," the inherent tension between "the dilatation of a creation" and "the precipitation of the fall."[9]

In a more conservative Catholic vein, and closer to Baroque than Renaissance poetry, Tasso's slightly earlier religious epic *Gerusalemme Liberata* (1575) was organized around the traditional distinction between town and country, that is, between the "city" as the focus of man's duty and symbol of order, and "nature" as the evasion of duty, acedia, spiritual wilderness. Beautiful Armida, representing all that is inimical to the City, inhabits a seductive garden associated with Venus and the pleasures of a Golden Age; but since the pagan classical dream has proven to be unreal, Tasso's hero Rinaldo, like Aeneas, ultimately returns to his duty toward the City, and Armida, like Dido motivated sacrificially by passion, here converts to Christianity. The Christianizing of romance to rival Heliodorus was Cervantes' goal in *Los trabajos de Persiles y Segismunda* (1617), which reshaped the adventurous journey into a pilgrimage from the north, the barbarian world of unbelief, to Rome, the center of the world of faith, symbol of the City.

Alongside the allegorical romances, the Renaissance produced works we can more properly designate as educational novels. Like the picaresque books, these evidence an urban rather than a courtly stamp. They tend to be more focussed on one or a few youths who enter the formative years and face certain, not always well-perceived choices crucial for their future. For example, Wickram's *Der Jungen Knaben Spiegel* (1554) presented the age's standard tale of two young men, the spoiled heir of a wealthy family of urban nobles, and his adopted brother, of humble caste but high principles. Gradually, the wastrel descends into the degradation of big city crime, while his persevering brother, inspired by his humanistic teachers, rises through knowledge and piety to become an important personage of the society. This was the bourgeois success story in a Protestant version — which still inspires many Americans and Europeans. Another form of the concentrated mirror was represented by Lyly's *Euphues or the Anatomy of Wit* (1578) which transposed the story of the educational experience of two youths to ancient Greece; transparent beneath the relabelling were the critique of contemporary institutions, such as the University of Oxford, and the treatment of fashionable cultural trends. As never fails in the course of time, the quester patterns and psychological apparatus of both the romance and novel underwent all manner of conflation.

In educational quester stories of the earlier seventeenth century, the drive toward encyclopedic inclusiveness often conflicted with mystagogic reductionism, as we see in even the title of Comenius' famous work, *The Labyrinth of the World and the Paradise of the Heart* (1623).

The more immediate influences were More's *Utopia*, Campenella's *Civitas Solis*, and Andreae's *Christianopolis* (1619). The new geopolitical and cultural picture of the seventeenth century is so complex that Comenius depicts the pilgrimage through its baffling diversity as an anxious groping in a maze; however, an inner principle of freedom mysteriously guides the searcher, who is secretly in tune with the purposes of Providence. Providence works through the unfathomable agencies of the constantly metamorphosing world drama, "a vast clockwork, fashioned out of divers visible and invisible materials." Without a named hero, the tour by Comenius takes us through a typology of stations and conditions of life in a city of men, rather than over the actual exotic topography of earth, exposes the deficiencies of such contemporary paths as alchemy, Rosicrucianism, etc., survives the threat of despair lurking in the perceived failure of the Reformation, and proclaims the universal inward church.

But it is a lucid outline of a contemporary spiritual dilemma, quite different from the mystagogic labyrinth of a work like Andreae's *Chymische Hochzeit Christiani Rosenkreutz anno 1549* (1616). To follow Andreae's plotline of sevenfold ascension and initiation, the reader must be schooled in sufficient lore to traverse with Christian a warren of hermetic signs and situations, including passage through the symbolic garden of the central Book IV.

Quite different in spirit from religious quester stories, and imaginatively closer to Renaissance romance, is the first great secularization of Renaissance psychology and cosmology accomplished by Marino's *Adone*, which starting in 1623 — eventually in some 41,000 lines — conquered all of Europe with its encyclopedic praise of the senses, the world, and life. For sheer plenitude of motifs from classical and Romanic literature in combination with secular sophistication, the *Adone* far outstripped older treatises on love such as the medieval *Libro de buen amor* and the *Roman de la Rose*. While the great Metaphysical poet Donne, too, could wittily appreciate the problematic dimensions of the age of Bruno, Galileo, and Campanella, Marino achieved his own Baroque synthesis by concentrating on already entrenched, favorite mythological subjects for the elite. In asserting the intellectual independence of the poet as creator, Marino simultaneously lent a new aesthetic value to the total educational repertory of sophisticated Europeans. Implicitly, one could now bypass any obligatory doctrinal key to the syncretistic heritage and construct a rational neomythic statement out of perceived patterns. The opening of canto 10 of the *Adone* apostrophizes divine intellect as the supreme virtue and Venus, the heavenly mother, as the attractive educative splendor toward which the mind strives — or, in Goethe's words two centuries later, the Eternal-Feminine which man discovers in the cosmos. Among the *maraviglie* or wonders Marino presents is the zeal of his epoch to fathom the movements of the heavens, and he explicitly praises Galileo and the telescope. We steep ourselves allegorically in the grotto of nature, where universal principles — time, fate, truth, and so forth — are discoverable. The pride in achievements starting with the Renaissance is unmistakable. Marino celebrates the sciences and arts, and their inventors from Prometheus over Gutenberg to the seventeenth century, confident his own age is erecting a new comprehensive model of the universe.

But it was Marino's mixing of pagan and Christian motifs — for example, his minute description in canto 16 of the parallels between the temple of Venus and a Christian church — which provoked the sharpest criticism by contemporaries[10]. His daring allusions to salvational history and ecclesiastical usages and ritual were condemned as incompatible with the dignity of a superior Christianity. The *Adone* connected two separate motivic complexes handed down in various ancient texts: Venus' warnings about the hunt and Diana's revenge on Adonis. The jealousy of the goddesses thus reflected in a fuller spectrum the conflictual experience of the creation incarnated in the aspects "virgin," "wife," "mother," in relation to "son," "husband," "father." Mythology became itself both a major subject and a source of conceptual leaps, but the capacity to formulate conceptual *pointes* was ultimately an affirmation of rational control of such deeply troubling as well as dazzling materials — a "continual psychological consolation" in the face of manifest principles such as Fate[11]. Unlike Ariosto and Tasso, Marino reworked the Neoplatonic notions of an earthly paradise and heavenly journey in his own Giardino del Piacere without obligatorily denigrating the sensual level; rather, he based his own poetic garden on the human body as truly a microcosmic model, the sensorium as the channel of love and the whole range of perception. Part I, cantos 1 through 9, ends with the union of Venus and Adonis in the garden of feeling, and Part II, starting with canto 10, brings the crowning of Adonis' experience in the realm of the senses through initiation to knowledge of the world of the spirit under the aegis of Aphrodite Urania; that is, transitory beauty conducts to intellectual beauty, the earthly to the heavenly paradise. At the same time, the life of the gods in the *Adone* reflected the grand style of seventeenth-century aristocratic circles, the hierarchy, ceremony, palaces, gardens, and luxury of a court-dominated society. Marino's cosmological vision would ultimately affect the world view of the high Baroque, as rationalism was extending its sway after the settlement of the wars of religion and with emergence of the modern European state system. And later poets, speaking in the eighteenth century to an anti-courtly bourgeois urbanity, would transfer the splendid refulgence onto the sublimity of nature at large, but Rococo eudaemonism would keep alive Marino's celebration of the senses.

Gracián's disillusionistic novel *El Criticón* (1619) yields a quite different idea of perfectibility through education. Starting from the island of St. Helena as a prelapsarian Eden, moving over the great cities of Europe through postlapsarian corruption, and terminating on a symbolic island of immortality, the journey of the wise Critolo, who travels as mentor unbeknownst to his uncivilized son Andrenio, allegorizes man's struggle to transcend animality. Spatially, the movement in the quest from Spain to Italy reflects the progress from nature to art, from mere body to mind, and from the lower state *hombre*, to that of *persona*. Madrid as mere court center must cede to Rome as the archetype of civilization. Temporally, the *Criticón* conducts us through the poetic stations of time and the year and the ages of man; this fourfold tropological cycle underscores the relentless imperative to cultivate personally one's finite humanity. In the *Criticón*, the achievements of superior human beings represent a resistance to the fall from a hypothetical ideal, a defiance of spiritual entropy. If Comenius' ecumenical pansophism spoke directly to radical, latitudinarian, and irenic Protestants eager to deal more tolerantly and empirically with God's nature, Gracián's prudentialism, too – though characteristic of the Counter-Reformation – often exercised an appeal across sectarian lines. Gracián's sense of man as an actor positing his own role amid vicissitude and the emphasis on fortitude had an epochal appeal for Protestant writers, much as had Lipsius' neo-Stoic teachings a generation before.

The *Criticón* was, in effect, the direct-line ancestor of the novel of education centered on a protagonist of education such as still would command respect at the close of the seventeenth century. The sophisticated technique of transposing the European present onto a remote past or into an exotic distance promoted the fusion of the novel of education and the treatise on human spiritual evolution. A stellar illustration is Fénelon's *Télémaque*. Finished toward 1695, this novel packed all the classical memories of Homer and Vergil into an educational-moral guide for the successor of Louis XIV. In searching for his father Odysseus, Telemachus wanders the ancient world mainly in the company of the sage Mentor (who is the goddess Minerva in disguise), experiences every kind of social and political arrangement, and succumbs for a while to voluptuousness, as one might expect of an island-hopping knight in the romance genre. What got Fénelon into trouble, however, were the transparent admonitions against haughtiness, absolutism, and warring exemplified by the unfortunate king Idoménée, i.e., Louis XIV. The actual Sun King was not of a mind to absorb Mentor's lessons on peaceful settlement of disputes, reform of the constitution and social mores, encouragement of the arts, industry, commerce, and agriculture, and other goals of good rulership.

By this time Fénelon was estranged from the now devout king on account of his sympathy with Quietism and, having been appointed Bishop of Cambrai, was effectively distanced from the court at Versailles.

The juxtaposition of the seductive island-paradise and the ideal city, Salente under Mentor, is the familiar contrast of labyrinthine erring and cultivation of the garden as the human estate. Fénelon thoroughly subordinated ancient mythology and history in a graceful new construct in the service of education.

We shall return to this significant juncture. But before doing so it is important to recapitulate with a sketch of the other two types of fiction: utopian vision and humoristic encyclopedism[12]. If any miracle could have seemed more fabulous than genuine reform, it was the news of a society that required none; this would be all the more startling if restless gadabouts happened upon it, and they did in Renaissance fiction. This strategy for expressing humanist aspirations took the form of imagining, in contrast to actual Europe, an alternative civilization which had retained the pristine impulse of the ancient tradition. The genre has ever after borne the name of More's *Utopia* (1516), purporting to relate the discovery of a peaceful, communistic republic somewhere in those vast oceanic spaces being opened by intrepid Renaissance explorers. According to the account transmitted by More, while the Utopians have developed the same principles in the arts and sciences as the Ancients and made all advances known to Europe such as printing, they have failed to evolve the tortured scholasticism or degenerate church of the Moderns. Rabelais next enshrined these humanist biases with radical energy in his mammoth five-part novel at mid-sixteenth century when he described how the young prince Pantagruel completed the fusion of the Utopian and the Dipsodic realms (that is, More's and Erasmus' teachings) in civilizing conquest.

Book I concludes with the collaboration of the older generation,

Gargantua and Friar John, in founding the Abbey of Thélème ("free will"), a utopian educational institution of revolutionary character not only to replace the corrupt, outmoded monastic and scholastic systems, but to serve as a model for the formation of a secular élite (ch. 52 ff.). In contrast to other utopian establishments, however, Rabelais forcefully advocates an open society governed by positive freedom and the imperative of self-perfection for both sexes. While acquiring the whole range of courtly graces, the Thelemites can repair to the core of the institution, its libraries in Greek, Latin, Hebrew, French, Italian, and Spanish. The new encyclopedic scope embraces the vital modern cultures. As Florence Weinberg has argued, Rabelais' Bacchic Christianity will be fulfilled through the striving of the Thelemites toward a fusion of the codes of Nature and Scripture, a rebirth of human glory after centuries of error and relapse[13]. But in the saga of the gigantesque race of Gargantua, whose ancestor supposedly survived the deluge by riding Noah's ark as if it were a hobby-horse, Rabelais also exhibits the caution of the maturing Renaissance. In the monumental series of expert consultations in Book III, he exploits with élan the ambiguity of the labyrinthine approach; finally it is the fool, Triboulet, who points the questers further. For a more programmatic exhibition of order, Rabelais fuses the older garden and city — as already noted — in a modern terrestial paradise, the élitist coeducational Abbey of Thélème. But the quest is far from completed. Book IV, which Rabelais dubs "continuation des mythologies Pantagruelicques" (Preface), adopts as its governing structure an intrepid neomythic voyage of exploration into recondite matters. Though "labyrinth" does not directly figure in Book IV's appended glossary of stimulating new terms — e.g., "microcosme," "hieroglyphicques," "symbole," "pyramide," "archetype," etc. — the progress of the novel amounts to jocoserious mystagogic ritual. In the larger course of the five Books, we are conducted through a maze of outmoded, intermediate, and beckoning forms and teachings into the core, a core which reissues into the plain reality of nature and history, the temple of the Divine Bottle being ubiquitous.

The controversial Cornelius Agrippa von Nettesheim (who captains the ship Alchemy in Rabelais's book IV) exemplified to his age the troubled magus who simultaneously denied the power of the mind to grasp ultimate reality, yet believed in the secret wisdom of an esoteric tradition and natural philosophy, as set forth in *De occulta philosophia*. Then he gradually questioned even the occult authorities and natural philosophy to which he had turned after bypassing conventional learning.[14] By 1526, with his treatise *De incertitudine et vanitate scientiarum*, Agrippa rejected the Platonic and Neoplatonic esoteric myth, the Hermetic writings, the Cabala, and astrology, but he later shrank back from his own destruction of the occult edifice in the hope the human soul might be the key to such secrets. Marlowe directly linked the crisis of Agrippa's thought with the Faust figure, a lasting archetype (if one may use the new-fangled term approved by Rabelais in his glossary). To the degree his conviction in man's centrality as magician faltered, Agrippa's belief that words and symbols possessed the power of the ideas they expressed gave way to questioning the conformity between the abstractions of the human mind and external objects, so that he denied any objective existence to the formulations of metaphysics, physics, astronomy, and mathematics. Besides alleging the untruthfulness and erring of virtually every revered ancient authority, Agrippa attacked poetry and history at large as mendacious, ridiculed the romances, and demonstrated the contradictions in moral standards from culture to culture, age to age, and the cruelty and deceit underlying the existence of social classes and legal systems. He anticipated the brooding of the pyrrhonist Montaigne, the empiricist Bacon, the humorist Cervantes over the enormous role of imagination and opinion in human experience.

As mentioned, the perplexity of human judgment in the new labyrinth of knowledge was, of course, a major theme of Rabelais' humoristic-encyclopedic novel, but Montaigne shifted the investigation of contradiction and uncertainty from the larger world onto an interior psychological and epistemological track in his famous *Essays*. In taking himself as his subject, Montaigne portrayed the psyche in a series of perspectivistic probes, catching its peculiar rhythms and habits in relation to the mysterious continuity of identity. Several features of the *Essays* advanced the Renaissance discovery of a labyrinthine principle to the Baroque threshold: First of all, the dramatic Baroque ego emerged, concerned with its own operations and vagaries in the flux of time as much as with the larger social or cosmological picture. Role-playing *per se* — and the ways in which people invent or inherit customs, ideas, and even language, all these being the outer costuming of a prodigiously inventive nature — became a primary topic. By the beginning of the seventeenth century the meditative capacity flourished through the thematics and forms of the world theater — in Shakespeare, Bidermann, Lope, Rotrou, Calderón, and others, for whom man was an actor, life a dream or vision[15].

Rabelais' romp through the wilderness of encumbering locutions of the Middle Ages and marshalling of more debonnaire Renaissance material exhibits the drive to erect a verbal counter-labyrinth, a logodaedalia[16]. But whereas Brant in the *Ship of Fools* (1494) feared the new sciences and the liberating invention of printing — which he linked with new urbanization, the advent of capitalism, and what would shortly be called Protestantism — just two generations later Rabelais was exulting in the revaluation of values that the new book-culture enabled and deliberately dispatched his own Renaissance protagonists on a symbolic voyage in quest of the meaning of renewed man. His attempt to shape a medium for dealing on a universal plane both with superseded (i.e., the long medieval interval) and with rediscovered time (i.e., the reinvoked exemplary ancient and early Christian heritage), constitutes a grand chord in the overture of the epoch of the novel. He bestowed new implications on the myriad choices and conflicts, the contradictions and absurdities of intellectual life and social custom, and the ageless lessons of nature. Rabelais' sovereign use of irony to create a new humorous literary doctrine, Pantagruelism, was readily identified with the honesty and modernity of the humanist ethos, as against a collapsing medieval order.

In a next step beyond Rabelais, Cervantes' intitial purpose in the novel *Don Quixote* — to champion humanist realism by attacking the mendacious medieval romance epitomized by *Amadis de Gaula* — yielded a secondary revelation. For in dealing with the suspect realm of fantasy, the great Spanish humorist inevitably built it into his masterwork as a paramount factor of human nature. Of course, this complicated involution was anticipated by Ariosto's already mentioned, deliberately medievalizing verse romance *Orlando furioso* (1532), which exploited the theme of splendid madness, under the pretext of urbane parody, to rescue essential poetic elements of romance and values threatened by the epochal changes of Renaissance society. Quixote's ultimate disillusionment with the power of chivalric ideals on which his conduct was premised, his abandonment of his own misprision of Orlando's story and other fictions, is therefore tragically shattering, even though in a strange mirroring his sober awakening and contrite death also stands as a final act of imitative fulfillment. We readers, too, must face in Quixote's humility a crushing defeat, painful acceptance of ordinary human reality with its burdensome imperfections and dullness. Like the contemporaries of Cervantes, we ponder our own involvement with his odd hero who is imitating, among others, an odd hero in an Italian work of literary art known to us as an urbane parody contrasting Renaissance sophistication and outworn medieval motifs. The era of book culture — that is, Western civilization as it had been transformed by the major technological tool of Humanism and the Reformation and Counter-Reformation — manifests its own problems distinctly in Cervantes' iconoclastic awareness of the already awesome printed parallel universe which has evolved: the now everywhere circulated and externalized, puzzling products of the human mind. Books, a key vehicle, measure, and even fetish of the Renaissance, have come to provide virtually in themselves a sufficient representative means to depict the systems of the mind and culture.

It is scarcely surprising that the moment of Cervantes' *Quixote* is also that of Shakespeare's *Hamlet*, that is, of a world-theater the main reference for which is the human institution and medium of theater. To the involution of book and narrative structure within the book by Cervantes corresponds Shakespeare's, Lope's, Rotrou's, and Calderón's obsessive Baroque involution of the play-in-the-play as an instrument for analyzing role-choice and identity; the intrusion of consciousness of the functions of actor and spectator is matched by the novel's self-reflection and the contrived presence in it of both its hypothetical variegated readership and the authorial mind.

Quixote has nothing else to do but err; he boldly resurrects the high office of being a knight errant, moving from encounter to encounter as in a romance. He draws into his orbit and implants a dream in the hearty man of nature, Sancho Panza; and eventually, as Book I is reaching its close, a whole troupe of sophisticates as well as village notables surrounds the stimulating anachronism, they spin complicated fictions to cope with his, and they discourse on the genres of their era and the nature of invention in a magnificent symposium on literary art. In Cervantes' *Don Quixote*, the mind by its own instrumentality (on the authorial plane) turned to a critique and assessment of itself, and this ironic stance in prose fiction was furthered by the new "theatrical" and "picaresque" forms of Baroque split consciousness. Ostensibly, Quixote errs, but not just absurdities, also gems of knowledge pearl from his lips in so doing. The wanderings of the *loco-cuerdo* or shrewd madman take us through all spheres and levels of Spain, and his aberrant behavior is the catalyst for our discovering in its amplitude a universe. The novel proved its adequacy to cope critically with the complexity of the larger scene of life.

Perhaps the best-known work of German seventeenth-century literature with a related ironic critique is that quintessentially Baroque novel, *Der abenteuerliche Simplicissimus Teutsch* [*The Adventurous German Simplicissimus*], which appeared wrapped in Cervantine layers of authorial masks in 1668. To the original five books, which suggested the rising and falling action of grand theater of the world and in counterpoint the falling, then rising plotline of the individual moral drama, the anonymous author appended a sixth book, the *Continuatio* which related the exotic ultimate hermitage of Simplex on a remote desert isle in the South Seas. Today we know the identity of the author, Grimmelshausen, and tend to associate him too eagerly with the famous frontispiece emblem, where in the Baroque satiric mode an odd composite being stands on the mask-strewn stage of the *theatrum emblematicum* and points quizzically at the plethora of emblems in the emblem book he holds in his hands, while we ponder the *subscriptio*, an epigrammatic poem about wandering and erring through the world and its four elements, yet finally finding rest and peace of soul. This is manneristically an emblem about an emblematic experience through art. Therefore we are missing the point if we look for some unity of character in the educational protagonist, according the Enlightenment conceptions of personality, rather than accept that the vagaries of his journey and even the often grim naturalism of witnessed disorders of the age constitute materials for meditative analysis. Modern critics have wanted to detect some influence of Cervantes, as well as the Spanish picaresque writers, in the consciousness of the first-person narrating voice and the ironic guidance through the tumultuous series of adventures and discoveries. However, as newer research indicates, Grimmelshausen was composing in another stage beyond the floration of the Cervantine and picaresque models, after the Spanish novel had left a deep imprint on French fiction and most notably contributed to the complex, encyclopedic disillusionism of another, then anonymous, major novelist, Charles Sorel, author of the *Francion*. Like Sorel, Grimmelshausen was striving for what he expressly labelled satiric truthfulness, a redemptive stripping away of costume, mask, pretence, an unabashed coming to terms with the criminal waywardness of his age after its enormous orgy of war-making.

There are several levels of esoteric reference for actions in the novel *Simplicissimus* both on the historical plane of Europe and on the personal plane of the narrator's life, which we eventually learn is specifically the story of the strange new type produced by the post-Reformation urban society, the artist-intellectual. A dense network of cosmological, astrological, and mythological motifs is woven through the details large or small of the novel, even though most details may strike today's readers as commendably hard data seen by a realist, a realist who then roguishly will take us on symbolic special excursions of obvious fairytale quality. Grimmelshausen certainly works with more immediately recognizable literary traditions of his day, as well. The more prominent thematics with which his novel opens include those of the quester-fool, still popular since the printing of Wolfram's *Parzival* in 1477, Brant's *Narrenschiff* (1494), Erasmus' *Encomium Moriae* (1605) and a host of other books; but the character of the storytelling is deeply conditioned by the early intrusion of a highly structured dream-vision in the generic mode of a Quevedo or Moscherosch, visited on the boy who becomes Simplex. The powerful disillusioning irony, with apocalyptic overtones, also appears in the two-tier narrating voice in the very first paragraphs.

We hear a picaresque speaker who is able to witness himself as actor and fool in the world drama as his erring occurs and to comment directly or obliquely on life's scene as the matured spectator who, implicitly, has already lived it.[17] Within distinct paradigmatic outlines, traced through profuse detail and over a perplex plotline, Simplex traverses in a wild skein of roads what turns out to be a necessary circle leading back to his origins[18]. When ejected from the instable representative paradise of country life into the turbulence of passion-wracked, strife-torn Europe, the very first refuge which the boy seeks out is ambivalent. He flees from the disrupted garden into the forest, that dark place in the middle of human experience, the labyrinth in which the exile must probe for a pathway. In the woods, at the witching hour, terrified of the threat from the wolf of whom he has been warned, Simplex is saved, symbolically, by the pious hymn intoned by the hermit who – in the close of the tale – will prove to have been his actual father. The hermit's woodland school, bringing the primary order of spiritual truth, remains the unimpeachable guide throughout; so does the earliest informed spiritual act, the work of art, the song as worship.

Therefore, as the novel progresses and Simplex undergoes his many transformations of role and gradually becomes a Hermes figure, we can read his stages of experience against a set of firm indices. From the garden (in its lower form as the simple village life, its higher form as heritage) through the labyrinth of the world, until his exit from the world, echoing Guevara's farewell, conducts him back into the garden – Simplex' encyclopedic tour is emblematic; it can be summed up in one or a few actual emblemata in popular pictorial collections. The climax of Simplex' social career as an opera star in Paris is explicitly portrayed as penetration into a dangerous labyrinth, as captivity in the Venus-Berg; his success is inversely a moral and an existential nadir. Then, to underline the slavational message, Grimmelshausen exploited in Book VI the new story-form of shipwreck on an island in the midst of that dangerous remoteness of the farthest ocean. This situation of extremity in the watery element is ambivalent sign both of Fortuna and of baptism. As I hope to clarify in due course, many later works of literature have so conditioned us that we feel no surprise upon learning that the thief, conman, and self-revealed author of fictions, Simplex, has left behind a spiritual biography and confession, inscribed on palm leaves, in the innermost retreat of the cave on his island from where the requisite Dutch captain carries them as a precious bequest back to Europe. The primary story of erring and wayfaring is superseded on the island by the announced form of the diary and mental exploration, the genre of interiorization. As the novel unfolds, Grimmelshausen manages adroitly to transcend all sectarian boundaries with his ecumenical pilgrim. Simplex has been tutored by Protestant pastors, has spoken favorably of the virtues of such extreme dissenters as the Anabaptists, has wandered with Herzbruder to the Catholic shrine of Einsiedeln where he undergoes conversion, explores the lands of heathen peoples, and dies in the image of his hermit father with Catholic aura, only to have his reliques translated by Protestant seafarers.

Simplicissimus is a colossal canvas of human disorder, the consequence of the Edenic Fall, during the Thirty Years' War. It is also passionately encyclopedic and reaches out to touch peoples beyond Europe. Before returning to this fact of a desire for a horizontally expansive universalism true to the altered world picture after so much European contact with exotic peoples, it is appropriate to remind ourselves of the unquenchable desire for an adequate "vertical" or developmental universalism. Grimmelshausen's novel appeared close to Milton's *Paradise Lost* of 1667 (revised 1674). If I turn aside briefly from the genre of the novel to this great epic, whose muse Milton dares to characterize as a divine voice, it is to see how out of a compact Biblical model a major Christian poet grandiloquently elaborates what is in essence a narrative fiction of development, with a dramatic struggle between good and evil at its core. As C.M. Bowra has said, Adam is the hero whose special case is pursued, as the grounding for the story of his descendants, and this plot must be read contrastively with the story of the fall of the angels.[19] In inversion, the magnificence of Satan's heroic defiance when he first asserts his own autonomous being gives way progressively to a tarnished ultimate role. Milton rejects the qualities of the ancient prideful heroic type in him and proclaims instead the resolute adherence to truth and love on the part of the loyal angels. Man's fall, however, summons forth nobility and courage, needed to endure and to merit redemption by accomplishing the race's education in history. When Milton dared to grapple with the paradox of the fortunate fall, he helped build a poetic bridge over which liberal Protestants had access to the modern world picture altered by science. Whereas worldly Marino kept the older Platonic-Ptolemaic spheres for their convenient poetic values in his cosmological epic *Adone* (1624 ff.), religious Milton enlarged the universe to accomodate the Copernican-Galilean shift and endowed its less definite vastness with awesome theatricality, the dizzying verticality of imagery of height and depth, and a sinuosity, obliqueness, complexity, and ambiguity both of language and patterns. When Milton demonstrated the serpentine style of Satan as subverter, he was also dealing with the mystery of the appearance of the involved, twisted, perplexing out of an essential harmony and purity, the potential for conflict but also for change and development.

Hence latent in the original garden of Eden and the initial perfection of Adam and Eve is the mutability which can flow from humankind's freedom. Extracting nuances from every garden of past literature, Milton succeeded in creating in his poem an earthly paradise which suggested a glory never to be forgotten, yet containing peril in its very beauty, the corrupting fullness. As Giammati has noted, we sense the restlessness which will trouble Eve in the patterns of nature fraught "with mazy error" (IV, 239). We see this in "the Serpent sleeping, in whose mazy folds" (162) Satan insinuates himself, this prelapsarian creature already being "In Labyrinth of many a round self-roll'd" (183).[20] Gradually Eve becomes lost in the mental maze and begins erring. The potential for evil is present at first sight in Milton's Eden even in the ambiguous golden aura of the forbidden fruit, and the echoes of Spenser's Bower of Bliss prepare us for the Fall, even though Milton's garden is originally perfect. The repercussions of narcissism, erroneous folding back upon one's own image, are first associated with Eve because of her role in the hierarchical order. God as creator is above man, and man in turn is above woman who is reciprocally dependent on him in order to bring forth her potential of forms, "Multitudes like thyself, and thence be call'd Mother of human Race" (IV, 474-475). Eve is associated with golden-haired, naked Venus (V, 380-385), but the implication already is the loss of the pristine purity; through her, reciprocally, Adam discovers appetite, makes wrong choices through sensuality, and "From Man's effeminate slackness it begins," as the Archangel Michael informs him (XI, 634). By direct allusions, Eve embodies an ambiguous spectrum of characteristics from Ceres to Circe even before the actual Fall.

Since the approach to Eden is a "woody Theatre" (IV, 141), our task — as in Baroque drama — is to understand the multiple perspectives on the action, to disentangle illusion and reality, to move spiritually over the flux of time, like "God beholding from his prospect high [...] past, present, future [...]" (III, 77-78). Satan is

> Assaying by his Devilish art to reach
> The Organs of her Fancy, and with them forge
> Illusions as he list, Phantasms and Dreams.
> (IV, 800-803)

The prideful dream, the false illusion one can be a God, is implanted in Eve who evidences a deficiency of reason as a check against error. Yet mysteriously, Adam has a comparable true dream on the day of his creation, waking to discover Eden as a copy of Heaven, and again when he dreams of a fairest creature and then first beholds Eve upon her creation from his rib (Book VIII). The relationship Adam-Eve mirrors symbolically the higher relationship Creator-Creation. Eve is on one level — and at one remove — only "Fairest resemblance to thy Maker fair" (IX, 538); on another level, she is the matrix through which love, though a unitary principle, will bring forth multiplicity. The "one flesh" of the primal parents images the paradox of a self-reflecting Godhead. So too the introduction of time into the eternal garden means not just captivity in history's labyrinth, but a pathway of education through history. In Book XII, Adam begins to grasp how a true guide, the Savior, will lead man back to paradise on a higher plane, and that there will always remain "a paradise within" (587).

In *Paradise Regained* (1671), Milton sang the further episodes in the plot line of religion, and the redemptive heroism of the Messiah as second Adam, born of the Virgin, second Eve. But the citation of the delusions, the twists and turns of idolatrous fancy among ancient peoples, is poetically as important in the complete record as are the providential wanderings of the Jews and finally the drama of the supreme protagonist Christ "in the wide wilderness" and "woody maze" of the world (*PR*, II, 232, 246). Among the temptations which Christ survives in Book IV are the summoned glory of Greece and grandeur of Rome — that is, the major classical heritages of the Renaissance. Even the noblest strains of philosophy, such as the teachings of Socrates, Christ dismisses as inferior to the "divinely taught" wisdom of the Hebrew-Christian continuum. When Satan flies near Heaven with Christ, the Holy City of Jerusalem suggests the future order safeguarded by the "True Image of the Father" (595).

Milton was writing for an age that obsessively practised the flights of perspectivistic historical imagination. In *Paradise Regained* perspectivism is employed to convey Christ's higher understanding and is a salvational weapon. But the considerable expansion of information on wholly alien civilizations, such as those of China and India, when added to the retrieved Egyptian and Near Eastern lore, not to mention the exotic observations resulting from contact with peoples of the newly colonized Western Hemisphere, was beginning to jeopardize the standard salvational history. As it became increasingly difficult to integrate materials into an old-fashioned coordination of relevant events and forms, the drive to find patterns in a universal history vielded the modern fields of comparative religion and anthropology. Symptomatic of the Northerm late Baroque was the grandiose novel *Arminius* (1679-80) by the Silesian playwright Daniel Casper von Lohenstein, directed at an audience already steeped in the notions of salvational history and of an ancient tradition, the transmission of secret or distorted wisdom. Lohenstein conflated the courtly novel of state, as exemplified by Barclay's *Argenis* (1621), the compendius French historical romances exploring every highway and byway of antiquity, such as Desmarets' *Ariane* (1632) and La Calprenède's *Cléopâtre* (1647), favorite ancient historians such as Tacitus, contemporaneous theoreticians of universal history such as Georg Horn and Samuel Borchart, the early anthropological speculations by such eminences as Kircher, prudentialist philosophers such as Gracián and Saavedra Fajardo, and other authorities — in short, an astonishing range of his age's total repertory. Lohenstein's encyclopedic complexity was greatly admired into the early decades of the eighteenth century, because it could appeal simultaneously at various levels both to traditional Protestants and to the bourgeoning rationalist camp. The *Arminius* compendiously transposed the cultural and spiritual situation of Europe and of the Germans in particular onto the axial moment of antiquity under Augustan Rome.

I have described elsewhere the baffling variety of data and multiple transformations of point of view in the *Arminius*, necessitating the reader's application of the principle of searching doubt.[21] Indirect guidance is offered in the thoughts and experiences of the exemplary educational protagonist, the Armenian philosopher prince Zeno, as he explores everywhere and everything in the ancient world. One illustration must suffice here of his retracings of many turns and deviations in the labyrinthine plotline of the human spirit and his affirmation of the survival of its scientific capacity. The essence is captured in the still widely anthologized poem from the *Arminius* titled "Aufschrift eines Labyrinths" (Inscription on a Labyrinth), which Zeno has read, in Egyptian hieroglyphics, over the entrance to the colossal memorial structure begun by Paraoh Moeris and continued by some ten further monarchs. As Zeno recounts, supposedly speaking in the first century A.D., the Egyptian labyrinth not only far exceeds in size and complexity the mere imitation by Daedalus on the island of Lemnos; the evolving Egyptian warren also represents the religious system through the various temples of the exotic Egyptian pantheon, the history of the land through its funeral sites, and geopolitical and cosmological realities of Egyptian being through symbolic patterns. Besides the direct mythological reference to Daedalus, emblematically the labyrinth as described in its own "inscription" is the world and the human body, macrocosm and microcosm; but it is much more, if we remember that in the novel Egypt is the model for man's earliest, and defective, efforts to erect a religious system. In a *tour de force* on the term *irr* (English "err"), now sounding like a preachment on deviation from the mean and the follies of the ages of man, now like a mystical vision of completion, Lohenstein's poem paradoxically aussures us, however, that the labyrinth is not a labyrinth if we are indeed searching:

> Wer aber durch den Bau vernünftig irregeht,
> Wird seines Heiles Weg, der Wahrheit Richtschnur finden.²²
>
> [But he who goes erring rationally through the structure
> Will find salvation's way, the guiding thread of truth.]

It is against this background — Fénelon's allegorical, typological transcriptions for a highly rationalistic readership and Lohenstein's ironc, janus-headed mirroring of habits ancient and modern — that eighteenth-century views of garden and labyrinth can be profiled advantageously. For by 1700 the key question has become that of explaining the variety of "mythology."

One of the most fascinating examples of the patterns of erring and wayfaring also marks a boundary for this essay. Daniel Defoe's *Robinson Crusoe* (1719) no longer quite qualifies primarily as a work of Baroque fiction, even through we recognize the vast Baroque emblematic world behind the startling clarity of the book's basic situations and setting.²³ Defoe had his own project to colonize the Orinoco estuary and Guiana, a region which he never actually saw; the vogue of travel literature would not have escaped this practical journalist. In any case he fused his interests in politics, religion, trade, military and other sciences — interests familiar in Bacon's *New Atlantis* — in the middleclass consciousness and voice of the self-styled wayward Englishman Robinson Crusoe. Crusoe is destined by his disobedience to probe the metaphysical implications of the solitude which being an outsider and exile entails and to experience the heaviness of material reality once the familiarity of home no longer conceals it. Moreover, Robinson is one of the first major protagonists in European literature to witness an actual juxtaposition of the state of archaic man and that of civilization and to know, as a felt reality, the existence of all time-layers of the human soul: from the anthropophagous savages of the Orinoco region, to the Moorish heathen, to the complexities of the centuries old Catholic and Protestant systems. Though of a generalized Protestant background (the family name was once German), Crusoe also acquires a separate identity as a Catholic in Latin America and establishes successful relations of trust with Iberian business partners. Slowly he connects his own maturing sense of the mystery of human evolution and its ultimately higher tendency with his fundamentally Protestant and Puritan concept of Providence. The ground-figure is his wanderlust, the yearning for adventure as a sailor and his heedless abandonment of solid prospect in a respected burgher family in orderly England. He addresses us with immediacy from the opening page in the first person, that is, in a modified picaresque voice, with which he narrates his acting out of sin and simultaneously moralizes about it. Everything Robinson does fits into generic frames of reference familiar from Baroque fiction: There is the adventure tale of Moorish captivity (familiar from Cervantes); there is the context of the saga of the early expansion of trade and of colonialism, including succinct notes on commerce, banking, communications, slavery, etc. But Robinson's story also unfolds as a special discovery tale: he meets primordial other worlds, and he plumbs his own inner world. Hence into the pseudopicaresque narration, after his stranding on the island, he introduces his journal like Simplex, the diary form that will be so potent in eighteenth-century sentimental writing. Robinson's self-observation and confession furthermore become intertwined with a second educational story, the special relationship to Friday, whose friend and mentor he becomes.

Teaching Friday to abstain from eating human flesh does not wholly alter the goodnatured savage; but it is a significant step in the larger scheme of things. Robinson himself learns much about fidelity from his Brazilian partner. Several episodes occur which cumulatively drive the lesson home. The unusual team of Robinson and Friday rescue beleaguered Spaniards, and the Englishman detects deeper qualities of humanity in them despite the bitter legacy of religious and imperial conflict between their home nations. They are integrated into his "new kingdom" as citizens. Contrarily, new dangers arise from the familiar and seemingly safe when mutinous English and Dutch seamen plot treachery; the malefactors are dealt with on a basis of natural law as dangers to the common weal. The survival of the contrite and relatively less guilty crewmen, who are allowed to stay on in the New World instead of being tried and hanged in Europe, amounts in practical social terms to "redemption." Out of the complex wayfaring of the astute, eventually wealthy Robinson, a picture of the awesomely farflung network of world routes and potential connections, resulting from Renaissance adventure, comes into view. The further symbioses which result from the new situations depicted fictionally by Defoe uncannily seem to presage the natural basis for the foundation of such nations as the United States.

Old error yields new ways. The inherent tension between the apparent mandate to "return" home and the attraction of new connections becomes an explicit theme late in the novel. By virtue of the inexorable effects of long absence, and as a product of his own considerable experience, the wanderer to remote edges of time and space, Robinson, cannot ever recapture his lost past in any satisfying way. He accepts alienation from England and its old ways as a condition of existence; his mind inhabits new realms, but he lives basically alone in his thoughts, without family or an older easier sense of clannish immediacy. Whereas Grimmelshausen's adventurer withdrew into the wooded hermitage of his noble father when he consciously bowed off the world stage, and this ultimate state of spiritual self-possession was recapitulated in Simplex' final hermitage on the desert island, Defoe's protagonist ponders for many years the savage place which once was only an emblem, but now is proving to be the real place of retesting mind, purpose, and nature. In the *locus amoenus* of Renaissance and Baroque literature, notably in pastoral isolation, sentiments could more readily be shared; but in the *locus terribilis*, the educational protagonist often faced the most dire threats by forces inimical to his humanity, usually the power of the untamed passions. In his wanderings he might mistake for a garden what was an entrapping labyrinth, but the point was to find one's way through and out of the labyrinth of the world and thereby restore the garden. Rabelais exulted in the quest. Cervantes raised the important questions about the nature of the mind which must act as guide through the bewildering evidence. Defoe imaginatively placed the mind in ultimate isolation and jeopardy for the necessary direct conversation with itself.

Notes

1 Bernal Díaz del Castillo, *Historia verdadera de la Conquista de la Nueva España* (ca. 1568, publ. 1632); Luis de Camoens, *Os Lusíadas* (1572): Richard Hakluyt, *The Principall Voyages, Traffiques, and Discoveries of the English Nation* (1558 ff.); Adam Olearius, *Offt begehrte Beschreibung der newen orientalischen Reise* (1647). The subtitle of this essay harks back to a keynote paper, "Garden and Labyrinth: The Idea of Development in Epic and Novel from the Baroque to Early Enlightenment," which I gave in 1978 at the University of Chicago's very stimulating week-long symposium on "The Baroque: Patterns and Concepts." The essay in its present form also benefited from the reaction of several audiences who patiently heard earlier versions or segments of earlier versions under the auspices of: the University of Paris-III (Sorbonne Nouvelle), Indiana University, and Purdue University in 1982; the Western Society for Eighteenth-Century Studies, meeting at San Francisco State University in 1983; the Comparative Literature Colloquium on Renaissance Literature at the University of Oregon in Eugene in 1984; Peking University, the Chinese Academy of Social Sciences in Beijing, Nanking University, and the Japan Women's University in Tokyo in 1985.

2 Gustav René Hocke, *Die Welt als Labyrinth: Manier und Manie in der europäischen Kunst von 1520 bis 1650 und in der Gegenwart* (Hamburg, 1957).

3 Hiram Haydn, *The Counter-Renaissance* (New York, 1950).

4 A. Bartlett Giamatti, *The Earthly Paradise and the Renaissance Epic* (Princeton, N.J., 1966). Also see Thomas Greene, *The Descent from Heaven: A Study in Epic Continuity* (New Haven and London, 1963), ch. 9. On the Renaissance aesthetics, vision, and paradigmatic understandings of sacred or paradisal space, see Terry Comito, *The Idea of the Garden in the Renaissance* (New Brunswick, 1978).

5 A good general treatment of the picaresque mode, from a comparative perspective, is Richard Bjornson, *The Picaresque Hero in European Fiction* (Madison, 1977).

6 My remarks on the Renaissance romance and novel in the next few paragraphs follow closely my paper "The Incorporation of History as Content and Form: Anticipations of the Romantic and Modern Novel," in *Proceedings of the 9th Congress of ICLA*, vol. IV, ed. by E. Kushner, M. Dimić, and Z. Konstantinović (Innsbruck, 1982), pp. 29-34.

7 *The Earthly Paradise*, p. 253.

8 *The Earthly Paradise*, p. 287 f.

9 Patricia A. Parker, *Inescapable Romance: Studies in the Poetics of a Mode* (Princeton, 1979), pp. 112 and 113.

10 The most satisfactory sympathetic treatment of Marino's views and poetic accomplishments is Helga Grubitzsch-Rodewald, *Die Verwendung der Mythologie in Giambattista Marinos "Adone"* (Wiesbaden, 1973).

11 On Marino's attempt to create a rationalistic "feeling" about existence that is conciliatory and balanced, cf. Grubitzsch-Rodewald, pp. 49 ff.

12 I have treated the basic forms of utopian literature at more length in my essay "Education in Utopia," in *Europäische Lehrdichtung: Festschrift für Walter Naumann zum 70. Geburtstag* (Darmstadt, 1981), pp. 119-131.
13 Florence M. Weinberg, *The Wine and the Will: Rabelais' Bacchic Christianity* (Detroit, 1972), ch. 5, "Man: The Abbot of Thélème and his Abbey."
14 A comprehensive treatment is that by Charles G. Nauert, *Agrippa and the Crisis of Renaissance Thought* (Urbana, 1965).
15 I treat this subject at more length in an essay on "Dream and Calculus in European Baroque Drama," in *Critical Dimensions: English, German, and Comparative Literature Essays in Honor of Aurelio Zanco* (Cuneo: Saste, 1978), pp. 154-173.
16 In an article entitled "Verbal Labyrinths in Sponde's *Stances* and *Sonnets de la Mort*," *L'Esprit Créatur*, 16 (1976), 134-152, Kurt Weinberg has examined the lyrical logodaedalia in which readers are induced to interpret lines vertically, as well as horizontally, and to move in a maze of antithetical directions over conceits which are startling for their unexpected metaphors, sound patterns, and syncretistic Humanism as elements in a paradoxical conceptualist game. Sponde's purpose was serious, to capture "in a labyrinth of multiple verbal mirror systems the Calvinist dogma of the Spirit relentlessly erring through the maze of carnal fantasies and appetites, with the terrors of death and physical destruction as the only dreaded, yet prayed-for exit to eternal peace (if not life)" (p. 152). I would add that in *Délie* (1544), an anagram for *L'idée*, Scève takes us into strange tracts of the soul, resembling now those mysterious, brooding landscapes – sometimes morasses – which appear in contemporaneous painting, and now the late-Renaissance parks in Italy where one wanders through sinous irregular paths past formations and objects symbolizing aspects of the mind and human development. In its highest reaches, the poem cycle *Délie* is organized emblematically, but the emblems are hieroglyphs, not mere allegories, and the logodaedalia is also a psychological maze. Góngora demonstrated – less gloomily – in *Las Soledades* (1613) how human language could be elevated to a plane of conceptual and verbal brilliance to rival the glories of nature, through dazzling syntactical and hermetic complexity. His lustrous artifices or words not merely suggested the "wonders" or *meraviglie* for which Marino, a poet of far simpler constructs, would be famed, but even foreshadowed Yeats' Byzantine corporeality and Mallarmé's Symbolist puzzles.
17 I have treated the connection of the picaresque and satiric novel in "Estebanillo and Simplex: Two Baroque Views of the Role-Playing Rogue in War, Crime, and Art (with an Excursus on Krull's Forebears)," *Canadian Review of Comparative Literature*, 9 (1982), 157-171.
18 The ground-figures of erring are treated by Rosmarie T. Morewedge, "The Circle and the Labyrinth in Grimmelshausen's *Simplicissimus*," *Argenis*, 1 (1977), 229-256.
19 C.M. Bowra, *From Virgil to Milton* (London, 1945), ch. 5, "Milton and the Destiny of Man."

20 For a fuller treatment of these themes, and Milton's poetic intricacy, consult ch. 6 of *The Earthly Paradise*.
21 I have treated aspects of this subject at more length in an article on "The Function of Myth in Lohenstein's *Arminius*: The Cases of Egypt and Prometheus," *Argenis*, 2 (1978), 187-228.
22 Cited from the two-volume facsimile edition by Elida Maria Szarota, *Grossmüthiger Feldherr Arminius* (...) (= Nachdrucke deutscher Literatur des 17. Jahrhunderts, No. 5) (Hildesheim and New York, 1973), I. 677a, lines 17 and 18.
23 The importance of typological thought and emblematic representation — i.e., the common Baroque literary heritage — is recognized by J. Paul Hunter, *The Reluctant Pilgrim: Defoe's Emblematic Method and Quest for Form in Robinson Crusoe* (Baltimore, 1966).

ACKNOWLEDGMENTS

I am grateful to the editors and publishers of the following books and journals for permission to reuse the indicated works:

"Education in Utopia," in *Europäische Lehrdichtung: Festschrift für Walter Naumann zum 70. Geburtstag*, ed. by Hans-Gert Rötzer and Herbert Walz (Darmstadt: Wissenschaftliche Buchgesellschaft, 1981), pp. 119-131.

"Cosmic Vision in Lohenstein's Poetry," *Neophilologus*, 53 (1969), 413-422.

"Primal Utterance: Observations on Kuhlmann's Letters to Kircher, in View of Leibniz' Theories," in *Wege der Worte: Festschrift für Wolfgang Fleischhauer*, ed. by Donald C. Riechel (Cologne: Böhlau-Verlag, 1978), pp. 27-46.

"Scientific Discourse and Postmodernity: Francis Bacon and the Empirical Birth of 'Revision,' " *Boundary 2*, 2 (1979), 119-148.

"The Rebel in Seventeenth-Century Tragedy," *Comparative Literature*, 18 (1966), 324-336.

"Andreas Gryphius' *Catharina von Georgien* als Geschichtsdrama," in *Das Geschichtsdrama*, ed. by Elfriede Neubuhr (Darmstadt: Wissenschaftliche Buchgesellschaft, 1980), pp. 119-131.

"Lohenstein's *Epicharis*: The Play of the Beautiful Loser," in *Studien zum Werk Daniel Caspers von Lohenstein, anläßlich der 300. Wiederkehr des Todesjahres*, ed. by Gerald Gillespie and Gerhard Spellerberg (Amsterdam: Rodopi, 1983), pp. 127-157; same as *Daphnis*, 12 (1983), 343-373.

"Dream and Calculus in European Baroque Drama," in *Critical Dimensions: English, German, and Comparative Literature Essays in Honor of Aurelio Zanco*, ed. by Mario Curreli and Alberto Martino (Cuneo: Saste, 1978), pp. 181-200.

"Pikara und Schelmin," in *Der deutsche Schelmenroman im europäischen Kontext: Rezeption, Interpretation, Bibliographie*, ed by Gerhart Hoffmeister (Amsterdam: Rodopi, 1986).

"Estebanillo and Simplex: Two Baroque Views of the Role-Playing Rogue in War, Crime, and Art (with an Excursus on Krull's Forebears)," *Canadian Review of Comparative Literature*, 9 (1982), 157-171.

"Erring and Wayfaring in Baroque Fiction: The World as Labyrinth and Garden," *Revue de Littérature Comparée*, 58 (1984), 277-299.

The illustration from Athanasius Kircher's *Turris Babel* is used with permission of the Lilly Library at Indiana University. The illustrations from John Wilkin's *Essay towards a Real Character, and a Philosophical Language* and Laurence Sterne's *Tristram Shandy* have been furnished by the Green Library at Stanford University.

INDEX

Aarsleff, Hans 111
Abraham, Claude K. 224, 251
Abrams, M.H. 118, 147
Agrippa von Nettesheim, Cornelius 68, 306f
Agrippina 156-59, 167, 195, 198, 202, 205, 223, 240
Aikin, Judith 196f, 201, 221f, 223f
Albertinus, Aegidius 293f
Alemán, Mateo 258f, 260, 261, 277, 280, 283, 293, 298
Alexander the Great 143, 195
Alfieri, Vittorio 154
Allen, Don Cameron 59
Alsted(ius), Joann Heinrich 27, 55f, 70, 79, 86, 148, 226, 249
Anaximander 54
Andreae, Johann Valentin 24-8, 81, 301f
Anouilh, Jean 250
Aquinas, St. Thomas 122
Arias, Joan 294
Ariosto, Lodovico 298f, 303, 308f
Aristotelianism 27, 35
Arminius 195f, 199, 218, 222
Ascham, Roger 15
Asmuth, Bernhard 59, 197f, 209, 221-24
Auerbach, Erich 143, 236
Augustus 46, 143, 194, 221, 317

Bacon, Francis 28-30, 121-27, 138, 140, 148, 150f, 227f, 251, 307, 318
Baker, Herschel 148
Bakhtin, Mikhail M. 11
Bandello, Matteo 285

Barclay, John 316
Barner, Wilfried 224
Barthes, Roland 146
Bataillon, Marcel 277, 289, 295
Bauer, Hermann 32
Bayle, Pierre 79
Beaumarchais, Augustin Caron de 269
Beare, Robert I. 106
Becan, Jan (Goropius Becanus) 99, 109f
Behar, Pierre 63, 66, 68-70, 84-6
Bekker, Hugo 166
Benjamin, Walter 171f, 184, 189
Berg,. Alban 273
Berkeley, George 135
Bible, Scripture 60, 91, 95, 126, 128, 147f, 171
Biblical figures
    Abel 100; Abraham 29; Adam 29, 58, 70, 76, 94, 101, 122, 155, 313-15; Adamic language 94, 96, 103, 106, 110, 131; Babel/Babylon 96-100, 109f, 120, 132; Christ 29, 39, 67, 71, 76, 315f; Daniel 54f; David 26, 94; Eve 41, 58, 314ff; Ham 102; Isaiah 64; Jacob 287; Japheth(ic) 99, 102, 106, 109; Joseph 286-88; Mary, Virgin 39, 41, 58, 67, 71, 75, 315; Mary Magdalene 65, 269; Moses 29; Noah 29, 55, 110, 219; Samson 193f, 218; Satan (Lucifer) 154f, 166, 313-15; Shem 102, 110; Solomon 29, 94, 95, 150
Bidermann, Jakob 225, 233, 247, 308

Bieman, Elizabeth 58
Bizet, Georges 273
Bjornson, Richard 260, 277, 278, 282, 293, 294, 321
Blackburn, Alexander 277
Boccaccio, Giovanni 37
Boehme, Jakob 68, 81, 89, 104, 109, 111
Bonaparte, Napoleon 144
Borchart, Samuel 316
Bowra, C.M. 313, 322
Boyle, Robert 127, 130
Braddon, Mary E. 275
Bran, Jerónimo de 289
Brancaforte, Benito 294f
Brancaforte, Charlotte 63, 84, 85
Brant, Sebastian 258, 279, 308, 311
Braunthal, Alfred 32
Brecht, Berthold 191, 262, 275
Brekle, Herbert Ernst 107
Brentano, Clemens 273
Brittanicus 240
Brockes, Barthold Heinrich 50, 72, 74
Brown, Norman O. 120, 147
Browning, Barton W. 83, 84
Bruno, Giordano 302
Büchner, Georg 185
Bunyan, John 228
Burckhardt, Hans 111
Burckhardt, Jacob 200
Burger, Heinz Otto 230, 249
Burney, Fanny 278
Buti, Francesco 284f
Byron, George Gordon, Lord 276

Calderón de la Barca, Pedro 177, 182, 225, 233, 235ff, 243, 247, 308, 309
Calvinism 18, 26-30, 41, 44, 70, 267, 322
Camoens, Luis de 297, 321
Campanella, Tommaso 22-4, 301, 302

Carr, Herbert Wildon 113
Cartari, Vincenzo 37, 39, 58
Castiglione, Balassare 15
Castillo Solórzano, Alonso de 260f
Causin, Nicholas 171
Cervantes Saavedra, Miguel de 126, 169, 226, 228, 238, 260, 261, 265, 283, 285, 287, 300, 307-11, 319, 320
Chaucer, Geoffrey 57
Chomsky, Noam 107, 131
Cicero, Marcus Tullius 19, 139
Clarke, Dana S. 249
Cleopatra 194-96, 221
Coleridge, Samuel Taylor 33
Colonna, Francesco 35, 57
Colum, Mary G. 120
Columbus, Christopher 23, 30, 297
Comenius (Komensky) John Amos 30, 79, 110, 111, 127ff, 130, 134, 149, 150, 301, 304
Comito, Terry 321
Conti, Natale 37
Copernicus, Nicholas 23, 36, 51f, 57, 69ff, 85, 314
Corneille Pierre 156, 173f, 183, 237-41, 250, 269
Coseriu, Eugenio 112
Courturat, Louis 110
Cromwell, Oliver 169
Crusius, Johannes Paul 111
Curras Rabade, Angele 111
Curtius, Ernst Robert 13, 230, 249
Cusa(nus), Nicholas (of) 35-7, 52, 57
Cyrano de Bergerac, Savinien 156-59, 166

Daemmrich, Horst und Ingrid 254, 277
d'Alembert, Jean Le Rond 56
Dalgarno, George 128ff
Dante Alighieri 141, 287
Dascal, Marcelo 107

d'Aubigné, Théodore Agrippa 250
Davie, Donald 135f, 140, 150
Davies, John 110
Defoe, Daniel 265-68, 269, 276, 318, 323
Delicado, Francisco 256ff
De Man, Paul 147
Desmarets de Saint-Sorlin, Jean 200f, 209, 211f, 216
De Mott, Benjamin 150
Derrida, Jacques 146
Descartes, René (Cartesian) 44, 72, 86, 104, 111, 121ff, 150f, 226, 238, 251
Díaz del Castillo, Bernal 297, 321
Diderot, Denis 271f, 276
Dietze, Walter 106
Diocletian 234
Diodorus Siculus 22
Donne, John 58, 65, 121, 226, 302
Dostoevsky, Feodor Mikhailovich 152
Dreike, Beate 111
Dryden, John 166
Du Bartas, Guillaume de Salluste 74
Du Bellay, Jean Cardinal 18
Dury, John 127, 149
Dyck, Joachim 60

Eco, Umberto 3
Eichendorff, Joseph Freiherr von 86, 273
Eliot, Thomas Stearns 117, 229, 232, 250
Elizabethan 40, 58, 162f
Elliott, Ralph W.V. 150
Emerson, Ralph Waldo 147
Encina, Juan de la 283
Epicharis 161-64, 193-224, 241-43
Epicurus 210
Erasmus, Desiderius 15, 18, 279, 305, 311
Estienne, Charles 37, 58
Eybl, Franz 65, 83

Faber du Faur, Kurt von 106
Feldman, Burton 60
Fénelon, François 15, 56, 304ff, 318
Ficino, Marsilio 54
Fischer, Anton 113
Flaubert, Gustave 274, 276
Fleischhauer, Wolfgang 188
Fleming, Paul 71f, 86
Fletcher, John 107
Fontane, Theodor 275
Foucault, Michel 147
Frege, Gottlob 111
Freud, Sigmund 113, 139, 239
Freyer, Hans 32
Frick, Karl R.H. 150, 224
Frye, Northrop 177, 190, 253, 276
Furrer, Rudolf 221

Galilei, Galileo 30, 70f, 218, 302, 314
Ganz, Hans 113
Gellert, Christian Fürchtegott 278
Georgi, David Samuel 24
Giammatti, A. Bartlett 298, 314, 321, 323
Gibbon, Edward 200
Gilles, Peter 16
Gilman, Ernest B. 33, 57
Girard, René 145, 152
Godwin, Joscelyn 107
Goethe, Johann Wolfgang von 31, 43, 272f, 302
Goldhammer, Kurt 86
Góngora y Argote, Luis de 282f, 322
Goodman, Paul 229f, 249
Gorman, Herbert 148
Gozzi, Carlo 269
Gracián, Baltasar 15, 65, 193, 221, 303ff, 316
Greene, Thomas M. 10, 321
Grimmelshausen, Hans Jacob Christoffel von 261-65, 279-82, 284-95, 310-13, 319, 320
Grubitzsch-Rodewald, Helga 321

Gryphius, Andreas 64, 66, 69, 78-81, 169-92, 197-99, 202f, 207, 219, 243, 258
Günther, Johann Christian 64
Guevara, Antonio de 280, 312
Guibbory, Achsah 123, 148
Guillén, Claudio 9, 254, 277, 278
Gutenberg, Johannes 30, 302
Guthke, Karl S. 32, 85
Gutmann, Joseph 113

Hakluyt, Richard 297, 321
Hall, Michael 110
Haller, Albrecht von 50, 59, 74, 82, 86
Hamann, Johann Georg 94
Hankamer, Paul 109
Hankins, John Erskine 38, 58
Hardy, Alexandre 250
Harris, Gary 64, 83
Harsdörffer, Georg Philipp von 74, 99, 105, 108-10, 285, 294
Hartlib, Samuel 30, 128, 149
Hassan, Ihab 119f, 147
Hauptmann, Gerhart 275
Haydn, Hiram 148, 298, 321
Hazard, Paul 229
Hederich, Benjamin 43
Hegel, Georg Wilhem Friedrich 122, 140, 152, 184
Heidegger, Martin 118, 120, 141ff, 152
Heinekamp, Albert 111
Heintz Günther 112
Heliodorus 300
Heninger, S.K., Jr. 32, 56ff
Herder, Johann Gottfried 94, 111, 112
Herzog, Urs 64, 83
Heselhaus, Clemens 172, 189f
Hieatt, A. Kent 37, 38, 39
Hobbes, Thomas 163
Hocke, Gustav Rene 297, 321
Hölderlin, Friedrich 152

Hofmannsthal, Hugo von 127, 148
Hofmannswaldau, Christian Hofmann von 64, 74, 82
Hoffmeister, Gerhart 9
Homer 304
Horn, Georg 316
Huberti, F.H. 112
Humboldt, Wilhelm Freiherr von 103, 105, 112, 138
Hunter, J. Paul 323

Ibrahim I 244f

Jacquot, Jean 166
Johnson, Lathrop P. 83
Jonas, Hans 141, 144, 152, 224
Jones, Richard F. 127, 149, 150
Jones, Rowland 110
Jones, Sir William 229
Joyce, James 117, 120, 127, 148, 273
Jung, C.G. (Jungian) 113, 239, 285, 287f
Juretzka, Joerg 194, 222
Just, Klaus Günther 167, 219, 220, 222, 223

Kafitz, Dieter 59, 221
Kaiser, Gerhard 189
Kant, Immanuel 60, 105, 111, 112, 140
Kantorowicz, Ernst H. 191
Kappler, Helmut 171, 188, 189
Katz, Jerrold J. 107
Kayser, Wolfgang 13, 109
Keith, Arthur B. 250
Kepler, Johannes 85f
Kerényi, Karl 287
Kermode, Frank 40, 58, 143
Kierkegaard, Søren 120
Kindermann, Heinz 166
Kircher, Athanasius 41-4, 59, 61, 89-109, 113, 132-34, 148, 189, 316
Klaniczay, Tibor 250

Klaj, Johann 110
Klein, Johannes 199-201, 222
Koschlig, Manfred 290f
Kuhlmann, Quirinus 59, 89-107, 148

La Calprenède, Gauthier de 316
Laclos, Pierre Choderlos de 271
Lal, P. 250
Lameere, Jean 32
Lawrence, D.H. 120
Leibniz, Gottfried Wilhelm Freiherr von 102-05, 107, 110-14, 121f, 131-34, 138, 148, 290
Lenders, Winfried 107
Levi-Strauss, Claude 131
Leopold I 196, 198, 208, 222
Lessing, Gotthold Ephraim 269, 272
Lindenberger, Herbert 177, 189, 191
Lipsius, Justus 67, 227, 304
Locke, John 104, 111, 112, 124, 131, 163
Loemker, Leroy E. 113
Logau, Friedrich von 71
Lohenstein, Daniel Casper von 30f, 41, 43-56, 59, 63-86, 161-64, 166, 167, 171, 182f, 187, 191, 193-224, 240-43, 269, 316-18, 323
López de Úbeda, Francisco 258-60
Lorris, Guillaume de, and Meun, Jean de 302
Lucian 16
Lucretius Carus, Titus 72, 78, 86
Lull, Raymond 90, 93, 112, 114, 128, 133
Lunding, Erik 171f, 207, 223
Lutheranism 18, 44, 70, 176, 197, 206f
Lyly, John 15, 301
Lyons, J. 108

Machiavellianism 163, 169, 179, 182, 194, 200, 221, 239, 243
Mackay, John Henry 151

Macrobius 68f
Mallarmé, Stéphane 43, 322
Mandel, Oscar 165f
Mann, Thomas 130, 273, 285-88, 292, 294
Manuel, Frank E. 150
Manuel, Frank E., and Manuel, Fritzie P. 32
Marino, Giambattista 30, 35, 40f, 69, 74, 86, 302ff, 314
Marivaux, Pierre de 269
Marlowe, Christopher 155f
Marshall, David 278
Martin, Vincent 57
Martin, Wallace 146, 151
Marx, Karl 140
Masen, Jakob 247
Masters, G. Mallary 33, 57
Matthieu, Pierre 200
Maupassant, Guy de 274
Mazarin, Jules 167
McCracken, George E. 113f
Melville, Herman 3
Merimée, Prosper 273
Meyer, Ahlrich 152
Meyer, Herman 11
Meyer, Leonard B. 136ff, 139, 150
Milch, Werner 86
Milton, John 3, 45f, 58, 69, 74, 124, 154, 211, 217ff, 228f, 250, 313-18
Mirollo, James V. 10
Molière, Jean-Baptiste Poquelin 269
Molina, Tirso de 165
Montaigne, Michel Eyquem de 227, 233, 250, 307f
Monteverdi, Claudio 197
Moore, D.M. 63, 84
More, St. Thomas 11, 15-18, 31, 301, 305
Morel, Jacques 166f
Morewedge, Rosmarie T. 322
Morton, John 16
Moscherosch, Hans Michel 311

331

Mozart, Wolfgang Amadeus 272
Müller, Helmut 63, 84
Münster, Georg 32
Mulagk, Karl-Heinz 221, 223
Musset, Alfred de 166
Mythology, mythological figures
  Adonis 38, 40f, 57, 76, 285, 288, 299f, 302ff; Aeneas 241, 300; Aesculapius 43; Anubis 40; Aphrodite (Venus) 38, 40f, 42, 46, 49, 57, 63, 73, 75, 80, 239, 241, 257, 258, 284ff, 288, 299f, 302ff, 312, 315; Apollo (Sol) 43, 58, 77, 100; Cadmus 30; Daedalus 317, 322; Demeter (Ceres) 38, 46, 257, 258, 277, 288, 315; Deucalion 50f; Diana (Luna, Cynthia) 39, 76, 303; Dido 85, 300; Dionysus (Bacchus) 34, 35, 37, 40, 58, 147, 166, 257; Eros (Cupid) 258; Heracles (Hercules) 48; Hermes (Mercury), Hermetic(ism) 45, 57, 68, 84, 91, 131, 219, 257, 286-88, 291, 298, 302, 307, 312, 322; Ishtar 277; Isis, Osiris, Horus, Typhon 37-40, 46, 47, 49, 58, 74; Krishna, Brahma, Rama 45ff, 229-32; Juno 75; Jupiter 40, 46, 212, 290; Minerva 39, 43; Minos 30; Oedipus 98; Orpheus 35, 47, 187, 284f, 288; Priapus 34, 38, 58; Prometheus 30, 31, 48-54, 68-70, 84, 219, 223, 302; Persephone (Proserpina) 38, 285, 288; Tammuz 277, 288; Saturn 76

Nauert, Charles G. 322
Naumann, Walter 13
Nelson, Benjamin 147
Nelson, Donald F. 287, 288, 294
Nelson, Robert J. 12, 230, 250
Nemoianu, Virgil 271, 278
Nero 162, 194-98, 201, 204f, 209, 210-15, 217, 219f, 222, 240-43

Neubauer, John 59, 114
Neuendorf, Klaus K.L. 107
Neukirch, Benjamin 74
Newton, Isaac 52, 54, 129f, 131, 135, 150
Nietzsche, Friedrich 51, 122, 141, 145, 152, 153, 166, 273
Nieuwelandt, Guilliam van 222
Nolte, Fred O. 111
Nostitz, Otto von 222
Novalis 144
Nuerner, Renate Elisabeth 111

O'Grady, Gene M. 106
Olearius, Adam 297, 321
Opitz, Martin 202
Osman II 203, 243ff
Otway, Thomas 163-66, 245-46

Papinianus, Aemilius Paulus 197, 243
Paracelsus, Bombastus von Hohenheim, Theophrastus 68, 71ff, 75-7, 86, 104, 109
Parker, Alexander A. 250, 253, 261, 276, 278, 282, 293, 294
Parker, Patricia 300, 321
Parsons, James 110
Pascal, Blaise 141f
Paterson, R.W.K. 151
Patzig, Günther 111
Paul, Saint 28, 34, 81, 143, 210f
Petrarch (Petrarca, Francesco) 72, 187
Philolaus 36, 57
Pico della Mirandola, Giovanni 297
Pictorius, Georg 37
Pindar 90
Piso, Gaius Calpurnius 205, 210, 223, 242
Platonism, Neoplatonism 34, 45, 54, 57, 65, 68, 73, 75, 80, 87, 89, 91, 102, 109, 141, 143, 144, 150, 204, 210, 303, 307, 314
Pope, Alexander 135

Porphyry 68
Postel, Guillaume 110
Pound, Ezra 126
Powell, Hugh 188
Pratt, Annis 227
Prévost, Marcel (Abbé) 269
Priestly, Joseph 110
Proust, Marcel 117
Ptolemaic 52, 68f, 314
Puccini, Giacomo 275
Pynchon, Thomas 146
Pyritz, Hans 86
Pythagorean 32, 34, 36, 42, 49, 54f, 86

Quevedo, Francisco de 255, 258, 259, 261, 277, 298, 311
Quine, Willard Van Orman 107
Quiñones, Ricardo J. 148, 249

Rabelais, François 11, 18-22, 26, 33-7, 52, 57, 121, 135, 228, 305-08, 320
Racine, Jean 153, 162, 183, 186, 191, 240, 269
Ramée, Pierre de la (Ramus) 128, 132f, 226, 238, 251
Ramsay, Andrew Michael 15, 54-6
Reiss, Timothy J. 250f
Rembrandt (Harmenszoon van Rijn) 227
Rice, Eugene F., Jr. 57
Richardson, Robert D. 60
Richardson, Samuel 265, 270
Richelieu, Armand-Jean du Plessis de 167
Rimbaud, Arthur 127
Rodriguez-Luis, Julio 254, 277
Rodway, Allan 120, 148
Rötzer, Hans Gerd 293f
Rojas, Fernando de 255-58, 298
Ronquillo, Pablo Javier 278
Rossi, Luigi 284f
Rossi, Paolo 114, 149, 151

Rotrou, Jean de 225, 234f, 249, 250, 308, 309
Rousseau, Jean-Jacques 50, 56, 86, 270
Ruiz, Juan (Archpriest of Hita) 302

Saavedra Fajardo, Diego 193, 221, 316
Sacher-Masoch, Leopold von 274
Sade, Donatien-Alphonse-François de 270f, 278
Saint-Lazare, Claude Malingre Sieur de 174, 189
Salas Barbadillo, Alfonso Jerónimo de 260
Sartre, Jean Paul 141
Scaliger, Julius Caesar 99, 101
Scarron, Paul 260, 269
Scève, Maurice 322
Schelling, Friedrich Wilhelm von 152
Schiller, Friedrich von 154, 160, 272
Schings, Hans-Jürgen 172, 189-91
Schleiermacher, Friedrich Daniel 146
Schmarsow, August 111
Schmeling, Manfred 250, 295
Schmid, Martin Erich 284
Schnabel, Johann Gottfried 30
Schöne, Albrecht 63, 84
Schopenhauer, Arthur 122, 229
Schottel(ius), Justus Georg 111
Schulenburg, Sigrid von der 111
Seidlin, Oskar 149, 188, 287, 294
Sejanus 156-59, 167
Seneca, Lucius Annaeus 161, 197, 201, 205, 208-13, 217, 223, 240-43
Sengle, Friedrich 170
Serres, Michel 114
Shakespeare, William 42, 58, 65, 154, 169, 191, 220, 225f, 230-32, 235, 236, 238, 269, 270, 292, 308, 309
Shapiro, Karl 148
Shaw, George Bernard 276

333

Sidney, Philip 58
Sieber, Harry 277
Singer, Irving 87
Skrine, Peter 222
Socrates 34, 45, 211f, 316
Soliman (Suleiman I) 203
Sophonisbe 193f, 202
Sorel, Charles 249, 260, 269, 285, 290f, 292, 293, 295, 311
South, M.S. 173, 179
Spadaccini, Nicholas 282, 295
Spanos, William 117f, 122, 146
Spellerberg, Gerhard 59, 83, 84, 221, 223
Spengler, Oswald 122
Spenser, Edmund 37-40, 42, 54, 299f, 314
Sperber, Hans 105
Spinoza, Baruch 55
Sponde, Jean de 322
Stackhouse Janifer G. 172, 189
Steiner, George 112
Stephens, James 124, 138, 148, 151
Sterne, Laurence 115, 127
Stirner, Max 140f, 151
Strasser, Gerhard 113f
Stoicism 64, 66, 68, 156, 161, 172, 197, 203, 209, 211, 225, 227, 241, 304
Sullivan, Gail 250
Susini, Eugène 189
Swift, Jonathan 135
Szyrocki, Marian 188
Szarota, Elida Maria 59, 63, 84, 172f, 189-91, 194, 221

Tacitus, Publius Cornelius 198, 201, 214, 240, 316
Tallement des Réaux, Gédéon 167
Tasso, Torquato 300, 303
Tesauro, Emmanuele 65f
Thackeray, William 273
Tisch, J. Hermann 58
Trask, Willard R. 249

Tristan L'Hermite, François 198, 201, 203, 209-12, 223, 241-44
Trousson, Raymond 32
Tonelli, Giorgio 60, 111
Toon, Peter 148
Turnbull, G.H. 149
Tymieniecka, Anna Theresa 113

Uhlig, Claus 58

Valentin, Jean-Marie 197, 222
Valle, Daniela dalla 244
Valle, Pietro della 189
Vega Carpio, Lope Félix de 159ff, 232-34
Verhofstadt, Edward 85, 207, 223
Versins, Pierre 32
Verstegan, Richard 110
Vespucci, Amerigo 16
Vickers, Brian 149
Vico, Giambattista 147, 253
Vida, Marco Girolamo 57
Villiers de l'Isle-Adam, Auguste 274
Vipper, Yuri B. 249f
Virgil (Vergil) 304
Voegelin, Erich 142-45, 152
Vondel, Joost van den 154f, 166, 171
Vorsterman, Lucas 289
Vosskamp, Wilhelm 63, 84, 86, 87

Wagner, Richard 152
Walker, D.P. 59, 103, 104, 108, 148, 150
Wallace, Karl R. 124
Warnke, Frank 245f
Waterhouse, Gilbert 31
Waterman, John T. 111
Webster, Charles 31, 130, 148, 150, 222
Webster, John 163
Wedekind, Franz 273
Wehrli, Max 85
Weidhorn, Manfred 249
Weier, Winfried 199, 202, 222

Weinberg, Florence 33, 35, 57, 277, 306, 322
Weinberg, Kurt 294, 322
Weise, Christian 246
Wellek, René 120, 148
Wentzlaff-Eggebert, Friedrich Wilhelm 63f, 80, 84, 189, 191
Wessells, P.B. 171, 189f
Weydt, Günther 285, 288, 294
White, Hayden 147
Wickram, Jörg 15, 300f
Wieland, Christoph Martin 32, 43, 54, 59
Wilkins, John 110, 115, 128ff
Wilson, Edward M. 295

Windfuhr, Manfred 85
Wittgenstein, Ludwig Joseph Johann 138
Wolff, Christian 107
Wolfram von Eschenbach 279, 311
Wollgast, Siegfried 85
Wundt, Max 108

Yates, Frances 31, 150, 151
Yeats, William Butler 322

Zahareas, Anthony N. 295
Zanco, Aurelio 295
Zola, Emile 274
Zoroaster 45, 54f, 77

STUDIENREIHE ZUR GERMANISTIK

Germanic Studies in America:

- Bd. 1 Nordmeyer, Rubaijat von Omar Chajjam. 2. Aufl. 104. S., brosch. und Lwd., 1969.
- Bd. 2 Richards, The German Bestseller in the 20th Century. A complete Bibliography and Analysis. 276 S., Lwd., 1968.
- Bd. 3 Germer, The German Novel of Education 1792-1805. A complete Bibliography and Analysis. 280 S., Lwd. 1968.
- Bd. 4 Gerlitzki, Die Bedeutung der Minne in «Moritz von Craun». 132 S., Lwd., 1970.
- Bd. 5 Bowman, Life into Autobiography. A Study of Goethe's «Dichtung und Wahrheit». 162 S., Lwd., 1971.
- Bd. 6 Putzel, Letters to Immanuel Bekker frim Henriette Herz, S. Pobeheim and Anna Horkel. 108 S., Lwd., 1972.
- Bd. 7 Geldrich, Heine und der spanisch-amerikanische Modernismo. 304 S., Lwd., 1971.
- Bd. 8 Friesen, The German Panoramic Novel in the 19th Century. 232 S., Lwd., 1972.
- Bd. 9 Novak, Wilhelm von Humboldt, as a Literary Critic. 142 S., Lwd., 1972.
- Bd. 10 Shelton, The Young Hölderlin. 282 S., Lwd., 1973.
- Bd. 11 Milstein, Eight Eighteenth Century Reading Societies. A Sociological Contribution to the History of German Literature. 312 S., Lwd., 1972.
- Bd. 12 Schatzberg, Scientific Themes in the Popular Literature and the Poetry of the German Enlightenment, 1720-1760. 350 S., Lwd., 1973.
- Bd. 13 Dimler, Friedrich Spee's «Trutznachtigall». 158 S., Lwd., 1973.
- Bd. 14 McCort, Perspectives on Music in German Fiction. The Music-Fiction of Wilhelm Heinrich Riehl. 154 S., Lwd., 1974.
- Bd. 15 Motsch, Die poetische Epistel. Ein Beitrag zur Geschichte der deutschen Literatur und Literaturkritik des achtzehnten Jahrhunderts. 218 S., Lwd., 1974.
- Bd. 16 Zipser, Edward Bulwer-Lytton and Germany. 232 S., Lwd., 1974.
- Bd. 17 Rutledge John, The Dialogue of the Dead in Eighteenth-Century Germany. 186 S., Lwd., 1974.
- Bd. 18 Rutledge Joyce S., Johann Adolph Schlegel. 322 S., Lwd., 1974.
- Bd. 19 Gutzkow, Wally the Skeptic. Novel. A translation from the German with an Introduction and Notes by Ruth-Ellen Boetcher Joeres. 130 S., Lwd., 1974.
- Bd. 20 Keck, Renaissance and Romanticism: Tieck's Conception of Cultural Decline as Portrayed in his «Vittoria Accorombona». 120 S., Lwd., 1976.
- Bd. 21 Scholl, The Bildungsdrama of the Age of Goethe. 80 S., 1976.
- Bd. 22 Bartel, German Literary History 1777-1835. An Annotated Bibliography. 230 S., Lwd., 1976.
- Bd. 23 Littell, Jeremias Gotthelf's «Die Käserei in der Vehfreude»: A Didactic Satire. 122 S., Lwd., 1977.
- Bd. 24 Carels, The Satiric Treatise in Eighteenth-Century Germany. 168 S., Lwd., 1976.
- Bd. 25 Lensing, Narrative Structure and the Reader in Wilhelm Raabe's «Im alten Eisen». 118 S., Lwd., 1977.
- Bd. 26 Profit, Interpretations of Iwan Goll's late Poetry with a comprehensive and annotated Bibliography of the Writings by and about Iwan Goll. 202 S., Lwd., 1977.
- Bd. 27 Hollyday, Anti-Americanism in the German Novel 1841-1862. 212 S., Lwd., 1977.
- Bd. 28 Horwath, Der Kampf gegen die religiöse Tradition. Die Kulturkampfliteratur Österreichs, 1780-1918. 295 S., Lwd. 1978.
- Bd. 29 Pantle, Die Frau ohne Schatten – By Hugo von Hoffmannsthal and Richard Strauss. An Analysis of Text, Music, and their Relationship. 256 S., Lwd., 1978.
- Bd. 30 Leckey, Some Aspects of Balladesque Art and their Relevance for the Novels of Theodor Fontane. 114 S., Lwd., 1979.
- Bd. 31 Thomas, Ordnung und Wert der Unordnung bei Bertolt Brecht. 141 S., Lwd., 1979.
- Bd. 32 Emmel, Weltklage und Bild der Welt in der Dichtung Goethes. Zweite, durchgesehene Auflage, 223 S., Lwd., 1979.
- Bd. 33 Stern, Hilde Domin: From Exile to Ideal. 93 S., Lwd., 1979.
- Bd. 34 Gellinek, Herrschaft im Hochmittelalter. Essays zu einem Sonderproblem der älteren deutschen Literatur. 180 S., Lwd., 1980.

Bd. 35	Weeks, The Paradox of the Employee. Variants of a Social Theme in Modern Literature. 160 S., Lwd., 1979.
Bd. 36	Mittelmann, Die Utopie des weiblichen Glücks in den Romanen Theodor Fontanes. 125 S., Lwd., 1980.
Bd. 37	Manyoni, Langzeilentradition in Walthers Lyrik. 128 S., Lwd., 1980.
Bd. 38	Helbig, G. E. Lessing: Die Erziehung des Menschengeschlechts. 77 S., Lwd., 1980.
Bd. 39	Schrader, A Method of Stylistic Analysis Exemplified on C.M. Wieland's 'Geschichte des Agathon'. 240 S., Lwd., 1980.
Bd. 40	Whitin, Der Wandel des Polenbildes in der deutschen Literatur des 19. Jahrhunderts. 208 S., Lwd., 1981.
Bd. 41	Fairy Tales as Ways of Knowing. Essays on Märchen in Psychologie, Society and Literature, ed. by Michael M. Metzger and Katharina Mommsen. 200 S., Lwd., 1981.
Bd. 42	Beckett, The Reception of Pablo Neruda's Works in the German Democratic Republic. 251 S., Lwd., 1981.
Bd. 43	Wiswall, A Comparison of Selected Poetic and Scientific Works of Albrecht von Haller. 432 S., Lwd., 1981.
Bd. 44	Cervantes, Struktur-Bezüge in der Lyrik von Nelly Sachs. 144 S., Lwd., 1982.
Bd. 45	Guthke, Erkundungen: Essais zur Literatur. 432 S., Lwd., 1983.
Bd. 46	Remak, Novellistische Struktur: Der Marschall von Bassompierre und die schöne Krämerin (Bassompierre, Goethe, Hofmannsthal). 130 S., Lwd., 1983.
Bd. 47	Laane, Imagery in Conrad Ferdinand Meyer's Prose Works. Form, Motifs, and Functions. 258 S., Lwd., 1983.
Bd. 48	Shaffner, The Apprenticeship Novel. A Study of the «Bildungsroman» as a Regulative Type in Western Literature with a Focus on Three Classic Representatives by Goethe, Maugham, and Mann. 178 S., Lwd., 1984.
Bd. 49	Gellinek, Pax optima rerum. Friedensessais zu Grotius und Goethe. 153 S., Lwd., 1984.
Bd. 50	Lewis, Eugene O'Neill. The German Reception of America's First Dramatist. 211 S., Lwd., 1984.
Bd. 51	Brüggemann, Drei Mystifikationen Heinrich von Kleists, Kleists Würzburger Reise – Kleists Lustspiel mit Goethe – Aloysius, Marquis von Montferrat. 220 S., Lwd., 1985.
Bd. 52	Weisstein, Links und links gesellt sich nicht. Gesammelte Aufsätze zum Werk Heinrich Manns und Bertolt Brechts. 517 S., Lwd., 1986.
Bd. 53	Allen, The Faust Legend. Popular Formular and Modern Novel. 178 S., Lwd., 1985.
Bd. 54	Hertling, Theodor Fontanes *Irrungen, Wirrungen:* Die 'Erste Seite' als Schlüssel zum Werk. 77 S., Lwd., 1985.
Bd. 55	Vogt, Vision and Revision: A Study of Inspiration in Thomas Mann's Fiction. 168 S., Lwd., 1987.
Bd. 56	Gillespie, Garden and Labyrinth of Time. Studies in Renaissance and Baroque Literature. 326 S., Lwd., 1988.

KRAUSKOPF LIBRARY
830.9 G412   STACKS
Gillespie, Gerald E/Garden and labyrinth

3 1896 00031 8224

830.9 G412   89-1511
Gillespie, Gerald Ernest
  Paul, 1933-
Garden and labyrinth of tim

830.9 G412   89-1511
Gillespie, Gerald Ernest
  Paul, 1933-
Garden and labyrinth of tim

WD